The series marks the culmination of several decades of research, and there isn't a sentence here that couldn't be footnoted to a person, a place, a moment that deserves our thanks. Hilary Clinton once said, "It takes a village to raise a child." As I get ready to send this series out into the world, all I can think is, "It takes a village to write Units of Study for Teaching Reading, 3-5."

Our thanks go first to our brilliant editor, Kate Montgomery. Kate was also the editor of the two *Units of Study for Teaching Writing* series. She and I developed this genre together, and I only agreed to tackle this enormous project after receiving a promise that despite Kate's new leadership role at Heinemann, she'd continue to be at the helm of this work. There isn't a word, a page, a decision, or a person connected to this series that hasn't run through her hands. How I honor her deft touch, which has brought shapeliness to the series, and her willingness to go to any lengths to meet and surpass the high standards that have become our trademark.

This book is dedicated to Jean Lawler. Each time that Kate and I have undertaken a *Units of Study* series, Jean Lawler has joined us at the helm of the *Units* team. Kate, Kathleen, and I could not have finessed this effort without her decisive and clear leadership, her keen understanding of this work, her unflagging attention to detail and above all, her steady kindness. Jean and Kate lead a whole team, and in subsequent Acknowledgements I'll introduce you to the others on that team who've been so invaluable.

At Teachers College, the one person who has been the sun, the moon, and the stars to this project is Julia Mooney, co-author of *Alternate Units*. Julia is writer-in-residence at the Project. Julia oversaw the operation, orchestrated the players, synthesized drafts, and above all, wrote alongside Kathleen and I. She helped us bring conference transcripts to life, she brought her knowledge of literary scholarship to the text, and she helped smooth out and clean up our prose. There simply aren't words enough to thank her.

The units, and indeed the reading workshop that is implicit in them, were first pioneered more than twenty years ago. At the time, Randy Bomer, Associate Professor of Literacy at University of Texas, Austin, Kathy Collins, author of *Growing Readers*, and Kate Montgomery, our editor, joined me as the leadership team behind this work and their influence is embedded in the very foundations of this work. Kathy has especially continued to bring her spot-on sense of kids to the endeavor, helping us bring our young readers to life.

The units of study in these books have been developed, piloted, refined by the entire Teachers College Reading and Writing Project staff over decades of work in thousands of classrooms. The ideas couldn't possibly have emerged from a lone writer or two, sitting at our desks. Instead, the ideas have come from the 60 staff developers who constitute the Teachers College Reading and Writing Project and from thousands of classrooms across the nation.

The TCRWP's staff developers meet for a full day, one day a week, to study research, to pore over data, to learn from each others and our teacher-colleagues' best thinking, and to over and over again, work towards creating more coherent, more powerful, more effective methods for teaching reading and writing. Our best-thinking about literacy instruction is always in the process of being pilot-tested and revised based on what works and what doesn't work. The series, then, owes its life to the staff of the Project. A few people have played an especially important role. We thank Laine Powell, Rebecca Bellingham, Lea Mercantini, and Melanie Brown for their research in our pilot classrooms and for joining us in the effort to collect, select from and organize children's work, book lists, anchor charts, and the like.

The Teachers College Reading and Writing Project is composed of not only a team of staff developers but also with a network of teachers, principals and superintendents, many of whom have worked shoulder-to-shoulder with us for years and have become some of the nation's wisest literacy leaders. Because Kathleen and I wanted to teach these actual units of study, as they are written, so that our books could show you the kids' work and our responses to that work, we asked six especially wonderful teachers, grades 3-5, to help up pilot these units of study in their classrooms and to allow us to study their children's reading. Those teachers, then, helped us rethink minilessons that didn't hit the spot, address gaps and add to otherwise revise based on the input from their students. We are grateful to those teachers—Katie Evan, Erin Hanley, Molly Feeney, Kathy Doyle, Sarah Colmaire and Randi Bernstein—and to their children. I describe these teachers in more detail in subsequent Acknowledgements. Their input has made these lessons far more responsive and more powerful, and their children's presence in the *Units* breathes life into the series.

Finally, I should address the nature of my collaboration with Kathleen, for it is that collaboration that brought this book to life. Kathleen is simply the best teacher of reading that I have ever known. She is Senior Deputy Director of the Teachers College Reading and Writing Project—a role that leads her to be at the cutting edge of all the organization's work with curriculum and methods. She has special responsibility for coaching and supporting the 45 upper grade staff developers in the organization. She also works extremely closely with teachers and principals in remarkable schools to help those schools continue their learning trajectories. Kathleen's focal schools serve both ends of the economic spectrum, and in both contexts, she helps people make dreams come true. Kathleen and I developed and revised the ideas in this unit of study together, we brought those ideas to life in classrooms together, and we learned from the students' work together. She was especially helpful in keeping the units grounded in very specific classrooms. My thanks, then, go above all to her. She has been a perfect partner.

The authors and publisher wish to thank those who have generously given permission to reprint borrowed material: STONE FOX. Text © 1980 by John Reynolds Gardiner

Contents

Introduction

The Unit in a Nutshell

n this, the first unit of the year, we launch the reading workshop. We pull out all stops in an effort to help all our students become avid readers. We wear a love of reading on our own sleeves, help students fashion their identities as people who care about reading, create a social life that revolves around shared books and, above all, we help students develop a sense of personal agency about their reading lives, taking responsibility for becoming the kinds of readers who not only make sense of books but who also let books change their lives. We meanwhile induct children into the structures, routines, and habits of a richly literate reading workshop. Students learn how to choose books that are just right in level and interest, to carry books between home and school, to collect and study data about their reading rates and volume, and they learn to push themselves to read with increasing stamina, fluency, and volume. In reading partnerships, children learn to retell and summarize texts and to share ideas that are grounded in the specifics of their books.

SOME HIGHLIGHTED SKILLS: *reading with fluency and stamina, monitoring for sense, retelling*

OVERVIEW OF THE UNIT

Tap Students' Energy for Reading by Inviting Them to Re-Create Themselves as Readers

At the start of the year, the goal is to help each child build a reading life and get started doing the work that readers do. We know that children will be creating identities, assuming roles within the classroom community, and we want to do everything possible to lure children to take on the role of being avid, powerful readers.

We start this by explaining that readers benefit from asking ourselves, 'When has reading really worked in my life?' Then, we figure out the conditions that allowed that reading experience to work so well—so that we can recreate those conditions. We channel these discussions so that we highlight whatever it is we plan to emphasize during this first month of the year. As readers reflect on what has worked for them, they also imagine what might work for them now and in the future. Then we can collaborate to make the classroom into a place where reading is the best it can be. Kids, meanwhile, also make places for reading in their homes; it is helpful to talk and think about developing habits, tools, and places that support reading not only in the reading workshop but also across people's whole lives.

Our goal is for each child to compose an identity of 'I am one who reads.' As Peter Johnston writes in *Choice Words*, "When authors write novels, they create characters—people who say this sort of

thing, do that sort of thing, and relate to people and things in these sorts of ways…This is not just what authors do, it is what people do with themselves. They narrate their lives, identifying themselves and the circumstances, acting and explaining events in ways they see as consistent with the person they take themselves to be…." (Johnston, 2004). It is this environment—of eager self-creation—that we want to create.

> *One of the most important ways in which we recruit kids' investment in reading is by asking them to play an active role in co-creating the reading workshop.*

As teachers, all of us have seen those nose-in-the-book readers who walk from their desks to the meeting area, nose still in the book, who only reluctantly and at the last minute lower the book to listen to what we have to say and even then, whose eyes shine through tears over the heartbreak and drama within the pages of their beloved book. For many of us, we've come to think that those True Readers are born that way—there is something different in their DNA. This unit and this year challenges that assumption, taking up the idea instead that reading—yes Real Reading, avid, Nose-in-the-Book Reading— is too important for us to relegate to DNA. And so, this unit is a time to help students to role-play their way into being the readers we long for them to become.

To one child we say, "I think that maybe, before now, you just didn't have the right books in your hands—but what I'm realizing about you is that when you do have the perfect book—you read non-stop!" To another reader we say, "The way you pay attention to people and really understand what makes them tick shows such a talent for deep reading. Reading *fiction* has everything to do with reading *people*—and your people-skills are going to serve you so well as a reader, you'll see." In these and other ways, we begin the year by doing everything in our power to help readers give reading (and themselves) a chance.

One of the most important ways in which we recruit kids' investment in reading is by asking them to play an active role in co-creating the reading workshop. With kids' help, we organize book bins and library shelves, combining books into text sets that capture their imagination. One bin may be titled, "Sad Depressing Books That Make You Cry and Cry" and another, "Light Sports Books." Kids will invent ideas for making reading 'hot.' One may suggest, as some of our kids have, that all the kids bring their best books in from home and then the class will organize shelves with titles such as "Daniel's Favorites" or "Tyrell's Best." A child who loves mysteries might agree to help decide on new mysteries to buy for the class, and

see if we can learn from what he does."

You may be surprised at this emphasis on inviting youngsters to take active roles co-authoring the reading workshop. With today's urgency to achieve, is there really time for this?

My answer is that today's urgency makes it more necessary than ever that we tap student motivation. Take a second to reflect on yourself as a learner, asking, 'When in my life has my learning curve been sky high? How can I create similar conditions for my students?" And I am very sure that if each of you think about those moments when your learning was off the charts, you'll think of a time when you pored your heart and soul into an endeavor and were willing to do so because this was work you chose to do, where your voice and contributions mattered, where you made decisions and watched the results of those decisions and then tempered what you were doing in light of what you were learning. Kids are not all that different than you and I. They, too, want to work with heart and soul on projects that matter to them, on work in which their voices and contributions matter. And their willingness to work hard, to persevere, and to remake themselves is critical to the success of our teaching.

The Logistics of the Workshop: Establishing Routines and Expectations

During the first few days of school, you will want to induct children into the routines and expectations of reading workshop so that they can carry on as readers and so that you are free to teach.

Learning the Workshop Rhythms

You'll teach children to gather quickly and efficiently for whole-class instruction, emphasizing the importance of children listening (and not constantly interrupting) during the minilesson. You'll teach children to expect that although the minilesson will be an occasion for them to learn a new reading skill or strategy, during any one day's reading time, they will need to draw on *many* of the skills and strategies they have been taught up to and including that day. You'll also induct children into the rhythm of reading, jotting a bit, then talking about their book, or their idea written on their Post-it, with another person.

to do book-promotion talks about mysteries. Another may suggest the class begin leaving Post-its on books that function like miniature reviews: "If you are the kind of kid who *loves* horses and wants to own the whole *Misty* series, you will *love* this book." Books, like movies, might get rated through a complex system of stars and numbers—developed, of course, by a youngster.

It is a small step to go from bringing out individualism within a reading class to helping support an interdependent, interpersonal community in which children with particular knowledge and skills teach others. The teacher's role, then, involves developing local experts, and also includes orchestrating classroom life so those local experts' talents become distributed. This might sound like: "Let's all see if we can study what Brian does to make time for reading at home and

DRAFT

Reading Lots and Lots

It is important that the logistics of the reading workshop support the essentials of reading—and nothing is more essential than kids having large chunks of time for reading. I discuss the importance of reading volume elsewhere in this book, but for now, it is important to mention that early in the year you will establish the expectation that during the reading workshop, every child will read, read, read, progressing through books that are just-right for that child.

Using Reading Logs

Whenever someone aspires towards a goal, it can help to collect data that provides feedback. People who want to run faster or to lose weight or to develop muscles keep scrupulous data, poring over the data to track their progress, and in the same way you will probably want to induct children into a system for collecting data on their volume of reading. During your first unit of study, then, you'll probably rally kids to become invested in reading logs in which they record the titles, levels, pages, minutes and places of their reading. Many September conferences will reference these logs. You might say, "I notice you've been reading faster. Has it been hard to hold on to the story as you read faster?" If a child's pace has slowed, you might ask, "What's slowing you down? I notice you read less today. What got in the way?" The log will also influence your observations. If you see from a glance at a child's log that the child is making slow progress through book, observe the child as she reads silently, checking if there are any noticeable reading behaviors that might be slowing the child down. Does the child move her lips while reading, move her head from side to side, point at words as she reads, use a bookmark to hold her place as she reads, or read aloud to herself? If the child does any of these things, you will want to intervene. Tell the child that he or she has graduated and no longer needs to do those behaviors.

Reading at Home

You'll also institute a system for a take-home reading. If nothing else, each child has a take-home book baggie. The important thing is that the child needs to read the *same* book in home and at school, carrying the book between places. Often teachers suggest that in a partnership discussion, children give themselves assignments in school, as in: "Let's read to page 75."

Working with Partners

At some point during this month, you'll establish reading partnerships, linking together children who can read the same books at roughly the same rate. These relationships have everything to do with building a culture that values literacy—the most important way to do this is to make reading into a richly social activity.

> *Unless children are reading books they can read with 95% accuracy, fluency and strong comprehension, it is superfluous to worry about minilessons that teach strategies for identifying with characters or developing theories!*

Usually classrooms do not have enough duplicate books for partners to read in sync all the time, but even a little of this is tremendously helpful. If partners can't read the same books, they can, and should, *swap* books. Even if partners are not reading the same book in sync with each other, they can support each other in a variety of ways. During reading, they can use Post-its to mark confusing words and during partner time, return to these places to word-solve together. They can mark places where they have strong reactions to the text, then one partner can read one of those sections aloud with strong feelings (good for fluency) and then they can talk about what happened in that section and why they reacted so strongly. Partners can listen to each other retell, asking questions to clarify and dig deeper into the story. You might want to teach your students the kinds of questions that could help them do this work. For example, it's helpful to ask questions about the main characters: "What is Mr. Putter like?" "Why did he agree to keep the dog?" These kinds of questions encourage a reader to not only explain what's happening in the story, but also to think more deeply about *why* those events are happening. In addition, these questions are ones children need to ask themselves as they read.

Choosing Just-Right Books

But reading won't amount to much until children are choosing just-right books. Unless children are reading books they can read with 95% accuracy, fluency,

DRAFT

and strong comprehension, it is superfluous to worry about minilessons that teach strategies for identifying with characters or developing theories! In another section of this volume, I detail procedures for assessing readers and matching them to just right-books. Those assessments occur at the start of this unit. Once you've determined books that are just-right for a particular reader, you'll probably give that child a personal bin or baggie in which he or she can keep a few just-right books. It helps to get the child started enjoying these books if you rave about a few you believe will be perfect for that child.

The books a child keeps in his or her bin will all be equivalent in level, save for two instances. First, an English language learner who is literate in his or her first language will read difficult books in the native language, and easier books in English. Second, when a child is transitioning to a new book level, that child's book-bin will contain books at both the comfort level, and the new instructional level. Ideally, the latter will be books you have introduced to the child; this works especially well if these are two or three books in a series, and you introduce, and even read aloud a bit from the first of those books.

Writing on Post-Its

By the end of the month, readers will do some on-the-run writing, probably on Post-its, as they read, and these will then be brought to the partner conversations. This writing work (brief though it must be) and the partner conversations (which will again be brief) are absolutely essential elements of a reading workshop.

These structures need to be in place by the end of the first week. You definitely don't have time to institute these structures gradually! It is often helpful for children to sit beside their partners during the reading workshop so the transition from reading to talking doesn't usurp valuable reading time (although sometimes this leads children to talk/read/talk/read throughout the reading workshop, which is not what you have in mind).

Teach Readers to Read with Stamina and Fluency, Monitoring for Sense and Using Fix-Up Strategies When Meaning Breaks Down

Every unit of study features a few especially essential reading skills. This unit spotlights the importance of reading with stamina and fluency and of using knowledge of narrative text structure to comprehend, recall, and retell books. Readers learn to choose just-right books and to read with alertness and engagement.

Engaging with Books

The first step toward helping students build their relationship to reading is to make sure that every child is reading with engagement. It is invaluable to steer children towards high-interest books and to talk up those books. When books are exciting, kids pick them up, start reading, and stay with them. Of course, part of this task also includes teaching kids when to put books down. If a child finds that reading a particular book feels like a chore, then he needs to recognize that something is wrong.

Empathizing With Characters

You'll help children experience the lost in a book feeling that is so essential to reading fiction and you'll support this engagement first and most by reading aloud to them, and teaching explicitly about the experience of participating in a book in this way. In order to encourage empathy with characters, you'll look up from your read-aloud and say things like, "He must be so sad," or "I was thinking about him all night…I'm so worried about him." You will help children care about characters by modeling how to talk and think about them as if they are real people. You will encourage children to turn-and-talk in ways that promote identification with the character. For example, you might say, "How do you think he's feeling right now? Turn and talk." Or, "I'm worried about her. Aren't you? Turn and tell your partner about your worries." Of course, the next step would be to urge each child to listen as if he or she were one of the characters. "Show me on your faces what Annemarie is feeling *now*," you might say. Or, a bit later, "Use your body to show me what's happening to Annemarie now."

Monitoring for Sense

You'll also teach children to monitor for sense, both by showing that sometimes as one reads aloud, something will happen in the book that makes us go, "Huh?" That monitoring for sense is a crucial part of reading, and you'll show readers that when the meaning of a text breaks down, and they say, "Huh?" they can then engage in problem-solving strategies to regain a hold on the text—or they can locate a more appropriate text. These are tall orders—especially considering that we are just getting to know the children!

DRAFT

Making Reading Lives

PART ONE

Learning from Best and Worst Reading Times

If I asked each of you to name your overarching goal for your children as readers, my hunch is that you'd answer, "I want my children to become lifelong readers." These are strong words; this is perhaps the most important goal that a teacher of reading could ever hold. You are saying, "Hold me accountable for my kids initiating reading in their own lived lives."

My worry is that sometimes we *say*, "My goal for my children is lifelong literacy," but then we end up teaching toward much smaller goals. I think it happens this way. We launch the year, hoping our kids will love reading. Within just a day or two, our hopes are dashed. It becomes clear that teaching reading will be about battling apathy, disengagement, and resistance. Meanwhile, we are surrounded with reminders that we will be held accountable for our children's progress in reading, and the thought scares us. If we are going to be held accountable, we are determined, therefore, to hold our children accountable, as well. And so we work zealously to

GETTING READY

- Create a class meeting area, framed by your classroom library, that ideally is carpeted and comfortable. At the head of the meeting area, place your chair and an easel containing a pad of chart paper with plenty of markers. You may also want access to a whiteboard. This space and these materials will be a part of your daily practice.

- You may want to establish temporary partnerships and a temporary seating chart until you have determined students' reading levels and can assign partnerships. Many of you will decide instead to just allow children to sit as they chose for now and to talk with whichever classmate is handy.

- On chart paper write, "This makes me think that to make reading the best it can be, I should…" You will point children's attention to this chart during the minilesson.

- Cluster kids' desks to form tables and place a bunch of books in a bin at each table. The books should be high-interest and either easy or just right for readers at the table. If you group children with an eye toward reading levels, remember these initial groupings will be temporary until you've actually determined reading levels.

- You may assign one child at each table to be a table monitor, who takes out and puts away book bins each day.

- Make sure there is a stack of Post-its near the book bin at every table cluster.

- Develop a system for children to check out and return books from the class library. For now, you may want to create a sheet at each table for children to sign out and sign in books. Later on, you'll probably want to think of a longer-term solution. Also, you may want children and their caregivers to sign a contract agreeing to contribute to the class book fund if the child neglects to return a book. If you decide to do so, you may want to send those contracts home today.

- See the *Resources* CD-ROM for additional examples of minilessons that show how repeating your teaching point several times enhances children's learning.

be sure that kids' reading is something we can see, check off, count, and measure. Meanwhile, for our children, reading becomes a process of answering questions, defining terms, listing traits, and filling in questions on ditto sheets. And pretty soon our teaching has lost touch with the goal of helping kids author lives in which reading matters. We are, instead, teaching toward smaller goals: Can children recall the name of the protagonist's sister, differentiate similes from metaphors, answer the cause-and-effect question at the end of the chapter?

> *I think that when we teach, we need to remember that human beings want to work with heart and soul on endeavors that matter.*

I am convinced that our teaching can be more powerful than this. I'm convinced that when children begin the year, resistant to reading, this is mostly because they've had few opportunities to build lives in which reading matters and fewer opportunities still to learn alongside a mentor who wears a love of reading on her sleeve. I'm convinced that if our real goal is to help children become avid readers, initiating reading in their own lived lives, then we need to give them the conditions that we, ourselves, want as readers—and these include time, choice, companionship, and opportunities to grow. I'm convinced that we do ourselves and our children a great disservice when we buy into the belief that they will only work hard if they're forced to do so.

Let me show you what I mean. Think of a time in your life when your work was as good as it can be. Actually do this. Thumb through your teaching memories, settling upon a time when your teaching felt alive and vibrant and good.

Now hold that time in your mind and ask, "What was it about that one time that made my work good? Why was that bit of work good for me?"

I'm pretty sure you are not saying, "Work was good because I could come in late, leave early, cut corners, slack off. No stress, no pressure. I could put my feet up on the table and munch chips." No. My hunch is that you are probably saying that your work was good when you poured yourself with heart and soul into an endeavor that mattered, when so much was expected of you that you weren't sure you could rise to the occasion, when your work added up to something big and beautiful. You probably thought of a time when your work was hard, but it was important, and it was yours. You were able to make decisions, to draw on your own strengths, to go for goals you chose.

I think that when we teach, we need to remember that human beings want to work with heart and soul on endeavors that matter.

In this minilesson, you do not make reading into something small. Instead, you say, "My goal is for you each to do nothing less than build a life in which reading matters." You say to children, "It is always, in life, *My Life,* by me." You say, "Go to it." Then you give readers books, time, company—the three things readers need most—and you pull your chair alongside them to learn how you can help.

DRAFT

MINILESSON

Learning from Best and Worst Reading Times

CONNECTION

Position children to think about their reading not as something that happens to them, but as something they have the power to make great. In this case, tell children reading can be good or not so good, and we can make it good from now on.

"Readers," I said. "Could I have your eyes and your attention, please?" I touched my eyes and then scanned the group as if collecting the children's attention. "I'll wait." I let the silence gather. "What I want to say is incredibly important so I need your eyes and your ears."

"Readers, notice that we have gathered as a community in a special place—our library; we're surrounded by books. I want to talk with you about reading, and about our lives. This will be a year when we all, every one of us, can make reading the best that it can be. We'll work on building our reading lives into exactly what we need them to be."

"I don't know each of you yet. I don't know the stories of you, Kobe, and you, Emma, as readers, or of the rest of you. But I know that for me, there have been times in my life when reading has been the worst, *the pits*—when reading has made me feel frustrated and bored. There have also been times in my life when reading has been *the best thing* in the world. This year, we're going to work together to make our classroom into a place that supports the reading lives we make so that our reading is the best that it can be. I'm not sure what we'll need to do in order to do that—we'll have to decide how our time will go, how our library will go, how our conversations will go. I will need your input, so you'll need to study how reading has gone for you, and how it could be better."

COACHING TIPS

Beginnings matter. We must open our lesson with a tone that expresses that the words to come are important. I do this by saying "Readers," and then I pause, scanning every face until all eyes are on me before continuing. Then I begin.

The way you talk to your kids in your minilesson matters tremendously. You need to figure out how to make these words feel right coming out of your mouth, or you need to change them so they work for you. Your attention needs to be not on your words, but on your kids and how they are hearing you. Think of this text like a blind man's cane. That blind man's focus needs to be through the cane and on the sidewalk itself, as if his fingertips are there on the sidewalk and the grass. If the blind man's focus was, instead, on the grip of the cane, then the cane wouldn't connect him to the world. In a similar manner, your attention needs to be through the words of the lesson and on to your kids; the words are only intended to help you reach them, not to become the new focus of your attention. You might glance at what I've written as you teach or (better yet) make your own version of it, but you need to lean forward, look your kids in the eyes, and talk intimately to them.

Don't be surprised that today and for a few weeks, you will find yourself struggling to figure out how you can use these books. We hope you'll eventually settle on several ways to use these books as you reach toward your goals for yourself and your students.

Name your teaching point. Specifically, teach children that people sometimes pause to reflect on our lives and then make choices and changes. In this case, we'll do this with our reading lives.

> "Readers don't just read books; we build reading lives, 'author' reading lives, in which reading matters. For each one of us, it is always "My Life," by me. And each one of us has choices. We can make lives for ourselves in which reading is the pits, or we can make lives for ourselves in which reading is the best it can be. Today, I want to teach you that to build powerful, wonderful reading lives, we need to reflect on our reading and then make wise changes so reading becomes the best it can be for each of us."

TEACHING

Set children up to notice that readers pause to reflect on times when reading has been the pits and times when it has been the best it can be. Recall and sketch a bad and then a good time, using this as an invitation to reflect and resolve.

> "When a person decides to be a singer or a soccer player, we do stuff with singing or with soccer, and then pull back and think, 'What's working for me? What's not working for me?' and we use our answers to those questions to help us author lives in which singing (or soccer) is the best it can be."

> "The same can be true for reading. We do stuff with reading, and then pull back and think, 'What's working for me?' 'What's not working for me?' And we use our answers to those questions to help us author lives in which reading is the best it can be."

> "Sometimes, when I am in the midst of reading, I pause and think, 'Is this working? Not working?' Other times, I think back over my earlier life as a reader. I remember particular times, and then think, 'Was that reading time working for me? Not working?' Watch how I do this, because in a minute, you're going to have a chance to do it too."

The teaching point is the crux of any minilesson. You signal that you are at this crucial part of the minilesson when you use the words, "Today, I want to teach you…." Say these words as if they have great weight, as if they will create a hush in the room and a deep attentiveness. Be sure your voice intonation changes and you use gestures to highlight the juxtaposition between reading that is "the pits" (spit that word out) and reading that is "the best it can be" (say this melodiously). You'll return to the phrase "the best it can be" often throughout this year since that is our over-arching goal.

In A Guide to the Reading Workshop, I explain that it is ideal for you to put each of these minilessons into your own best words. Make your own adaptations. The exception to that may be the teaching point, at least for a time. Until you are accustomed to the minilessons, you may find you either read the teaching point, or better yet, say it by heart. We want to keep these teaching points brief, interesting, and usable again and again. You'll find the teaching point will be repeated within the minilesson because we are trying to put words in kids' mouths—minds—so that they can remember them later, so they can use these lessons about reading (and life) over and over again throughout their lives.

The teaching method I will use in this minilesson is demonstration. I'll dramatize the way I go about doing what I hope children will do. Usually a demonstration is preceded by the teacher telling children what it is the teacher notices and what they'll be able to do afterward with what they notice.

Demonstrate your recollection of bad and good times reading by thinking aloud.

"So, let me think about a time when reading didn't work for me. Hmm… I'm thinking back to when I was your age. Let's see… When was reading pretty much the pits for me? Oh! I know!"

In this instance, I am thinking aloud in front of the kids. It is as if I have opened my brain up so kids can see me in the process of mulling over my memories. Whenever I think aloud, I try to signal that this is what I am doing. I'm no longer reading the words of the book. My eyes look up toward the ceiling; my voice conveys that I am musing.

"When I was your age, this girl in my grade—Gretchen Sarnejoki—was into this science fiction series. She carried thick books around like they were the coolest things."

If, as you tell your story, you hear talking, you might look in the direction of the children who are talking and stare hard at them, putting your finger to your lips. And then quickly get back to what you were doing.

"One day, I asked to borrow one of Gretchen's thick books. I couldn't even read the characters' names. It was awful. I kept falling asleep. But I carried that book around for weeks, pretending to read it. That was one time when reading was the pits."

I decided to illuminate the fact that sometimes readers try to impress others and sacrifice their reading lives as a result because I expect many children in the class do just that. You can share your own reading story, of course, but try to share a vignette that is detailed and brief—a tough combination—and that resonates for your kids.

In this minilesson, the children each sketch a positive memory of reading and then share the story of that moment. The fact that children sketch rather than simply recall these memories adds complexity to the minilesson because it means that youngsters need pen and paper on hand. You can forego the sketching if you decide to do so and rely only on children's memories, instead.

"Of course, there have also been times when reading was the best it could be. Let me think of one time in particular. Oh! I know! When I was a bit older than you, I read a book called *Exodus.* Late at night after my mom called, 'Turn off the light,' I kept reading by flashlight under my covers. I remember reading faster and faster, my heart pounding, desperate for the kids in the story to escape the Nazis to reach safety! And I remember longing to be part of a cause like theirs. Now when people ask me how I came to be a teacher, I sometimes say, 'Because of the book, *Exodus.*' It taught me that I want not just a job but a mission. That book was so important to me. It's easy to see that that was a time that reading was the best it could be for me!"

This personal story, and consequently the minilesson, is longer than ideal, but it is crucial to start the year off by being real with your children. You may decide to extend your own reading story just a bit, as I have. Be mindful, though, that the choice to keep kids in the meeting area comes with at a cost: less time for children to get lost in their own reading. You will always want to crop every possible minute from a minilesson. Be sure you don't get into a back-and-forth exchange during your minilesson since that will usurp kids' reading time. Use every possible device to keep your minilessons as brief as possible—while still making them powerful.

"The important thing, readers, is that we not only pause to remember, or to notice, whether reading is or is not working for us. We also mine those times for insights on how reading should go in our lives. We go from noticing that our reading is working or not working to thinking, 'This makes me think that to make reading the best it can be, I should…' (and I gestured at the words I'd written on chart paper). [Fig. I-1]

This makes me think that to make reading the best it can be, I should…

"I'll show you what I mean. When I think about that time I pretended to read one of Gretchen's books even though it was totally confusing, I wonder what I can learn from that. Never to borrow Gretchen's books? Never to read fat books? That's not it at all. Never to read science fiction. No, that's not what made it awful. Now that I'm saying it out loud to you all and really thinking about it, I'm realizing that the heart of what made that reading experience the pits was that I was faking it. I was trying to impress people, trying to be cool, carrying a thick book around, but it ruined my reading life since I couldn't really read it. This makes me think that to make reading the best it can be I should not fake reading. I need to have the courage to say, 'This is too hard for me' if it is too hard for me! Or 'I like mushy romance stories!' if I like them, even if other people don't."

Debrief, naming what you have done that you hope children will learn to do also.

"Readers, I hope you notice that readers don't just *read*. We also build reading lives for ourselves. To do this, we pause to reflect, 'When was reading the pits for me?' and 'When was it the best it can be?' And then we figure out how these reflections can help us learn how to change our reading lives for the better." [Fig. I-2]

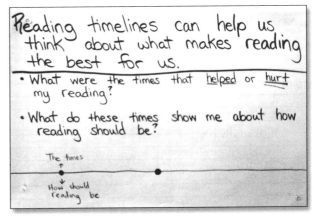

Figure I-1
If you ask children to timeline their lives as readers, you can then help them mine those timelines for insights that can inform the new year.

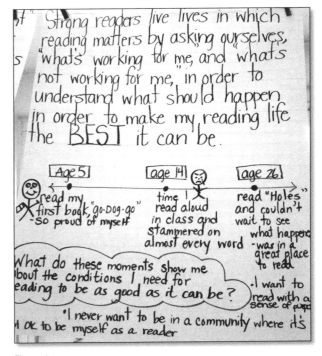

Figure I-2
By asking children to reflect on their reading lives, recalling what has and has not worked, teachers set the tone for the unit. This conveys the message that *this* year, in *this* room, reading will be great.

ACTIVE INVOLVEMENT

Invite readers to try the process you've demonstrated. In this case, ask them to start by remembering times in their lives when reading either worked or did not work for them, and talk about that one time.

"So, let's try that. Right now, will you think back over your whole life as a reader? Think of the bad times, when you felt horrible as a reader." I paused and let them actually leaf through memories. "Thumbs up if you've thought of at least one time when reading was the pits for you." [Fig. I-3]

Figure I-3
Knowing that Grace struggles to find a quiet place suggests she may benefit from working in a "private office" within the classroom.

When you teach minilessons early in the year, you are not only teaching the specific content of the day; you are also teaching your kids how minilessons tend to go. You are teaching kids the roles you hope they'll play in these minilessons. You may want to watch a minilesson on the DVD to see ways in which you can handle the predictable problems. For example, you'll want to think now about what you will do when a kid blurts things out in a loud voice.

Notice in this minilesson that when we want children to do some mental work, it helps to leave space for it. Silences are very important; they signal "Do this now." When you ask kids to think and then you stop talking, the resulting pool of silence means that you expect the voice in each child's mind must be his own voice, not yours.

Notice that I often ask children to use a thumbs-up gesture to signal when they are with me. I expect children will keep their raised thumbs close to their chests so they don't create a hands-in-people's-faces effect. I definitely do not wait to be sure every child has produced a thumbs up before I proceed. I tend to expect well over half the children will signal they are with me, and then I move on.

"Now think of a time in your reading life when reading was just about the best it can be. Think of a particular time, perhaps a particular book." I paused and let children do this thinking. "Thumbs up if you've thought of one time when reading really worked for you." I noted many thumbs going up. *[Fig. I-4]*

"Will you find someone sitting next to you and talk to that person about the time reading worked and made that one time so great for you as a reader? Or talk about the time reading didn't work and what made it the pits for you as a reader." After a moment, I pointed to the chart from earlier and called out, over the buzz, "This makes me think that to make reading the best it can be, I could…." I provided them with time to make some resolutions based on what they'd figured out.

When we first taught this session, we asked children to sketch out the bad and good memories they selected to help them hold these long enough to reflect upon them. We later decided this extra step—the sketching—was probably not helpful, because it didn't seem to be a technique children would use again to help them make decisions about how to change their lives. In life, we use mental recollections and conversations to inform the present and future, not sketches.

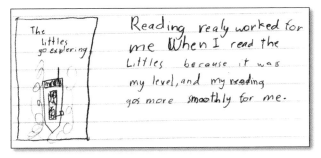

Figure I-4
When students articulate what works for them when they read, they take ownership of their reading lives.

Today, when readers turn and talk with a neighbor, they create very temporary arrangements. To keep things straight, I refer to these as reading friends or neighbors, and not as reading partners. The latter term is reserved for the more formal, long-term arrangements that you'll establish once you've assessed readers and know those who are reading books at a similar level of difficulty, you'll establish long-term partnerships. In this book, I establish these partnerships in Session XI. (This gives you a deadline for assessing your readers.) At that time, for example, two children who are reading books that are level S/T might become partners. Ideally, I partner children who are friends already or who are likely to become friends because I want them to know the joy of sharing books with a friend.

Debrief, citing what a child said and emphasizing that your students' ideas will shape what the class does this year.

"Readers, can I have your eyes?" I paused and waited for their attention. "I heard Gabe reflect on a time that reading went well for him. It was last summer at his grandma's house in Montana. He decided what was so perfect about that reading time was that he had a quiet place for reading. So Gabe's got the idea that this year, he could create a place for reading, a very quiet place, at home. Gabe, I hope you *also* make a very quiet place for reading here at school!"

"The rest of us might want to think about Gabe's idea; we too could set up spots for ourselves where we can go to read. Gabe also said it was great when he had four Matt Christopher books in a big pile, and he's given me the idea that this year, maybe we should each have a short stack of books beside us as we read—books to look forward to next! I know many of you have come up with other ideas about what you need for reading to work for you. We'll need to build our lives to make sure we're working with those ideas!" *[Figs. I-5 and I-6]*

I like to sit back and relax with a good book. nobody talking and the cricks chirping and the cars Zooming past my house. I like to conlde with a blankat. It was nice

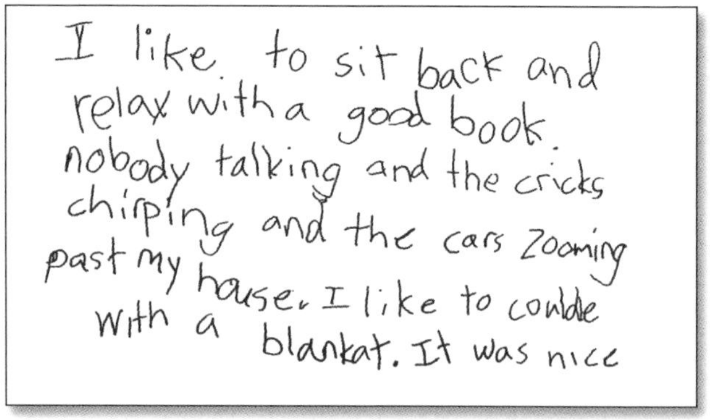

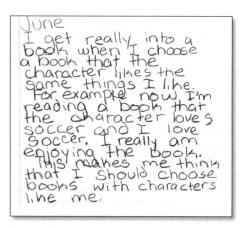

Figure I-5
Children's reflections on their reading lives reveal a lot about them as readers.

June
I get really into a book when I choose a book that the character likes the same things I like. For example now, I'm reading a book that the character loves soccer and I love soccer. I really am enjoying the book. This makes me think that I should choose books with characters like me.

Figure I-6
When children talk about times when reading has worked for them, they help you create a buzz around reading.

LINK

Send children off to read, helping them manage the transition.

"On this very day, you are going to have time to read—and to think about what works for you as a reader. Table 1, I've put together a bin of books that I know you're gonna love. There are old favorites here, and some quick reads that you can zoom through. There are probably also some books that make you say, 'No way! This one does *not* feel right for me.' That's fine because you are the boss of building your reading life. You can go back to your table and get started reading from that bin."

After that group dispersed, I talked in a stage whisper to the readers remaining in the meeting area, knowing what I said was heard across the room. "Look, Isaac has already settled into reading! So has Tyrell! Let's see how the other readers at Table 1 start reading."

Then I dispersed children from another two tables, saying, as they traveled to their seats, "I can't wait to watch *you* settle into reading." Eventually, all the children were sent back to read. As I moved among the tables, I said to all the children, "I'm looking for nose-in-the-book reading." I tapped one child's book as if you signal, "eyes here." I made a "What's going on?" gesture to another child as if asking, 'Why aren't you settled into the seat?'

Remind children that whenever they are trying to improve at something, they can pause to ask themselves, "Is this working for me?" or recall a time it has worked. Then, they can figure out what supported the success and build that into their lives.

After a bit, I said, "Readers, after you've read for a bit, pause and think to yourself, 'Is this reading working for me? Not working for me?' because you need to author a reading life for yourself. And you have choices. You can make a life in which reading is *the pits,* or you can make a life in which reading is *the best it can be.* And you will be the author of your reading life forever and ever, not just today, and not just in this class— you always have that strategy to use, of looking at your bests and worsts, then making wise changes so that reading becomes the best it can be."

Notice that you have reiterated the exact words you used in your teaching point. Minilessons rely on oral language to communicate and most orators know repetition is important— hence King's repetition of "I have a dream…" or Kennedy's of "Ask not what…but ask…." When you repeat the exact words of your teaching point many times, your words stand a chance of becoming part of your children's thought processes, and a part of their language. Plan to return to the words of previous teaching points throughout the unit of study and the year. (See the CD-ROM for other examples.) [Figs. I-7, I-8, and I-9])

CONFERRING AND SMALL-GROUP WORK

Manage the Workshop By Filling It with Respect for Reading

As you launch your first day of your reading workshop, your goal will be to create a well-managed workshop that brims with reverence for reading and to help each of your children feel recognized and at home within this workshop.

Manage Through Creating a Reverence for Reading

It may feel as if you are being pulled between the contrasting goals of, on the one hand, establishing the management structures that will keep your children working productively and, on the other hand, instilling reverence for reading. The secret is to convey to children that the reason they need to use every minute of time with care is because the reading workshop provides such a precious opportunity to read. During the first day, convey an enormous sense of urgency. "This reading workshop time is so incredibly precious. I can't wait for all of you to have this chance to read."

> ### MID-WORKSHOP TEACHING POINT
>
> #### Readers Choose Several Books at a Time So We Always Have One to Read
>
> "If any of you finish your book and need to choose another one, would you let me know because I'd love to help steer you to some great books. And as I get to know the books that you want to read, I might even suggest you start reading with one particular reading partner, someone I think might like the same sort of books."
>
> "And after I've met with you and given you a book bin for yourself, when you *do* go to the library, I suggest you choose a couple of books to keep in your bin. If you choose three or four books at a time, think of it like you have a short stack of books on your bedside table, waiting to be read. That way when you finish one book, you can go straight to the next without delay. When you choose a stack of books, think about choosing books that go together: three books in a series, or three books by an author, or three dog stories. That's what lots and lots of readers do. Of course you'll also remember to choose books that you can read easily and smoothly. You can resume your reading."
>
>

Today and throughout the first portion of the year, you'll want to provide scaffolds that help children transition from the meeting area to their own independent work. After you send children off from the minilesson, you will probably circulate quickly, using nonverbal signals to draw their attention toward reading. A child is still chatting with a classmate; I catch her attention, make a "shh" gesture, and pantomime opening a book as a way to say, "Get started." I leave a quick note folded on another child's desk: "Reading time is precious."

Of course, once you've circled the room, settling children, you'll want to pull in to talk with individuals. Before you draw a chair close to a child, think for a moment about your goals. All of us, when we enter a new community, are given the chance to reauthor ourselves—in this case, help children who have always seen themselves as resistant to reading see themselves and portray themselves differently. Remember educator Jerome Harste's wise advice: "I see our job as teachers as that of creating in our classroom the kind of world we believe in and then inviting our children to role play their way into being the readers and writers we want them to become."

Especially during these early days of the year, I try to follow Dr. Spock's advice. He wrote, "Catch children in the act of doing good." I sometimes alter his advice to say, "Catch children in the act of *almost* doing good." For me, this means that if I see a child who appears to be daydreaming instead of reading, I am apt to say, "Oh my goodness. That book has gotten you thinking so, so much! I can just see the wheels of your mind churning. The same thing happens to me when I read—sometimes my mind gets so full of thoughts that I need to put the book down for a second and just think."

If I notice that a few children at one table are not focusing on reading—one is staring off into space, another is flipping though books in the table-top bin, and a third is adjusting her watch band—when I approach the group, I'll let them see me coming and correct their behaviors so that I can say, "I noticed that a few of you had taken a little break from reading and just now, you got yourselves started reading again—all on your own. That is so smart. Sometimes we *do* take a quick break from our reading to gather our thoughts or to think about what's going on in the book, and it is just the smartest thing in the world to be able to say, 'Break's over,' and to get back to work. I'm really impressed that you are the kinds of readers who can say, 'Break's over' and return to your book."

If I see Tyrell and Gabe wrestling over a book from the series *The Secrets of Droon*, I will *not* say, "Will you two quit fighting and do some reading? You are always coming up with some excuse not to read!" Instead, I'm going to interpret the event, to them, as one involving reading and the best of intentions, saying: "I'm not surprised you are wrestling for the chance to read a favorite book. I know just how that feels—I have so many books I'm dying to read, too, and it's so frustrating when someone else wants the same book!" Of course, you'll still need Tyrell and Gabe to find a way to settle the matter between them. So you might say something like, "I bet you can figure out a way to settle this ol''two-readers-want-the-same-book'problem quickly so you won't miss precious reading time. Take a second and figure it out quickly." Even while ending a tussle, you can convey confidence that your children are eager learners, good citizens, and responsible decision makers. Once Tyrell and Gabe solve the problem, I can tell the class in a mid-workshop teaching point, "Listen to this reading problem and solution Tyrell and Gabe just worked through!" I can explain in short that in life, it sometimes happens that two people are dying to read the same book, and that's what had happened with Tyrell and Gabe. I can shine a spotlight on the fact that they resolved their struggle on their own, saying "Eventually, though, they worked it out. Tyrell offered to be next in line for the book and Gabe said thanks, 'and when you read it I'll show you the really cool parts!'"

In countless ways, then, I'll coach children toward working productively while also conveying the message that I know they love reading and that they are no doubt dying to use every minute to read, read, read. It is crucial to work toward creating a culture in which reading is valued. You can do this by shining a spotlight on whatever children do that matches our hopes.

Help Each Individual Child Feel Recognized as a Reader

As you confer with children, you'll want to compliment the child in such a way that you help that child construct a positive self-concept as a reader. As you do this, you can also help the whole class see that there are lots of ways to be successful as readers within your class. For example, if you sit beside a child who keeps reading even after you've signalled you want to talk, you can help the child see his actions as significant. "You finished reading that passage before looking up. You seem to be the kind of reader who gets really drawn into a book! I bet that when I say, 'Let's gather in the meeting area,' you'll be the sort of reader who walks over like this. (I act out a child who walks, nose still in the book, to the meeting area.) Am I right? Is that the kind of reader you are?"

You may notice a child looking for a second book by an author she read recently, and you might seize this opportunity to address the whole class for a moment. "Jasmine just asked if I could help her find another book by Judy Blume because, as Jasmine put it, she was 'whisked away' by *Fudgeamania.* When we love a book, it makes sense to look for others by that author since it's likely we'll love those too. And Jasmine just told me that she'll read this second book differently than the first because now she'll notice how it fits with the first book, and she'll notice the ways Judy Blume tends to write, in general. That makes sense, doesn't it? If you are reading a second book from one author, you might borrow Jasmine's technique of thinking, as you read, about all the books the author has written." The truth, of course, is that you had this idea well before Jasmine, but in every way possible you'll want to help children feel as if their good ideas are shaping the reading community within the classroom. Especially in the case of quiet children like Jasmine, you'll want to make a big deal of contributions they make to the community that might be overlooked.

Another way to support a child's developing notion of herself as a reader is to connect the work she does in her life with the work she does in her reading. For example, if Brianna selected as her favorite part of her book a passage that contained details about relationships and very little action, I might say, "Do you know how unusual it is for a reader to say that his or her favorite part is a bit of text where there is no high drama, no fast-paced action—where instead of *action,* where there is *interaction?* I have a hunch that you are a people-person in life as well as when you read. I've noticed you watching kids in the class, noticing how others act and probably, how they feel, and my hunch is that you read people in books that same way. That is a really cool gift, a talent, and it probably makes you into a thoughtful and sympathetic reader."

You might feel uncomfortable deducing these sorts of things from just the page that a child has selected as a favorite, but you could do a lot worse than going around the classroom, saying to kids, "I've been watching you and it seem to me that you are the kind of reader who has learned to. . ." and then coming up with something wonderful to say about each child. You will certainly see more in your children if you aim to tell them something beautiful you notice about their relationships with reading. Then, too, you'll be conveying to children that their actions matter to you, that you want to get to know them, that you see great possibilities in them, and that they have talents, proclivities, ways with books that even they may not yet have recognized. Does one child hold a book carefully, respectfully, suggesting this is a person who knows that books are nothing to snuff at? Say so! Does another child walk quickly from the meeting area to his or her reading spot, not wasting a precious moment of reading time, suggesting he knows how to use his every moment really well? Tell him! When you pull your chair alongside one reader, does she say, "I'm okay, I don't need a conference. This is a good part." As if waving you away? Does another child laugh aloud as she reads? If so, tell these chil-

dren that you've noticed these crucial signs of engagement, and that these signs suggest they are definitely putting in the effort it takes to making reading the best it can be!

TEACHING SHARE

Readers Learn More from Best and Worst Reading Times

Help children develop systems for managing their reading lives. In this case, suggest they use Post-it notes to mark their places.

"Readers, can I stop you? We just have a couple of minutes before it is time for math. I know your minds are full of ideas about whatever you're reading. Right now, place a Post-it note—there should be some in your tabletop basket of books—in your book at the spot where you're leaving off, and jot your name on it. The Post-it note will be a bookmark so tomorrow you'll know where to start reading. Put your book back into the tabletop basket and then come join me in the meeting area."

Ask children to continue practicing the strategy introduced today, offering a way for them to use it more deeply. In this case, push them to think exactly how they can make their reading lives stronger based on their reading experiences.

"We've been thinking a lot today about the ways in which reading has worked well for us, and ways it sometimes has not worked well for us. Right now, I want you to talk once more about a time reading was great, or a time it was the pits. And this time, when you talk, be sure you add a little extra depth to your conversation, pushing yourself to think (and I gestured to some bullet points I'd written on the chart), 'This makes me think that to make reading the best it can be, I should….'"

On this first day, the children and I convene in the meeting area for the teaching share, but often I will conduct the share while they're still in their reading spots. For now, they'll sit next to anyone, but eventually, I will direct children to sit beside their long-term reading partners. I'm convening them today because one of my biggest goals right now is to bring the class together as a community.

> **This makes me think that to make reading the best it can be, I should...**
>
> - Find some great books
> - Find a quiet place and time without distractions

"So let me show you what I mean: One of my best reading times was that time I told you about when I read *Exodus* under the covers. I know that time was great because I loved the book I'd chosen, but it was also great because it was totally silent in my room in the middle of the night, and there was nothing distracting going on around me—in fact, the covers blocked out everything except me and that book! Now, you all have done some remembering like that, and here's the part where you have to push yourself extra hard. You'll want to add more thinking: 'This makes me think that to make reading the best it can be for me, I need to not only find some great books, I also need to find some times and places that are very quiet and don't have a lot of distractions. So reading at the bus stop, which I had planned to do, might not be the best for me after all. It might be that I need to plan to read late at night again. I'll have to think more about that.

Now, did you see what I did? I tried to stretch my idea of what makes reading good for me into now. Okay, it's your turn to do it. I'll give you and your neighbor a few minutes to talk, and then we'll gather back together. Go ahead."

Ask children to share their thinking in twos. As they do so, coach them to push themselves to use the strategies more deeply so that they can do this today and forever.

I listened in as Fallon talked with Sam. Fallon, chewing on the end of a red braid said, "I think reading works for me when I don't have to sit at my desk. At home, I always stretch out on my bed or the couch to read. It's more relaxing that way." She flopped back on the rug dramatically, arms crossed behind her head. She added, "This makes me think…um… we should be able to sit where we want during reading."

This is the first share of the year, so I want to make sure they have an opportunity to actually share with each other. It's a prompted share in that I gave them a prompt that will get them started and will guide their conversation. This can be a helpful scaffold for a while until children are used to talking about their reading, but you should expect that before long, share sessions will be less scaffolded and less controlled. You'll also notice this share matches the mid-workshop teaching point and the minilessons. This, again, is meant as a means for providing support.

Sam didn't respond immediately but stared up at the ceiling for a minute. He leaned forward, his small hands pressed to his temples. Then he spoke slowly, deliberately. "For me, reading works best when I am in a series, like *Harry Potter*. I really like those books."

"What do you like about them?" I prompted, knowing Sam was still thinking.

"Well, it's like you get to travel into this whole other world. And when you read another book in the series, you already know all about the world and how it works. And you know the characters too, and how they change—like in *Harry Potter*, they all grow up and they do different things at school and learn new magic. Some people get bored by series books but I don't. This makes me think that we should be able to choose what books we read."

Convening the class, I said, "Readers, as I listened in to you, I took notes. You're teaching me the things I need to consider as we coauthor our year of reading. When I hear many of you say things like, 'Reading works best when I can choose my own books,' it makes me think that this year you need choice. When I hear you say, 'I like to talk about my books because it helps me understand them,' this makes me think that maybe we should get reading partnerships going. When I hear that you don't like books about the olden days, this makes me think I need to teach some strategies for reading books that are set in different times because I'm pretty sure I could help you find ways to like those books. We've got so much to think about! Remember, whenever you want to grow at something, in reading or in anything else in your life, you can always think back on your experiences and figure out from them what actions you can take to improve in that area! This is not just something we do today; this is a strategy to take with you your whole life."

Don Murray, the father of our understanding of teaching the writing process, has often said that any course in reading and writing whose goal is to empower children must begin with silence—a silence children must fill. During this first day, you have not exactly been silent, but you have conveyed to children that this is their year, their reading time, and that your job will be to help them make reading into something that works for them. Conveying this message needs to be a big part of what you aim to do over these first few days.

Be sure you actually take notes as children talk with each other so that you can cite their words. Your attentiveness to their achievements will make a world of difference.

First Things First

I wrote *Living Between the Lines* when my sons were three and five years old. In the book, I told the story of teachers in schools with which I worked writing a letter home to their students' parents, asking the parents to write in return, sending the teacher a letter introducing their son or daughter. I enclosed the letter a group of teachers had sent home. It went like this:

> Dear Parent,
>
> I'm writing to ask you to help me become a partner with you in your child's education. I will only have your child for a short time in this trip through life—just one fleeting school year—and I want to make a contribution that lasts a lifetime.
>
> I know my teaching must begin with making your child feel at home in my classroom, and with helping all the children come together into a unique learning community made up of particular, unique individuals, each with his or her own learning style and interests and history and hopes. Would you help me teach well by taking a quiet moment to write me about your child? What is your youngster like? What are the things you, as a parent, know that would be important for me to know? What are your child's interests? I want to know how your child thinks and plays and how you see your child as a learner and a person.

In that book, I included a few of the responses, letters the teachers received such as Barbara Novak's that began, "As I begin to think and write about my one and only child, my first thought is to thank you for wanting to receive my insights on him. I've just watched Joshua and his two cousins set up a lemonade stand on a warm Saturday afternoon. I love the excitement, gleam, and joy he's experiencing as he sets out to do business…". The letters that the teachers received were each utterly distinct, yet each letter was filled with a reminder of the infinite preciousness of this one individual in the eyes of those who love him, love her.

A year after *Living Between the Lines* was published, the day came when I stood at the end of my driveway, my son at my side, waiting for the flash of yellow through the trees to tell me the school bus was rounding the bend. It pulled to a stop in front of us, and I kissed Miles goodbye, gave him a last squeeze, and watched as he clambered up the tall steps, turning to give me that last smile. I walked back to the house, wiping the tears from my eyes, remembering the words of author Elizabeth Stone who said, "Making the decision to have a child is momentous. It is to decide forever to have your heart go walking outside your body."

Then that afternoon, while checking the time, waiting, waiting, for that flash of yellow to round the bend and for Miles to be home again, I went to the mailbox. And in it was a letter from Miles' teacher. I opened it, and began to read:

> Dear Mrs. Calkins,
>
> I'm writing to ask you to help me become a partner with you in your child's education. I will only have your child for a short time in this trip through life—just one fleeting school year—and I want to make a contribution that lasts a lifetime….

How I laughed aloud to see my letter coming back to me! That hadn't been my plan, it had been in the book simply as an example, but I, for one, didn't care. The invitation was there, and how glad I was to sit at the kitchen table, and begin to put my child onto the page. I made a copy of the letter I wrote—it's in the file bearing my son's name, the one with all the little certificates and love notes and dried clover from all those years. The other day, when Miles left for the West Coast, for his first grown up job, I went through that folder again and found the letter I'd written to his teacher. It is eight pages long! How Miles' teacher must have hooted and hollered to see my tome in her mailbox! But how important it was for me to be able to say, "Let me tell you about my son…" and to put him on the page, in all his complexity.

On these first days of the school year, when the pressure to assess kids and match them to books looms so very large, it's good to get letters from parents that remind us of how this child plays and works. If Ms. Grimes was going to teach Miles, it was good for her to know that he was making a Roman Road smack in the middle of our lawn, with a layer of pebbles and then a layer of mud, poured into a makeshift frame

DRAFT

he created with a ladder, lying flat. I will never forget the author Avi's words to teachers: "If you are going to teach me to read and to write, first you need to love me."

So our first job, as teachers, is to fall in love with each and every child—right away. That is not always easy at the very start of the year, when we are still mourning the loss of last year's kids, but the truth is that youngsters know when they are surrounded by positive regard, they know when they are in a place in which they can take risks, reveal their vulnerabilities, aspire towards big goals.

I recommend you find ways straight away to invite your students to teach you who they are, what they care about. During those first days of the school year, when no one is yet accustomed to sitting at a desk all day anyhow, set children up to do the things that will help you construct a sense of this child as a reader, a writer, a person. Perhaps you'll want to ask children to draw pictures of one time in their lives when reading was the best it could ever be, and one time when reading was the worst it could ever be. The important thing won't be the pictures, but the shared stories that children swap about their reading histories as they share those pictures. Perhaps you'll want to give each child a square of the bulletin board, and ask the child to bring in stuff that shows her history, his history, as a reader. Imagine if you were asked to fill a square of the bulletin board with things that show *you* as a reader…which books, of all that you have ever read in your whole life, would you choose to put into that square? What ways of responding to reading would go there? It's not lightweight work to take the time to construct images of who we are as readers, and to put those out into the world.

Perhaps you'll ask each child to read something—perhaps a poem, a picture book—and to leave Post-its that show what that child was thinking, and then you can teach children to conduct reader-studies, noticing the kinds of thinking that each tends to do. This would allow you to begin to develop some language about how each of your readers is different from each other reader in the sorts of thinking that the child tends to do. "You've got this way of reading and asking questions that get right to the heart of everything. It's such a special thing because you take us into really deep conversations with those questions. I hope over the year, you teach us all about how you do that." That child might be reading books that are the least complex of any being read in the class, and yet the child is not

just a level—she is also an inquirer, and a teacher of inquiry to the class. From the very start, then, you will want to highlight that readers are more than just a text-level. Once you match kids to books, chances are good there will be talk such as, "I'm an N reader." You'll want to have the goods to counteract that, at least a bit. "You are also our class expert on the sports page, aren't you? I can't believe that you actually read it every single day before you even come to school!"

Once you've allowed each child to begin to tell you the story of who he or she is as a reader, then yes, I also believe it is urgent to match kids to books and to get each child reading texts that are roughly in that child's reading range. You may be uneasy about matching children to books—and believe me, you won't be alone in that. I do not know anyone who thinks that leveling books is a science or that efforts to use running records to match kids to the level of text difficulty they can handle is anything but a rough approximation, a way to generally steer kids towards books that are apt to be within their range. But most of us believe this work can be empowering, when done in a system that is imbued with respect and appreciation for each individual. And we believe that because reading matters, doing whatever it takes to get the books that kids can actually read into their hands matters too.

Before You Begin: Leveled Books and a System for Assessing Readers

As I've written about in *The Guide to the Reading Workshop*, there are certain aspects of assessment that need tending to even before school begins. (You will have all the work you can handle in these first few weeks of school with these twin tasks of establishing the foundation of your reading workshop and of assessing your readers, so any work that you can do before the children walk into your room—grab the opportunity!)

You, and hopefully your colleagues as well, will need to have already chosen a system for leveling books, whether it is based on the Fountas and Pinnell system or the DRA system, and you will need to have already leveled a portion, perhaps two-thirds, of your classroom library before the children arrive in September.

You also will need to have already established a system for assessing readers. Again, as I've written more about in *The Guide to the Reading Workshop*,

Fountas and Pinnell and DRA each have assessment tools available that can help with this, as does the Teachers College Reading and Writing Project website *http://frog.readingandwritingproject.com/assessments.html*. With the help of one of these sets of tools, and your already leveled books, you will be all set to begin assessing your readers, even on the first days of school.

Assessment Goal for the First Weeks of the Year

In these first weeks of school, our first priority will need to be matching each child with a book, a stack of books, really, that he or she can read. This is not the time to dive into conducting any one assessment in depth, discovering every detail of that reader's strengths and preferences and needs. For now, it is more critical that we buzz through the whole class, conducting quick assessments with lots of students, assessments that allow us to make sure that all the students are launched into reading just right or even easy books. It's more important that we get everyone reading, and better yet, reading with a partner at about the same text level, than that we collect complete, detailed, perfect data on each child. We'll need to aim for every child to be roughly assessed within the first two and a half weeks of the school year. There will be plenty of time afterward to conduct more detailed, rigorous assessments and to follow up on all the questions that our initial assessments will provoke. We need everyone reading, right away, so that we can teach.

This emphasis on conducting lots of assessments quickly and efficiently cannot, however, mean that we stop the assessment of a child once we find the first level where she reads at 96% accuracy and adequate comprehension. At that stage, the assessment is not accomplished! To find a reader's just right text level, we will need to continue assessing her reading as she works with increasingly difficult texts until her comprehension of the text begins to break down, in other words, until her "ceiling level" is established. This means that we also cannot chop off or even cut short the part of the assessment where we assess understanding. Assessments that consider only accuracy and not comprehension are utterly worthless—reading is not reading if a child does not understand the passage enough to retell it and to answer a few literal and simple inferential questions.

What Does the Assessment Work for the First Weeks of the Year Look Like?

No matter which of the several assessment tools you and your colleagues have chosen, the assessment work of these early weeks will be essentially the same: we'll be taking informal running records.

Here's the process in a nutshell. We will give a leveled text to a child to read. Meanwhile, we'll hold a form that reproduces a portion of that leveled text. On this form, we will note exactly what the child says and does as he reads the text. We'll note not only if child has read the words on the page correctly, but also if the child corrects himself or substitutes in words to take the place of the words in the text. Then, we'll ask the child to retell the text, and we will ask a few simple questions about it. Using a set of criteria that we've decided on previous to this, perhaps as part of the assessment tool set we've purchase or adopted or invented, we'll determine if the child has understood the story well enough so that we can ask him or her to try the same process again, with an even harder leveled text.

Using records from the previous year or some quick questions and casual observations, we should be able to start the process with a text that is slightly too easy for the child to ensure the child will have great success and be at ease for the assessment. Once we've figured out the text level that is just right for the child, we can show him how to find books at that level in the classroom, or we can offer him a stack of books to choose from. The child will then be able to keep a short stack on hand, perhaps in a bin or baggie, to read for the coming weeks.

As I've mentioned in *The Guide to the Reading Workshop*, Marie Clay, the founder of Reading Recovery, has written a short, accessible book on this topic, *Running Records for Classroom Teachers*, and if you don't have an assessment tool that guides you through this process, I suggest that you learn to conduct running records from the master by referring to this book.

A Sample of a Beginning of the Year Running Record

Here is an example of a running record a teacher conducted at the very beginning of her school year. You'll see that she is abbreviating the analysis of the details of his miscues and is instead looking for wider patterns in his reading—is this text level comfortable for him, yet still challenging enough for him?

DRAFT

Leveled Text Excerpt and Tyrell's Reading and Retelling

In this case, the teacher is using forms she downloaded from the Teacher College Reading and Writing Project website, and you could do this too if you are not already using another assessment system. Or, you can simply make a photo copy of the leveled text you are about to give the child so that you can have something on which to mark the child's reading, and something to leave in the folder you are creating for him as a record of the assessment you are conducting.

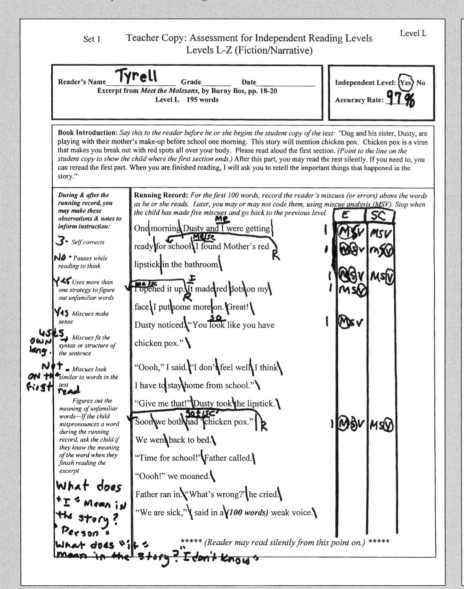

Set 1 · Teacher Copy: Assessment for Independent Reading Levels · Levels L–Z (Fiction/Narrative) · Level L

Reader's Name **Tyrell** · Grade _____ · Date _____
Excerpt from *Meet the Molesons*, by Burny Bos, pp. 18–20
Level L · 195 words

Independent Level: (Yes) No
Accuracy Rate: **97%**

Book Introduction: *Say this to the reader before he or she begins the student copy of the text:* "Dug and his sister, Dusty, are playing with their mother's make-up before school one morning. This story will mention chicken pox. Chicken pox is a virus that makes you break out with red spots all over your body. Please read aloud the first section. *(Point to the line on the student copy to show the child where the first section ends.)* After this part, you may read the rest silently. If you need to, you can reread the first part. When you are finished reading, I will ask you to retell the important things that happened in the story."

During & after the running record, you may make these observations & notes to inform instruction:

3 – Self corrects

NO – Pauses while reading to think

Yes Uses more than one strategy to figure out unfamiliar words

Yes Miscues make sense

uses own lang. – Miscues fit the syntax or structure of the sentence

Not on the first read – Miscues look similar to words in the text

Figures out the meaning of unfamiliar words—If the child mispronounces a word during the running record, ask the child if they know the meaning of the word when they finish reading the excerpt

What does "I" mean in the story? "Person"

What does "it" mean in the story? "I don't know"

Running Record: *For the first 100 words, record the reader's miscues (or errors) above the words as he or she reads. Later, you may or may not code them, using miscue analysis (MSV). Stop when the child has made five miscues and go back to the previous level.*

One morning Dusty and I were getting
ready for school. I found Mother's red
lipstick in the bathroom.
I opened it up. It made red dots on my
face. I put some more on. Great!
Dusty noticed. "You look like you have
chicken pox."

"Oooh," I said. "I don't feel well I think
I have to stay home from school."

"Give me that!" Dusty took the lipstick.
Soon we both had "chicken pox."
We went back to bed.
"Time for school!" Father called.
"Oooh!" we moaned.
Father ran in. "What's wrong?" he cried.
"We are sick," I said in a *(100 words)* weak voice.

***** (Reader may read silently from this point on.) *****

"We can't go to school," Dusty said.
Father nodded. "You are right," he said.
"It looks like a bad case of chicken pox.
You will have to stay in bed."
Father looked worried. "I am afraid it
will be boring for you," he said.

Father brought us
cakes, mint tea,
and books.

We were very happy.
I purred like a cat.
"This is heaven,"
Dusty said. "I
never felt so
good being sick!"

But when Mother came home after work,
she called for us. This is it, we thought.
Now we're in trouble! *(195 words)*

Total miscues including self corrected: **6**

Self corrections: **3**

Miscues reader did not self correct: **3**

Accuracy Rate: Circle the number of miscues the reader did not self correct.

100%	99%	98%	97%	96%
0 miscues	1 miscue	2 miscues	3 miscues	4 miscues

96%–100% accuracy is necessary to determine the reader's independent reading level. Try a lower level text if the reader made 5 or more miscues.

* *If the child makes the same miscue repeatedly, count it as one miscue.*

Literal and Inferential Retelling or Summary

Say, *"Please retell the big or important parts of what you just read."* Write notes regarding the student's retelling or summary on the back of this page. If the student has trouble getting started, prompt him/her to look at the text. Say, *"What happened first?"* Make a note that you prompted the student. Some students will retell the story sequentially in response to this prompt, while others will summarize the gist of the story. Either response is acceptable.

Use the Retelling Rubric and Sample Student Responses to determine if the child's retell and response to the comprehension questions are acceptable. If a student is not able to retell but is able to answer the comprehension questions, note that this student will need extra work on how to retell a story.

The boy and the girl got "sick" w/ chicken pox. They stayed home from school. Then they played in mom's lipstick to show they had chicken pox. Mom got mad. They had fun being sick.

Set 1   Teacher Copy: Assessment for Independent Reading Levels
Levels L–Z (Fiction/Narrative)

Comprehension Questions Section: Analyze the student's retelling/summary to see if it contains information that answers each question below. If a question was not answered in the retelling, ask it and record the student's response.

1. *Literal Question:* How does Dug get the red dots on his face?

Dug got "sick" w/ chicken pox. He used lipstick.

2. *Literal Question:* Where are Dug and Dusty supposed to be?

In school but they are playing sick.

3. *Inferential Question:* What do you think is going to happen when Dug and Dusty see their mom?

Their mom will be mad because they played with her make up.

4. *Inferential Question:* Dusty says, "I never felt so good being sick!" What do you think Dusty meant by saying this?

They had fun playing sick.

Oral Reading Fluency Scale – Circle the Appropriate Level

Fluent	Level 4	Reads primarily in larger, meaningful phrase groups. Although some regressions, repetitions, and deviations from text may be present, these do not appear to detract from the overall structure of the text. Preservation of the author's syntax is consistent. Most of the text is read with expressive interpretation.
	Level 3	Reads primarily in three or four-word phrase groups. Some small groupings may be present. However, the majority of phrasing seems appropriate and preserves the syntax of the author. Some expressive interpretation is present; this may be inconsistent across the reading of the text.
Non fluent	*(Level 2)*	Reads primarily in two-word phrases with some three or four-word groupings. Some word-by-word reading may be present. Word groupings may seem awkward and unrelated to larger context of sentence or passage. Beginning a little expressive interpretation, frequently first seen when reading dialogue. *staccato*
	Level 1	Reads primarily word-by-word. Occasional two-word or three-word phrases may occur—but these are infrequent and/or they do not preserve meaningful syntax. No expressive interpretation.

Adapted from: U.S. Department of Education, Institute of Education Sciences, National Center for Education Statistics, National Assessment of Educational Progress (NAEP), 2002 Oral Reading Study.

Final Score

(Yes) No   Was the reader's accuracy rate at least 96%?
Yes *(No)*   Did the reader read with fluency? (a score of 3 or 4 on the Oral Reading Fluency Scale)
(Yes) No   Did the reader correctly answer *at least 3* questions in the Comprehension Questions Section?
(Yes) No   Did the retelling/summary express the important things that happened in the text?

Is this the student's independent reading level?

- If you did NOT answer "yes" to all four questions in this **Final Score** box, try an easier text. Keep moving to easier texts until you find the level at which you are able to answer "yes" to all four questions in the **Final Score** box.

- If you circled 4 "yes" answers in the **Final Score** box, the student is reading strongly at this level. However, it is possible that the student may also read strongly at a higher level. Keep moving to higher passages until you can no longer answer "yes" to all four questions. The highest level that showed strong reading is the independent reading level. For example, you might find that you answered "yes" to all four questions in the **Final Score** box for level P, then a "yes" to all four questions for level Q, but only three "yes" answers for level R. Level Q is the highest passage on which you were able to answer "yes" to all four questions in the **Final Score** box. Level Q is the current independent reading level for the student.

Drawing Some Conclusions Based on Tyrell's Running Record

As we can see from the teacher's records, Tyrell read this passage with only 3 miscues that he didn't correct, and only 2 of those miscues didn't quite make sense in the passage. This is a high accuracy rate for him reading at this level—97%, in fact. His reading however, did not sound smooth—it was staccato, and his phrasing was awkward and unrelated to the meaning of the passage. Did he understand the passage well and just not read aloud well? The teacher asked him a few quick questions: "Who is 'I' in the passage?" and "What does 'it' mean right here?" and from his answers, it was hard to tell if he understood the passage.

Tyrell's retelling of the passage is a bit scrambled, but on the whole, close to the text. He answers three of the four comprehension questions correctly, but one of the inferential questions he misses. Taking all this into account and following the formula applied to running records, this text level, text level L, could be Tyrell's reading level for the time being. Although Tyrell's comprehension and facility with this text was not extremely strong, his teacher still wanted to try one text level more with him, in case he could manage that one too. She gave him an excerpt to read from text level M, but it quickly became clear that his accuracy would not hold him at that level, so she broke off the assessment before completing it.

Tyrell's teacher explained to him where in the classroom he could find some level L texts, and gave him a stack to look through for himself, choosing some to reserve in his own personal short stack.

Assessments on a Shoestring

Of course, even conducting these super-efficient, slightly abbreviated, informal running records, it will still take you two weeks before you have gotten to every child. What will you do to support matching children to texts when you haven't yet gotten to them? There are several other ways to make informed guesses about children's text level, quickly. Of course, these assessments are much less reliable, but they are only intended as stop gap measures, until you work your way over to each child.

Teach children the "3 Words" guideline. Dick Allington has invented a quick, rough rule of thumb: If there are more than three words on a page that you don't know, that text is probably not just right for you. While, of course, this is only

DRAFT

meant to be the roughest of rough guidelines, it can be a help to your readers. We could teach them this guideline and let them self-assess the level as they begin choosing books for themselves.

Set up tables of children likely to be at a certain level, give them the books, and observe. You'll be surprised how much you can estimate about a just-right reading level for a reader from across the room! Are the children engaged? If not, quickly modify your guesses about levels until they seem to be. You'll get to a fuller assessment later.

Ask a child to tell you about the last book they read that they loved, then give them more texts at that level. Of course, this won't always work, but it does sometimes. If a child has not been reading or decides to claim a popular book that is not truly one he's either read or enjoyed, this will fall flat. Sometimes, though, a short conversation is all it takes to make an educated guess.

Rely on last year's level. If you have records from the child's teacher of the previous year, try that level. Likely, it will be easy for the child, and therefore, a much better match for the child than a book that is too hard.

Find help from other adults. Is there a reading specialist, an intern, a student teacher who could help assess readers in these first weeks? Could any of those people, or others, help if you set up a few training sessions open to professionals across the district?

Expand the time in which you conduct assessments. Use every moment of your day, even considering borrowing a few children before school, during lunch, at recess, during an assembly or other period. Could you assess a few children during orientation in the late summer, or in the evening just before a Beginning of the Year Parent Night?

Cluster children and estimate the right level for them, watching to learn how they fare. In *The Guide*, and in the conferring sections of this part of the unit, I suggest that, just for a week, you may want to cluster read-

ers that you estimate might be at about the same reading level at a table together with a basket full of books that you suspect will either be just right or too easy for them. Include a few books that are harder, as well. As you assess other readers, watch what's going on with these clusters—you'll see quickly if anyone seems notably stronger, or seems adrift. Don't hesitate to use imprecise observations like these to streamline your more formal assessments.

Explain the logistics of the assessments to the readers in clusters. When you conduct assessments, bring a cluster of children to your area, and then you can explain what you'll be doing just once to the whole cluster of children. After your explanation, you can ask all but one child to turn away and continue their independent reading as you turn to the first child to be assessed.

Conduct two assessments in tandem. During the running record process, a child reads aloud a leveled passage as you mark their reading, then the child continues reading that passage silently. While one child is silently reading the rest of the assessment passage, try asking a second child—one who is likely to be at the same level—to begin their reading aloud. Then, as the second child continues reading the passage silently, you can turn back to the first child.

I've written about some of these and other ways to streamline running records in the conferring and small-group sections within each session, and you will no doubt invent your own ways. For now, though, let me say that while you assess your individuals, conducting some form of running records, the whole of the class will meanwhile be reading books at levels that you ascertain from whatever data you have—conversations with colleagues, test score levels—and are apt to be in the ballpark for your particular readers. From a distance, you can scan the scene as readers read these leveled books, and you can look for signs of engagement or disengagement that will let you know whether the book a child is holding is at least roughly appropriate for that child.

IN THIS SESSION,

you'll teach students that readers know it's important to occasionally stop and analyze our reading and then make resolutions to let it change how we read in the future.

DRAFT

Making Honest, Important Reading Resolutions

here's nothing like the start of a new school year—or of a new initiative. One of the great joys of teaching is the fact that every year we have the chance to start again, with renewed energy and resolve. We as teachers all know the excitement of new school supplies, squeaky clean notebooks and plan books, newly waxed classroom floors, clean desktops, and a whole host of new names on a new class list. Who are these children? What will they be like, and how will they work and play together as a group? We anticipate the year with butterflies of anticipation.

Of course, we are nervous and excited not only because we wonder who the children will be. We are also wondering who we will be during the year ahead. We face the new

GETTING READY

- Prepare a pocket folder for each child, perhaps labeled "My Reading Life," containing a stapled-together packet of blank reading logs. Either you or the child will also want to stash a collection of blank sheets of paper in this folder. This will serve, for the time, as a stand-in for the reading notebook that you'll eventually give each child. Some of you may decide to launch the notebook now.

- Provide each table with a stack of small Post-it flags for marking favorite passages during today's reading time. Another option is to ask children to supply these for themselves. Either way, you will not want to distribute Post-its each day.

- Suggest that children store a pen and some Post-its, which they will need for this and for future minilessons, in their pocket folders.

- You will probably want some Post-its and pens on hand to distribute to the children who don't bring them this first time.

- You'll want access to either blank chart paper or a whiteboard to write log information during the share.

- At the end of today's active involvement, you will ask children to write their New School Year's resolutions perhaps on strips of paper. In which case, you will need to cut white construction paper into strips and bring those strips with you to the meeting area.

- Look at your classroom arrangement and identify an area in which you can conduct assessments.

- Prepare to assess at least four or five readers with running records during this workshop session. You will probably assess all the readers who are clustered around one tabletop book basket, and they will probably be readers who read in roughly around the same range of text difficulty. You'll want to know the texts you are asking them to read and to duplicate enough forms so you have enough for each child.

- Consider how children will carry their books and other reading materials between home and school. We've suggested giving each reader a gallon-size plastic baggie, although there are other, more stylish options, as well.

school year asking ourselves, "Who am I as a teacher? Who will I be this year?" After all, if the class will come together like a drama, with each person stepping into the role that will become his or her part to play, we will also be assuming a role, becoming a character. One of the beautiful things about our profession is that we have a chance each year to remake ourselves.

> *After all, in order to set realistic, meaningful goals, both we and our students need to reflect on our strengths, weaknesses and hopes, and then we need to make manageable action plans that will help us reach our goals.*

If you haven't had a chance prior to now to imagine ways in which your teaching will be even better than it was last year, it's important to take that time now. You may be tempted to spend your free time cleaning the supply closet in your classroom or searching for that one perfect read-aloud that you know is somewhere. But the truth is that the supply closet can wait, and so can the search for the perfect book. The single most important thing you can do right now is to plan to become the teacher you want to be. If you don't have a dream, as they sing in *South Pacific*, how will you make a dream come true?

In our attempts to shed old skin and to become the teachers we aspire to be, many of us begin each year with a little list of New School Year's resolutions. We hope to be more organized in our teaching, so we scan teacher supply stores looking for the just-right plan book that will help us reach our goal. We want our teaching to be more responsive to our kids, so we resolve to interview each of our children at length so we come to know that child as a person. The important thing is that we not only make resolutions, but we act on them, figuring out systems, methods, and mentors that can help us achieve those goals.

Just as it is important for us, as teachers, to nurture dreams for ourselves, so too, it is important for us, as teachers, to nurture the dreams children have for themselves. And now, the start of the year, is the perfect time to invite children to imagine the ways they'll change in the upcoming year.

Children, like teachers, enter the new school year with butterflies in their stomachs. "Will my friends be in my class? Will my teacher be nice?" youngsters wonder. Lurking beneath these questions, there are other questions that are rarely articulated but even more real. "Who will I be this year, in this class? What is the story of this world that I'm joining, and who is the character that I will play?"

To imagine the ways they want to grow and change, we need to help students devise systems, plans, and mentors so they can reach their own goals. The process of coming up with New School Year's resolutions can be nothing more than a cute way to fill those empty September bulletin boards—or it can be a way to help children author their own lives. The thinking work behind creating and keeping resolutions is serious mind work and life work. After all, to set realistic, meaningful goals, both we and our children need to reflect on our strengths, weaknesses, and hopes, and then we need to hone those into manageable action plans that will help us reach our goals.

Whenever any of us aspires to shed the old skin and to become someone new, it helps to be surrounded by a supportive community of people who are engaged in similar lifework. In this lesson, you will help children rise to the occasion of this new beginning.

# MINILESSON

Making Honest, Important Reading Resolutions

CONNECTION

Tell children that teachers make New School Year's resolutions in September, at the start of a fresh year of school, and give an example of one of yours. Suggest that your students can do the same each year.

Before the children convened, I said, "Readers, join me at the rug. Please bring your book and a pen."

"Readers, eyes this way." I noticed that Lily was sitting with her back to me, absent-mindedly twirling her hair, chatting with a friend. I touched her shoulder, so she'd know to pay attention, meanwhile addressing the whole class. "Eyes this way."

Once I had everyone's attention, I leaned forward and talked directly to the class in a manner that suggested I was sharing a secret.

It doesn't matter what words you use to gather kids' attention as quickly as possible, but we recommend using concise phrases and using them consistently. In these first few days of school, it's vital that children learn that when you say, "Eyes this way," (or whatever cues you use), this is not an optional thing to do. To convey this, I suggest waiting so that you only continue once everyone is onboard. I don't want to embarrass Lily in front of the whole class, yet I want to hold her accountable to the task at hand. I want to be sure to help her develop the habit of getting ready right away. I also want the other children to see that "Eyes this way" means all eyes this way.

"Can I tell you a secret about teachers? Don't tell them I told you this, but September is like New Year's for teachers. You know how people make New Year's resolutions in January—like 'I'm going to run every day' or 'I'm going to stop eating hard candy' or 'I'm going to start keeping my room clean'? Well, every August, right before school starts, many teachers make New *School* Year's resolutions, hoping that we'll have the best year ever. I do this too. This year, I promised myself to keep track of all of the books I read aloud, recording them in this notebook. I decided to do this because I want to make sure I'm reading aloud a more balanced diet, one with different kinds of texts. I also promised myself that I'd interview you all because I want to listen to true stories of your life and to use your ideas in my teaching."

One of the most important jobs that this portion of the minilesson needs to accomplish is that it must connect us with kids. Of course, there are many ways to draw in kids. One, for example, is to tell a personal story. ("Can I tell you about something that happened to me, long ago when I was about your age? One day, I...). Another way to connect is to show children that you have thought long and hard about them, trying to select the right thing to tell them. ("Last night, I lay in bed thinking and thinking about what the one, most important, suggestion I could make might be. And finally, this morning when I was eating my breakfast, I realized that I do have a tip that I can give to you as readers, a tip that I think will make a world of difference. Are you ready to hear it?") This minilesson demonstrates yet a third way to draw in readers: I act as if I'm sharing a secret. Who doesn't want to hear a secret?

My larger point is that as you read through these sessions, you'll want to become accustomed to seeing each session as not only the story of what I did when teaching a class of children, but also as a template for how minilessons might go. If you notice a minilesson begins with a story that seems to have very little to do with reading, then it will help if you deduce from that example a transferable point that often, when teaching the mind work of reading, we talk about something that is not reading, and then draw a parallel to reading. Today, I shared one particular secret—that grown-ups make New Years resolutions. But had I decided that the minilesson would launch partnerships, I could have turned this to be a secret about partnerships. "Can I tell you a secret?" I'd have said. "Grown-ups don't want to read all alone. Most grown-ups have a reading friend."

Name your teaching point. Specifically, teach children that it is wise to seize opportunities, like the start of a new school year, to look backwards into one's history and forward into one's hopes.

"I'm telling you this because people who take care of themselves—as athletes, as musicians, and as readers, too—know that it is important to sometimes stop and say, "From this moment on, I'm going to...,' and then we name our hopes, our promises, our New Year's resolutions. After that, we make sure that important resolution changes how we live in the future, so that our resolution will come true. Readers do that too. We stop, we promise, and we look forward, saying, 'from now on I....'"

"Yesterday, we talked about how looking at best and worst times can give us ideas for ways we might change our lives. Today, then, we can figure out exactly which big changes we most want to work toward and some of the ways we can get there."

Teaching

Teach children that new resolutions can make a big difference if they are important and realistic. Show children how you go about making such resolutions.

"Since we are building a reading life that is the best it can be, we will need to occasionally stop, think of best and worst times, and bring in more of the best, *and* we'll need to occasionally stop and decide on resolutions for ourselves. The thing is—we can make those resolutions and they can mean very little, or we can make them and they can make an enormous difference. Let's think for a few minutes about how to be sure that we become the sort of readers who really, truly *do* build spectacular reading lives."

Notice that today's session fits tongue and groove into yesterday's. You should be accustomed to minilessons that are extensions of each other. Notice that I return to the key phrases from Session I's teaching by referring to our resolutions. Obviously, if our teaching is going to make a lasting difference, then kids need to carry what we say from one day to the next. Many children aren't accustomed to teachers and curriculum that accumulates, however. Part of what you are doing during these earliest sessions is that you are inducting children into the norms and customs of workshop teaching—in this case, getting them used to the idea that the lessons from each day are carried forward, not left behind.

"Resolutions should be *important*. If I really do want to author a rich and interesting reading life, then my resolutions need to help me make *important* progress toward that goal. I can't have ten goals—but I can make sure I'm steering myself in a direction that I think matters."

"Resolutions also need to be *realistic*. For example, I know it would be really great if I kept a record of *everything* I read—not just the texts I read aloud. Then I could really make sure that my reading life is balanced, and that I read across a wide variety of genres. But I am not organized enough to keep a record of every text I read—that is just too ambitious for me. It's more realistic for me to aspire to record the texts I read aloud to you."

"So let me think, for a minute, about an important goal, one that will take me far—but one that is also doable, realistic. While I think of a goal for myself, think of one for yourself, too, because in a minute you're going to have a chance to share an important goal you have for yourself."

There are many studies that list the skills of proficient readers. Interestingly, those studies rarely cite "initiates reading" or "reads with stamina" or "makes time for reading" within the list of skills. Instead, these reports say that proficient readers visualize, ask questions, infer, determine importance, and interpret. Proficient readers do those things—but they also carry books with them, reading often in a day. They read for long stretches of time when possible and have friends with whom they discuss texts. You'll see, therefore, that this series of books supports the proficient reader's full repertoire of skills, strategies, and life habits.

"Hmm…What I'm thinking is that I'm the sort of person who loves to read, if only I allow myself to do it. Sometimes, though, I end up postponing reading 'til just before I go to sleep, and then my problem is—I *do* go to sleep. I open a book to read, and my eyelids start drooping. Has that ever happened to any of you?"

"So I'm going to make a goal. In the year ahead, I want to read for more time every day. Specifically (I like to do that with my goals—to make them very specific), I've decided I'm going to try to read at least thirty more minutes than I usually do, each day. It used to be that I'd only read right before bed but now I will plan to read at other quiet times in my life—maybe at the waiting room at the doctor's and dentist's office? That's always quiet. And also, when I *do* read before bed, I'll go to bed earlier, so I won't be so sleepy, or I'll sit in a chair rather than lying down so I don't fall asleep."

Debrief. Describe the parts of your demonstration in a way that will help children transfer the outline of your thinking into their own minds. In other words, describe the strategy in a way that will be useful beyond this situation.

"Did you notice that to make a resolution, I thought about something that would really help my life? (Frankly, for me, the most important thing of all is making time for reading, finding time to read more each day.) I also set a goal that is realistic, not too far from what I've been able to accomplish already: Thirty more minutes isn't *that* much more. And, I tried to come up with some specific ideas for how I'll meet my goal—like suggesting maybe at the end of an evening I need to sit up in a chair to read instead of lying down in bed."

ACTIVE INVOLVEMENT

Ask children to make their own New School Year's resolutions. Ask them to share with a neighbor.

"Now it's your turn to begin thinking about your New School Year's resolutions. Take some time to think about something important you'd like to change about your reading life." I let some silence permeate the room, and then as I continued to speak, I did so in a way that suggested children would still be mulling this over as I spoke. "It helps to be completely honest with yourself about the strengths and weaknesses of your reading life and of yourself as a reader. Remember to think about something you could *do* in the year ahead that would make an important difference."

Notice that I often include parenthetical tucked tips into my minilessons, and usually these parenthetical comments extrapolate larger, more transferable points out of the minilesson. These tucked tips are not always in parentheses, but they generally feel as if they are included to enrich the main drift of the lesson.

Note that after demonstrating, I routinely step back and name what I've just done in a way that is applicable to another text, another person, on another day. I hope this will make my teaching explicit and transferable.

During the silence, I try to think of another goal I could adopt that would help my own reading. I've found that even when the room is silent and everyone is thinking, I can provide a powerful model if, instead of using the time to cast an eagle eye over the classroom, I actually sit in front of the children and do the mental work I hope the kids will be doing. As I do this, I am still taking stock of the children and estimating how many are with me.

Noticing that a fair number of children didn't seem to have any idea of how to make resolutions, I began providing more scaffolding. I say, "For some of you, your goal might be to get back into reading series books, because you notice when you are into a series, you tend to read a lot. Some of you might resolve to take more time choosing good books so that you don't just plug along through books you don't like." [Figs. II-1, II-2, and II-3]

"Okay, turn and share one of your New School Year's resolutions with a neighbor. Tell your neighbor your resolution and talk over some specific ideas for how you might actually go about reaching your resolution." [Fig. II-4]

Restate, with scaffolding if necessary, some of the New School Year's resolutions you've overheard children make. Propose a public holding place for all the resolutions.

"Readers, eyes up here. How inspiring you are! I heard so many ambitious, wise, honest resolutions. I heard one of you say that it's been hard to concentrate when you're reading. So you plan to work on really focusing while reading, and you'll need to get a reading spot that allows you to be alone. That's such an honest resolution. I heard one of you saying you wanted to try reading science fiction since so many of your friends have enjoyed it and you've never tried it. That could be a fun goal to fulfill! I'm thinking we could keep track of our reading resolutions on a bulletin board. Sometime today, during reading time or later, let's each of us record our most important reading resolution on one of these white sheets of paper." I held up strips of paper I'd cut. "We'll make a big display of them. That way we can look back on them and say, 'We've almost met all of our goals!' And we can say, 'I can help Kobe or Gabe or Kaylie meet a goal if I….'"

As they talk, I pay close attention, listening for resolutions that apply widely to the class—these resolutions I would prepare to share. If the resolutions children talk about don't seem developed enough to actually have traction in readers' lives, you may want to provide more scaffolding for children. For example, you might say, "You are on such a smart track when you say you want to be a better reader. What do you think are some specific ways you could do that?"

> My goal is to take my book I'm reading with me wherever I go so when I'm on the subway, I'll have my book.

> My goal is to find text I love because then I'll want to Read. I'll ask my friends about texts they really like.

> I'm going to read as many just right books as I can.

Figs. II-1, II-2, and II-3
These students are making goals and plans that reflect the conversations occurring in their classroom.

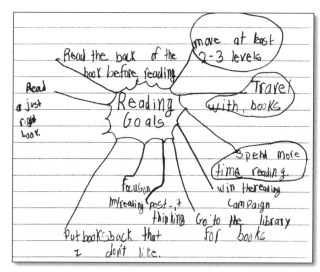

Figure II-4
In some classrooms, students made webs and lists of their goals, rallying them around the important work of authoring their own reading lives.

Link

Send children off to resume reading. Ask them to flag sections in their books that they particularly like.

"So, as you will every day, today you'll have time to read. I know each of you used a Post-it note as a bookmark. Please leave that marker on the page where you *begin* reading today, because later you'll calculate how many pages you read in a day."

"Keep your resolution and ideas about how to make reading the best it can be in mind, today and from now on. You are in charge of your own reading, so make wise decisions!"

"You will also see that I left some special flag-like Post-it notes in your bin of books. As you read today, would you flag places in your book that you especially like—just two or three places."

"Tables 2 and 3, you can go back to your tables and get started reading. Let's watch and see if these readers immediately get their books from the bin and read." As the children settled into their work, I chronicled what I saw. "Look, Josh is already looking for a page he can flag! Sam's reading, but he's got some of those Post-its ready at his side. Wow, look at Table 2. The whole table full of kids is already reading!"

Then I signaled that Tables 4 and 5 could get started. "I can't wait to watch you settle into reading." When several children didn't move efficiently to their reading spots, I walked over to them and quietly said, "Let's not waste another second of reading time. You've had enough time to settle. Please take your book out and begin reading" As soon as readers at Tables 4 and 5 were seated, I signaled for the children still remaining on the rug to move to their reading spots.

During the share session at the end of today's workshop, children will be asked to fill out the first entry in their reading logs, so it will be important for them to maintain a record of the page on which they started reading. If you notice some children neglect to leave their Post-it on the page where today's reading began, remind them to do so as you confer.

Notice that in today's link, you send children off to read. You don't send them off to do the work you demonstrated in today's minilesson—although of course that work now becomes part of their repertoire. But your minilesson is not an assignment channeling children toward the work of the day. The content you teach in one day's minilesson needs to last a lifetime.

There is a saying: "What you expect, inspect." Your children will learn to read from reading itself. So, you need to pay attention to kids actually doing the work entailed in reading

You'll notice that I pay a lot of attention to transitions. This is temporary. A month from now, the minilesson will end with a send off: Off you go! But for now, I'm apt to send children from the meeting area to independent work one table at a time, and to do this sort of sportscaster talk, naming what I see children doing as they move from the meeting to independent reading. I definitely do not want children to return to their seats and sit idly until I'm able to give each child a personalized jump-start. In classrooms where teachers take the time to teach children how to get themselves quickly to their independent reading, this transition can take a minute or two. In other cases, transitions can take away ten minutes of precious reading time. So don't hesitate to convey very clear expectations—go so far as to model how a reader walks quickly and directly from the reading area to his or her seat.

CONFERRING AND SMALL-GROUP WORK

Learn Tips for Making Your Assessments as Efficient as Possible

You will need to decide whether you must spend another day rallying children's enthusiasm for building a reading life or whether you can now shift toward a focus on assessment. If you decide on the former course, you might ask children to read aloud favorite passages (they will have flagged these) and then use this as a way to talk up each child's identity as a reader. "So you're the kind of reader who appreciates. . . ."Meanwhile, you can note the child's ability to read a text at that level. That is, if you see a child reading a level T text with gusto, then a day from now, when you take running records of this child's reading, you'll know to start at or beyond that level.

In his book, *What Really Matters for Struggling Readers,* Dick Allington presents research that demonstrates that when children do not have the opportunity to read lots and lots of books with ease, their reading suffers in dramatic ways. Once you have read those studies, I expect you'll feel as urgently as I do that you need to conduct quick assessments so that you can expeditiously match children to books they can read with at least 96% accuracy, fluency, and comprehen-

sion. Many children lose ground dramatically during a summer without reading. You can't afford for them to continue that downward slope once the school year has begun.

Aim to assess all your children within the next week. That timetable may take your breath away, and yes, it is possible to proceed more slowly, but you should feel very uncomfortable if your plan is that your children will spend weeks holding books they can't read.

In *A Guide to the Reading Workshop,* I outline a streamlined way to conduct initial assessments. Essentially, you'll need to rely on scores from standardized tests, on data from your children's reading during the previous year, and on your quick assessments done as children read from table book baskets to estimate the approximate level of text difficulty that each child can handle. If the child can read the passage with accuracy, fluency, and comprehension, progress up levels until the child reads a passage that is too hard, at which point you'll examine the child's "miscues" to glean what it is that the child can and can't do at the too-hard level.

MID-WORKSHOP TEACHING POINT

Readers Talk About Our Goals

"Readers," I said, in a voice that was intended not as a show-stopper, but as a voice over, accompanying their work, "In two minutes, we'll stop to talk. You will need to have flagged a passage you love." After another minute or two, I said, "Right now, find someone beside you with whom you can talk. Shake hands—don't leave anyone out." They did this as a way of making the links official, and I gestured for a few children who would otherwise have been left out to become triads.

"Each of you should have been checking in with yourself today as you read, thinking, 'How is reading time going for me today? What can I do to make reading time as good as it can be?'"

"Will one of you tell the other how reading has been going and what you have done to make it as good as it can be?"

As children talked with each other, I said, over them, "When you talk with a friend, make sure you lean across your desks so the other person can actually hear you, and make sure you don't mumble into your collar. These need to be real conversations."

Children talked for just a minute or two. "I know you both may not yet have had a chance to share—that's okay. Some days, one person will talk, other days, another will. " I noticed some children were still talking, so I paused. "Eyes up here." Once the class was absolutely silent, I continued, "I love the way you are making decisions so that reading works for you—

continued on next page

Use Every Available Minute and Person to Help Conduct Initial Assessments

Try to assess at least five children a day so that within just over a week, each of your children will be reading from his or her own bin of just-right books, sharing that bin with a matched partner. This is an ambitious goal, but it is possible.

It helps to start with the decision that your assessments needn't be perfect. Although you will eventually want to secure detailed information about children, especially your strugglers, for now you need to conduct initial assessments that are designed to get every child in the class reading books that are in the ballpark of just right for that child.

Use every minute and every spare set of hands to make sure your kids are assessed immediately. Ideally, your school has a reading specialist who can help teachers with assessments. If that's not the case, then consider other professionals. If your school works with student teachers, you could ask the university to teach methods of assessing readers early on in their methods courses so student teachers arrive with experience conducting and analyzing running records. If the university is not prepared to do this, then you might set up training sessions for student teachers within (or across) schools in your district. In many schools, music, art, and science classes may not yet have been launched, and ESL and speech teachers may not yet have their full complement of children. Ideally the principal will call, "All hands on deck," and recruit folks to join in the emergency effort to get all children's reading off to the strongest possible start. This plan may sound as if it imposes a heavy load on your colleagues; that is true, but at the same time, the school will be sending the message that all teachers are reading teachers.

> ### MID-WORKSHOP TEACHING POINT
>
> *continued from previous page*
>
> because after all, *you are the author of your reading life.* You are the boss of your life. If the book you are reading is too hard for you—you don't have to come and ask me if you can switch. No way—*you* are the author of your reading life! And if you want to reread the funny parts of your book—do you need to raise your hand and ask? Of course not. Because *you* are the author of your reading life, you will make these decisions."
>
> "Are you ready to do something that I absolutely love doing as a reader?" They nodded. "I absolutely love turning to my reading friend, someone who truly cares about reading as much as I do, and saying, 'Listen to this amazing part of my book.' Then I read that part to my friend and we talk about it. (When we have time it is especially fun to then *reread* the part in an even better way, this time reading to bring out the coolness—the funniness, or the excitement, or the beauty.) Right now, will one of you go to a part you have flagged and
>
> *continued on next page*

Consider assessing outside the regular school day. Can you bring in a couple of children before school or during lunch? Perhaps children from three classes can convene in the auditorium for a giant chorus practice, and the teachers from those classes can use that time to assess, assess, assess. Perhaps there can be a mid-day recess for this first week of school, with a handful of children from each class staying in each day for intensive assessments. All of these tradeoffs will be worthwhile ones.

In some schools, at least some children in each classroom will be asked to come to school during the week or two before the year begins for an orientation session. As part of these sessions, the reading specialist or literacy coach or an especially skilled classroom teacher conducts an assessment. This, then, means that the school principal can be assured that at least those children are well-matched to books and will travel an appropriate course. Hopefully, if a few children enter the school year already matched to books, the teacher can use these children as gauges. If a child reads as well as one who has been assessed as reading *Magic Treehouse* books and other level M books, then that other child, too, will probably be reading a similar level.

Bring a Cluster of Children to You and Assess One Child While Others Are "On Deck"

The reading workshop itself can provide many opportunities to assess. In *A Guide to the Reading Workshop,* I suggest that for just a week or two (no longer), you may want to seat children so that those who seem to be somewhat similar to each other as readers are clustered at a table with a basket full of books that you suspect will either be just right or too easy for them. Include a few books that are harder, as well. As you move among these children and observe them working with books that are at similar levels (with a few noted exceptions), you'll find that, even before you take each child aside for a more formal assessment, you'll be able to ascertain each child's relative abilities reading those books. This will help you hone in on each child's just-right reading level. That is, although you will have seated children at a particular table because data suggests they'll probably be similar, you'll find one who seems notably stronger, or one who is struggling much more. Although the judgments you'll be making will be extremely crude, don't hesitate to make observations such as these and to use them to inform your work with running records. Doing so will streamline your formal assessments, saving time and angst for everyone.

When you are ready to conduct formal assessments, I strongly recommend that you bring three or four children (who you believe will be reading at the same level) to the place where you'll be doing this assessment. If you bring one child alone, then you need to tell that one child what you'll do, then work with him, then send him back to his seat, get another child, wait while the child makes her way to your area, explain what you will do all over again, and so forth. More time than you realize can be consumed with the logistics. If you bring a cluster of children to your area, then you can explain what you'll be doing just once to the whole cluster of children, and then steer three children to turn their backs to you and to read their independent books, while meanwhile, you work one-to-one with a child who reads the assessment passage aloud.

I recommend that you start, always, by asking the child to read a passage that you believe will be a bit easy. It is depressing for a child to begin with a too-hard text and to regress down levels toward easier and still-easier texts. If, as the child reads along, you notice the child struggling with several words, then do not wait before intervening to say, "Thanks.

continued from previous page

MID-WORKSHOP TEACHING POINT

read it aloud. Don't read more than, say, two paragraphs. Then will the two of you talk about what makes that part good? If you have time, reread that part really, really well."

After a bit, I said, "It is time to return to silent reading. You have already read for fifteen minutes. Notice how many pages you read in that time. Now, you'll have another fifteen minutes for reading. If you read the same number of pages, what page will you stop on? Mark that part with one more Post-it note, sort of as a goal post. You know how some athletes run every day, pushing themselves to run faster and farther, and that way they strengthen their muscles? Readers sometimes do the same thing, pushing ourselves to read a bit more. Go ahead and get started."

Can we try something different now?" If the child generally reads correctly, without becoming derailed by more than a few unfamiliar words, then you'll want to take great care to notice the child's fluency. Does it sound as if the child is talking? It should. If it is apparent that the passage is *way* too easy, you could pause mid-way and say, "Thanks. Can we try another passage?"

Once the first child has read 100 words aloud to you while you have recorded the child's miscues (more on this in a minute), the child can shift toward reading the remaining portion of the selection silently (although, in an ideal world the child would actually read the *first* half the passage silently, and the *last* half aloud). Meanwhile, you can tap the shoulder of a second child and get that child started reading what will presumably be the same passage. Now you will record what this second child does with the first 100 words, just as you did with the first child, only on another piece of paper. By the time the second child passes the 100-word mark, you should see the first child has finished up reading the entire passage, and so you can return to the first child, this time asking comprehension questions. In this way, you can assess two children at one time, while another two are waiting in the wings.

You may worry that the children could possibly overhear each other's reading but frankly, if you turn children so their backs are to you and to the child who is reading aloud and if you get those children who are not being assessed at the moment immersed in their chapter books, very few will care to listen to a friend's reading. Even if they *do* glean a word or two, this won't allow them to fake being able to read something that they can't read.

The advantage of asking several children to read texts that are in the same range is that *your* preparations for the day's assessment work will be much easier. *You* need only read and think about a couple of passages.

Then, too, watching roughly similar children handle the same passage differently will help you discriminate among the reading abilities and imagine the partnerships you'll soon establish.

Corners You Can't Cut: Analyze Miscues As the Child Reads a Slightly Too-Hard Text

A word of caution: Often you'll find that there is not a lot to record. The child's reading may well be practically flawless. You may be tempted to declare that you have found the child's just-right level. But remember, you can't determine a child's just-right level without determining the ceiling for that child. So if the child reads one level flawlessly, you need to move to a higher level, and even perhaps to a third level, progressing until the child encounters a text that is too hard—and at that point, you *will* find yourself recording ways the child struggles. That is, if there is not a lot to record, you need to progress to higher reading levels so that you reach a place where the reader does make a significant number of mistakes. Only then will you be able to analyze the sources of information that children do and do not draw upon when reading slightly too-hard texts. This knowledge will help you know how to help the reader's process.

It is always eye-opening to notice what the child does and does not do when he or she is reading a text that is too hard, so this final running

record will probably reveal the most to you. It will show you not only that this level is beyond the child's reach, but it'll also show you what falls apart first for this child. The child's miscues will act as windows, helping you to see what the child holds onto, and lets go of, once the child's reading begins to break down. Until the child makes miscues, you won't be able to see whether this is a reader who holds onto *meaning* at all costs, generating words that make sense but do not match the actual letters on the page, or whether this is a child who holds onto the *visual* aspects of reading, diligently saying the sounds of the letters but letting go of meaning. You need to know what it is that each of your readers does and does not do when a text becomes hard if you are going to help each reader develop the capacities needed to tackle those just-too-hard texts.

You will need to make a decision whether, once you have assessed children, you want to channel the children whom you have assessed to select a stash of just-right books from the classroom library or whether for now, you'll simply want them to make good selections from those tabletop baskets, saving the opening of the library (Session VIII) for when the whole class has been assessed.

TEACHING SHARE

Readers Keep Records and Research the Ways Our Reading Changes

Distribute pocket folders containing blank reading logs, and ask children to record, study, and talk together about their data.

"Readers, you have now read for another fifteen minutes—so you've read a half hour in all. Will you use a new Post-it as a bookmark. Bring your book and a pen with you, and come to the meeting area. Tables 1, 2, and 3, come quickly please. The rest of you get ready to join us in a minute." Once half of the class had settled in the meeting area, I signaled for the other readers to assemble.

"Class, I'm giving each of you a pocket folder, entitled "My Reading Life." This is going to be *your* folder to hold the tools that will help you study your reading life—what's working, what's not working, how you can make it the best it can be. This isn't a way for me to keep track of you; it's a place for you to be honest about your reading, a tool to help you grow as a reader and to make your reading life your own. This folder has a packet of blank reading logs—I'll tell you about this in a moment—and blank sheets, which will be used to collect your jottings and sketches. You will keep this "My Reading Life" folder the whole year—using it in class and then bringing it home every night—and it's important that you have it with you here every day."

"Let's open up our folders to the reading logs." I searched the rug to see that every reader's packet of reading logs was on his or her lap. "Eyes, please." I waited. "Your log looks just like a packet of paper, but this will be the single most important paper that each one of you will have this year. You'll end up with about thirty sheets like this one. These will allow you to keep track of and to study your reading."

"Let's fill in the first entry on your log together. Write today's date (I wrote it on the white board) and record an *S* because we are reading in school (not an *H* for home). Write the title of the book you have been reading and the author—write two titles and authors if you finished one book and started another, and if you aren't sure of something leave it blank for now. Then look for the color dot on the spine of your book and record that color in the square on your chart marked *Level.* We'll talk about levels later. Record, too, the page and time at which you started and finished reading—I'll write today's start and finish times on the board so you can just copy them. Use your Post-it notes to figure out the page on which you started reading today, and the page on which you finished reading. *[Fig. II-5]*

"Today, you read for thirty minutes, so record that in the Total Time column. Here's the important thing. When you have finished logging your reading, study your chart. Do some math with your data. Think about how much you read in the first fifteen minutes—it won't be on the chart, but you have a Post-it note in the book to show that—and how much you read in the second fifteen minutes. Was one more or less than the other—and why might that have been the case? In a minute, I'm going to ask you to share what you observe about yourself with someone sitting nearby. For now, just study your log." After a minute of silence, I said, "Thumbs up if you noticed something," and when half the class indicated they'd noticed something, I said, "Tell someone near you what you saw." *[Fig. II-6]*

Teachers, it's important to emphasize that these logs are tools for self-reflection. It is very easy for children to feel as if these are the teacher's way of checking up on them, and of course the great risk is that children will start fabricating these logs, recording whatever they think you want to hear. Because children will keep the logs out on their desks every day as they read, it won't be easy for them to exaggerate the amount of reading they do at home. If they exaggerate the number of pages they read at home, then during the independent reading workshop, they will need to jump ahead in their reading, leaving great gaps in the text. You'll want to make sure the logs are out while children read, and that you look at them, to make them trustworthy.

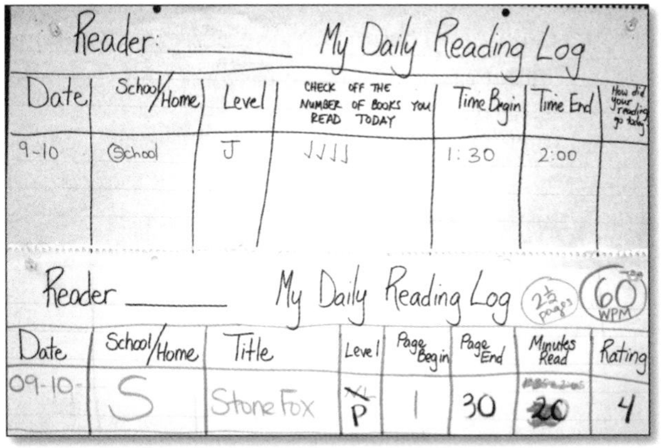

Figure II-5
Children reading books leveled A–J will often read several books during one day's workshop, so listing titles and authors for each may be too time-consuming.

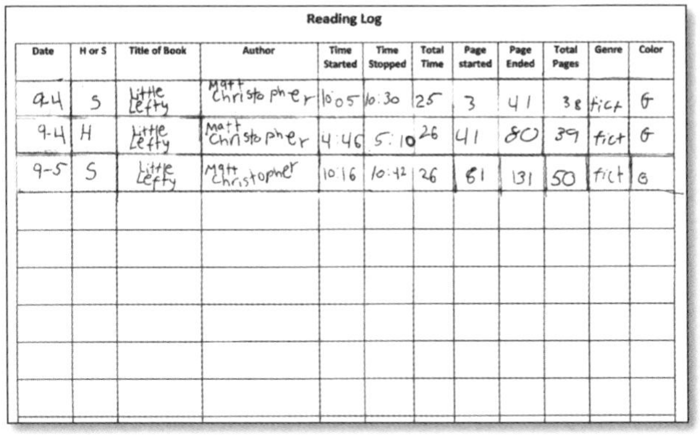

Reading Log

Date	H or S	Title of Book	Author	Time Started	Time Stopped	Total Time	Page started	Page Ended	Total Pages	Genre	Color
9-4	S	Little Lefty	Matt Christopher	10:05	10:30	25	3	41	38	fict	G
9-4	H	Little Lefty	Matt Christopher	4:46	5:10	26	41	80	39	fict	G
9-5	S	Little Lefty	Matt Christopher	10:16	10:42	26	81	131	50	fict	G

Figure II-6
Of course, the real treat is the opportunity to put a log smack in the center of a reading conference.

DRAFT

I listened in as Grace said to Izzy, "I noticed that I read twenty-six pages in thirty minutes. That is just about one page a minute. Wow, I'm pretty fast, aren't I?" She smiled, clearly pleased with herself.

As children talked with each other, I voiced over, "Wow! Some of you are coming to discoveries about how much of a page you tend to read in a minute! Some of you are noticing differences between how much you read today and how much you usually read. Some of you are comparing logs and noticing that you read differently depending on the book. Because you are the author of your reading life, you are going to study the records you keep across the whole year. And the records might just help you think about the goals you already set for yourself and about new goals you *might* set for your reading."

Channel children to begin carrying books between home and school, recording home reading on their logs. Ask them to make and sketch a reading place at home.

"Class, I'm going to give each of you a big plastic bag so you can take the book you were reading today home and continue reading it tonight. Put your reading folder with the logs right in this baggie and tonight be sure you record your start and finish times, and the number of pages read. It will be really interesting to see whether you read more at home or at school, won't it be?"

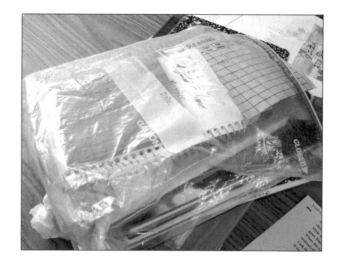

"One more thing. Readers, when you read tonight, will you keep in mind that readers don't just read books. We author lives in which reading matters. And one way to do that is to think about how you can use what you know about yourself as a reader to make sure that you make wise decisions. Yesterday, some of you wrote that you realize you need quiet places to read—so tonight, when you are reading, find yourself a quiet reading place. You might have to move a lamp, or to establish some family rules like "No Bothering Me When I….'"

"Would each of you be willing to sketch a picture of yourself reading tonight and show in the picture what you do to make reading work for you? Bring that sketch, your reading log, and your reading book with you to the meeting area tomorrow. You'll take your book baggie home every night, because you'll want to be reading at home every night. As soon as you walk in the door of our classroom tomorrow, the first thing I am going to ask you is, 'Do you have your reading book baggie?' *Do not* forget it!"

Not only do I want children to conceive of themselves as avid readers at home as well as at school, but I want these conceptions to become the reading roles and identities that children take up for themselves. I make a big deal out of remembering to bring book baggies home and back to school every day. My dramatic reactions to children who forget are sure to be effective reminders for the future.

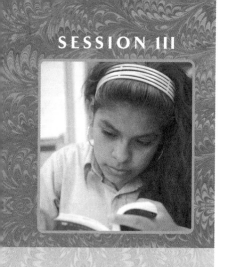

IN THIS SESSION,

you'll teach children that readers learn to recognize books that are on our own personal level so we can spend a lot of time reading smoothly, with accuracy and comprehension.

DRAFT

Finding Tons of Just-Right Books

ime is precious. If you think of it, in life, time is all we have. What you and I do with our time is what we do with our lives. How crucial it is, then, that we, as teachers, take great care with the most precious resource that has been entrusted to us: our children's time.

First-year teachers sometimes approach teaching worrying over how they'll fill up the time, but after any of us has taught for even just a few months, we realize that the central challenge in teaching is not to fill time, but rather it is to use every minute as wisely as possible. When the job is to teach reading, there is not a lot of debate over the wisest possible way to invest children's time. If our goal is for children to grow as readers, the one single thing they most need is time to read.

Alan Purves, a great reading researcher, has said, "Trust the books and get out of their way so they can teach." He is right, of course. Children learn to read above all from doing just that. There are countless research studies and indicators

GETTING READY

- Ask children as they enter the classroom in the morning, "Do you have your reading baggie, your book, and your log?" If a child has left his or her reading materials at home, act as though it's a crisis. Suggest the child phone home to ask an adult to bring the forgotten reading materials to school (although you know that won't actually happen). Do this publicly so other children see that forgetting their books or their logs is regarded as a crisis. Don't shrug off this situation saying, "No big deal. Read something else for now."

- Set up one child to demonstrate how she determines whether a book is too hard or just right for her. You will want to select a child who represents the general skill level of most of the children in the class—one who also has a strong self-concept. You would not want this reader to be one who struggles with reading.

- Select two books, one that is too difficult for your volunteer to read, and one that is just right.

- Ask children to bring their pocket folders to the meeting area. These should contain children's logs, Post-its, and a pen. Ask children to also bring their books. You can take this opportunity to tell children that they will be responsible for remembering to bring their reading materials to the meeting every day.

- Prepare a T-chart entitled "Signs to Watch for When Choosing a Book" with two columns—"Too Hard" and "Just Right." You'll fill in this chart quickly in the midst of the teaching portion of today's minilesson. Readers will then add to the chart later in the minilesson.

- Allow the children the same time interval to read their books today as you did yesterday, so they can compare the volume of reading they did yesterday with the reading they do today.

- During conferring time, be prepared to do book introductions for children who are having difficulty finding just-right books.

- You will want to be sure you have a stopwatch or a clock with a second hand available when you help children calculate reading rates during the share.

- See the *Resources* CD-ROM for materials such as a form that helps children capture the information they are gathering about their reading lives and for examples of book introductions.

that confirm this. Data collected through The National Assessment of Educational Progress—the one test that is often referred to as "the nation's report card"—show that at every grade level, students who read more, in school and at home, are the ones who receive higher scores. Stephen Krashen's reviews of research on comprehension show that of all the reading comprehension tests that collect data on volume, 93% of them report the same findings: students who read more achieve higher scores.

> *If our goal is for children to grow as readers, the one single thing they most need is time to read.*

These findings are hardly surprising. After all, reading is a skill, just like playing the oboe and swimming are skills, and any skill is developed over time, through practice. There is very little that a teacher can do from the front of the room that will make a child into a good swimmer or a good oboe player. Instead, to become skilled, the child needs to swim or to play the oboe. In the same way, the child needs to read. Researcher John Guthrie goes so far as to show that for a child to maintain his or her level as a reader, she needs to read, to actually do eyes-on-print reading, for two hours a day (at home and school, across all disciplines). Think about that. If *Stone Fox* is a just-right book for a reader, he should finish it in an hour or, at most, two hours of reading. Even if he spends half his total daily allocation of reading time reading books in the content areas, this would still mean he needs to read between three and six books the length of

Stone Fox in a week. Remember that this is so that children can *maintain* their reading level. If a fourth-grade reader reads at a second-grade reading level, to begin to catch up, the child needs to read well over two hours a day! In too many classrooms, in the name of reading instruction, class time is consumed with literature-based arts and crafts projects, with book-based games and puzzle exercises, and with talking about texts. Reading instruction can't usurp time for the one thing children most need—time for reading.

Our first goal in the teaching of reading needs to be to get books that kids can actually read into their hands—books they can read with at least 96% accuracy—and to encourage children to spend increasingly long blocks of time reading, reading, reading. Your message for this session is this: readers need to read, read, read, pushing themselves to read with increasing stamina. Yet remember, your goal is also to help readers take responsibility for authoring their own reading lives, so today's minilesson on reading with stamina, and doing so for increasingly long periods of time, needs to rally children to take this on from the heart, as part of their own agendas.

When children have books that are just right for them, this goal is easy to reach. The reader who shudders when Matilda encounters Ms. Trunchbull isn't thinking about the amount of time he still needs to spend reading, or the number of red-dot or green-dot books he has read. This reader doesn't need us to tell him to find moments for reading throughout his day. This reader, instead, comes just a hair away from being late to music because he had to finish the chapter before galloping down the hall to join his class en route to Room 223. He joins the back of the line, and his best friend turns to ask, "You done with the book yet?" The class is entering the music room, so there isn't time for conversation, but our reader mouths, "You can have it tomorrow" and gets a thumbs-up in response. Such is the success when readers find the books just right for them.

MINILESSON

Finding Tons of Just-Right Books

CONNECTION

Ask readers to share logs and sketches with a classmate, researching their reading habits at school and at home.

"Readers, when you come to the meeting area, please bring your book baggie with book, your folder (with a pen and Post-it notes), and the sketch you made last night. You will need to bring your reading materials with you to the meeting area every single day. Today is the last time I'll remind you to bring them." Once children had convened, I said, "Thumbs up if you remembered to keep track of the page and time at which you started and stopped reading last night?" I looked out at the sea of thumbs and responded, "Look how many of you remembered! I'm dying to know if any of you noticed patterns in your reading. We'll talk about that in a minute." *[Fig. III-1]*

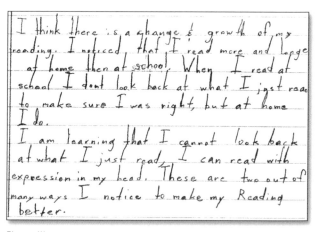

I think there is a change & growth of my reading. I noticed that I read more and longer at home then at school. When I read at school I dont look back at what I just read to make sure I was right, but at home I do.
I am learning that I cannot look back at what I just read, I can read with expression in my head. These are two out of many ways I notice to make my Reading better.

Figure III-1
One student's reflections on his reading life.

"You also brought in sketches of yourself reading. Hold those up so we can admire them." They did so. "Before we talk about our logs and sketches, we need to study them, to study ourselves as readers. As you study your data, put a star wherever you find something interesting that you're dying to talk about. In a second, you'll have a chance to talk." [Figs. III-2 and III-3]

Figure III-2
A reader's sketch showing where she does her best reading can provoke insights about how to make classrooms support equally grand reading.

You will want to help children glean insights from studying their logs. For example, did they get through approximately the same number of pages at home and at school? You may find that some children did very little reading at home. Be sure you don't criticize kids for this, especially at this point. The point is that we are interested in the data. It is critically important that kids put the true information into their reading logs. We don't want any child to think it's best to pretend.

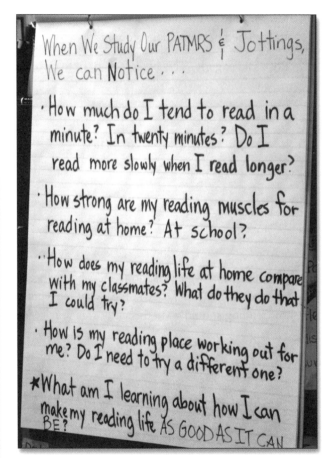

Figure III-3
Again and again, we want to encourage children to reflect on their lives as readers, noticing what works and what is a struggle, and figuring out ways to make reading the best it can be.

"Readers, what insights are you growing about yourselves as readers? How much did you read at school? At home? What does the sketch reveal when you look at it alongside your log? What am I learning about how I can make my reading life as good as it can be? Turn and tell the person sitting beside you something that you have realized."

I listened in as Malik said to Rosa and Aly, "My book was so exciting and I was reading like I was on the edge of my seat. I couldn't stop!"

"At the start of my book, it was sorta slow," Aly said. "But I'll read faster today because now I'm into it. I'm always like that. Once I'm into a book I can't put it down!" She straightened her shoulders proudly.

Rosa said eagerly, "This book feels right to me. I can read it, so I like it."

Rosa is an English language learner. In a recent study, Linnea Ehri found that English language learners who were enrolled in a tutoring program made the most gains in their reading achievement when they read high-success texts. The tutoring program was successful because the students were reading books they could read with 98% to 100% accuracy. This growth in the students' reading was not achieved when the students were given more difficult texts. The bottom line seems to be that the more time students spend with texts they can read with a high level of accuracy, the more effective and rewarding reading will be for them, and the more they will enjoy it, and the more they will then read.

I coached into the conversation. "Talk about whether you have kept your New School Year's resolutions so far. Ask, too, whether what you've noticed gives you ideas for how reading should go in this class, this year." *[Figs. III-4 and III-5]*

I read better at home when my brother goes to soccer practice.

I like reading at school because it's quiet.

Figure III-4   Figure III-5
Asking students to jot about circumstances in which reading works best for them reinforces habits such as claiming a comfy chair as a regular reading spot. Environment is an important factor in making a successful reading life.

Provide a context for the day's teaching point by telling children that before you can turn over responsibility for choosing books, they need to know the research on reading.

Before the conversations had subsided, I intervened. "Readers, can I have your eyes?" I added, "I've been thinking and thinking about the ideas you've shared for how we can make this year, this class, into a type of place where reading works for you. Most of you have been saying that reading will be the best for you if you can choose what you will read."

"I lay in bed last night thinking about your proposal, worrying. It's a big deal for a teacher to hand over to kids the job of deciding what you'll read. *Teachers* are usually the ones telling kids what to read, where to start and to stop reading. Then in bed last night, I thought to myself, If I tell kids, 'Read this, sit here, read for this long, then do this,' even though you *might* have a very good reading experience, I still won't be teaching you to author reading lives *for yourselves*. If I make all those decisions, how am I helping you make wise decisions for yourselves as readers?"

"So, readers, I am going to turn the job over to you. I'm going to mostly let you be the boss of what you read and of how much you read."

"*But* I can only give you that responsibility if I first teach you what experts, wise teachers and reading researchers, have found. And this is it. This is hugely important, so listen up."

This first part of a minilesson is called the connection *for good reason. The lesson can't come out of the blue. Youngsters deserve to know the context that led you to decide to teach this content. As part of that, you are apt to reference how today's work connects with yesterday's work, or (later in the year) with last month's work.*

More importantly, there is another connection that needs to happen right now. You need to connect with kids. There are always a million things competing for kids' attention, and it is no small feat to convey to kids, "You need to listen." Over time, you'll watch me use countless strategies to get kids' attention. In this minilesson, I want these children to know that I lay in bed the night before, thinking about them, that the teaching I'm doing emerges from tons of thought. I want them to know that a minilesson is part of a long-running conversation between me and them.

When a team of teachers piloted a draft of these minilessons, many of them reported that it felt a bit over the top to talk to eight- and nine-year-olds about "building a reading life." The teachers commiserated a bit over the looks that kids gave in response to this speechifying. "My kids looked at me like this," one of the pilot teachers shared, and made a vacant, wide-eyed look that said, "Huh? Whaaaat?" After the first sessions were piloted, we planned to revise them so there would be less rhetoric about authoring a reading life. Much to our surprise, however, by Session V or VI, the teachers had changed their minds completely, saying things like "Oh my gosh. All of a sudden it is clicking! The kids are completely invested in building their reading lives, and they understand now what we are trying to do together this year." And by the end of the year, the group all came to the same conclusion: The single most powerful thing about the year had been the way the kids embraced the idea that they are the authors of their own reading lives. We've made the decision, then, not to scale back aspects of these early lessons that might, at first, seem a bit much. So my advice is this: Try to teach as if your kids are totally taking in what you are saying. As when you read aloud a poem—more of the message gets through than you realize.

Name your teaching point. Specifically, teach your children that readers need tons of high-success reading and explain what that means.

"Today, I want to teach you that reading researchers have found that all of us—you and me, both—need tons and tons of high-success reading to grow as readers. We need tons of time to read when we are not fussing over hard words, when we are not stopping and starting and stopping again, when we don't need to furrow our foreheads. We need lots of mind-on-the-story reading. Today, I want to teach you how to recognize the kinds of books that are at your own personal level—ones you can read smoothly, with accuracy and comprehension."

Teaching

Chronicle what one child does to test whether a book is just right or too hard, recording onto a T-chart clues we all use.

"Readers, many of you already came to the same conclusion that reading scientists, reading researchers, have come to as well. Over the last few days, when you recalled and reflected on your reading experiences, many of you said that reading works for you when your reading feels almost like you are talking, or being talked to, because it is so smooth. And reading doesn't work for you when it is halting and slow. You aren't reading researchers, but you have discovered something really huge about reading. When we read slowly, the text can be hard to follow, to hold onto."

"So if you are going to be the boss of your own reading life, if you are going to make decisions about what you'll read, I need to teach you how to check whether a book is a smooth read—whether it is just right."

During today's mid-workshop teaching point, you can ask kids to time themselves reading for a minute. Some researchers say that to understand a text, it is necessary to read it the speed of speech, which is at least 120 words a minute.

There are not endless options for methods you can use in the teaching components of a reading minilesson. In Sessions I and II, you used the teaching method of demonstration. You demonstrated one way a person can pause to recall a reading episode and to mine that episode for insights. This time, the method you'll use is one we refer to as explain and show an example. Of course, in this instance, the example is a child doing a demonstration: Izzy will reenact how she goes about testing whether a book is just right or too hard for her.

"Izzy has got a stack of books here that she already knows she is interested in—she'll read them all eventually! Now she's going to check out whether any of these books might be just right for her. Let's learn from how Izzy figures this out. Let's watch for signs that suggest that a book is too hard or is just right for her. I'll write down signs we see to help us all do this."

As I spoke, I revealed a T-chart entitled "Signs to Watch for When Choosing a Book," which was divided into two columns: "Too Hard" and "Just Right." Izzy stood in front of her classmates (one of her favorite places to be!), picked up *The BFG* by Roald Dahl (level U), and checked out the dot on the book jacket's spine: pink dot. She began to read haltingly, and with a robotic voice:

> Sophie couldn't sleep a brill. . . brilliant moon. moonbeam, was shining. . . slanting
> through the curtains. A gap in the curtains. It was shining on her. It was shining
> right on to her. Pillow. The other children in the dorm. . . dorm. . . dorm-ite-ory
> were—had been asleep for hours.

As Izzy read, I jotted notes about the signals that showed the book was too hard for her.

Signs to Watch for When Choosing a Book

Too Hard   **Just Right**

- Don't understand
- Have to read slowly
- Can't read with expression
- Keep getting stuck†

When Izzy finished reading, she shook her head as if to say that no, the book was not just right for her, and she put it away.

You should be sure you have set up the child beforehand who will demonstrate and that he or she understands the point of the lesson. It's best to select a child who probably represents the reading level of most of the readers in your room, not a struggling reader.

The child shouldn't read more than three sentences or so in either the just-right or the too-hard book, or this will consume too much time.

Sometimes children become accustomed to reading in a staccato, robotic manner and do this even when they could read fluently. I remember conferring with a struggling reader who read aloud to me from her independent book in a very choppy, very word-by-word fashion. When I asked, "Does that sound like a just-right book?" I assumed she would say it was not just right, however she did not see a problem with her reading. She thought the book was perfect for her. I realized then that she was so accustomed to struggling through her books, that she did not realize what it means to read with fluency. Today's lesson may seem obvious, but to many children, it won't be obvious at all.

Name what you hope children noticed, emphasizing tips that are transferable to their own experience.

"Readers, did you notice that Izzy didn't need to read much before she knew the book was too hard? And even though she got most of the words right, she knew this wasn't right for her. She read slowly, she got stuck on words, and she stopped a lot. She definitely couldn't read with expression or with meaning—what she actually said didn't even make sense. So Izzy did smart work to stop herself after a couple of sentences."

It is helpful to show that a child can get the words correct without the book being just right. Choose demonstrations that make the points your kids need you to make.

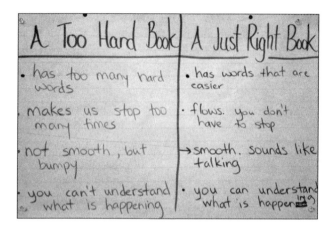

ACTIVE INVOLVEMENT

As the child moves to test a second (and just-right) book, transfer the job of listing indicators that a book is just right or too hard to children. Ask one child to compile indicators on the class chart while others jot on their own papers.

Izzy watched for my nod, and then picked up *Matilda* (level S), again checking the spine and noticing a red dot. Before she began reading, I passed my marker to Jasmine, who stood tall and poised, as always, next to the chart, and I signaled that each child in the class needed to also be a researcher. "On a blank piece of paper in your reading folder, jot signs *you* see that show that this is a just-right, or a too-hard book," I said. This time, Izzy read with unmistakable ease and pleasure, her confident voice reflecting the drama and dark humor of the page.

> *It's a funny thing about mothers and fathers. Even when their own child is the most dis… disgusting little blister you could ever imagine, they still think that he or she is wonderful. Some parents go further.*

You may wonder what the child is supposed to make of the color dot on the spine of the books. "Did I miss something?" you may be asking. "What is Izzy to make of the color dot on her book's spine?" The answer is that no, so far I haven't discussed this with children, and would just as soon not, for the time being. Remember that by now, fewer than half the class will have been assessed, so the gradations of levels, each marked with a different color, won't matter a lot yet, except, perhaps, to a child who came from a class with a leveled library. It's okay to let this be ambiguous for now.

Izzy looked like she was ready to continue reading, so I tapped her on the arm to signal that I wanted to talk to the class now. "Readers, let me give you just a second more to finish jotting the signs you saw that this second book was too hard or signs that it was just right." Then, I quietly helped Jasmine add to the chart on the easel.

After a minute, the class called out other indicators for Jasmine to add to her list. Soon the chart looked like this:

Signs to Watch for When Choosing a Book

Too Hard

- Don't understand
- Have to read slowly
- Can't read with expression
- Keep getting stuck

Just Right

- Understand
- Find it funny or infuriating, etc.
- Get most words right
- Read fast and smooth
- Read with expression easily
- Read noticing punctuation

While I worked quietly with a few children, I heard some comments about how the dots had helped Izzy predict that one book was apt to be too hard and another, just right. I wanted to provide some language around book levels without devoting a great deal of time to them. "We'll talk more about the dots later, but they are like those signs on a ski mountain," I added. "When I see a trail marked with a blue circle, I know I'll have a good trip down. When I see trails marked with a black diamond, I know that if I go forward, I'm taking my life in my hands!"

Often, I give children who are a bit more serious, like Jasmine and Izzy, the chance to be in the spotlight.

LINK

Remind children that readers need tons of high-success reading. Send them off to get books from table baskets and to persevere for at least twenty minutes.

"Since I'm going to hand over to you responsibility for choosing the books you'll read, you need to keep in mind that reading researchers have found (as many of you have found, too) that we each need to read tons and tons of books that are easy for us to read, easy enough that our reading flows smoothly and sounds (in our mind) like regular talk. Today we noticed that when we are doing just-right reading (I pointed at the chart), we don't get stuck on words, we read mostly fast and smooth, we read attending to punctuation. Above all, what we read makes sense."

"When you go off to read today, you'll want to go back to the book you read yesterday and last night at home. As you resume reading, make sure that this is a just-right book for you. If it isn't, switch to one that is. If it is, record the page number at which you start reading onto your log. You'll need to keep your Reading Life folder near you on your desk as you read because I will definitely want to study the data when I talk with you."

"So from now on, today and forever, when you are thinking about making your reading stronger, keep in mind that you won't get better by reading the hardest book in the world—many people, adults too, think that! The truth of the matter is that you get better by doing lots and lots of reading in which you really understand the text. This doesn't mean you read books for babies, and it doesn't mean you never challenge yourself with a text that is a bit too hard. This means you mostly read just-right books, and you read avidly, hungrily, whenever you can. If you do that, you will absolutely get stronger as a reader, and you'll feel it happening quickly."

"Let's read. You'll have a chance to keep track of the number of pages you read again today and to study yourself. I'll be interested to see if you again mark parts you're dying to share. I hope so! Tables 3 and 4, off you go. Now, the rest of you."

These findings echo Tim Rasinski's research on reading and fluency. He has said that every study of reading volume shows that struggling readers spend markedly less time reading than proficient readers. Furthermore, it is the strong level of engagement in high-accuracy reading that enables readers to utilize all of their reading skills at once, and improve their fluency and build comprehension. Yet when struggling readers are exposed to only a limited amount of that high-accuracy reading, they do not develop the skill set necessary to excel at the rate they need to in reading. This is a call to action. As much as we want our readers moving up levels, we also need to shower them with praise for reading book after book on their just-right level.

You will notice that I talk about kids reading for forty minutes. There is an advantage to keeping the time spent reading in school consistent. To nurture your kids' interest in researching themselves as readers, let them see their own growth easily! If you keep the timeframe for reading consistent—forty minutes for reading in all, then kids will easily see their reading stamina increase. This also will make it more likely that they do settle down to read— and because you want to spend your time assessing readers yet want a productive, quiet tone in the reading workshop, it is especially helpful right now to have a technique for channeling them to actually read. On the other hand, it is crucial that when the class becomes frayed, you stop reading time. It could conceivably be that at this time in the year, your kids can't hold it together for forty minutes. You may need to extend reading time slowly, adding a couple of minutes every day, scaffolding readers until they are reading for the intervals you expect.

Teachers, you'll be asking children to contrast the number of pages they read today (not including your teaching time of course!) with the number of pages they read during the same time interval yesterday. For this reason, it's important that children have the same amount of reading time as they had yesterday. Later, you'll want to extend the reading time by a few minutes both before and after the mid-workshop teaching point.

CONFERRING AND SMALL-GROUP WORK

Turn Even Your Resistant Readers into Nose-in-the-Book Readers

How crucial it is for you to approach your year really, truly believing that you can turn apathetic, disengaged readers into avid, engaged readers. And you can. Over and over, I've seen teachers who turn kids around, and frankly, who do so in very short order. Within a month after the start of the school year, you can absolutely counteract the idea that reading is dull. You will actually see lethargic, resistant readers turning around before your eyes.

Wear a Love of Reading on Your Sleeve and Rally Kids to Love Reading Too

First, and I mean this with all seriousness, you need to believe it is possible. Before you can lure your kids to be nose-in-the-book readers, you do need to trust that this can happen. Then, you need to wear a love of reading on your sleeve. If your own relationship to reading is shaky, then give reading a new chance—you may want to start by reading some terrific children's books. Try books by Katherine Paterson, Karen Hesse, Jacqueline Woodson, or any other author who appeals to you and to your kids. Reread books you once loved and haven't read since you were a child. Try to let reading become a special part of your own life. And be public about your reading life.

Assume that your children will love reading. If a child says, "I didn't get to read last night," act like it must have been a rough night for the youngster. "You poor kid! I hate it when I have to do so much junk that I don't get my own time to read." If a child doesn't like a book, act like this is a crisis. "Oh my goodness—you definitely don't want to read a book you don't love! Let's find a book that you won't be able to put down."

Then, too, you need to notice all the little signals that you give out that carry the message that reading isn't wonderful, and stop giving those signals. Don't say, "I know the book is boring, but you have to force yourself to get through twenty pages." Don't say, "You have to work at it. I know it is hard, but this is good for you. When you grow up, you'll be glad you forced yourself to read as a kid."

Even when you wear a love of reading on your sleeve, there will be

---

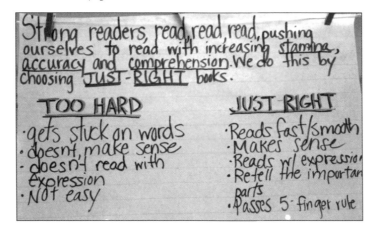

> ### MID-WORKSHOP TEACHING POINT
>
> #### Readers Check To Be Sure a Book Is Just Right
>
> "Readers, use a Post-it to mark where you are stopping, then eyes up here, please." I waited. "I need to tell you I saw readers today making really smart decisions. Some of you researched yourself and realized you were running into about five hard words on every page. You could figure out many of those words if you really worked at them, but it is hard to understand your reading, let alone enjoy it, when you keep starting and stopping. So it was really smart of you to say, 'This book will probably be just right for me in a month, but for now, I'm going to read a whole bunch of slightly easier books.'"
>
> *continued on next page*

---

some children who aren't swept up. You will want to look each of these children in the eyes and acknowledge that their spirits are low at this point. And then say, "This year will be totally different." These children need to feel you understand their resistance or their struggle and that you are still confident you can help them find books that will put them on the road toward becoming strong and passionate readers.

Use Book Introductions to Help Readers Warm Up for Reading

One of your first priorities will be to help children find books that will be right for them. Here are some things we've found work often (not always, of course!) with struggling readers.

- Resist the impulse to select your own favorites; figure out which books might become *their* favorites.
- Make sure to offer books that will be easy for the reader.
- Try short books with short chapters.
- Try books with plenty of white space and pictures.
- Try books in which the main character is the same age or older than the reader.
- Try books with action-packed plots.
- Try a book that offers social rewards—it's popular or respected in the class or school.
- Try books with language that is accessible, realistic, kid-friendly. (Often the most accessible books will be mysteries, humorous books, or thrillers.)

MID-WORKSHOP TEACHING POINT

continued from previous page

"Right now, will you and a neighbor get together? One of you take the role of researcher, one the reader. Thumbs up if you will be the researcher. Thumbs up if you will be the reader."

"Okay, for the next few minutes, let's have the reader continue reading your book, only this time, read it aloud. And researchers, you see if the reader's book is just right, or if you think it might it be a bit too hard. Use the chart if you need to. If it might be too hard, signal me, and I'll bring your reader a somewhat easier book, and you all can research whether the reader's reading gets smoother and makes more sense with that easier book."

"So right now, readers, start reading where you left off. And researchers, think if the book seems just right." As children read and researched, I provided a few readers with somewhat easier books. After a bit, I stopped the class. "Researchers, before you can really know if the book is just right, you need to talk about the book, and you need to make sure the reader understands and is interested in the story. But for now, we are not going to check on that because it is time to get back to reading. Readers, you need to ask yourselves, "Was the book making sense to me? If not, signal to me. And those of you who were the researcher—use these research questions to check on your own book, and signal to me if *you* think you might need a different book. I've got some really good alternative books here, and I can help you find a great book for you, quickly."

- If possible, read a chapter aloud to the child—or at least read the first page aloud.
- Aim to set each resistant reader up with a stash of likely to be great for him books—it may be fun for some children to roam through scores of books, looking for the perfect one, but for children who haven't enjoyed reading, this can be daunting. This reader will welcome a bin full of especially high-interest, socially popular, accessible books.

Strong, as well as resistant, readers profit from book introductions. For all readers, an introduction can help the reader grasp the plotline of the story, but for strong readers, introductions also help them grasp the significance of the story. For an example of a book introduction that does this, turn to the *Resources* CD-ROM.

TEACHING SHARE

Readers Reflect on Reading Goals, Sometimes by Noting Our Reading Volume and Pace

Ask students to study their reading logs and build some theories about what they've noticed. Ask readers to share and discuss their thinking.

"Readers, can I stop you? We are not going to gather on the carpet for the share today. Before you do anything else, will you enter this next stretch of reading into your log? Look at the number of pages you just read in these forty minutes, and compare them with the number of pages you read yesterday during forty minutes. Now see what patterns you can find or what theories you can build. Think also about your New School Year's resolution." After a moment of silence for thinking, I said, "Please share with a classmate what you noticed." [Fig. III-6]

I then listened in as children talked with their peers. Zayd said enthusiastically, long legs splayed out under his desk, "I noticed that I can read a page a minute. This means I can read almost a book a day, if I pick little ones. I think I can read more this year than before."

Sam said, "I was reading really slowly at first, but then I quit that book. It wasn't so good. I'm reading a different book now, and it seems like I keep going faster and faster through it because it's so good!"

After children talked for two or three minutes, I said, "Readers, earlier today, we acted as reading researchers, studying what Izzy did to choose a just-right book. And then you had a chance to study your partner, right? Now you're acting like researchers again, only this time you are studying *yourself* as a reader. Today many of you—like Izzy—figured out a book that is at a just-right level of difficulty for you. As we go through this year, you'll see that your just-right level will keep changing and you'll see that you can read more and more pages at a time, too. You'll feel your reading become stronger as the year progresses."

> I can see signs of change +
> growth. Some signs of growth +
> change is that I am reading long
> & more. Plus I am read alot
> stronger.

Figure III-6
Could anything be more important than reading with stamina and volume? Readers learn to read by reading.

I'm imagining that some of you may be squirming a bit at the repeated emphasis on reading more, and reading faster, and on the importance of levels and accuracy. You may be thinking, "Where's the role of reading for the love of it?" You may long for more talk about character, quests, life lessons and the like. Please trust that all of that will come. It seemed to Kathleen and to me that it was important to get some of the foundations in place from the start—and there is overwhelming evidence to suggest that youngsters grow from reading a huge volume of just-right books. Even if you decide that you'll eventually lighten up on any effort to channel children to books at this or that level, you'll probably want to wrest kids away from the all-too-common syndrome of spending months inching through books that are way too hard.

Reading Faster, Stronger, and Longer   **DRAFT**

IN THIS SESSION,

you will teach children that readers take off the brakes as we read, sometimes picking up our reading pace a bit, so we can take in both the details and the whole of what we are reading.

On a recent school visit, my colleagues and I stopped at the sound of catchy music and laughter emanating from one classroom. A dance class was in session, and we stopped to watch. A lithe instructor would turn off the music every few minutes, and in this brief silence, the class would reenact the steps, aiming to get "nine-ten-eleven-*clap*-turn" right. Soon, the instructor would holler an approving "Go!" and turn the music back on. When a dancer missed a step, the music soon pulled him or her back into its pace and rhythm. The dance, ultimately, was more about fluidity of movement than about individual steps.

In our teaching of reading, so intent are we on the instruction of steps that sometimes we forget to turn the music back on. Almost all our students have mastered the small steps: sounding out words accurately, decoding phonetically, moving through each word as it comes. But to make reading work, you'll want kids to pick up the rhythm and pace of what reading should feel like, to experience that words on a page become images in our mind until we're immersed in the story. "Faster," you'll urge, *not* because you want lightning-speed readers who zip through word lists or texts (far from it!) but because choppy, word-by-word reading deters

GETTING READY

- Create bookmarks for readers containing tips for reading strong and long to distribute during the active involvement.

- Make a chart titled, "Reading Fast, Strong, and Long" that contains the reading tips for use in the active involvement and mid-workshop teaching point.

- Bring copies of books representing varying levels of difficulty, such as *Henry and Mudge, Stone Fox,* and *Hatchet.* If you do not have these books, then select three books from your library that reflect similar levels of text difficulty.

- Scan the group once your readers have convened to be sure that each reader has brought reading materials, including a book, their "My Reading Life" folder, Post-its, and a pen. You will have set children up to do this today without requiring a reminder so that this aspect of the workshop becomes automatic and does not require your attention. If a child has not brought his or her materials, you'll want to make an especially big deal out of it so that others understand the importance of being prepared at the beginning of each day's work.

- See the *Resources* CD-ROM for a bookmark sample and a running chart to be used in the active involvement.

- Before the next session, Session V, you need to read aloud the first chapter and the first several pages of Chapter 2 in *Stone Fox.* If you decide to weave a different read-aloud into this unit, you'll need to have decided the portion of the book you'll incorporate in the minilesson and have read up to the selected passage.

comprehension. In effect, you're saying to your kids, "You can stop decoding now, and start reading." You're asking them to make the jump from recognizing single words to understanding clusters of them. And, as you urge children to read more pages—more quickly, more deeply—you aren't introducing three enormous goals in one minilesson but the three faces of *one* singularly important goal—*fluency.*

> *To make reading work, you'll want kids to pick up the rhythm and pace of what reading should feel like, to experience that words on a page become images in our mind until we are immersed in the story.*

This minilesson, then, is about reading in a way that allows kids to take in more text. It is about reading with *prosody*—rhythm and sound in one's heads—about deep immersion in the meaning of reading. Of course, this in itself necessitates a fast pace. Imagine having to listen to someone who talked very slowly, stretched and repeated her words, pausing multiple times within a single sentence. Not only would you be unable to sustain a conversation with such a person, but you'd be bored and frustrated, regardless of the content of the talk. It is the same way with readers. Until the pace of reading picks up to provide a steady flow of meaning to engage the brain, books will be tossed aside not long after they've been picked up. You'll want to remove all the brakes and obstacles to reading so that kids can achieve and sustain this optimal, crucial pace.

Reading researcher Keith Topping tells us that fluency is "the extraction of maximum meaning at maximum speed in a relatively continuous flow, leaving spare simultaneous processing capacity for other higher-order processes." Indeed, if we were to read with our fingers trailing under words as we mouthed them to ourselves, obsessively rereading to get every word right, we'd be held up from *thinking* about our reading, so caught up would we be in decoding. Before we can aim high in our teaching, hoping to have a classroom where kids analyze, evaluate or theorize as a result of reading, we'll have to teach this pace. "Read faster, stronger, longer," we say. It is a simple-sounding message, but it can make all the difference to the quality of reading our kids are doing.

DRAFT

 # MINILESSON

Reading Faster, Stronger, and Longer

CONNECTION

Review the big ideas from recent reading workshops, emphasizing children's thinking about their reading and their goals for the coming school year.

"Readers, it is still the very beginning of school, and you've learned so many important things about yourselves as readers. You've thought very hard about what makes reading work well for you, and one of the things I've heard many of you say is that this year, you'd like pick your own books to read. This will help make reading the best it can be. As you choose your books, you'll follow the wise advice of reading researchers who have discovered that to become powerful readers, readers need to read tons and tons of books that are just right."

"You've also been analyzing your reading logs, and many of you were surprised to notice that you do not read all that many pages, even though you're reading the whole time during our workshop. What great noticing—so honest. Yesterday, someone said it this way: 'I feel like I want to read stronger and longer, like a super reader!' I thought of those words a lot last night, and I realized that this is a great goal for all of us to work toward!"

Name your teaching point. Specifically, tell children that today you'll teach them that readers take off the brakes as we read, letting ourselves flow.

"Today I'm going to teach you a few tips that you can use to become readers who read faster, stronger, and longer. Readers take off the brakes as we read, picking up our reading pace a bit at times, so we can take in what we are reading more fully—both the details and the whole."

As you know, there are several different ways teachers can approach the connection portion of a minilesson. In the connection that follows, I've briefly reviewed some of the big ideas we've covered in the last few days. I list these big ideas quickly rather than eliciting them from students. In another month or two, I might set students up to generate these with a partner, but for now, I'm still trying to induct students into the pace of minilessons. At this point, if I begin a minilesson with a question such as, "What are the big ideas we've learned?" and give students time to raise their hands and respond, it's highly likely that the focus of the minilesson will become blurred, and the minilesson will run long.

TEACHING

Rally kids to adopt the goal of reading longer, stronger, and faster. Then offer them some ways readers can make progress toward this.

"Imagine that I'm your reading coach right now. You're about to go off to read, and I'm giving you some tips to remember so your reading will be faster, stronger, and longer, too. As I give you these tips—things I've learned about reading from researchers—your job will be to listen and to think, 'Might any of those suggestions be just right for me?' If so, try them."

"Back when you were beginning readers, you learned to do some things that were helpful because you were just learning, sort of like using training wheels when you were just learning to ride a bike. But just like training wheels are put away, some of our old reading habits need to be put away, too. Watch me show you how a beginning reader might read, and then watch me demonstrate how an experienced reader, one who reads strong and long, has learned to read, and see if you can notice the difference."

Selecting one of the books I had brought to the meeting area, I read a sentence twice, first as a novice, pointing under the words with a finger and mouthing quietly as I progressed. Then—letting children know I was switching—I read as an expert reader, without the use of my finger and without mouthing. "When you were beginning readers, your teachers may have taught you to point under the words, whispering the words to yourself, and to use a book mark to hold your place in a story. Those were great strategies for you when you were a beginning reader, but you have graduated. You are *way* past that stage. Doing those things now slows you down. So, put those strategies away, just like you put away training wheels! I know kids who sit on their hands for a day or two to keep from pointing at the text. So our first tip is this: To read faster, stronger, longer, remember not to point under the words with a finger or a bookmark and remember not to whisper or form the words with your mouth while you read."

It is remarkable how many readers continue to use these beginning reader behaviors even when the behaviors pull the readers down. Sometimes teachers even encourage readers to use a bookmark or a finger to trace progress through a text. I think the reason some teachers ask for this is that these actions make reading visible, and therefore allow a worried teacher to know if a child is actually reading. The youngster who mouths words or uses a finger to track print can show an observing teacher that he or she is actually reading, and my hunch is that this can make the teacher feel more accountable. Although it is totally understandable for a teacher to want proof that a child is actually reading, it will, in fact, hold a reader back when the child uses a bookmark or a finger under the line of print.

Several times, the founder of Reading Recovery, Marie Clay, has visited our classrooms to help my colleagues and me develop the strongest ideas for supporting readers. On one visit, Marie said, "It is almost never the case that a child needs to read with a bookmark under the line of print—Maybe one tenth of one percent of readers need those bookmarks, and even then, they need to follow, not precede, the child's line of sight or they'll prevent the reader from looking ahead, something that is crucial for the child to read punctuation."

"The next tip is harder to show, but no less important. Reading researchers have found that some readers reread, or look back, as many as twenty times while reading even just one page! These are usually just tiny look-backs, rereading a few words here and there, and usually the readers who do this are looking back to check that they have gotten a firm grasp on everything. But the important news is this: If you are one of those readers who always puts on the brakes as you read, always double checks that you are right, always looks backwards, you need to stop putting on the brakes, and to let yourself whirl through the story. If you really try to focus on understanding what's happening and reading on to the next part, you'll find that you don't need to keep checking back—you'll get into the flow of the story better without check-backs. So tip number two: As long as you understand the basics of what's going on in the story, read forward instead of rereading or looking back."

"Finally, the third tip I want to share is that we read faster, stronger, and longer when we read with more expression, more feeling. This might seem odd. Wouldn't it slow you down to read a story really well, almost like you are reading it aloud to the class? But the thing is, when you're trying to read with feeling, the story will speed you up. If you want to work on reading with more expression and more feeling, practice by rereading parts of a story that you especially love, parts that are full of action or emotions. So again, tip number three for reading faster, stronger, and longer: Read with expression and feeling. Your reading should sound, in your mind, like a professional storyteller is telling a story to you. Even if you don't actually hear a voice in your mind when you are reading, you need to let yourself develop a sense for the tone of the words."

It may help for you to use your own fingers to signal that you are progressing to yet another item in this list. Then again, you could keep a running list on chart paper, recording just a word or two for each of these strategies, so that your record keeping doesn't overwhelm the minilesson. If you decide to keep a running chart, the chart in the active involvement (which is also on the CD-ROM) might help.

There are several more tips and suggestions I could offer, but it felt like we reached a critical mass of content at this point. Alternatively, I could have chosen to share only one or two tips in this lesson. I would have made that decision if I felt that I was losing the students' interest and attention.

ACTIVE INVOLVEMENT

Give each reader a bookmark, listing advice for reading strong and long. Ask them to reread and discuss the tips on the bookmark, choosing one to implement.

"Readers, I just gave you several different suggestions about reading faster, stronger, and longer. I'm going to give each of you a bookmark that contains these suggestions. When you get your bookmark, turn to someone and read aloud each bit of advice, saying more and thinking more about how that piece of advice will help you." Then I distributed bookmarks that contained these pointers. [Fig. IV-1]

Reading Fast, Strong, and Long

- Follow words with eyes, not finger, bookmark, or voice.

- Guard against constant, tiny look-backs. Read on, read on.

- Read with feeling so you hear a read-aloud voice, or feel the tone, in your head.

"Now, take another moment to look over your bookmark. Ask yourself, 'Which one of these strategies will I try today in order to read longer and stronger?'" If you don't point at words or whisper read anymore, you're unlikely to need that tip, so you'll probably find another one to try. Think about yourself as a reader, and then make a thoughtful choice. This is like making yet another New Year's resolution. Put a little check mark next to the bit of advice you are going to try, and if you don't feel as if one of these strategies fits for you today, turn this bookmark over and write something you think could help you read longer and stronger, not just today, but forever."

The teachers who piloted these units found the bookmarks to be a big hit with their students. The bookmarks became little treasures for the students, something they enjoyed holding on to and adding to.

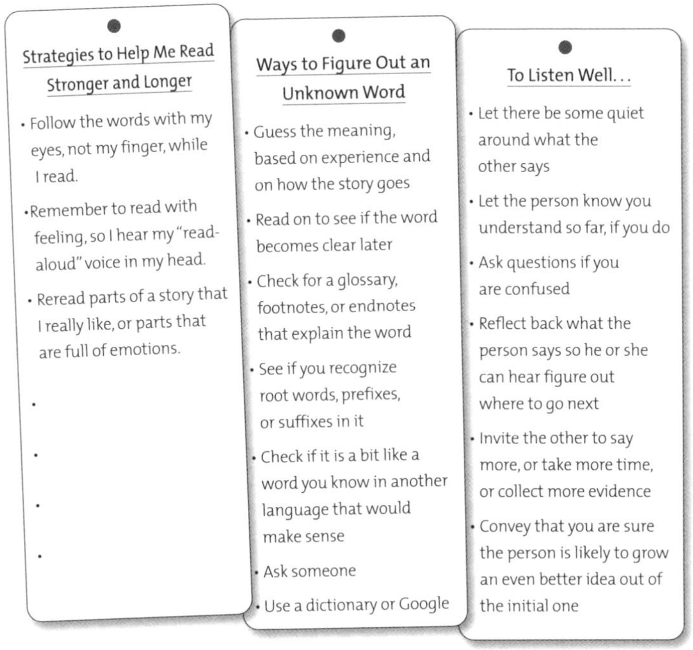

Strategies to Help Me Read Stronger and Longer

- Follow the words with my eyes, not my finger, while I read.
- Remember to read with feeling, so I hear my "read-aloud" voice in my head.
- Reread parts of a story that I really like, or parts that are full of emotions.
-
-
-

Ways to Figure Out an Unknown Word

- Guess the meaning, based on experience and on how the story goes
- Read on to see if the word becomes clear later
- Check for a glossary, footnotes, or endnotes that explain the word
- See if you recognize root words, prefixes, or suffixes in it
- Check if it is a bit like a word you know in another language that would make sense
- Ask someone
- Use a dictionary or Google

To Listen Well...

- Let there be some quiet around what the other says
- Let the person know you understand so far, if you do
- Ask questions if you are confused
- Reflect back what the person says so he or she can hear figure out where to go next
- Invite the other to say more, or take more time, or collect more evidence
- Convey that you are sure the person is likely to grow an even better idea out of the initial one

Figure IV-1
Teachers make charts more portable and personal by converting portions of them into bookmarks that young readers keep close at hand as they read. Often some bullet points are empty, leaving room for the reader to invent.

Link

Ask readers to fill in their reading logs and then to begin reading, using one of the tips for reading strong and long. Urge readers to sustain their focus for longer today.

"Readers, before you do anything else, get out your log and fill in the starting time and page number. As we're working on reading stronger and longer, we will want to reflect on our reading lives. Once you've recorded your starting time and page number, get started reading, right here in the meeting area. As you read today, and whenever you read, try the advice you've marked on your bookmark to get yourself reading stronger and longer. When I see that you've settled into reading, I'll tap you on the shoulder and send you back to your seat so you can continue."

"Today, push yourself to read for longer without getting restless. We have been stopping after about fifteen or twenty minutes. Our goal today will be to read for twenty-five minutes before we come up for conversation. This first stretch of reading will be longer than the reading time we've been having, and you'll probably get to read a whole bunch more of the book! Let's get started."*[Fig. IV-2]*

During the link, I articulate again what I have taught, reminding children that this is a strategy they can use for the rest of their lives. You will note that the words "Whenever you read…" are used often in the beginning or endings of a minilesson. Note, too, that I reference teaching points from previous days and books from previous days too, because I want all that work to continue to stay alive in the classroom.

One teacher who piloted the units created a goal sign she hung in the classroom that stated the amount of minutes the class was reading and what they would be reading by the end of October.

Figure IV-2
One teacher hung this sign on her classroom door in September and used it to rally her students to read strong and long.

CONFERRING AND SMALL-GROUP WORK

Set Both the Whole Community, and Each Reader, on a Right Course

During the first few days of the school year, even when you are not officially assessing readers, you'll be watching them read to understand them better and to guide them toward productive pathways. When you are not conducting running records, you'll need to move among your readers. You can do this in a half-hearted fashion, regarding this as just a breather in the midst of your assessments, or you can do this with a sense of purpose, power, and engagement.

You don't want to fritter away the brief intervals in which you are not collecting running records.

Support Engagement in Reading

From the beginning, you need to be absolutely certain that during reading time, your kids are reading. Now is the time to establish classroom norms, and one of them must be "During reading time, we read." Stand back and look over the classroom, making sure you see eyes on print, all around the room. Count how many children are actually reading at any one time; if fewer than three quarters are doing so, invest more time in settling the

children down, supplying them with high-interest and easy books, and establishing the tone that you want for the classroom.

If you see problem areas in the classroom, research the larger issue rather than simply rushing about trying to make things right. If children are out of their seats, roaming the classroom, this should surprise you. After all, you will have put a basket of books at the center of each table and asked children to select books from that container, so you shouldn't see children going to the classroom library yet. You haven't asked for any writing, so you should not even see a line at the pencil sharpener, grinding pencils into stubs. If you see children wandering the room, this should spur questions.

While you address problems, it will also be critically important for you to study and spotlight what's working. Identify readerly behaviors, saying to one child, "You are working so hard at getting a stack of just-right books!" and then suggest others follow suit.

Some readers will appreciate a straightforward challenge. For exam-

> ### MID-WORKSHOP TEACHING POINT
>
> #### Readers Vary the Pace of Our Reading in Response to the Text
>
> "Readers, eyes this way. Before we do anything else, notice how many pages you just read in twenty-three minutes. Were you pushing yourself to read faster, stronger, longer? Tell the person sitting near you whether you did anything differently today. If you did, tell your neighbor what it was."
>
> After just a minute for the children to buzz back-and-forth with each other, I gathered their attention. "Readers, today, in our lesson, I taught you three tips for reading faster, stronger, longer. But you know what? As I listened to Lily read, she helped me remember another tip."
>
> "Are you ready for tip number four? Here goes: Lily has found, and reading researchers agree, that readers often read some sections of a text quickly and some sections slowly. Usually when you get to a part of the story where it's pretty clear what is going on, and especially if there is a lot of dialogue, a lot of talk, a reader moves through that part quickly. For example, Lily came to a part of her book where the author talks about how the main character, Clementine, from the book *Clementine*, is rambling about her day not going as planned and about how she once again is having a not so good day. That wasn't new news for Lily— she knows Clementine will often talk at length about how the plans she sets out to accomplish rarely happens as planned—so she whipped through that part. But then Lily came to a section of the book in which Clementine starts getting herself into another sticky situation by cutting off her own hair, so Lily needed to catch the details, because this was new information. So, what Lily and the researchers are suggesting is that you can zoom through some
>
> *continued on page 56*

ple, after reading Richard Gentry's research on reading volume, I started to worry that a number of kids simply weren't reading enough. I mulled over how to handle this and decided to stop pussyfooting around. I met with two children who had each been inching through different books, and I said, "I'm concerned. I looked over your logs and saw you have each been reading your books at a pace that will result in each of you spending about ten days on one of these books. There is a researcher who has recently found that kids need to read the books you're reading, books like *The Shoe Shine Girl* and *Donavan's Word Jar* in about three days, when those books are at the just-right level, not ten days. I know that is more reading than you have been doing—but could you try it, just to see? Could you give yourself a goal of reading forty pages tonight, not fifteen?"

The kids were skeptical. "I don't know," they said, eyeing each other and giggling.

"Why not try it? That's what goals are for. You try to reach them," I said. "You try, try, try. Then tomorrow, we can see. If it was impossible, we'll change the goal."

The next day the kids came bounding into the classroom, books waving, hollering, "We did it! We did it!" I learned from those children. Sometimes we need to be more willing to ask a lot of our kids. *[Figs. IV-3 and IV-4]*

MID-WORKSHOP TEACHING POINT

continued from page 59

parts of a book. And other parts require slower reading. So on our chart, 'Reading Fast, Strong, and Long,' I'll add tip number four, on the chart paper I added 'Read some parts of the book faster, especially when it's clear what's going on.' Then I said to the children "you can add that tip to your bookmarks too, at the end of today's workshop, when you're filling out your log."

Reading Fast, Strong, and Long

- Follow words with eyes, not finger, bookmark, or voice.

- Guard against constant, tiny look-backs. Read on, read on.

- Read with feeling so you hear a read-aloud voice, or feel the tone, in your head.

- Read some parts of the book faster, especially when it's clear what's going on.

"Right now, look back over the last page or two that you've been reading, and decide whether there are some fast-read sections in those pages and some slow-read sections. Give me a thumbs up once you have decided."

continued on next page

Channel Children to Outgrow Early Reading Habits That No Longer Help

Of course, as you move around the room, settling children down, you'll also want to help children use strategies and tips from your first few minilessons. Stand back and scan the room to find the children who are still moving their lips or sliding their fingers under words as they read. These can be hard habits to break, but if your children are reading books that are level H and above (and chances are good that they will be), then these vestiges of early reading are holding their reading back. If you notice a child or two still using those early reading behaviors, you may decide to work with that child in an individual conference, and you might rely on a form of conferring that I call *coaching*.

In such a coaching conference, you don't stop what the child is doing to interview and then instruct. Instead, you simply listen to the child read and then whisper prompts into the child's reading. To one child you might say, "You are moving your lips as you read. I bet you can hear the words in your head and that you don't actually need to say them in your mouth. Try it." Then, after watching for a few seconds, you can whisper, "I knew you could do it" and, after watching another minute, "That's it," or "Keep it up. You'll find you read much faster now." To the next child, you might voice over, "You are sliding your finger under each word. I bet you can read with your eyes only. Let me see you read with your eyes only." If you see his finger creep back out, touch his hands, perhaps saying, "Sometimes it helps to sit on your hand." Again, watch for a few seconds and then whisper, "Keep reading, using your eyes." If you see several children needing similar instruction, you may want to gather them into a small group. You might begin by saying, "Readers, I've been watching you, and I can see that you need a little more help breaking your finger pointing and whispering habits that used to help you, but don't any more. Today, I want to remind you of two very simple things you can do. . . ."

continued from previous page

MID-WORKSHOP TEACHING POINT

After a minute or two, when many thumbs were raised, I said, "Show someone sitting near you a passage that you think deserves to be read quickly, and then try reading that part aloud, reading it quickly. Then show each other a passage that seems to be asking to be read slowly, and try reading that passage slowly."

After a minute or two, I said, "Let's resume reading. Remember to read faster, stronger, longer, *and* now you know for today and for forever, you can take cues from the text to know when you can read even faster and when you might need to slow down a bit."

"By the way, you all still have Post-it flags in your tabletop baskets. Remember that two days ago I suggested you read, noting the really great parts so you can share them with each other. When I suggest something one day, I am not making a one-day suggestion. I am saying, 'This is something good readers sometimes do, on any given day.' So again, as you read, you may want to note or flag parts you love so you can share these later today with your partner or someone else. Sharing great parts is something you can do throughout your reading life."

Channel Children Toward Just-Right Books

During the first few days of the year, you'll also use conferences as a way to channel children toward just-right books. On one of the first days of this year, for example, I approached a table full of readers, and said, "Readers, can I have your eyes and your attention. In a second, you can resume your reading, but when I tap your shoulder, read aloud a little bit. Then I'm going to ask whether your book is a good fit or not." As the group resumed reading, I tapped Grace and she read four lines aloud rather quickly. I stopped her and she said yes, the book seemed like a good match because she could read it easily, only getting stuck on a couple of words. Since I was assessing fluency as a measure of books being just-right and Grace seemed to read fluently, I tapped the next student.

Gabe took a turn reading to me. I had recently assessed Gabe as a level N reader. He was actually able to decode higher-level books, but I found that even in level O books his fluency broke down to the point of creating serious gaps in his comprehension. When I saw that he was reading *The Tales of a Fourth Grade Nothing* by Judy Blume (hunched over the book, his thick bangs hanging so low over his eyes I marveled he could see at all), I suspected that he would benefit from a little support with choosing just-right books. When I asked him to read out loud, he did so slowly and haltingly. I asked, "So Gabe, do you think this book is a good fit?" He nodded, saying he thought the little brother was funny. I cut to the chase: "Gabe, let me teach you something about a good fit. It should sound like you're talking. It should be smooth like this (I picked up his book, *Tales of a Fourth Grade Nothing*, and began to read it smoothly). Did it feel smooth like that when you were reading just now?"

"Not really," he said, looking a little downcast and pulling on the cuffs of his pants.

"Well, I'm so glad you were trying it out. Now you know, right? Now you can tell that before you dive into *The Tales of a Fourth Grade Nothing*, you might want to warm yourself up with some easier books. Then when you're ready for *The Tales of a Fourth Grade Nothing* you'll be able to really get into it." I looked in his table book bin for books that were Ns—three levels easier. I pulled *Julian's Glorious Summer* from the bin, saying, "Maybe you can begin reading another funny book—this book is in the *Julian* series by a great author, Ann Cameron." Then, bringing out another book,

I said, "Or you could try one of these." I showed him books from the *Amber Brown* series by Paula Danzinger. "Amber is always getting into funny situations in these books. Why don't you decide on a book from one of these two series, and plan on reading a couple of books that go together from that series. I bet that by the time you finish with those, you will find that this Judy Blume book is just right for you." Then I added, "After you pick one and get started, I'll come back and listen to you read."

I then motioned to the two children from that table with whom I hadn't read. "I'm going to move to a different table, but would you two do me a favor and check *your* books yourselves. I know you can do it. And if it isn't just right, get a different one."

When you want to confer to help children select just-right books, you can conduct your research by looking at student logs as well as by listening to children read aloud. You can learn a lot by simply taking note of the number of pages a child has read during the first minutes of any one day's reading workshop. Since children should have their logs out on their desks, it should be easy for you to research and give compliments. "Kobe," I said. "Can I stop you for a second?" He nodded. "I noticed that you have already read thirteen pages today. At this pace, you might be able to read almost forty pages today! Wow, that is impressive. You must've gotten right down to reading and gotten lost in the story."

Kobe turned his Yankees cap backwards, a little shy about the compliment, saying, "Yep, this book is easy for me so I read it really fast." I was pretty sure that in fact the book was not easy for him, but I let it go, and celebrated his sense of accomplishment.

Looking at his log to study the patterns of his reading since he began the log, I said, "I notice that this is your third quick book in a row; you have just about read a book a day. I read a lot of really quick books when I am at the beach in the summer, like you're doing now. It makes sense for you to do this at the start of the year so you get back into the swing of reading. At this rate, you'll have read five books by the end of our first week of school!"

Figure IV-3
Amber is finding a way to let books matter in her life.

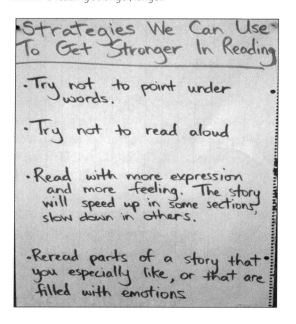

Figure IV-4
Andrew is reading stronger, longer.

TEACHING SHARE

Readers Can Use Research on Volume to Help Us Revise Our Goals

Share reading researchers' findings about the pace of reading.

"Readers, I want to tell you about some research that a scientist who studies readers has done. The guy's name is Dick Allington. You know how some scientists study butterflies and some study the algae in lake water? Well, Dick Allington studies kids—kids like you. And he and a friend of his have some findings about what kids need to grow strong as readers. These findings have gotten teachers really talking and thinking a lot about how we teach reading. So I thought that because you are sort of helping me figure out how our reading time should go, you might want to hear his findings. You ready? I'm going to tell you this researcher's findings about kids and reading, and then ask you to look at your reading log and to think about your reading life, and see if his advice might help you think about your New School Year's resolutions."

"Okay. So one thing he has found is that if you are reading a book like *Stone Fox* (I held it up)—or another book that is just about that long and that hard—and if you are reading the book silently, to yourself, not in a read-aloud where we keep stopping to talk, it should take you about an hour and a half—or a couple of days of reading time, at the most, to read the whole book. If you are reading a longer book like *Hatchet*, it could take you up to a week to read the book (and four hours of reading time) but no more."

Allington cites research by Gentry who has said that if you read a book such as Henry and Mudge, *it should take you about ten minutes to read. And if you can read a book like* Stone Fox, *it should take you about an hour and a half to read. If you can read a book such as* Hatchet, *it should take you about four hours to read. There is nothing magical about the particular book Gentry cites.* Henry and Mudge *is a level J book, approximately forty pages long with a few sentences on a page.* Stone Fox *is level P, with eight-two pages.* Hatchet *is level R with 192 pages.*

"He also said that kids should generally aim to read about fifteen pages of whatever book you are reading in about twenty minutes of time. That rule-of-thumb doesn't always work. You could read a bit faster or a bit slower, but that is the pace most people should expect of our reading."

You'll notice a lot of talk around students as reading researchers. The teachers who piloted these units found that rallying students around researching their own reading habits creates a strong sense of pride in the students' reading lives. Talking about experts in the field of literacy shows children that their work is important and that there are reasons why we teach them each and every strategy.

Ask students to apply what they've learned about the research to their own reading pace, as represented in their logs.

"So right now, quietly look over your log and think about your own reading—how much you read, when you read, your struggle to find books that are just right for you but that you also want to read. Use the flag Post-its from your bin to note interesting things you notice on your own reading log. Think about your reading goals for yourself. In a minute, you'll have a chance to talk with someone about your thoughts." I paused until they seemed ready, and then gave them time to talk to one another. [Figs. IV-5 and IV-6]

After a few minutes I stopped the children and reminded them to read tonight with their goals in mind.

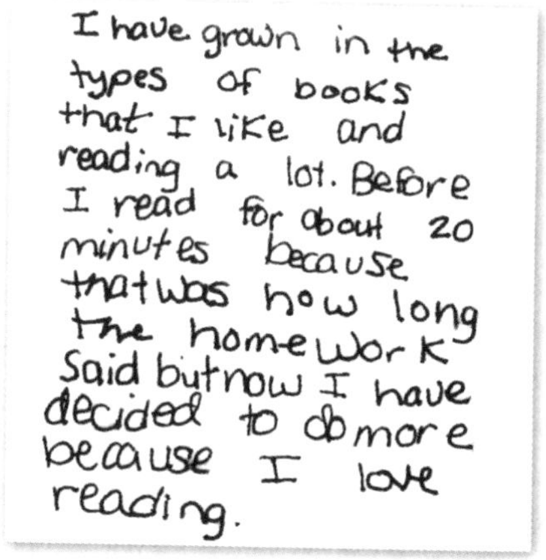

I have grown in the types of books that I like and reading a lot. Before I read for about 20 minutes because that was how long the homework said but now I have decided to do more because I love reading.

Figure IV-5
If Grace is reading beyond the assigned amount, this signifies a big change in her disposition toward reading. She used to read just enough to meet the requirements of an assignment, not a moment more. Even if she is just role-playing being someone who now gets lost in books, it's worth celebrating the identity she's choosing for herself.

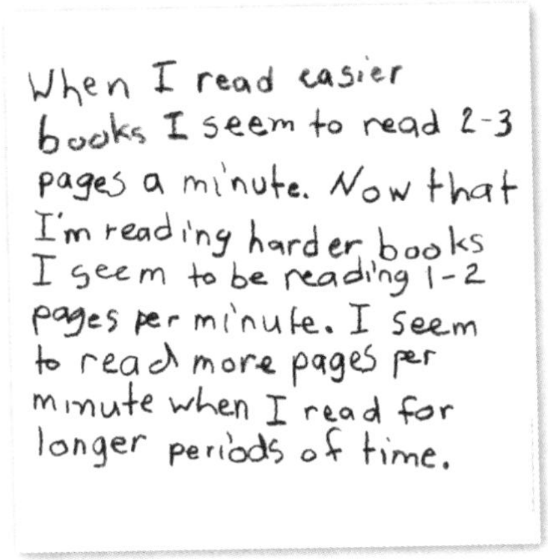

When I read easier books I seem to read 2-3 pages a minute. Now that I'm reading harder books I seem to be reading 1-2 pages per minute. I seem to read more pages per minute when I read for longer periods of time.

Figure IV-6
There is traction, accountability, and detail in this observation. Aly actually studied her data, prompting surprising insights.

DRAFT

Awakening Ourselves to the Text

IN THIS SESSION,

you'll teach students that readers learn to pay attention while reading, rather than reading quickly as if on autopilot, so that the words matter.

I recently reread Gary Paulsen's beautiful book, *The Monument*. In the book, Mick, an artist, is hired by the sleepy mill town of Bolten, Missouri, to make a monument that represents the town. He takes his sketchpad and, with Rocky, an adopted kid with a bad leg, trailing behind, he moseys through the town, taking it all in. Reading Paulsen's book, I felt as if I was with Rocky, following behind Mick, and as if he was helping both of us see that town as if for the first time. Rocky talks about this kind of seeing, saying,

> Sometimes you don't see things and time will go by and by and then you'll look and see it. In the orphanage we always thought Sister Gene Autry was kind of ugly because she had such a square face and big jaw. But later and still later after I was adopted. . . I would sit and think of Sister Gene Autry as being kind of beautiful. . . . That's what happened now, while I was following Mick. I'd been in Bolton for years, and … thought I knew everything about it…but I was wrong….

Mick went through the town like a chalk storm, the little colored bits in one hand and tablet in the other….And he would stop and draw…. Once he saw something small, some little thing I couldn't see. He lowered to his hands and knees and crawled into a shrub by the Walters's place dragging the tablet behind him…."Come see—come see. Oh, it's the most lovely thing, the most lovely, lonely thing of all. Come see."

GETTING READY

- You need to have read aloud Chapter 1 and the first several pages of Chapter 2 of *Stone Fox* prior to this minilesson.

- In this minilesson, you will read from Chapter 2 of *Stone Fox*. If you've selected a read-aloud other than *Stone Fox*, pace yourself so that you've stopped your reading just before a passage you believe you can read in two ways: first, as if you are on autopilot and then with full attentiveness.

- Scan the group to be sure that children have brought all of their reading materials with them to the meeting area. If a child has forgotten, let her know that she should not need reminders. By attending to these and other routines, you enable children to become responsible, autonomous members of the community.

- Before Session VI, you'll want to finish reading aloud Chapter 2 and read up to the selected passage in Chapter 3 that is included in Session VI's minilesson.

DRAFT

…I scrabbled down—it was hard because of my leg—and I looked in. Light came down through the bush and shone on a small place, just a little circle inside the bush, and there was a tiny cross, made of popsicle sticks where one of the Walters kids had buried a gerbil or a dead bird.

It didn't matter what was buried there. Not to Mick. He pulled the pad in with him and I watched him make the light and the little circle and the two crossed popsicle sticks. While he worked I saw his face and he was crying…. I could see it then, see the sadness of the little grave and the way the light hit the popsicle sticks.

As I read this, I could see it too, the little leafy enclave, the lopsided popsicle-stick cross. And I saw myself, too. Somehow, reading that book, and reading other books, too, makes me see my own life as if for the first time. Reading wakes me up, when I let it. "Great literature," Donald Hall, the poet laureate, has written, "if we read it well, opens us up to the world and makes us more sensitive to it, as if we acquired eyes that could see through things and ears that could hear smaller sounds."

Reading well has a lot to do with those moments that jolt us awake. I was at the hairdresser last August. My cell phone, on the counter beside me, vibrated, and I thought, "It is 8 AM. Who could be calling at this hour?" Then I remembered my son Miles would be driving home from an all-night computer party. I picked up the phone.

"Mom. I fell asleep driving. I was in a really bad accident."

I walked out of the hairdresser, my hair half cut, and drove through town. From far away, the whole street was blocked off with scarlet cones and that yellow tape they use when someone has died. The policeman came to my car window. "Road's closed, there's been a bad accident."

"It's my son," I said, hardly believing this was me, saying those words. I watched the man's face turn white. He stepped aside, moving the cone so I could drive up the hill."

At the top of the road, overturned cars and ambulances were everywhere. Miles was there, too, bloody. I wiped the blood off and saw the wounds weren't deep. I retrieved his glasses from the wreckage, and learned the others were okay, too. Everyone was okay.

> *Reading well has a lot to do with those moments that jolt us awake.*

And then I breathed. I remember breathing, and thinking I hadn't breathed since the call came. I breathed, and I took in the blue, blue sky, and thought, "I will never again take this world for granted. I will never again walk through a day without my heart hurting at the unspeakable beauty of it."

So often, I'm so busy that it is as if I'm made of smooth steel. Hurrying here and there with my cell phone and my email and my voice mail and my appointments and my busy, busy schedule, so proud of my busyness. As Maxine Kumin, the poet, says, "I am so busy living the life of mother and wife that I don't have time to unfold—it's all in the pleats."

And so I read and write. I read and write to see more, hear more, think more, feel more, live more. And, aspiring to read as well as I can, I gather the kids close and tell them that my New School Year's resolution is to read myself awake.

MINILESSON

Awakening Ourselves to the Text

CONNECTION

Tell children a story about a time when you or others took in with deep attention someone else's words, someone else's story, and let it change the way life unfolded.

"Readers, I want to tell you a true story. A while ago, I visited another school. The principal saw me come in and said to me, 'What lucky timing! Do you want to visit Room 203? They are celebrating their writing.' Of course, I love hearing kids' writing, so I hurried to the room. When I got there, a girl named Marisol, dressed in her Holy Communion finery for the occasion, was just taking her place at the front of the class. Her memoir went like this:

> I'm the kind of girl who has never had a birthday party. I live with my aunt. She cooks macaroni for me and tells me to get going and where have I been? She doesn't think about my birthday. Last summer, I went back to the Dominican Republic and my baby sister—she's big now—and they gave her a party. No one could tell I never had one.

> Soon I will be ten. I pretend there will be a party and the kids will come, and we'll play "duck, duck, goose" and we'll listen to the radio and there'll be a pink cake, "To Marisol." But then my dream ends. I'm the kind of kid who never had a birthday party.

I know this is a long story, and you may skip it. The story is not essential to the work you are asking kids to do. This is more about preaching than teaching. I've included it because the past few sessions made reading seem like a muscle that needs development, like a job that needs to be tackled. I wanted to start this session with something inspirational. In our teaching, we are always running from one side of the boat to the other. That is, sometimes we will focus on phonics, sometimes on comprehension. Sometimes we will convey reading in a cold, muscle-developing way; sometimes we'll convey it in a warm fuzzy way. I felt this minilesson needed a bit of the warm fuzzy.

"A week later, Marisol turned ten. And all the children, their parents, their teacher, and a colleague of mine, gave her a big birthday party in the park. There were pink balloons hanging from the trees, and a pile of presents, and those great big fifth graders played 'duck, duck, goose' and listened to the radio. And there was a pink cake—and on it the words, 'To Marisol, for all the birthdays that you never had.'"

"Back in the class, the kids talked about how it had been the words in Marisol's memoir that gave them the idea for something as big as a birthday party. And they talked about how words, how other people's stories, can do that. They talked about the fact that on July 4th, what we celebrate with parades and fireworks, is a time when some people went into a very little room and put some words on a piece of paper—The Declaration of Independence—and a nation was born. A nation was born from people putting words on the page and letting those words matter."

Explain why you chose to tell a story about taking in words (and texts) with deep attention, giving them the power to change lives.

"I am telling you this because it seems to me that we sometimes forget that words matter. We read them like they are just little ink marks on the page, our eyes running over them, with nothing happening in our brains. This morning, a child from the class next door announced, 'I read fifty pages last night!' We were both really excited, because fifty pages is a lot. But when I said, 'So what happened in the story?' the kid answered, 'Uhh. . . .' He added, 'I read it—I just can't remember it now.' We talked about how reading isn't just eyes on print; reading is meaning making and reading is letting what you read change your life, change your work, change your thinking. That boy and I realized that *sometimes,* we get to reading so fast that we forget to really take in what the words say. We aren't poised to let them change us."

Even in presidential debates, people find that anecdotes are often more persuasive than arguments. In this anecdote, an unnamed child goes from celebrating the vast numbers of pages he has read to realizing that in fact, he didn't really take in what he'd read at all. It all slid right past him. I hope that as I tell the story, children will identify with him; I hope they'll connect. This is, of course, the goal for the first portion of any minilesson.

"This happens to me not only when I read, but also when I drive. Yesterday, I got in the car to drive to the store. I drove along, drove along, drove along, and then, I pulled into the school parking lot! I thought, 'Whoa! How'd I get here?' and I realized I'd been driving as if I was on automatic pilot, not paying attention. And sometimes I do that when I read. The other day, when I went to find where I left off in my reading, I started looking through the pages to see which ones I'd read and realized they *all* seemed vaguely familiar, but mostly new. I hadn't *really* read any of them. I'd just flown past them.

This connection contains three or four stories, any one of which would have been sufficient for the minilesson. Become accustomed to seeing times when the minilessons in this series contain an excess of examples, and know that this leaves you in the position of being able to draw from among all the stories here that will work for you. Then again, the stories should help you think of your own stories, and yours will always be the best.

Name your teaching point. Specifically, tell children that we need to guard against reading just to get it done, and to instead read with deep attention.

"So today, I want to remind you that when we read, we need to guard against just whipping through the words, reading on autopilot. Instead, we need to pay attention, making sure we are reading in such a way that we let the words matter."

TEACHING

Point out that you aim to read yourself awake. Demonstrate reading first on autopilot, and then catch yourself and reread, this time envisioning and responding with attentiveness.

"Have you ever heard a person say, 'I read myself to sleep last night?' Well, in my life, I try to be the kind of reader who reads myself *awake*. When I read, I want it to feel almost like I'm in a gigantic 3-D movie—one with surround sound! A famous fiction writer, John Gardner, once described reading by saying, 'We read a few pages at the beginning of the book and suddenly we find ourselves seeing not words on a page but a train moving through Russia, an old Italian crying, a farmhouse, battered by rain. We read on—dream on—not passively but actively, worrying about the choices the characters have made, listening in panic for some sound behind the fictional door.'"

"I'm going to read the upcoming bit of *Stone Fox,* and I want you to watch what I do to be sure that I don't just whip past the words, reading on autopilot. As I read, give me a thumbs up if you think I am reading with my mind on fire and a thumbs down if you think I am reading on automatic pilot." Opening the book, I began to read the upcoming page in a rambling, racing sort of a voice.

> It was now the middle of September. The potatoes they had planted in early June took from ninety to hundred twenty days to mature, which meant they must be harvested soon. Besides, the longer he waited, the more danger there was that an early freeze would destroy the crop. And little Willy was sure that if the crop died, Grandfather would die too.

Yesterday's minilesson encouraged children to read faster, stronger, and longer. Today's adds a caveat, saying, "faster, stronger, and longer, yes, but not without attention!" Reading on autopilot will be a term that echoes not only throughout the minilesson (we try to repeat the teaching point a couple of times in any minilesson), but also throughout the Units of Study for Teaching Reading *and the year. When we teach kids to guard against reading on autopilot, we are teaching them one of the most important reading skills there is to teach: monitoring for sense. It's an awareness that one has not made sense that triggers the use of fix-up strategies. When we teach, we give kids a meta-language so they can guide their own reading lives.*

You can crop any section of any of these minilessons to suit your children. One of the teachers who piloted these sessions teaches in a third grade inclusion classroom, and she acted out the words from Gardiner's quote 'not passively but actively' and ended the Gardner quote early, cropping out all mention of 'worrying about the choices the characters have made,' and about 'listening in panic for some sound behind the fictional door.' You could go farther and remove Gardner's quote altogether. These will be the sorts of decisions that you make as you adapt these minilessons for your children.

A friend of Grandfather's offered to help, but little Willy said no. "Don't accept help unless you can pay for it," Grandfather had always said. "Especially from friends."

Then I paused, looked out at the children who were signaling with thumbs down, and then I made my own thumbs-down gesture. As if I caught myself in the act of reading on autopilot, I said, "Whoa! I was just racing past the words. That wasn't even reading." Backing up, I reread, this time fully attentive to the text, imagining the action as it unfolded, using gestures and pauses and emphasis to demonstrate that the words weren't passing me by—that I was understanding the import of the words.

> It was now the middle of September. The potatoes they had planted in early June took from ninety to hundred twenty days to mature, which meant they must be harvested soon. Besides, the longer he waited, the more danger there was that an early freeze would destroy the crop. And little Willy was sure that if the crop died, Grandfather would die too.
>
> A friend of Grandfather's offered to help, but little Willy said no. "Don't accept help unless you can pay for it," Grandfather had always said. "Especially from friends."
>
> And then little Willy remembered something. His college money! He had enough to rent a horse, pay for help, everything. He told Grandfather about his plan, but Grandfather signaled "no."

I reacted strongly and visibly to this unexpected reaction from Grandfather: "What?!"

> Little Willy pleaded with him. But Grandfather repeated "No, no, no!" The situation appeared hopeless.

I shook my head sadly and sighed.

> But little Willy was determined. He would dig up the potatoes by hand if he had to.
>
> And then Searchlight solved the problem. She walked over and stood in front of the plow. In her mouth was the harness she wore during the winter when she pulled the snow sled.

In this teaching component, I contrast a don't-do-this example with a do-this example. I often use contrast to show children what I hope they will do, set against what I don't want them to do. In most instances, I will exaggerate the differences, making the "don't do" example especially flat and the "do-this" example especially alluring. This is a technique we use often. I find the presence of contrasting examples pops out the differences between what I hope readers do and what I hope they don't do.

You don't need to act out every single bit of the story; that does not display deep comprehension to the children. Certain parts of every text are worth pausing for, or acting out, and others are meant to be background; extra attention to them disrupts the balance of the unfolding story. Reading well aloud is not easy, and might take some rehearsal.

Name what you just did in a way that is transferable to other texts and other days.

Looking up from the book for a moment, I said to the class, "Are you noticing how I am reading attentively, trying to picture the story in my mind, and reacting to everything?" Then I tucked my head back into the book and continued reading aloud.

> Little Willy shook his head. "Digging up a field is not the same as riding over snow," he told her. But Searchlight just stood there and would not move. "You don't have the strength, girl." Little Willy tried to talk her out of it. But Searchlight had made up her mind.

I looked up with relief, "So Willy's problem is solved, it looks like!"

ACTIVE INVOLVEMENT

Set children up to try reading with their minds awake, envisioning and reacting to their own independent reading texts.

"Listen closely now, because it is your turn to try reading yourself awake. Will you get out *your* book, and while sitting right here, will you read on from wherever you left off? Sit here and read, like you did yesterday in the meeting area. Remember to use the tips from yesterday, too—the ones on your bookmark. But today, be especially careful to not let yourself start flying past those pages, reading on autopilot. Instead, read with full attention, making a movie in your mind and giving yourself time to react to what happens."

As children read quietly, I occasionally whispered for the room to hear, "See what the words are saying. Hear the characters." Then after a few minutes, I voiced over again, saying, "Pay deep attention as you read. Make sure you are wide awake to what is going on." Then, to a nearby child, I added, "React. How does this make you feel?"

When it comes time for the teaching component of a minilesson, the teacher needs to think, "What teaching methods will I use?" In this minilesson and in most, you will demonstrate. To think about what it means to demonstrate, imagine you are teaching a child how to put on a shoe, and you are demonstrating as a way to teach this. You would start with the shoe off and proceed in a step-by-step fashion, articulating the steps as you do them. You would probably say things like, "First, I . . ." and you would do whatever you named. You would probably tuck in little hints such as, "Notice that I don't squish down on the heel." The teaching in this minilesson, too, relies on demonstration and has a lot in common with the teaching you'd do to demonstrate how one puts on a shoe. As you read this teaching component, think about ways this bit of teaching is illustrative of a kind of teaching you see repeatedly in these books.

You should notice that I'm not reiterating what I've just done, although I usually do so in minilessons. The read-aloud passages make this minilesson long as it is, so I'm making choices to abbreviate.

I could have asked the children to read the next passage of Stone Fox, *but that would only work if the whole class could read that level of text difficulty.*

Teachers, you may feel a bit uneasy because the teaching you are doing in this minilesson probably feels inadequate to the job. The kids have a lot to learn, and your minilessons are only just a start. Rest assured that the teaching point of this minilesson will be a motif across the whole year.

I crouched next to Malik and asked him to share his thoughts. Malik was reading *James and the Giant Peach,* which was an easier text than he usually reads. He'd just read the part where the main character, James, goes on his adventure with all the insects. Malik tugged on the tassels of his ubiquitous hoodie. "James is really excited about his journey and feels free for the first time in his life." Malik then put his hands on his hips and stuck out his chest, showing that James was proud and fearless, flashing a bright smile.

I gestured for him to read on and moved to listen to another cluster. I could tell that Tyrell was struggling; he had his finger out under the words, and his face was scrunched in concentration. I decided to do a little coaching, saying, "Reread that part, and this time, let's you and I try to read smoothly and also pay attention to what's going on. You don't need that finger! Try it." He read, a bit more smoothly and with much more expression. I said, "Holy Moly! Did you hear that difference! I could pay much deeper attention to that! This time, I'll read it, and again, let's really *feel* what it's saying." After taking a turn reading, I reminded him to keep doing that kind of thinking as he read on his own.

After a few minutes, I intervened. "Readers, I hate to interrupt. Will you give me a thumbs up if you kept yourself attentive, if you were wide awake to the text?"

Teachers, always during the active involvement section of a mini-lesson, you will want to listen in on the work of one child, then another. One of the reasons that you'll have a seating chart for your meeting times is that you'll want children like Gabe and Tyrell to be within reach so you can keep especially close tabs on their understanding of and engagement in your minilesson.

LINK

Synthesize yesterday's teaching point about reading quickly with today's about not reading on autopilot. Urge readers to read quickly and attentively, reacting to the text.

"So readers, from now on, whenever we read, let's remember that yes, we want to push ourselves to read stronger and longer, but we don't want to read like we're on autopilot. Instead, we want to be the kind of readers who read ourselves awake. To do this, we need to be sure that we are truly feeling, deeply reacting to what we read."

"Remember, when you get back to your seat, you need to fill out your reading log, noting the starting time and page. As you read today, be sure to flag parts of the book that are important. Let's also flag pages where you found yourself to be especially wide awake, where it is almost as if the print has been written in bold letters. You are going to have a chance to share those parts from today with each other later."

This link spotlightsthe importance of readers drawing on their full repertoire of strategies. It is common for teachers to misunderstand reading and writing workshops and to think that minilessons are a time to demonstrate a strategy that we then assign to children, telling them all to practice that one strategy during that one day's workshop. Such an understanding allows the teacher to hold tight to many norms of traditional instruction, where teachers dole out little one-day assignments to children, who then do as they are told. Reading and writing workshops are different. Minilessons allow teachers to teach a strategy that then becomes part of readers' growing repertoires of strategies. Each day, readers above all continue their important work of reading and, in the writing workshop, of writing, and as they do so, they draw upon their full repertoires of strategies to accomplish their important purposes.

CONFERRING AND SMALL-GROUP WORK

Teach Yourself—and Your Students—To Confer

You'll no doubt continue to spend the bulk of your time during the reading workshop cloistered with a small group of children, listening to one and then another read leveled passages. Hopefully, you'll also have a bit of time before or after your assessment work to do some conferring. As you confer with children, you'll probably want to brush up on your own skills at conferring. Remember, as you do this, that you are not the only one learning to confer. Your children, too, need to learn how they can play the roles they are expected to play in conferences. Help them by giving them little pointers along the way.

Research To Understand the Work Each Reader Has Been Doing

Your conferences will usually begin with research. Your temptation might be to research *what* the child is reading. My general suggestion is to avoid a lot of talk about the text itself until you have established a purpose for that talk. You'll fashion a direction for the conference from hearing about the work the child is already doing as a reader, the thinking the child is doing, and the strategies she is using. So I suggest you begin your confer-

ence not by asking, "What are you reading?" and "What's your book about?" but instead by asking, "What have you been thinking about as you read?" or "What work have you been doing as a reader?" or "How's your reading been going? Are you trying anything new as a reader?"

When you ask questions in hopes of learning about a child's reading, the child will often feel a bit unsure how to answer. After all, many people are not accustomed to responding to a question like "What work are you doing as a reader?" Expect, therefore, that your child might respond with a plot summary or a book evaluation. Alternatively, the child might sort of shrug and look like a deer in the headlights.

Either way, you'll want to help the child know the sort of response that you're expecting. If the child launches into a long-winded retelling of the book, for example, you will probably want to interrupt, and say, "What you are doing right now is retelling the book, and it is true that readers sometimes think back over all that has happened in a story, and we sometimes tell each other the plot of a story. But just now, when I asked, 'What are you working on as a reader?' what I am

---

> ## MID-WORKSHOP TEACHING POINT
>
> ### Readers Read Ourselves Awake and Talk Back to Texts
>
> Speaking without drawing children's attention fully away from their reading, I said, "Readers, in a moment I am going to stop you. Before I do, make sure you have flagged a part of the book where you found yourself really sitting up and taking notice, where it was almost as if the print was written in bold. If you haven't *found* such a part, you can *make* it. *You* can make almost any section of a book important if you really, really pay attention to it."
>
> After readers had another minute to read, I said, "Let's stop now. All eyes up here." When I had the class' attention, I said, "I want to remind you that there's reading, and there's *reading*. You can read in a 'Let me just run my eyes over this page' sort of a way, or you can sit up and take notice. I want to challenge you to really, truly read today. A man named Paulo Friere said it this way, "Reading is not walking on words. It's grasping the soul of them." That is what you are being asked to do today—and everyday."
>
> "And here are my tips about how to do this. First, you need to choose. You need to decide, 'Am I going to read, or to *read*?' And frankly, there are parts of a book that you fly over, and there are parts where you need to sit up and take notice—just like there are parts you read quickly and parts you read slowly."
>
> "And second, when you find a part that matters to you, what makes that part matter is not just what the author wrote. It is also what *you* bring to the page. *You* make that part huge by talking back to it—by saying, 'Oh no!' or, 'The same happened to me,' or 'Watch out!' You make that part huge not only by talking back to it, but also by laughing aloud or practically crying."
>
> "I know you already flagged a part of your book that mattered to you. Now I want you to reread that part to yourself, and really, truly let the words in. See them. Hear them. Let them
>
> *continued on next page*

wondering about is whether you are trying to do specific stuff to read well." I might at this point gesture toward a chart that records things that the class has been studying. Those charts will be minimal at this early point in the year, and there won't yet be a lot of language about reading floating around the classroom, but still, I'll reference whatever is available. I might, for example, say, "For example, have you been pushing yourself to read a bit more, or have you been thinking about what makes reading work for you and then doing more of that?" You might want to suggest other ways that readers could talk about their reading, saying something like this: "When I think about the work I am doing as a reader, for example, sometimes I find that I am too critical of books, that I read just a tiny bit and think, 'This is boring.' And so I've set goals for myself to give books more of a chance, to try to not be so quick to judge a book.' Do you see how I'm talking about *my goals as a reader,* not just talking about what happens in my book? That's the sort of thing I am dying to know about you right now. What are you working on as a reader?"

After a child begins to answer, telling me what he or she has been working on as a reader, I follow the child's lead. For example, if the child says, "I'm trying to read faster," then I'll ask, "What specific things do you

MID-WORKSHOP TEACHING POINT

continued from previous page

remind you of one time in your own life. Think about what the character is probably thinking, feeling. And this time, will you talk back to that part of the book? I put some Post-it notes in the center of each table. Take a couple Post-it notes and as you read, get yourself to talk back to the passage (or two). And this time, record what you are thinking on your Post-it notes and attach them to that part of your book.

"Then you can continue reading, but as you read, look for another section or two of the book that again, is almost written in bold ink. And again, when you read that other section, leave space not only for the author's words, but for your response, using Post-it notes." You'll share the passages and your response to them at the end of today's workshop. *[Figs. V-1, V-2, V-3, and V-4]*

Figure V-1

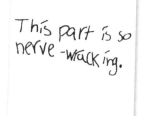

Figure V-2

This reader is reading on the edge of his seat. He'd benefit from nudges to elaborate or to speculate how the tension might be resolved. Readers can be nudged to use writing about reading as an invitation to not only record but also to extend their thoughts.

Figure V-3

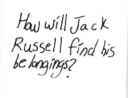

Figure V-4

Already at the start of the year, Amber's predictions are grounded in text evidence. Soon she'll generate multiple possibilities and imagine not only what but also how things will unfold.

find you can do to get yourself reading faster?" If the child doesn't know, I'm apt to say, "Will you read aloud a bit, so I can try to understand what you do?" When I set the child up to do some reading while I watch, I have hunches in mind that inform my observation. For example, when I listen to the child read aloud, because I know she is working on her pace, I'm apt to watch her phrasing, her attention to punctuation, her attentiveness to pace of reading. As the child reads, then, I'm conducting some follow-up research. Although the child will have pointed me toward one line of work that she's pursuing, I'll research other aspects of reading too. If the child is just starting a book, for example, this will make me curious about the amount of previewing the child does. I might say, "I want to learn a bit more about your reading. Can you pretend you were just about to read this new book and show me how you get yourself started on a new book?"

That is, although I follow whatever lead the child gives me, I also try to contextualize the information I learn by gleaning other sorts of information about the child's reading. I'm apt to look at the log and see the number of pages a child has read in school and at home. I'm apt to look also at the books the child has read and notice what I can about the child's choices. Early in the year, there may only be a few Post-it notes that reveal the child's thinking as he or she reads, but if there are any such records of the child's thinking, I study them, noticing especially the sorts of thinking that this reader is apt to do often. "You just read this passage," I could say, "What were you thinking as you read that?" I may ask some questions to learn how a child sees that passage fitting with the whole of the text.

This research takes about three minutes of time, and as I'm conducting the research, I am thinking about what I can compliment and what I can teach. I usually compliment first, and I try to name something that the child is doing that seems to be at the top of the child's game. I'll discuss these compliments in more detail later, because they are important. I usually want to support the new risks the child is taking. I also want to support hard work. Sometimes I compliment work that the child may not actually be doing yet, but is gesturing toward. "I absolutely love the way you. . . ," I'll say. I try to push myself to say five or six sentences about whatever it is I admire, going on and on at some length about it. Over time, you'll hear lots of examples of ways in which I do this. For now, the main thing for you to know is that I aim to name what the child has done in such a way that the child is apt to do it again, on another day and in another text, and I also aim to build the child's sense of identity and agency as a reader.

Name Your Teaching Point and Demonstrate, or Otherwise Teach, the Reader, Coaching the Child to Try What You've Taught

Then I teach, and when I teach, I try to preface my teaching with an explicit teaching point. For example, if the child has been pushing herself to read quickly and has not spent any time on book orientation, I might preface the teaching part of the conference like this: "Lily, since you always jump into your books headfirst, there is just one tip I could give you that I think might help you with your goal of reading faster, and it might also help you to be sure you are really thinking about the whole of your book as you read. Could I give you one tip?"

After she nods, cocking her head to the side and shifting around in her seat, I'd say, "You are so intent on racing to the words, on pushing yourself to read a ton—and these are great goals—that you are skipping past something that most of us do at the start of reading. Even when we want to read quickly, most of us take a second at the start of a book and at the start of every day's reading time to look over what we're about to

read, thinking, 'What's coming ahead for me as a reader?' People call this 'book orientation.' I think it will *really* help you if you take a minute at the start of every day's reading to do a teeny bit of book orientation."

Then I'd want to show the reader how to do whatever it is I am hoping the reader will do. In this instance, I'd say, "Let me show you how I get ready to read," and then I'd do a book orientation, musing aloud to myself as I notice things. After I demonstrate, I try to name what I've done just as I do in a minilesson, only the explicit teaching in a conference is especially abbreviated. "You try it now," I say, and I ask the reader to try the strategy out while I'm sitting by her side. I want to see her begin to do the work on her own, praising her effort and ability and guiding her along.

End Your Conference, Reminding the Child This Will be Useful Other Days with Other Texts

Then it is time to end the conference. I usually do so by recalling both the compliment and the teaching point, urging the reader to draw on both these things often during reading. I also want to remind the reader that we all have so many choices of how to best spend our time during reading workshop, and I add the new thing I've taught to the child's repertoire.

TEACHING SHARE

Readers Find Opportunities to Read Aloud and to Share Bits of Texts that We Love

Tell children a story that helps them push themselves harder, even if they think they understand the work they are trying to do.

"Readers, can I stop you? Let's stay right where we are right now—but I need all your eyes." I waited. "When I was a child, my mother used to take me out onto the tennis courts and hit the ball to me. Time after time, I'd swing away and the ball would whiz past me. Time after time, my mother would yell, 'Keep your eye on the ball.' I always wanted to call back, 'What are you talking about—keep your eye on the ball? Of course, I'm keeping my eye on the ball! What do you think I'm doing, watching birds?'"

"But then one morning, something amazing happened, something altogether different than anything I'd ever experienced. On this particular morning, the ball came across the net toward me, and I watched it descend to the court, then bounce up, and then hang suspended in the air for an instant before it arched down toward me. Standing there, I saw the ball as it hit my racket strings, as it made that lovely reassuring thwack, and as it now spun back toward my mother's side of the court. And I realized that I'd never before kept my eye on the ball. I'd never before followed the ball so intently that I actually saw it hit my racket. I'd never before followed my mother's coaching."

"Today, I haven't been saying, 'Keep your eye on the ball.' Instead, I've tried to say, 'Read the words. See them, hear them, make a movie in your mind, react to what you see and hear. Read yourself awake.' I know that at the start of today, you probably thought, 'I'm doing that,' but I hope you are getting the idea that really great readers see more in a text, hear more in a text. *And* I hope you are also learning that really great readers think more and feel more in response to reading."

This teaching share and many others ask children to find selections they like and to read those aloud to each other and then discuss them and read them aloud again. There are a few reasons why we are returning to this so often. First, we have been amazed to see how wildly popular this is with kids. They enjoy reading to each other, especially when there is no assessor in sight. They know what is expected of them, and almost every child seems to feel that he or she can be successful at this. The kids are engaged and active and productive and on-task. Then, too, there is an increasing body of research that suggests that children need authentic opportunities to read aloud and reread aloud and reread aloud again texts that they love. Tim Rasinski encourages teachers to make songbooks and recruit kids of all ages to sing along. He loves it when children rewrite verses, adding their own spins on those songs, and he rallies kids to sing those homemade songs with gusto and pleasure. He encourages teachers to find opportunities for informal reader's theater, for oral renditions of all sorts. His advice is this: "Remember, practice does not make perfect. Perfect practice makes perfect!"

Because it is early in the year and because the demands on your time are especially strong right now, you will not have had a chance to show kids a million marvelous ways to share books. So for now, you'll want to keep your teaching simple and keep kids' work as engaging as possible. It is for those reasons that we return often to share sessions that invite kids to, well, share.

Ask children to share their work of the day with a partner. In this case, ask them to share reading with deep attention, allowing themselves the space to respond to the text.

"Right now, please find that section of your book where you read yourself awake and read that aloud to a neighbor. Read like these are the most important words—the richest words—imaginable. And not only read the section well, but then afterward share the response that you jotted on a Post-it note, and talk as deeply and completely as you can about what you feel and think about that passage." [Figs. V-5 and V-6]

After a few minutes, I closed the reading workshop by saying, "Readers, you have shared the words in your books in a way that brought them to life for your partners. You are certainly reading yourselves awake! You talked about parts that stand out to you—that feel as though they're written in bold. When you bring these books home tonight, remember that you will read parts that stand out to you. When you get to a passage that feels as though it is written in bold letters, is to react to that passage with your own important thoughts." [Figs. V-7 and V-8]

I think that it was nice of Ms. McNicklas helped the "pet Finders" by driving them around.

Figure V-5
With coaching, this reader could use more precise language to grow insights and ideas.

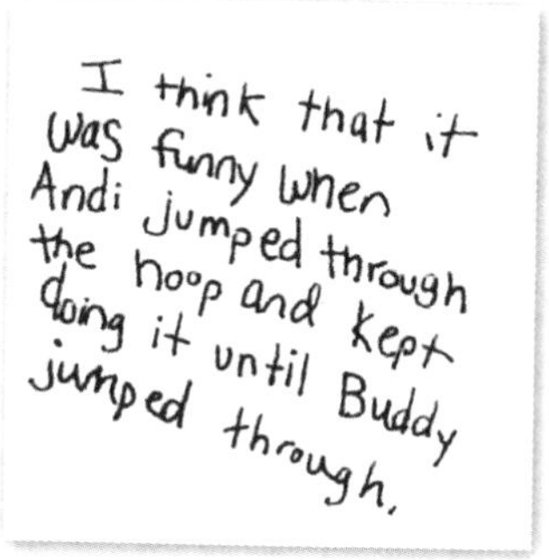

I think that it was funny when Andi jumped through the hoop and kept doing it until Buddy jumped through.

Figure V-6
Humor is a great comprehension monitor. When readers laugh aloud as they read, the text is registering.

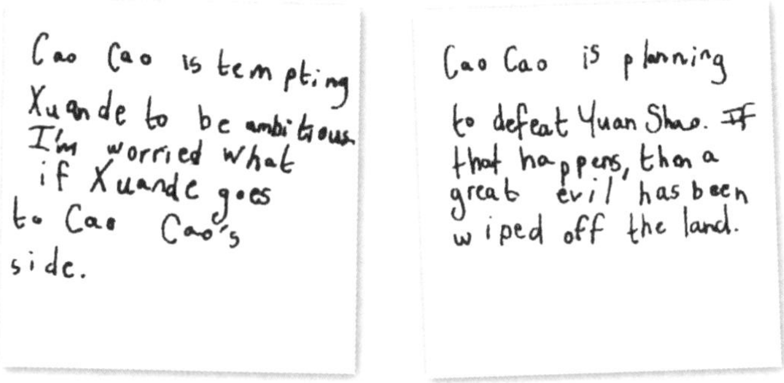

Cao Cao is tempting Xuande to be ambitious. I'm worried what if Xuande goes to Cao Cao's side.

Cao Cao is planning to defeat Yuan Shao. If that happens, than a great evil has been wiped off the land.

Figures V-7 and V-8
This reader is responding emotionally to the text. If you teach children to be wide-awake readers, they learn to step into a character's shoes, to imagine what might happen next, and to empathize.

Making Texts Matter

PART TWO

DRAFT

Holding Tight to Meaning

n Session IV, I mentioned that as this unit and this year unfolds, you'll want to become accustomed to standing back every once in a while to observe your readers during independent reading. Remember that we, as teachers, can learn so much by simply standing in the doorway of our classroom and looking in at our kids. Throughout the year, we need to be mindful of how much actual reading kids are doing. Do some heads seem to be moving like revolving fans? Do some children seem to develop urinary track infections, visiting the bathroom again and again, whenever it's time to read? Chances are those kids are not holding books that are a good fit for them.

As you observe your readers, develop the habit of thinking, "In what ways does my reading curriculum—my mini-lessons, my homework assignments, my one-to-one work—lift the level of what kids are doing right now during independent reading?" If you have focused on readers pushing themselves to read longer, you should see evidence that children can already sustain a focus on reading for longer periods of time. If, while introducing books you have talked

GETTING READY

- You need to have read the rest of Chapter 2 and the first several pages of Chapter 3 in *Stone Fox* prior to this minilesson.

- You'll be reading aloud a portion of Chapter 3, "Searchlight," of *Stone Fox*, unless you have selected a different book to read with your class. If you are relying on a different book, select a passage to read aloud that is written in a way in which you can easily make a mental movie as you read the first portion of the passage, but then something happens (such as a jump in time) to make your mental movie "blurry."

- Consider marking up your copy of *Stone Fox* so that you are reminded where you want to do your think-alouds and to prompt the students to turn and talk.

- Create a chart titled "When Our Mental Movie Grows Blurry" to use during the teaching component of today's minilesson. Keep it out of view until then.

- Create a chart titled "Ways You and Another Reader Can Share Your Reading Lives," leaving room on the bottom of the chart to add in some of the kids' responses during the share. Again, keep it out of view until the right moment.

- Before teaching the next session, Session VII, you will need to have read up to the part in Chapter 7, "The Meeting," that begins with, "Little Willy loved dogs...." If you've selected a different book as your read-aloud, you'll need to have read up to a place where you can imagine demonstrating what happens when a reader's mental image breaks down—a place that might be confusing.

up the value of reading several books by an author, for example, then as you watch kids work during independent reading time, you should see them initiating their own author studies, looking between one book and another by the same author. That is, you need to always expect that your teaching will affect what kids do during the independent reading workshop. If your teaching and your curriculum don't affect what kids do during this time, then chances are

> *If your teaching and your curriculum don't affect what kids do during this time, then chances are good that your teaching will not affect what kids do during their own lived lives as readers.*

good that your teaching will not affect what kids do during their own lived lives as readers. And if that is a case, you need to wonder what the point of your teaching is.

So far, you will have taught children to leave Post-it notes as bookmarks, to think about how much they read and to aim to read longer, to notice what works and what does not work for them as readers, and to make choices so that reading works. And you will have taught them to read themselves awake. During independent reading, then, you should see them drawing on all this work. Notice that all these lessons leave a great deal of control in the hands of the learner. I have relearned the importance of this from the work I have been doing lately, not as a teacher, but as a daughter.

Over the past few years, my tough, stoic, Rock of Gibraltar mother has had one physical crisis after another. She's been in and out of the hospital with seizures, strokes, GI infections, a dislocated hip, and a dozen other things. She's been battered by the storms of life. Recently, I was there to bring her home from the hospital, and this time, she was in bad shape. For a few days, it seemed as if she might roll up in a little ball, losing her grip on life.

I will not forget one afternoon when I watched her haltingly make her way across the kitchen to the coffee pot. She got the empty pot out of its place in the machine and slowly made her way to the sink, where she filled the pot halfway, then shuffled across the room toward the coffee pot. She poured the water into the appropriate compartment in the coffee machine. Mum's arm strength, though, wasn't what it had been, and the water ended up pooling on the counter, dripping into a puddle on the floor.

At this point, I jumped up, ready to help, but my father signaled no, and engaged me in a lively conversation. Out of the corner of my eye, I noticed Mum was slowly making her way to where a towel hung, getting the towel, and then dropping the towel onto the pool of water. With one toe, she moved the towel about, sopping up the water. Then, still leaning on her walker, Mum made her way slowly back to the sink to repeat the whole ordeal. Again the water splashed all over the counter and pooled around Mum's feet. This time, it was impossible to ignore the situation.

My father leapt to his feet, strode across the room, grabbed the perfectly good coffee pot, and heaved it into the trashcan. "That dang thing has been leaking for weeks. I'm sick of it," he said, and within a few minutes he'd left the house to get a new coffee pot. An hour later, Dad returned with a scientifically chosen coffee pot containing an extra-large opening for the water.

I learned a lot from the way my spendthrift father supported my mother during those days when she needed help. Dad was adamant that hovering and micro-controlling weren't going to help. Above all, we could not compromise Mum's sense of personal agency. The doctors told us she needed to eat, so Dad and I began getting out two bins of yogurt, leaving one of the containers of yogurt and a spoon

near Mum as we ate our own with great relish. She needed to eat—but no matter how much she needed more calories, it would not have been a good trade off for us to begin feeding her as if she was a baby bird. In the end, nothing matters more than that we support a person's grip on life and leave the person's sense of personal agency intact.

I tell you this because sometimes I think we are so concerned about making sure that readers' growth in reading is supervised and supported at all times that we risk sacrificing their sense of personal agency—their grip on life. We are so worried that every reader may not be growing stronger every minute—reading exactly the right things, practicing with the right muscles, engaging in the right conversations, developing the right skills—that we sometimes forget that kids are not going to have vibrant, strong reading lives if we take away their ability to make decisions and to act in proactive ways to author their own lives. If, in school, we always tell children, "Sit here. Read this. Look for that. Mark this. Then talk about that," then how will we teach children to compose lives in which reading matters? Don't we need to give children some choices so that we can teach into those choices and so that children know that they can be proactive authors of their own lives?

MINILESSON

Holding Tight to Meaning

CONNECTION

COACHING TIPS

Remind children that yesterday they learned to guard against reading on autopilot. Tell them that readers often recall our reading by recapping the big things that happened.

"Yesterday we learned that it is important to guard against reading on autopilot, and instead to read ourselves awake, creating movies in the mind. In a few minutes, you will continue reading where you left off last night. Before we read on in a book, it can be helpful to remind ourselves of what was happening in the story when we stopped reading. Readers usually do this by scanning through the pages we've read, storytelling them to ourselves. As we do this, we think things like, 'Oh yes, I remember how it all started.' We recall what we just read, telling the parts in sequence."

"Let's practice by getting together with someone and storytelling the part we have read so far in *Stone Fox*. You will sort of tell the sequence, the timeline, of the big things that have happened. I'll get you started."

"Willy, a boy who lives alone with his grandfather on a potato farm in Wyoming, discovered that his grandfather wouldn't get out of bed. So he got Doc Smith, the town doctor, to come and she . . . Now take it from there."

I listened in as children talked with each other. Then convening the group, I repeated

You'll see that the connection in today's minilesson is long and involves kids actually trying some things out. The architecture of the minilessons can't be a straitjacket.

You may notice that I have mentioned retelling but have not taught children anything about how to retell. One of the challenges in teaching reading is that kids are always engaged in the whole shebang of reading. "Lines of development" can't easily be isolated and separated out from the rest of the braid of skills that comprise reading. As a result, it will be the case that again and again in your teaching, you'll mention an aspect of reading growth, giving a nod to that aspect's place in the overall scheme of things—without necessarily spotlighting that particular line of work at that particular time. I do not focus on retelling yet because the children are not yet in sustained partnership relationships, so any press to retell a book would seem like a mere exercise, something to do to prove they can do it but for no natural purpose. Later in this unit, kids will be paired into long-lasting partnerships, and then I will use partnerships as a reason for (and a context for) retelling.

This is a very unusual connection because it includes some active involvement. At the beginning of the year we have a lot to get going. You will teach retelling later in this unit, so don't worry if the children still have a lot to learn about it.

Notice how I got the children started on the retelling, thereby making it much more likely that they would be able to continue the retelling successfully. It is important for us to provide children with assisted practice. When we start doing the activity that we want children to do, passing the baton to them midway through that activity, is an extremely effective scaffold.

my start to the retelling and signaled for Isaac to add onto it. He said,"Doc Smith says Grandfather doesn't want to live anymore, that he wants to die."Then I signaled for Izzy to continue the retelling. She added that Little Willy decides to dig up and sell the potatoes, using Searchlight to help. I said,"You all seem clear about what's happened in *Stone Fox* so far. Sometimes, though, we *aren't* as clear about what's happening in a story and then we need fix-up strategies.

Name your teaching point. Specifically, teach children that when readers encounter confusing parts in books, we draw on strategies to clarify the meaning.

"Specifically, today I want to teach you that readers sometimes pause when we become confused in the text we're reading. We'll be reading along, and then the text turns a corner, and suddenly we're not quite sure what's going on. It's as if the film breaks in the mental movie we're making. When that happens, readers say,'Huh?' and we continue reading, asking, 'What's going on?' The details sometimes help, and sometimes we need to reread."

Teaching

Explain that the structure of this minilesson is different than usual. It will contain a long read-aloud. Set children up to make mental movies as they listen.

Then I continued."Instead of a regular minilesson, I'm going to do some reading aloud, and I'll teach today's minilesson inside the read-aloud. Remember, as we read, we need to pay attention, to be wide awake, and to make movies in the mind. Remember, too, that some parts of a story need to be read quickly—and I think we may be in one of those parts. Reading a little bit quickly may be the best way to hold onto the mental movie, I think. Let's try it. If the story gets confusing, stop me."

"I'm going to read aloud from where we left off in *Stone Fox*. As you listen, remember to make a movie in your mind." I began to read Chapter 3,"Searchlight,"the passage describing Willy and Searchlight racing against themselves just for the fun of it. I read faster and faster as Searchlight ran faster, and, as I read, I showed I was reacting internally to the content of the passage.

One of the most important lessons you can teach kids is that of monitoring for sense. Your previous lesson was on guarding against reading as if on autopilot, and this minilesson returns to this skill. If kids don't realize they have lost comprehension, then knowing dozens of fix-up strategies will be all for naught because they won't reach for those strategies.

The teachers who piloted these lessons found that during a lesson like this, one that requires reading aloud longer chunks of the text, it was helpful to mark each teaching move in their own copy of Stone Fox. *That is, they marked each place in* Stone Fox *where they thought aloud and each place where they asked children to turn and talk.*

You'll notice that I explicitly tell the children how this minilesson will be different from a regular lesson. This lets the children know what to expect.

Over and over again, you'll see that demonstrations begin with me telling children what I'll be teaching and how I want them to watch. Next I teach the content, and then I recap the strategies, emphasizing the sequence of steps. Finally, I give children the chance to put the strategy I've just demonstrated into action for themselves. This lesson follows most of these patterns.

At a little before six each day, little Willy would position his sled in front of the old church on Main Street. Today again he waited, eyes glued on the big church that loomed high overhead.

Searchlight waited too—ears perked up, eyes alert, legs slightly bent, ready to spring forward.

B-O-N-G!

At the first stroke of six, Searchlight lunged forward with such force that little Willy was almost thrown from the sled. Straight down Main Street they went, the sled's runners barely touching the snow. They were one big blur as they turned right onto North Road. And they were almost out of town before the church clock became silent again.

I paused and looked up from the book. "I can see they're racing, can't you? I'm wondering, are they racing against anyone or are they racing themselves, just for the fun of it? Let's read on and see. Notice as the actions get faster, my voice gets faster. I have no brakes on!" I resumed my reading, hurrying my voice and leaning in as I read on.

"Go, Searchlight! Go!" Little Willy's voice sang out across the snowy twilight. And did Searchlight go! She had run this race a hundred times before, and she knew the whereabouts of every fallen tree and hidden gully. This enabled her to travel at tremendous speed even though it was getting dark and more dangerous.

Little Willy sucked in the cool night air and felt the sting of the wind against his face. It was a race all right. A race against time. A race against themselves. A race they had always won.

I looked up, eyeing the kids significantly, as this passage now answered the question I'd raised.

The small building up ahead was Grandfather's farmhouse. When Searchlight saw it, she seemed to gather up every ounce of her remaining strength. She forged ahead with such speed that the sled seemed to lift up off the ground and fly.

The most important thing about reading aloud well is that you must be there. Your focus must be through the words to the scene, the drama, and you must be there. You're watching Searchlight, poised on the starting line, all muscles.

You hear the "bong" and you lunge forward as you read.

As I read aloud, I almost try to act out the words with my voice. I may even free one hand to act as though I were Little Willy holding Searchlight's reins. Sometimes, I might pause to fill in the sensory gaps that might not be explicitly stated in the text, but right now, the text begs me to read briskly. Finally, I name what I have done.

In addition to marking the places where you will go between reading and teaching, you may also want to write notes about what you will say in this minilesson onto Post-it notes and stick them inside your copy of Stone Fox, *so that when you "realize" (as you will during the teaching portion) that your mental movie is blurry, your teaching will still feel authentic to children because you will not need to switch back and forth between the published minilesson and your copy of* Stone Fox.

"Thumbs up, readers, if you can see this, if you are making a mental movie."I scanned the rug. Thumbs popped up everywhere. I continued to read.

> They were so exhausted when they arrived at the house that neither of them noticed the horse tied up outside.
>
> Little Willy unhitched Searchlight, and then both of them tumbled over onto their backs in the snow and stared up at the moon. Searchlight had her head and one paw on little Willy's chest and was licking the underside of his chin. Little Willy had a hold of Searchlight's ear, and he was grinning.
>
> The owner of the horse stood on the front porch and watched them, tapping his foot impatiently.

I pause twice here, first to remind our community of learners that I had answered an earlier wondering, and also to model how swiftly strong readers can verify a wondering with a quick mental note. The second time I pause, I both confirm for myself that kids are indeed making mind movies and set them up for the more confusing parts I'm about to read.

When you reach a confusing part of the read-aloud text, demonstrate your confusion. Say "Huh?" Then explicitly name the strategies readers can use to reconstruct meaning.

I looked up from the book."Did your mental movie get blurry?"I asked, incredulously, my voice reflecting that I, for one, couldn't quite picture what was happening."Give me a thumbs up if you are having trouble picturing this. What kind of guy is this, and where did he come from."Most thumbs went up."Are we picturing him like a postman or a cowboy or what?"Sometimes when things get confusing, I read on for a bit to see if the confusion clears up. Let's try it. Listen closely."I resumed reading.

> Chapter 4: The Reason
>
> "GET OVER HERE!"The voice cut through the air like the twang of a ricocheting bullet.

During this passage, the last paragraph comes out of nowhere— "Huh?" and must confuse any attentive reader. Let your voice reflect this confusion, and literally follow the line with, "Huh?"

I express more confusion over the image:"What?"

> Little Willy had never heard a voice like that before. Not on this farm. He couldn't move.

Putting the book down, I shook my head and looked at the class. "Readers, let's stop. I'm totally confused. Aren't you?" I reread the last few lines, my voice accentuating the way in which the events in the story seemed to come out of nowhere.

"Readers, I'm realizing that this is not the only time that this has ever happened to me. In other books, too, I sometimes read along, watching my mental movie, when all of a sudden I think, 'Huh? What just happened?!' It's like all of a sudden the film in the movie projector that is my brain suddenly whirls into a blur and I lose track of what's going on. Has that ever happened to any of you when you are reading?" Many children nodded in assent.

"When we read and meaning breaks down—when our mental movie gets blurry—there are things we can do to clarify the picture. I've created a chart that can help with this work." I revealed and read from a chart titled "When Our Mental Movie Grows Blurry."

"When we come to confusing parts in a story, we can do several things to clear them up. The first and most important thing we can do is to *notice* we are confused." I pointed to the first item on the chart. "Good readers are aware when a story suddenly turns a corner like *Stone Fox* just did. We *think*, 'Huh?' Usually we then continue reading, aware that we need to figure out what just happened, aware we need things to get clear. Paying attention to the details helps. And *sometimes* we need to go back and reread to see if we missed something.

When Our Mental Movie Grows Blurry

- *Realize it. Ask, "Huh?"*
- *Continue reading, asking, "What's going on?"*
- *Look at details.*
- *Ask, "Could it be that . . . ? Or could it be . . . ?"*
- *Reread, if necessary*

Notice how I am setting up the conditions in which the strategy I plan to teach—one related to fixing up meaning when it falls apart—will be useful. Whenever I teach a strategy, I tend to begin my demonstration before the time when I encounter some trouble and then show that when I encounter a need, I reach for a strategy. I do try to show readers how they can recognize when it is time to pull a particular strategy out of their repertoire. In a minilesson, I am not only teaching how to use a strategy but also when to use it.

GOOD READERS...

- Don't whip through words like you're on autopilot. We need to pay attention—making a mental movie as we read. Then, we rewind and retell the story to ourselves.
- Remember the characters name, we describe them, and the setting.
- Notice when they are confused and read on asking, "What's going on?" OR we go back & reread

Active Involvement

Demonstrate reading on, asking "What's going on?" Try to reconstruct meaning and help children do the same.

"So readers, let's start by reading on, because that's usually the first strategy a good reader tries. But remember, we're going to read on with that question, 'What's going on?' in our minds. I pointed to the second item on the chart.

I resumed reading. I reread a bit of the passage, just to regain momentum, and then pressed on. As I read, I continued to demonstrate being confused and responding to that confusion.

> "GET OVER HERE!" The voice cut through the air like the twang of a ricocheting bullet.
>
> Little Willy had never heard a voice like that before. Not on this farm. He couldn't move.
>
> But Searchlight sure could.
>
> The owner of the voice barely had time to step back into the house and close the door.

I looked at the children with a puzzled face. "Who is this person that would go into Little Willy's house? Thumbs up if you have any clue what's going on." Most thumbs were down. "Let's read on to see if we can figure it out."

I resumed reading, adding in my responses to the text as I read.

> Searchlight barked and snarled and jumped at the closed door. The door opened a crack. The man stood in the opening. He was holding a small derringer and pointing it at Searchlight. His hand was shaking.
>
> "Don't shoot!" ("Oh, my goodness!") "Don't shoot!" Little Willy yelled as he reached out and touched Searchlight gently on the back. The barking stopped. "Who are you?" (I paused.)

Be sure that you are actually doing the sort of thinking you hope your kids will do. If you want them to be puzzled over how this section fits with the text, you need to be puzzled. Even if you explicitly say, "I'm confused," you should act confused, too. The children will see this and they'll join you in your confusion and in your efforts to clear up the confusion.

I exacerbate the confusion and then show kids that my response is to read on, trying to figure out what is going on.

When you read that this strange man held a gun, pointing it at Searchlight, you'll want to become that man for just an instant and to aim low toward the dog.

"Name's Clifford Snyder. State of Wyoming," the man said with authority. He opened the door a little farther.

The man was dressed as if he was going to a wedding. A city slicker. He was short, with a small head and a thin, droopy mustache that reminded little Willy of the last time he'd drunk a glass of milk in a hurry.

"What do you want?" Little Willy asked.

"*Official* business. Can't the old man inside talk?"

I closed the book and said to the class, "Is it becoming clearer, do you think? I'm beginning to piece things together, to have at least *some* guesses about who this man might be. It's all still hazy in my mind, though. Let's think about the clues we have about what's going on. Remember that as we read stories, just as in life, sometimes we have to entertain several options, thinking, 'Could this guy be . . .' or could he be . . . ?'"

As you read, be sure to alter your voice a bit to reflect the voices of the characters. Mr. Snyder will sound authoritative when he announces his name and, in a bit, disrespectful when he refers to Willie's grandfather, "The old man is . . . ." He'll sound pompous when he says he is here on "official business."

Ask children to tell a partner what they make of the confusing part. Share what one or two say, showing that readers construct tentative theories. Then read on, helping children listen with a theory in hand.

"Turn and tell your neighbor whether you have any clue about what could be going on. Who might this man be and why might he have come to the farm? Remember, the chapter is called 'The Reason.'"

Be willing to alternate your speed so you read somewhat quickly—and other times, slowly, with poignant pauses. Don't be afraid to add small gestures.

Children turned and talked.

After a few minutes I said, "Readers, listen to what Fallon and Sam were talking about. Fallon said, "When we heard he works in town and he came to talk to the grandfather about serious, official business, we got the idea that maybe he is part of why Grandfather doesn't want to live. Maybe he is going to take Willy away from Grandfather and put him in foster care." And Sam said, "We thought maybe Grandfather did something illegal because the man has a gun and is dressed like he's going to a wedding. We figured he's wearing a suit. And so then we figured that this guy is a detective who's come to question Grandfather."

Again, I am scaffolding for children, making them put the strategy I'm teaching into action. I allow them time to pull the information together.

"Readers, you all came up with such great ideas about who this man might be. It seems like you used another strategy on the chart, looking closely at details to form an idea." I pointed to the place on the chart that emphasized the importance of details. "You noticed the clothing the man is wearing, the gun he's holding, and the fact that he's on 'official business,' and you hypothesized that perhaps Grandfather has done something illegal. Good job, readers! Let's read on, holding onto our ideas. As we read, we'll see if our theories are justified."

I resumed reading, repeating just a line so the children could follow the text.

"Can't the old man inside talk?"

"Not regular talk. We have a code. I can show you."

As little Willy reached for the door, Clifford Snyder again aimed his gun at Searchlight, who had begun to growl. "Leave that … *thing* outside," he demanded.

"She'll be all right if you put your gun away."

"No!"

"Are you afraid of her?"

"I'm not … afraid."

"Dogs can always tell when someone's afraid of them."

"Just get in this house this minute!" Clifford Snyder yelled, and his face turned red.

Little Willy left Searchlight outside. But Clifford Snyder wouldn't put his gun away until they were all the way into Grandfather's bedroom. And then he insisted that little Willy shut the door.

Grandfather's eyes were wide open and fixed on the ceiling. He looked much older and much more tired than he had this morning.

When children do good work, I try to name what they have done well in such a way that the action I support is transferable to another day and another text. Here, I say that I like the way the children pay attention to details to form a big idea, and then I cite examples of the details. You'll do this one teaching move—naming what someone has done in a way that is transferable to another day—over and over, and you'll do this in conferences, minilessons, mid-workshop teaching points, and teaching share sessions.

You won't discuss this now, but you might notice that passages that might seem, at a glance, to be relatively insignificant ones can actually be windows that help readers see right into the insides of characters. Willy's strength and tenacity come through in this passage when he ignores Clifford Snyder's statement that he is not afraid of Searchlight.

"You're no better than other folks," Clifford Snyder began as he lit up a long, thin cigar and blew smoke toward the ceiling. "And anyway, it's the law. Plain and simple."

"What? I'm confused again. Let's read on and see if our mental movie clears."

Little Willy didn't say anything. He was busy combing Grandfather's hair, like he did every day when he got home. When he finished he held up the mirror so Grandfather could see.

"I'm warning you," Clifford Snyder continued. "If you don't pay…we have our ways. And it's all legal. All fair and legal. You're no better than other folks."

"Do we owe you some money, Mr. Snyder?" little Willy asked.

"Taxes, son. Taxes on this farm. Your grandfather there hasn't been paying them."

I paused and said to the children, "Is it clear now who this man is?" When the children nodded, I did so as well. "We know who Clifford Snyder is and why he has come, don't we? And I'm not sure, but I think maybe we even know why the grandfather has given up on life."

Notice that I am again demonstrating that readers notice instances when the text becomes confusing and ask, "What?" We need to demonstrate that readers take action when they don't understand.

Willy's actions are remarkable and give a window into his character. A strange man comes into the house, screaming, and Willy goes about his ritual of combing his grandfather's hair.

LINK

Recap what you have taught and then send children off to continue reading, reminding them to draw on all the strategies including this newest one, as needed.

"Readers, we've learned over the past few days that it is important to press ourselves to read a bit more quickly, and certainly we were able to speed up during parts of this read-aloud. But we have also learned that we need to be careful to not read on autopilot, letting the words slip past us without us really taking them in. We've been trying to read ourselves awake by creating a movie in our mind's eye. And we've learned that even when we are really attending to a story, sometimes the story will turn a corner and we, as readers, lose track of what is going on. When that happens we need to say, 'Huh? What's happening?' Usually we can read on, with questions in mind, looking for details that help clear up our confusion, and pretty soon things become clear. If they don't, we reread." *[Fig. VI-1]*

"Remember, before you read today and every day, you may find it helpful to remind yourself of where you left off last night by scanning through the pages, storytelling them to yourself. Fill in your logs, and then get going. Try to read yourself awake—using your Post-it notes to help you talk back to what you are reading. You'll have a chance to share those later. And if meaning breaks down, I know you'll say, 'Huh?' and that you'll have strategies to draw upon."

When I recap things that I hope children have learned, I am apt to gesture to the chart that lists these things. I want children to be reminded that all of the strategies they've learned earlier are still relevant—and that the chart serves to remind them of all they've learned. Notice that charts always have a title, and the title generally captures the big goal. Then the chart lists strategies. Sometimes each bullet represents the small steps in the sequence that is outlined across the chart as in the "When Our Mental Movie Grows Blurry" chart. Sometimes, instead, each bullet represents a different optional strategy. In this instance, the information in a bullet is generally written in a step one, step two, step three fashion.

This link illustrates the cumulativeness of your teaching. The link leaves the reader with a repertoire of skills and strategies to draw upon.

Figure VI-1

This "pop quiz" was one teacher's way of helping her students monitor for sense as they read.

CONFERRING AND SMALL-GROUP WORK

Work with Strugglers in Ways that Help Them Accumulate Texts

Now that you have launched the year, and most of your children are able to carry on during reading workshop, you will probably want to begin paying special attention to the children who struggle at reading. This section will capture one conference in great detail. As you listen in on this conference, attend to the content, but also notice the structure of the conference because it will illustrate the structure of reading conferences in general.

By Teaching Cause and Effect, You Help Children Link One Chapter to Another

Children reading books at levels K, L, and perhaps M are apt to be novices at reading books in which the story develops across several chapters. Until recently, these children have probably been reading episodic chapter books such as *Frog and Toad*, in which each chapter is a self-contained story. They've probably already ventured into series such as *Henry and Mudge* and *Mr. Putter and Tabby*, where the chapters build upon each other but where the combination of short chapters, few characters, and high picture support all work together to scaffold the reader. As these readers move toward chapter books such as those featuring Junie B. Jones, Judy Moody, Marvin Redpost, and the like, they sometimes need help holding the whole of the story in mind across chapters and days.

As I drew my chair in alongside Tyrell, I saw he was reading the second chapter of *Marvin Redpost: Alone in His Teacher's House*. I was happy to see that Tyrell, who had recently been reassessed as a level M reader, was tackling this new series. I expected he'd love it. "Tyrell, may I stop you for a

---

> ### MID-WORKSHOP TEACHING POINT
>
> #### Readers Monitor for Sense and Activate Problem-Solving Strategies When Meaning Breaks Down
>
> "Readers, I have to stop you. I just saw Emma doing something incredibly smart. She was reading along, turning one page, then another, then she stopped, looked up like this (I looked up at the ceiling as if musing over something) and then she did this (I showed how Emma paged backwards a bit in her book, and then resumed reading.) When I asked Emma what she'd just done, she said, 'I was reading, and then I realized that it seemed like the text had totally changed, for no reason. So I thought, 'Huh? Did I miss something?' and then I went back and reread, and I figured out that I'd just let one part get past me. Now the story makes more sense.'" As I spoke, Emma nodded her head, affirming my account of her work.
>
> *continued on next page*

---

moment?" I asked. "Put your finger where you stopped reading." I often ask children to do this when they've been reading silently because it helps me see exactly where they are in the text. Tyrell, after a little bit of searching, put his finger at the bottom of the first page of the second chapter. As Tyrell showed me where he was in his book, I was already recalling all I know about readers who work with texts at this level and about Tyrell in particular. "Oh, you've just started Chapter Two, 'The Key.' Tell me what's been going on."

"Well, they're waiting in the parking lot." he said.

"Uh huh." I looked at the text myself, skimming it to glean a quick sense of what was happening at that moment. Meanwhile, because I was preoccupied for a second, I did not immediately respond with an extension question. Because I held back, Tyrell was given a bit of time to realize, without my prompting, that it would be a good idea to elaborate. The little circle of silence around his brief plot summary gave him the responsibility to say more on his own. Tyrell added more detail to his first comment. "Marvin and his friends are looking at people's cars." I looked at Tyrell with a 'say more' expression on my face. He added, "It's teachers' cars."

Often when talking with a child, the youngster will say something I do not understand, and I find it helpful to reveal my confusion. If I want children to monitor for sense as they read and listen, then I need to do the same thing, and I need to let children in on times when their words don't make sense to me. "I don't get it," I said. "Why are they waiting in a parking lot and looking at teachers' cars?"

Tyrell paused for a moment. "I forgot," he said, looking uncomfortable and using his thumb to flip the pages of his book and make a breeze. At this point, one of my hunches was confirmed. He could profit from help pulling the threads from one chapter into the next. Knowing that the research phase of my conference had been short, but feeling fairly confident of the direction that had emerged, I made the decision to teach him to "accumulate the text."

Putting my hand on his briefly to stop the page flipping that he probably wasn't even aware he was doing, I said, "It's such a good thing that you noticed that you forgot why Marvin and his friends were there!" I said, even though I knew that he'd only recognized the gaps in his understanding because of my insistence on him producing a summary that made sense. Wanting to help him role play his way into being the sort of reader who monitors for sense, I said, "You are smart to realize that when a reader doesn't know *why* people are doing something, that's a good clue that the reader has dropped important stuff, and so it's a good time to look back and collect what's been dropped." I always want to dignify reading work, and to especially dignify readers using fix-it strategies when meaning falls apart, so I added, "This happens to me sometimes at the start of books. I am meeting so many new characters and learning so many new details that sometimes I find myself dropping—forgetting—important information. This happens to you too, right?"

Tyrell nodded, seeming a little relieved to have this out in the open. "'Cause sometimes I don't really get it, like why they're out there in the parking lot."

"When I realize I'm forgetting stuff and I don't even know why people in my books are doing things, I start using the ends of chapters as stopping places. At each end-of-the-chapter, I look back and think, 'Hmm, what's been going on so far?' And then, in my mind, I sort of write a little summary

of that chapter. This helps me carry that information, that summary, with me into the next chapter. This makes it easier to make connections between chapters, seeing ways one chapter sets up the next chapter." This was, in a sense, my teaching point for the conference. I was careful to be explicit and to talk in a way that would be applicable not only to this day and this text, but to other days, other texts.

"Let's try it together," I said, knowing that actually I'd probably begin by doing a bit more demonstrating before shifting to engage him in scaffolded work. "You already finished Chapter One so. . . ."

Tyrell knew what to do and was already flipping back to the end of the first chapter. As he did this, I coached him, whispering, "Hmm, what's been going on. Let's skim through the chapter to remind us."

We looked through a few pages together, reading silently. I touched a part or two of the text, as if marking my place while I read those parts, knowing I was also drawing Tyrell's attention to them. After we read silently alongside each other for a minute, I looked up at him, as if to say, "You start."

Tyrell began, "Well, Marvin's teacher is going away and there's going to be a sub."

"And I can see that some of the kids are excited about that. I wonder why?" I mused, "I ask that 'why' question all the time, don't you? Why are they excited for the sub?" I then flipped back into the chapter, studying it for a second to understand the characters' motivations—and to show that these are found in the text, not in thin air. Pointing to a line of the text that helped a bit, I said, "I'm looking to see if they are excited because they think they'll get to fool around more if there's a sub."

I looked for causes for actions that take place later in the book because I wanted to teach Tyrell that it helps to think between one chapter and the next, and I wanted also to give him specific tips, as well as the more gen-

---

MID-WORKSHOP TEACHING POINT

continued from previous page

"I hope all of you keep track of your storyline. If you find your storyline breaking down, you can do like Emma did and reread, or you can press on, reading with a question in your mind. If you think of it, it'd be great to mark the confusing passage with a 'Huh?' Post-it note so that when I confer with you, or when you talk with a classmate, you can point out places where you caught yourself feeling confused, and then you can show me how you solved the problem." [Figs. VI-2 and VI-3]

Who is talking?

Figure VI-2
It's sophisticated to ask who the narrator is in a story. You could teach this child a new literary term.

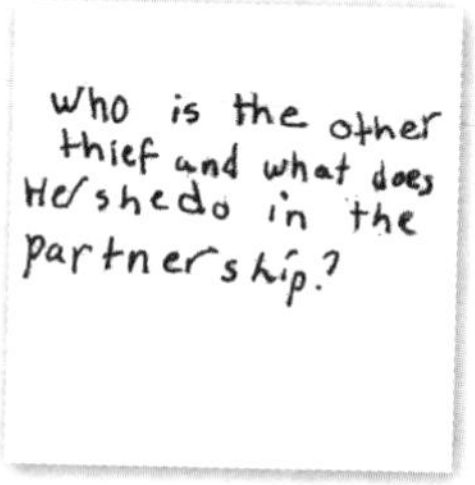

who is the other thief and what does He/she do in the partnership?

Figure VI-3
If a reader regularly jots questions on Post-its, you can suggest to him or her to take the next step and begin answering the questions.

eral teaching point. One hugely important way in which one chapter links to another is that the earlier chapter reveals the causes for actions that happen later. In this instance, I did not ask Tyrell to supply the causes for subsequent actions because although I have described this as "let's do this together," I knew that I had yet to demonstrate that skill. I planned to carry much of the load at the start of our shared work. So as we reviewed the preceding chapter, I used thinking aloud to demonstrate the way I went about speculating over a character's motivations. And then I tried to turn more of this work over to Tyrell.

"Do you think there are other reasons that explain why the kids are excited to have a substitute teacher, or excited that their teacher is going away?" I mused, as if unsure myself of what these could be.

"Oh yeah, also Marvin is excited 'cause when the teacher's away, she wants Marvin to take care of her dog. She's going to pay him money," Tyrell said, getting into the groove. "Marvin is going to her house to meet Waldo."

"Oh, right. I see right here she says, 'I'll meet you in the parking lot in twenty minutes.' You are right! So this time, looking back has helped us answer that question of why was Marvin in the parking lot, right?" I added.

"Yeah, and Nick says he's the luckiest kid, Marvin is."

"What a thing for Nick to say. I wonder why he thinks that?" (See how I keep asking that "why" question?)

"Maybe Nick is jealous or something that Marvin is going to get paid money." Tyrell said.

"Tyrell," I said, knowing it was time for me to end the conference. "I love the way you don't just talk about *what* the characters are doing and feeling. After you say that Nick is jealous, you think about *why* that is the case. And the author doesn't come right out and tell us, does he? So we have to sort of guess, like you just said, '*Maybe its because. . . .*' That is really smart work."

To make sure that Tyrell extrapolated lessons that could pertain to another book and another day, I said, "Tyrell, you are reading stories that go across lots of chapters now, and it is easy to forget parts of them as you go from one chapter to the next. So remember to pause at the end of each chapter and to recall what just happened, carrying that information with you as you read on. And when you find a character doing something, ask, 'Why is he doing that?' If you have no idea, that's a clue that you are probably forgetting parts of the story. You probably need to look back." Tyrell nodded and got back into his book.

Look Reluctant Readers in the Eyes and Recruit Their Willingness to Try

As you confer with readers, you'll want to keep an eye out for disenfranchised readers. You'll probably want to talk candidly with them—one at a time, away from an audience. Early in the year, I'd gotten the hunch that Kobe was going to foot drag a bit when it came to reading. During the very first week of school, he'd sometimes taken on a "don't bother with me" demeanor. On this particular day, he sat in his chair, slouched low, spinning his book around on the desk. He wasn't disruptive, just disengaged. In fact, he seemed to try to make himself invisible.

I knelt beside his chair, clip board on my lap, and said, "What's up, Kobe?" He shrugged. "You still reading *Hatchet*?" I asked. Still in his slouch, he held the book up vertically on his table so I could see it. Still no words. "How's *Hatchet* been for you? In fact, how's *reading* been this year?" Kobe shrugged, and I kept looking at him expectantly. I struggled to hold back from jumping in with another question.

"Reading's boring." Kobe looked past me as he answered, eyes on the clock.

"I see. When I hear people say that, it could mean lots of things. It could mean that they haven't found their Most Amazing Book Ever yet; it could mean reading is sort of hard and not fun, all work and no payback. When people say 'reading is boring,' it could mean tons of things. I want to know what it means to you."

"Well," Kobe said. "I finally got into this book, it's turned out to be okay, but most of the books I read are boring."

"Kobe, listen to this: This is just the start of our reading time together. I don't know you well yet, but I guarantee that I will get to know you well and when I do, I'll be able to show you books you'll love. I mean—maybe I won't be able to find those books, but I promise I'll work like crazy to show you books that are as good for you as *Hatchet* and even better, but you have to promise me something, too."

"What?" Kobe said, looking at me for the first time.

"Kobe, you have to promise that you'll be willing to give this a go. We can make this work, I guarantee. Are you with me?" He smiled begrudgingly, and shrugged. 'Yeah?' he said, unsure, but leaving the door open a crack.

 TEACHING SHARE

Readers Take the Time to Look Back Over What We've Read, Collecting Our Thoughts and Planning How We Will Talk about Books

Tell readers they can take on the responsibility of choosing what they'd like to talk about related to reading. Remind them of their work so far this year that might merit talk.

"Readers, I need your eyes. Stay where you are. Today's share will be at your places. But I need your attention for a minute." I waited. "I know that usually during our share sessions, I have channeled you to think about something, like your New School Year's resolutions, times when reading is and is not working, patterns you notice by studying your log. But I have been remembering that earlier this year when I asked you to think about what works for you as readers, some of you said that you like to be able to choose what you want to talk about. So let's try it—and I will research how this goes, okay?

"Today, you can choose what you want to talk about—and you can talk with your whole table or with one neighbor. Just decide, as a table, how you'll do it and, of course, do not leave anyone out."

Revealing the chart, "Ways You and Another Reader Can Share Our Reading Lives," I said, "This lists the ways you've shared reading so far this year, but you can invent new ways too, if you want. Just make sure you and your friend agree. Then before you start sharing your reading, take a second to look back over what you've read and collect your thoughts. I'm going to research what you do to share your reading lives."

This chart will resurface in Book 2 and will serve as an anchor chart for the first two units. You'll want to introduce it, therefore, with some fanfare and to make it a big deal that readers will be responsible not only for studying their reading lives on their own, but also for being able to articulate their reading lives to a neighbor or a friend. Later on in the unit, when children are assigned long-term partners, they will continue this sort of reflective discussion with that person.

Ways You and Another Reader Can Share Your Reading Lives

- *Talk about your reading volume. How much do you tend to read in a day? In a minute? How might that amount be changing, and why?*

- *Talk about home reading versus school reading. How are they the same? Different? When, where, and for how long do you tend to read at home? At school?*

- *Talk about a great book and then think, "Why do I like this book so much? How can I find more books like this?"*

After listening in on one conversation after another for a few minutes, I called for the group's attention, and said, "I know you'd like to keep talking, but reading time is over. You can finish talking about this on the playground. I spotted a number of you really poring over your logs and then discussing things you noticed, just like scientists who look for patterns in the things they study. So we need to add something else to our chart." I added the following:

- Study your logs like scientists and discuss the patterns you see. Then talk about making your reading lives as good as they can be.

"Readers, fill out your logs." I wrote the opening and closing times for that day's reading time on the whiteboard and then walked the room, complimenting a couple of readers as they filled out their logs. To one child I said, "Jasmine, I noticed you read five more pages than you did last night in the same amount of time. You must have really pushed yourself as a reader today!" I gave another child a thumbs up for reading twice at home.

Ways You and Another Reader Can Share Your Reading Lives

- Talk about your reading volume. How much do you tend to read in a day? In a minute? How might that amount be changing, and why?

- Talk about home reading versus school reading. How are they the same? Different? When, where, and for how long do you tend to read at home? At school?

- Talk about a great book and then think, "Why do I like this book so much? How can I find more books like this?"

- Study your logs like scientists and discuss the patterns you see. Then talk about making your reading lives as good as they can be.

Teachers, you'll notice that the chart "Ways You and Another Reader Can Share Your Reading Lives" and this discussion suggest that readers can talk with "a friend." You'll want to use the term that you've used in your teaching. When children turn and talk and do not yet have long-term partners, are they talking to a neighbor, a classmate, or who? At this point, my expectation is that some children have been assessed and are now reading from a bin of leveled books. You may or may not have set these readers up with partners who read the same level texts.

I am aiming to do several things at once here. First, I want to validate children on their reading work thus far. Second, I want to communicate to readers that my role is not to check up on kids' reading logs. By framing my feedback in positive ways, even if the progress a reader made was very small, I am earning the trust of children who may be tempted to view the reading log as a less meaningful, obligatory document. Instead, I am setting children up to view this record as a tool for reading progress and reading growth.

Readers Can Share Our Reading By:

* Showing a friend a well-written or funny or weird part of a book, reading that part aloud, then talking about it.
* Talking with a friend about how much you've tended to read in a day, in a minute. How might that amount be changing, and why?
* Talking with a friend about home reading and school reading. How are they the same? Different? When do you tend to read at home? Where? For how long? How well does it work for you?
* Talking about a great book, and then think, "Why do I like this book so much? How can I find ones like it?"

DRAFT

Welcoming Books

IN THIS SESSION,

you'll teach students that readers can choose how we feel about books, either reading them like gold or being a curmudgeon toward them.

t is important to me to equip youngsters with practical strategies that will allow them to pursue important principles. You'll see that minilessons provide explicit instruction in the strategies that young readers need to monitor for sense, to retell, to read with fluency, and to infer and predict and synthesize.

Yet, if you listen closely to the lessons, you'll also notice that a big portion of teaching is not explicit. Under the radar of these minilessons, you'll see that we are not only trying to teach children to read well; we are also teaching them how to love reading. We are teaching them to let books and characters into their hearts and their lives. After all, a joyful attitude and satisfying experience with reading will contribute

as much to developing a lifelong relationship to reading as will a high level of technical reading proficiency.

I'm reminded of a childhood friend of mine who studied piano. She learned to play beautifully and performed in a variety of venues to critical acclaim. When I recently attended a conference in her city and stopped by her home, I was surprised that she didn't have a piano. I mentioned this, and she said that she hadn't played for years. She said that although she learned to play well, she never learned to love playing. She never learned to find a place for the piano in her life. I contrast her with another family friend. Although he never had formal instruction, he's learned to play the guitar, ukulele, and mandolin, and he and a group

GETTING READY

- Prepare to read from Chapter 7, "The Meeting," of *Stone Fox*. Specifically, you'll want to start your read-aloud in the minilesson at the passage that begins, "Little Willy loved dogs." If you're reading a different read-aloud book, you can select almost any especially powerful passage to incorporate within this minilesson. During the minilesson, you'll read a passage in a disengaged way and then you'll as if the text were gold.

- If possible, make a copy of the text you'll read for each child for use in the active involvement.

- Pick a section of your mentor text to reread during the teaching share.

- If you decide to lead a small group on fluency after the minilesson, be sure to read the conferring section and follow the process. Notice that you'll make two charts of a small passage, each chunked differently.

- Continue to take note of rituals that you began earlier and hope are now solidly in place. Notice that children are coming quickly and directly to the meeting area, taking their seats without a fuss, transitioning smoothly in and out of turn-and-talk work and so forth.

- See the *Resources* CD-ROM for additional resources such as the *Stone Fox* excerpts.

of friends get together regularly to play music together. Almost every day, he picks up one of his instruments and plays for a stretch of time. He tells me that music is one of

> *We must not only teach children how to read well; we must also teach children how to love reading.*

the great joys of his life. For him, the challenge of mastering new chords and songs is exhilarating. We must not only teach children how to read well; we must also teach children how to love reading.

One of the ways we can show children how to love reading is to teach them that reading can matter in their lives. We can show them how to open their hearts and minds to the characters and stories they are reading. We can teach them that reading is not just figuring out the words but it is also the hard work of finding a way to make the story matter.

In this session, we move this idea of allowing a story to matter from an implicit nuance of our teaching to an explicit teaching point. We show children how to read with an open heart and mind. We suggest that some readers read like curmudgeons, while others read as if the book is gold.

For many teachers who piloted this series, this session was their absolute favorite. Why? We do not know. But teach it with full confidence, expecting that this lesson will reverberate in your classroom for a very long time. Months from now, children will continue to take pleasure in the word *curmudgeon*. Hopefully, they will also grasp the deeper, larger lesson, which of course is a lesson not only about reading, but also about life. We must each decide: Will I be the kind of person who sees the donut—or the hole?

DRAFT

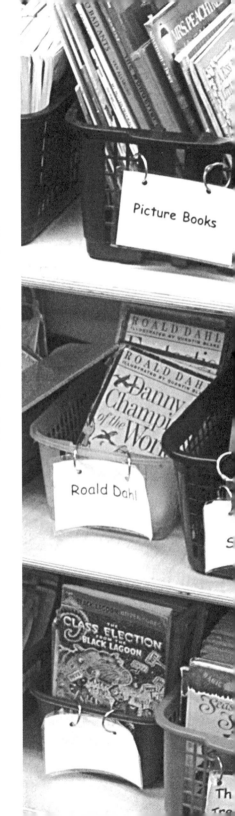

MINILESSON

Welcoming Books

CONNECTION

Set children up to learn that they can read like curmudgeons or they can open up and let books and reading matter to them.

"Readers, before I begin, I want you each to have an excerpt from *Stone Fox*. We have read this passage before, but we are going to reread it again today in the minilesson. For now, just put it down in front of you, and I will let you know when you need it."

"Readers, do you know what a *curmudgeon* is? A curmudgeon is a cranky person. He or she lives life in a cynical way. You might even have a neighbor who's a curmudgeon. You wouldn't dare go trick or treating at a curmudgeon's house, because if you rang the doorbell, he'd probably say, 'Get off my porch. Don't you dare ring my doorbell again!'"

Name your teaching point. Specifically, tell children that we need to let books in if they are going to matter.

"Today I want to teach you that readers must choose what our relationship toward books will be. We can be a curmudgeon toward books. Or we can let books matter to us, reading them like they're gold."

TEACHING

Read a selected book in a disengaged way, showing children that readers can take in books like this.

"Let me show you what it's like when I read a bit of *Stone Fox* like a curmudgeon." Shifting into the role, I picked up *Stone Fox* and said scornfully 'What kind of title is that—*Stone Fox*?' Then I looked closely at the photo of Searchlight pulling a sled and

We don't want to shy away from using sophisticated vocabulary with our children, but we want to make sure that they understand what we are saying. Notice how I explain what a curmudgeon is by defining it and then giving an example. It is a terrific word.

Of course this session picks up where the previous session left off. Anything that is worth teaching will need to be revisited.

said, "*Another* dog book. I get so sick of them." I turned to near the end of Chapter 7, "The Meeting," and began to read in a cranky, disinterested voice, hemming and hawing as I read.

> Little Willy ("Another weird name.") loved dogs. ("Ugh, he's not my type, I can tell already.") He had to see the Samoyeds up close. They showed no alarm as he approached, or as he held out his hand to pet them. ("This is so boring. The only thing that's happening is he's petting dogs. Big whoop.")
>
> And then it happened.

I stopped reading and yawned and looked around the room.

Exaggerate your negative attitude toward the book through word choice, intonation, gestures, and facial expressions. This will help your children get the point of this lesson. This dramatization also makes the minilesson funny. Who says that the teaching of reading has to be so serious? Even though I am being over the top, I am exaggerating a true relationship with reading that I know some of my children have. I want them to see themselves in me and rethink the way they approach books. I want them to know that it's up to them to change their relationships with books.

Active Involvement

Set children up to continue reading, with disengagement, the text you've begun reading, this time to each other.

Then I said, "Get with a reading friend. One of you pick up the text in front of you and read as a curmudgeon to your classmate. Remember to sound cranky, as if this is the worst book you've ever read."

As children read aloud to each other throughout the meeting area, I added a little drama. In a voiceover, I said, "Boring," and yawned, playing up the feigned disengagement, channeling readers to do the same.

"Readers." I waited until eyes were on me. "You sounded like the most bored, disengaged, cranky curmudgeons I've ever heard! That was kind of fun, but the truth is that some of us sometimes actually *do* approach books like that!"

It may be that some of your children won't be able to read Stone Fox *because the book is too hard for them, thus you may instead ask children to read their own books as if they are curmudgeons as we do here. Also, notice that only one person in a duo needs to read aloud. You could suggest children get into groups of four, with one of the foursome doing the reading as another way to be sure you aren't channeling a child who can't read this to feel embarrassed.*

DRAFT

Set children up to read the next section of text as if it is gold. Start them off by reading a few lines of it aloud yourself.

"Now, change your mindset, and this time, read the next section of the book as if it were gold. Let me show you what I mean." I picked up the book and read the next bit with gestures and facial expressions that reflected rapt attention to the content. I took in every word on the page and did all I could to experience Willy's feelings and emotions.

> Stone Fox stood tall in the darkness and said nothing. (I shook my head.) Searchlight barked outside. The Samoyeds barked in return. (Using my hands to represent some of the barking dogs, each coming from different corners of the night, I helped children hear the chorus of dogs.)
>
> Little Willy continued, (I looked up as if I was Willy talking to Stone Fox) "I'm going to race against you tomorrow. I know how you wanna win, but . . . I wanna win too. (I pointed to myself.) I gotta win. (I clenched my fist.) If I don't (I lowered my voice) they're gonna take our farm."

I grabbed my chest and shook my head.

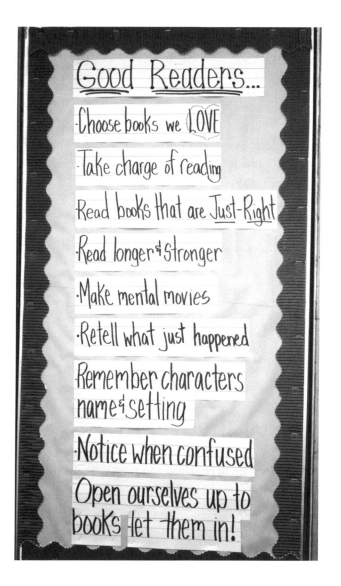

I stopped and said, "With the person next to you, continue on, reading as if it is gold."

After they'd had some time to read, I stopped them. "Readers, when we read a book like it's gold, it's more than just reading like we're interested, or reading with expression. It's also being open to the story and letting whatever happens to the characters happen to us, too. It's letting a book really *matter* to us."

During this active involvement, listen to as many children as you can "reading like gold." Your children are trying to read the best they can, so this is a good time to assess for fluency. As you move from group to group, write down the names of the readers who could benefit from small-group instruction on fluency. After you give the link of the minilesson, you may decide to keep a cluster of children who need work on fluency with you for some small-group work.

LINK

Send children off to read their independent reading books, reminding them they can choose to read those books like they are gold.

"That was beautiful! So, readers, we can approach a book like a tough-skinned curmudgeon, or we can approach a book expecting it to matter. Right now open up your own books and start to read them like gold. I will tap you on the shoulder when it's time for you to go back to your seat. Don't forget to fill out your logs when you get back to your seat, and then to continue to read your book as if it is gold."

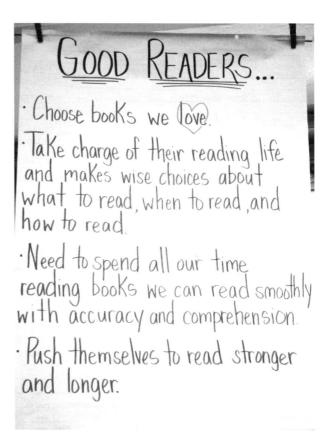

CONFERRING AND SMALL-GROUP WORK

Teach Readers to Read Texts Fluently and Like They Are Gold

A Strategy Lesson to Support Fluency and Making Meaning

During today's minilesson, you will have heard many children reading aloud. If you had a chance to notice a few children who could use a bit of support with fluency, then you might convene a five-minute strategy lesson with those children. You will definitely want to tackle the high-frequency word work and decoding work that gets in the way of students' reading with automaticity. This strategy lesson however, is designed to focus on parsing, helping students outgrow choppy, robotic-sounding reading. Before sending children off from the meeting area to read independently, you might say, "Will these readers remain on the rug?" and then list the names.

I usually begin any strategy lesson by telling children why I've convened them. "Readers, I didn't send you back to your seats after the minilesson because when I was listening to you reading like gold, I noticed that you weren't quite reading like you were talking." I picked up *Stone Fox* and said, "You sounded something like this, 'I'll win. . . . I'm going to . . . beat you. Stone Fox . . . remained . . . motionless. And . . . silent.'"

> ### MID-WORKSHOP TEACHING POINT
>
> #### Readers Abandon Books that Turn Us into Curmudgeons
>
> "Readers." I waited for all eyes to be on me. "I bet some of you are wondering what to do if you've tried everything to make your book work for you, but you just can't seem to find any gold in it. It probably makes sense that if you're almost done with the book, you should finish it. But if you're not close to the end, you have a tough decision to make. You don't want to become the kind of reader who starts books and gives up on them easily. But you also don't want to be trudging your way through the book, feeling like a curmudgeon. If you ever find yourself in this situation when you really feel you need to put a book down, you need to know that is okay. Deciding to stop reading a book that doesn't feel like gold is a lot better than continuing to read like a curmudgeon. I just ask that you let me know if you are about to abandon a book so we can figure out what's going on, and so I can help you make sure your next book is one you can read like gold. Let's get our eyes back into our books and continue to read our books like they are gold."

"Did you hear how I'm pausing so much between the words that the meaning gets confusing? Didn't the part I just read sound confusing to you?" The children nodded.

"It should sound smooth, like talking. Listen as I reread these lines without so much pausing, trying to sound like I'm talking." I reread the same lines, but this time I read them smoothly.

Usually in strategy lessions, after demonstrating what I hope children will do, I invite them to do it. Strategy lessons follow the same pattern as minilessons, although the teaching portion of a strategy lesson will be teensy weensy and the active involvement, substantial. Because I pre-planned that I'd teach this strategy lesson, I came prepared, having rewritten part of the passage children already read aloud onto chart paper. This time, I chunked the text into short phrases, almost as one might write a poem.

"See how I broke the sentences up? Almost the way one might write a poem? The white space represents places where I think you'll want to pause instead of pausing after every word or every couple of words."

"I'll win.

I'm gonna beat you."

Stone Fox remained motionless.

And silent.

Willy backed over to the barn door,

still holding his eye.

"I'm sorry we both can't win,"

he said.

Then he pushed open the barn door

and left,

closing the door behind him."

I'll win. I'm gonna beat you."

Stone Fox remained motionless. And silent.

Willy backed over to the barn door, still holding his eye.

"I'm sorry we both can't win," he said.

Then he pushed open the barn door and left,

closing the door behind him.

In a strategy lesson, as in a minilesson and a conference, I aim to be as explicit as possible about what I want to teach. "Today we're going to work on getting our eyes to grab for more words at a time. That will help us pause less and sound smoother when we read, so that our reading sounds like we're talking. Let's read this together and try to pause only at the ends of these lines. I put a pointer at the beginning of the sentence and began reading it, signaling for the children to join in unison.

"Let's try it again. Don't pause until you get to the last word on each line, and then as you are saying that last line, move your eyes quickly to the next line. Okay, here we go."

I began by joining with the group, but then let them continue without me while I listened in until I was sure that each child was reading the chunks fluently.

I'd prepared another chart with the selection written into larger chunks, giving the students more to "grab with their eyes" on each line. "Let's try it again, but this time, (I turned over to the next piece of chart paper), let's try to have our eyes grab for more words so we pause less. We want to sound smooth like we are talking. Let's give it a go." I pointed to the first line and said the first word and stopped reading myself so I could listen as the children carried on.

"Read it a couple more times, and then I'll come back and listen in. You want to make your voice smooth as if you are talking." Just before I slipped away I quickly coached one child, saying, "Put the words together," and another, saying "Faster," and then "That's it, try it again, really thinking about what you are saying."

In a minilesson, it is important to wrap up the lesson by restating the teaching point and asking children to continue the work as they turn to their independent reading. A strategy lesson ends with similar instruction. Of course, one day of small-group support is just a start, so I'll plan to convene the group again in a few days. Also, I know that when I confer with any one of these readers, I will make sure I ask that child to read a bit of his or her story so I can continue to teach into fluency. When I form permanent partnerships, I also know that I'll ask these children to read aloud to each other often.

TEACHING SHARE

Readers Sometimes Share Favorite Passages, Reading Them Aloud As If They Are Gold

Demonstrate a way readers share their books: by reading aloud a cherished passage.

"Readers, when I absolutely love passages in a book, I mark them so later I can share them with others, and I'm pretty sure you're the same!" I reread a passage from Chapter 2 of *Stone Fox* to make my point.

> It was now the middle of September. The potatoes they had planted in early June took from ninety to one hundred twenty days to mature, which meant they must be harvested soon. Besides, the longer he waited, the more danger there was that an early freeze would destroy the crop. And little Willy was sure that if the crop died, Grandfather would die too.
>
> A friend of Grandfather's offered to help, but little Willy said no. "Don't accept help unless you can pay for it," Grandfather had always said. "Especially from friends."
>
> And then little Willy remembered something. His college money! He had enough to rent a horse, pay for help, everything. He told Grandfather about his plan, but Grandfather signaled "no." Little Willy pleaded with him. But Grandfather repeated "No, no, no!"
>
> The situation appeared hopeless.
>
> But little Willy was determined. He would dig up the potatoes by hand if he had to.
>
> And then Searchlight solved the problem. She walked over and stood in front of the plow. In her mouth was the harness she wore during the winter when she pulled the snow sled.

Ask students to share a cherished passage with a partner.

I let my voice trail off and then I said, "Why don't we each find a part of the story where we let the book in and it mattered to us. Reread it to yourself as if it was gold and then, in a minute, let's read those parts to each other. We could even swap books and read each other's parts as if they are gold. I will give you a few minutes to prepare."

After a few minutes, I said, "Readers, let's read a part that mattered to you to a classmate. Remember to read it like it's gold."

A few minutes later, I voiced over, saying, "Readers, I was listening in and some of you weren't reading your passage as if it mattered to you, as if it was gold. Try it again."

Today's minilesson and teaching share address reading with fluency. If you have many children with fluency issues in your class, make sure you tuck fluency in every opportunity you can to support this skill. Since children are reading parts that mattered to them, they should be able to read with expression that conveys the author's meaning. In the teaching share, I interrupted and asked the children to try again so that their second or third efforts would be smoother and more meaningful. The more frequently a child rereads something, the more fluent the reader becomes.

Introducing Ourselves to Books

IN THIS SESSION,
you'll teach children that strong readers create a buzz about the books we love, and do this by summarizing and excerpting those books.

Already in this book, I have quoted the great reading researcher, Jerome Harste, who once said, "I see our job as creating, in the classroom, the kind of world we believe in and then helping our children role play their way into being the readers, writers, and learners that we hope they will become." It is for good reasons that this quote is something of a refrain in this unit, because the unit's goal is to help each young person feel proactive and optimistic as he or she goes about the work of constructing a life as a reader. At the start of the unit of study, you invited children to reflect on times when reading has and has not worked for them, and then to use the insights gleaned to think about how, this year, they can each author a rich reading life.

Asking children to reflect on their histories and to talk about their hopes was an inspirational activity for the start of a school year, but if it is going to be more than that, then you need to remember that when we teach, it is almost as if the classroom community is the cast of a giant play, and each child has a role in that play. If a child feels that his role is to be the class rebel, the child will assume the part. If a child feels that her role is to be the sci-fi fanatic, she will assume that role. As teachers, it is tremendously important that we help all our children see themselves as—take the roles of—readers. Some may be avid readers of the sports page and sports stories—they're readers. One reader may be known throughout the class as an avid reader of vampire books. You can help her enrich that identity over time, but

GETTING READY

- Before today's minilesson, you may want to have a ribbon-cutting ceremony to mark the library opening. In any case, you'll want to give at least some of your children time to peruse the library since the session relies upon them having spent time trying to choose books from the library.

- By today you will have assessed all your children, which will allow to you move the books from the table bins to their rightful places in the classroom library.

- Have your personal reading log on hand to use in the teaching part of this minilesson. Be sure your log contains books you want to promote to the class. You'll use your log as a tool to make a book recommendation.

- Make the chart titled, "How to Create a Book Buzz" to use during the teaching component of the minilesson.

- Plan a book recommendation that you'll outline during the teaching share.

DRAFT

for now the important thing is for each child to feel that he or she belongs *somewhere* in the great wide world of reading. Reading is so fundamental we must do everything possible to help each and every child see himself or herself as a kind of reader.

> *By recruiting kids to help us build a classroom setting that is conducive to reading and writing, we also help them imagine themselves living productively in that space, we help them rehearse for the roles they'll assume.*

Before the curtain opens on the drama of a new year, it is important that children work with us and with each other to create the setting. By recruiting kids to help us build a classroom setting that is conducive to reading and writing, we also help them imagine themselves living productively in that space, we help them rehearse for the roles they'll assume.

After I published *The Art of Teaching Reading*, I decided I would turn over a new leaf. I would no longer be a workaholic. I'd get a life. I'd even go so far as to entertain, to cook festive meals. But you can't just *decide* to become a cook. First, you need the proper kitchen. So, I hired one of those fancy kitchen consultants to come to my house and help me decide whether my new counters should be granite or Corian and whether I needed an island with a second sink. The kitchen consultant who came asked me all sorts of intrusive questions. She said, "Tell me, Lucy, when you cook, how many people tend to prepare the meal?" She even said, "Describe a typical meal for you and your family."

I did not know what to tell her. I definitely did not want to say the truth—that only one of us cooks at a time. I knew if I told her that cooking in my family tends to amount to one of us pouring the cereal into a bowl and then adding milk, I would never get one of those islands with a second sink in it. Finally I blurted out, "I want the kitchen for the me I am going to become, not for the me I already am!" She looked at my curiously, like I was speaking another language.

But kids get it. Kids know that when they are invited to stay in during recess time to help prepare the library, they are rehearsing for the moment when they can use that library. When they think about the categories of books they want in a library, and join in the search for the books that belong in bins bearing titles such as "Light Sports Books," "Cousins to Harry Potter," "Roald Dahl Books," and "Boy Alone in Woods, Needs No-one Books," they know all this is preparation for something grand that will happen soon.

DRAFT

MINILESSON

Introducing Ourselves to Books

CONNECTION

COACHING TIPS

Share a story illustrating how one child created a buzz around a book for another child. Tell children that friends can be good resources when all the books seem like strangers to us.

"Readers, this has been an exciting morning. It is so great to have our classroom library up and going! This morning, I listened in as some of you explored the library. What I noticed was that there is almost too much in the library, right? When the books are strangers to us, it's hard to see what's there and to make good choices. I saw some of you flipping through basket after basket, overwhelmed.

"Then I heard Aly trying to decide whether to read *The Lion, the Witch and the Wardrobe*. She said out loud, 'What is this? I don't think it's my kind of story' and moved on to another one. This must have caught Josh's attention because his eyes lit up and he said, 'Wait a minute, that's just as good as *Harry Potter*!' Aly squinted her eyes at Josh and said, 'Really?' as if she didn't *really* believe him."

"'Oh yeah,' Josh said. 'It's totally exciting, with magic and some scary parts. And there's a whole bunch in the series. You should read it.' And then Josh told Aly a bit about the book, and a bit about what it would feel like to read it. He told her to stick with it past the first chapter—that chapter didn't hint at how much adventure would be coming up."

Then I said to the class, "And do you know what happened?" I turned to Aly. "Aly, tell the class what you did next."

"It's totally my new favorite book now!" Aly said. "Josh was right. It is like a cousin to *Harry Potter*. There's a group of kids living half in a human world and half in a magical world who have to save the day by going after the evil queen. I love it!"

Teachers, your classroom library may have been open all year long, so you may not have the opportunity to stage an official grand opening ceremony, complete with a ribbon cutting. And of course, the session does not rely upon today being the opening for your library. But another year, I do recommend keeping the library off bounds during the first two weeks of the year so that you can create a grand event and a drum roll that combine to give the library a halo. In general, when planning units of study, it takes thought and discipline to withhold some things from kids so those things can be revealed and brought center stage later.

Aly is off the charts in her abilities to tackle complex texts, and for her, the level that someone has ascribed to a book is totally irrelevant. The Narnia books are generally thought of as level T texts; there is certainly no thought that these are too easy for Aly. You'll probably have some children for whom book levels seems inconsequential.

It's not by chance that I use this example. The Harry Potter books are almost a rite of passage for many children, so I know that likening C.S. Lewis' books to Harry Potter is sure to draw children's attention. I'm also hoping that children will think about categories of books as they recommend books and as they decide on books to read.

"Readers, that introduction is something that happens all the time between readers. We introduce books to each other. What Josh and Aly did was so grown-up. Josh didn't just say, 'Read this, it's good.' No, he gave Aly a real reason why she might like it. He introduced her to the book, like you might introduce one friend to another. He created a little buzz of excitement around the book for her. That's what readers do with each other. When we find good stuff to read, we introduce other people to it, we create a buzz of excitement around it, and the next thing you know, six other people who were strangers to it before are now reading a book we discovered. Watching you this morning, I realized that the way to open a library is not with a ribbon cutting ceremony. Instead, the way to open a library is by introducing each other to books, and creating book buzzes!"

Name your teaching point. Specifically, teach children that strong readers create a buzz about books we love.

"Today, I want to teach you that readers create a buzz about books we love so that those books will be exciting, not strange, to others. To do this, it helps to talk about the sort of readers who will like a book, to summarize the book (without giving too much away!), to read a little bit aloud to others, and above all, to tell them why the book is special." [Fig. VIII-1]

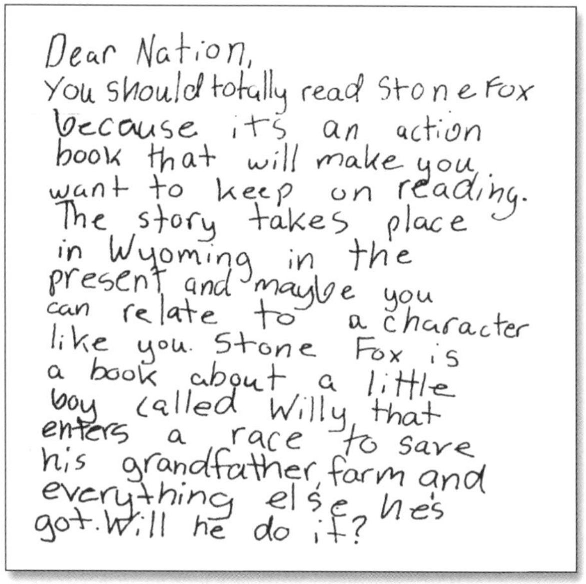

TEACHING

Give an example of a book recommendation, demonstrating the steps involved in creating a book buzz.

"Readers, I want to give you an example of what a great book introduction might sound like—one that will create a buzz! My sister left a message on my cell phone this morning, asking me to make a book recommendation for her son Kyril, who is about your age. I'm going to plan what I'll say right now. Listen and notice the steps I go through to introduce him to a few books and create a buzz? I'm pretty sure that this chart (and I reveal a chart) shows the steps I take when recommending a book, but I may have missed things I do. As you see me take a step, count it across your fingers and if I do things that aren't recorded, we can fix the chart later."

Dear Nation,
You should totally read Stone Fox because it's an action book that will make you want to keep on reading. The story takes place in Wyoming in the present and maybe you can relate to a character like you. Stone Fox is a book about a little boy called Willy that enters a race to save his grandfather, farm and everything else he's got. Will he do it? He's

Figure VIII-1
In one classroom, children decided to fill the classroom with written book buzzes. Not surprisingly, a few children decided the book they most want to promote was *Stone Fox*. Note the opener—this reader believes his words will have an impact!

It's natural to recommend things we love to others, and it's natural to shy away from the complete unknown until we know a little something about it. Adults do this all the time. We recommend restaurants, vacation spots, movies, politicians, and we take the recommendations and seek the advice of others. Young children, too, make recommendations. They rave about movies, music, food, games, toys, and on and on. In this session, I'm hoping to expand their repertoire of recommendations to include books. You might call your students' attention to sources of book reviews such as www.spaghettibookclub.com or www.kidsbookshelf.com. Keep in mind that a book recommendation, when well done, is almost like an oral book review, and that's an important genre to learn. So, this session will serve many purposes.

"First, I need to think about my nephew Kyril, and his reading life. Remember, Josh knew that Aly loved Harry Potter books, so that's why he thought she'd like the Narnia books? So let me think of Kyril. Hmm. . . . Last month, when I last saw him, Kyril was enjoying The Wayside School books. That makes me think that he likes funny books, and books about kids nowadays doing everyday sorts of things. That also gives me an idea for how hard the books are that he likes to read. I know lots of books that are approximately that level of difficulty (and if I didn't, I'd direct him to someone who could help.)" I paused and gestured toward the first bullet on the chart, reminding children to note when I'd demonstrated one of the chart's bullet points."

How to Create a Book Buzz

- *Think about the person who wants a book recommendation.*

- *Think about the person's reading life—you may have to ask some questions.*

- *Choose a book for that person, remembering the books you know.*

- *Tell the person why you think this book might be a perfect fit.*

- *Summarize a bit of the story, highlighting the parts the reader will like.*

- *Read aloud a tiny excerpt that reveals something enticing about the book.*

- *Talk about why the book is irresistable.*

I think it is very helpful for a teacher to have a bibliography in mind that says, "If the reader liked ____, then he or she is apt to like ____, ____, and ____."

I opened my personal reading log in which I had jotted notes about relevant books. "Now watch me scan my reading log to remind myself of books I could recommend." I ran my finger along my log and stopped at a title. "This is the one—*Diary of a Wimpy Kid*," I said. "I loved that one and it is sort of like *The Wayside School* books, only funnier, I think, and it's even more popular with kids."

"Okay, I've chosen a book." I gestured to the chart and looked to see if children had noticed that I'd completed the second step. Next, I'll want to give Kyril a quick summary of the story. I'll summarize it as if it were gold, highlighting the parts of the book that will especially appeal to him, but making sure I don't give away the ending. Let's see, I'll tell him that *Diary of a Wimpy Kid* is the story of this boy named Greg whose mom makes him keep a diary in which he records all the funny things that happen to him in school. Secretly, he'd like to be popular in school—he rates himself 52nd in popularity (see how I added tiny details)—but right now, he's mostly just trying to avoid both schoolwork and all the big, hulking bullies in middle school. The book has a lot of cartoon illustrations, and the writing is hilarious."

"Next (pointing to the fifth item on the chart), I often read aloud just a tiny section to give the person a feel for the book. You know how when you go to the movies they show previews for upcoming movies? I'm going to choose an excerpt to read that I hope will get Kyril excited about the book. Let's see here. . . . This part would give Kyril a glimpse into Greg's friendship with Rowley, his best friend. Rowley doesn't have a clue about how to be popular." I flipped through the book, stopping at a part I thought was humorous:

> We were getting our stuff from our lockers at the end of the day, and Rowley came up to me and said—WANT TO COME OVER TO MY HOUSE AND PLAAYYY?
>
> I have told Rowley a billion times that now that we're in middle school, you're supposed to say "hang out," not "play." But no matter how many noogies I give him, he always forgets the next time.

I'm deliberately showcasing a book that will be accessible to the readers in my class who resist reading. These are the children who especially need books.

My point is that we can lure someone to read a text by sharing parts that will draw people in. Select a section you believe kids will enjoy. The section of choice was not a cliffhanger, but I know Kyril wants very much to fit in with the crowd, and I hoped this passage would resonate for him.

"And finally, I want to tell Kyril why the book matters to me, why it is special. I need to think about why I love this book." I held the book in my hands, turning it over a bit, mulling over why I love it. "I think *Diary of a Wimpy Kid* matters to me because I can really relate the main character, Greg. He is short and wimpy and he acts like the class clown. I think he does that 'cause he is feels bad about himself. I was insecure when I was little, so I think Greg reminds me of myself."

ACTIVE INVOLVEMENT

Set children up and ask them to give book introductions to each other.

"So, readers, right now while you sit here, I'm going to ask you to try recommending a book to a classmate. Pair up with a reading neighbor—someone you've worked with before, whose reading you know well and who seems to read books that are about as hard as the books you read. Shake hands, so I know you are in pairs. Don't leave anyone out—threesomes are okay too."

"You just watched me create a buzz about a book that I love, and now it's your turn to try it with a person near you—someone who tends to read similar books. One of you will recommend a book to the other. Decide which one of you will do the recommending." I gave them a minute. "Recommenders, eyes up here," I said and waited. Think about your classmate's reading life. Ask a question or two if you need to do so." I waited, then continued. "What kinds of books does your reader tend to like? Get the reader's tastes in your mind. If you are not sure, then quickly ask your reader for his or her all-time favorite book. Now, scan through your reading log—and remember reading you have done before this class, too—and think about a book you have really liked, one that you think would be a good fit for your reader."

As you show children how to sell books, you are also aiming to sell a book to them! It goes without saying, then, that you'll have greater success with this lesson if you pick a book to recommend that speaks to children. We read fiction for many reasons, but perhaps the most compelling one is to find something that resonates for us—a character, a storyline, or a combination of the two.

You'll notice that when children are making book recommendations, I direct them to reference their logs. I am doing this in part because I'm trying to maintain a spotlight on this tool and to show children that it is useful to them—not just a form of accountability.

The method of teaching that you are using in this active involvement is one that I refer to as coaching. It is the same method used in coaching conferences. You are essentially giving voice-over prompts as directives, walking kids through a sequence of steps in a new activity, and leaving time between each prompt for them to do a bit of thinking.

"Now, take a moment and in your head summarize what your chosen book is about. You won't be able to choose an excerpt to read aloud right now, but you can think to yourself, 'Why does this book matter?'"

"Right now, create a book buzz for your reader. Tell why you chose the book, summarize it in a way that will help the person want to read the book, and read an excerpt. Tell why it matters to you."

I listened in as children made book recommendations. As they talked, I coached them by saying things like, "Sarah, make it sound good!" or "Joel, just a quick summary. You don't need to go into tiny details," or "Gabe, don't forget to say *why* you liked it so much!"

LINK

Remind children that they can both recommend books to each other and ask classmates for book recommendations.

After a couple of minutes, I gathered everyone's attention again. "So readers, I felt the energy in the room rise—you created buzzes around some books, for sure! Listening to you recommend books made me want to go right over to the library and find those titles even if I've already read these books a hundred times!"

"You are going to read tons of books this year—and some of them will be ones you love. From now on, remember that if you like a book a lot, it will really help your friends and our class if you create a buzz around it. And if you want to choose a new book to read but feel a bit lost, ask a friend to introduce you to one. Today you learned how, and if you ever forget, our chart, 'How to Create a Book Buzz,' can remind you."

I always want the charts to be living, functional documents, so I refer to them often. Once the information on a chart has been internalized, I'm apt to store the chart out of sight. It's inevitable that those old charts will be brought out again at another time, to be revised. Of course, you may want to find ways to provide tiny copies of charts to children. Some kids tape charts into their reading notebooks, hang them beside their homework area, or turn them into bookmarks.

CONFERRING AND SMALL-GROUP WORK

Teach Children to Share to Their Thoughts about a Book, and to Share Them with Others

In a great many schools, every year brings new initiatives, new programs, new mandates. Teachers become accustomed to attending the Superintendent's Conference Day at the start of each school year, and hearing, year after year, about new directions, new priorities. We hear the words, "This year…" and brace ourselves, thinking, "Please, please, let him announce, 'This year, we'll continue doing the same ol' things.'" We long for time to revisit, to rethink, to extend, to deepen.

After a while, experienced teachers come to realize that underneath the veneer of new initiatives that come and go, the real work on teaching continues, and it has everything to do with inviting kids to do some work, and then studying what kids do in order to figure out ways to lift the level of their work. The key to powerful teaching lies in a teacher's attentiveness to the work that her children produce, and the teacher's willingness to assume responsibility for ratcheting up the level of children's work in ways that effect not today's product, but the learners entire future.

There's lots of talk about data-based instruction. Every district is flying this flag. But I see far too little evidence that instruction is really data-based.

MID-WORKSHOP TEACHING

Readers Read with Other Readers in Mind

"Readers, eyes this way. If you're reading a book that you feel is buzz-worthy right now, give me a thumbs up. Wow, that's more than half of you! Great. Sometimes you might know right away that it's a buzz-worthy book, but other times, you need to read a lot of the book to know."

"I want to share something important that Jasmine just said about her book. When I asked how her reading was going, she said, 'Great. I love this book.' I said, 'It's buzz-worthy?' and her eyes twinkled as she nodded her head up and down. Then she said, 'I think Grace will love it because it's about this kid who loves his dog so much, and Grace loves her dog so much. I think she will really get into this one.' Jasmine's insight made me realize that when we create a book buzz, it helps to think about why *we* like a book, but also to think about why *someone in particular* might like the book. When Jasmine said, 'My book is about a child who loves his dog. I think Grace will love this book because she's so much like the main character,' it was as if Jasmine was creating a book buzz with Grace in mind. As you read, you might do that too; you might think about a specific person who will especially like a book. You might read and find yourself thinking, 'Hey, I bet So-and-So will really get into this because he plays hockey just like this character does.' You can always put a Post-it note on the cover to remind yourself to recommend the book to the person you have in mind."

You may be sputtering in protest and wanting to tell me about the ways your school's obsession with test preparation has taken over everything. But blanketing a school in one-size-fits-all test prep materials is the opposite of what it means for our teaching to be data-based. Data-based instruction means that we must actually look at the data—at the products, the work that kids do, and we think, "What exactly does this show? What patterns do I see? Where is there evidence of good work and what can I learn from that evidence? Where is there evidence of problematic work, and what can I learn from that evidence?"

I am all for data-based reading instruction, as long as we collect a variety of data and it is data that we trust and data that reflects our priorities. Certainly as part of this, we need to look—really look—at the evidence we have of the thinking children do on the run as they read. This means we need to pay attention to their Post-its and logs entries, as well as their talk about texts. And we need to believe that what kids do is amenable to instruction and that we can ratchet up the level of their work through clear, responsive teaching.

Small-Group Instruction that Supports Readers in Using Post-It Notes to Hold on to Their Thoughts About a Story

Chances are good that your children's Post-its will be depressing to look at. Many won't have recorded any thoughts at all and those who have at least tried to capture their thoughts on this form of marginalia will often report on what the book actually says, rather than reflect on the content. You could race from one child to the next, encouraging each one to talk back to the text he or she is reading. But you'd be repeating yourself in lots of conferences, and when you find yourself doing this, it's usually wiser to convene a small group.

I approached a small table of five readers and immediately checked to see if one or two readers had been capturing their own ideas on Post-its, in which case those readers could mentor the others. No such luck. So I decided to confer with one child publicly while the others watched. "Readers," I said, "I am noticing that many of you don't have much of your thinking jotted onto Post-its. I want to try something. For the next few minutes while you're reading, push yourself to have an idea about what you read and then jot your idea on a Post-it note. Then keep reading, perhaps growing another idea. After a bit, I'll work with one of you while the rest of you watch. What you see me do here, you can bring to your own reading." The children agreed with the plan and settled back into their reading.

After a half minute, I saw Sam jotting. I asked, "What are you thinking?" and he read aloud quietly from the book itself. After he read a paragraph, I said, "What did you jot?"

"I think he's old fashioned. He's kind of like my dad."

I made sure the others in the group were listening, and continued to work with Sam.

"Yes, I noticed it says right here in the text that he's old-fashioned, doesn't it! You must have read closely to remember that detail. Now, as you read on, carry the idea that he is old fashioned with you, and see if you can grow *your own thinking* about that." Sam read aloud a few more sentences, and I stopped him and said, "What are you thinking now about the character being old fashioned?"

"Well, he is not only old fashioned, but he also likes things his way."

"What does all this make you think about him?"

"He is a picky person?" Sam said, his rising intonation suggesting he wondered if his thought met with my approval. *[Fig. VIII-2]*

"Sam, you've taken a couple of thoughts you're having about a character and mixed them together to get another idea and this new idea—that he's picky—isn't in the book, is it? Terrific! But the way you said 'He is a picky person?' (I copied his questioning intonation) makes all of us (I checked in with the other listeners) think that you're not quite sure if he's picky or not. You said it like a question, right?"

Sam nodded his head. "Yeah. I mean, the old people that I know are often picky and since he's old fashioned it's like he's old. But I'm not really sure."

"Okay, so why don't you jot your hypothesis—your tentative idea— with a question mark and stick the Post-it in the book. If we had a way to make copies, I'd tell you to stick a second copy of the Post-it onto your hand, and to keep an eye on it as you continue to read. But we can't make copies so will you leave it on the book and also remember it? I bet you'll get some more ideas about this hypothesis of yours and develop other ideas as well. What you will be doing is just what readers do. As we read, we form ideas about the people we are coming to know in a story by collecting all of our thinking and putting our ideas together, then by carrying that bigger idea with us as we read on, expecting it will change. Off you go. Keep it up."

After these few minutes with Sam, I turned to the other children in the group and processed what they'd just seen, asking them to try to do similar work while I coached into their efforts.

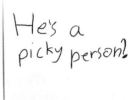

Figure VIII-2
It's a step forward for Sam to generate an idea that is not actually stated in the book. Now he needs to carry the idea forward as he reads, letting it become more complex.

Conferring that Supports Children Who Need Help Having Thoughts as They Read

You may find that some children whip through books without taking the time to pause and react to the story. They may be deep into a book, but when you interrupt them to ask what they are thinking about the story, they shrug.

When Emma finished a fast-paced bit of reading aloud, I asked what she was thinking now, based on her reading. She seemed flustered, as if I'd put her on the spot. By this point in the year, I'd come to realize that Emma generally aims to please; I speculated that in her previous school she may have been held more accountable for reading correctly and smoothly than for generating original ideas.

"Emma, can I tell you something? I've read books like this one, books I love and just want to devour, reading faster and faster! Is that how it is for you in this book?"

She nodded. "I really want to finish it because I want to get to the next one," she explained, referring to the next book in the series.

"Well, what I've learned is this: When you're reading with that urgent sense of wanting to know what's going to happen next, and when you're thinking about the next book, you miss some treasures in the book you're reading right now. It's like when people drive fast to get someplace. They are so focused on getting to the destination that they don't even notice the scenery they are zooming past. It's good to be able to read like you're doing, but most of the time you'll want to read in a way that really allows you to notice what's going on in the book *and* what's going on in your mind. Instead of racing through the words, it's usually more pleasurable to pay attention to your thoughts."

"You mean like taking a break sometimes?"

"Well, let me show you. Listen to me read part of *Stone Fox*, and I'm going to have thoughts." I reread from *Stone Fox*, thinking aloud and jotting on a Post-it note. "Did you see how I read a bit and when I had a reaction that seemed important, I jotted it on a Post-it note? I didn't let my reaction whiz past as I raced on and on and on. I caught a dawning thought and held onto it on this Post-it note. Why don't you go back to the beginning of the chapter you're in and reread, this time, trying to catch and hold onto dawning ideas. I'll stay for a bit to listen in and see how it goes for you."

Emma read aloud a couple of paragraphs about the doctor's advice to Willy, and then looked at me and said, "That wasn't really nice for her to say!"

"That's such interesting thought," I said, trying to show that her idea was worth contemplating. I repeated her thought. "Why *do* you think the doctor would say something not nice?" I mused, as if I had no real answer to that thought. "Do you think she is unkind, or what might it be?"

Emma paused, clearly thinking. Then she took a big breath, as if about to burst into an answer.

Pushing a Post-it in front of Emma, I said, "Just write it on your Post-it note, and keep reading. As you read on, remember, your amazing ideas can be the start to a whole journey of thinking. It helps to ask yourself further questions, like 'Why did she (or he) do that?' Keep up your amazing thinking!" Of course, I knew I was overstating the brilliance of her ideas, but I wanted Emma to realize that in this class, she could shine not just by reading quickly but also by thinking deeply.

I knew that Emma would need lots more help thinking about her characters and her books. This relationship with books would only become a habit if she received lots more practice. I made a note to check back with Emma in the next few days and wondered if I should be helping her partner, Izzy, to do similar work or to function as a thinking-mentor for Emma.

TEACHING SHARE

Readers Can Introduce Books to Ourselves

Tell students that they can introduce books to themselves, and create a buzz for themselves, not just others. Demonstrate this with a book they're apt to like.

"Readers, let's gather back together. Everyone please bring your books with you." Once children had settled in the meeting area, I said, "Today we talked a lot about creating a book buzz and sharing our enthusiasm for books with others. That's a generous thing to do as a reader. But you know what? Don't forget to be generous with yourself. Treat yourself well as a reader, too. What I mean is that you can create a book buzz for *yourself*. You can get *yourself* introduced to a book, get *yourself* enthusiastic, too. Watch me. I'm going to flip through my book bin and I'm going to show you how you can create a book buzz for yourself.

I flipped through the books and picked out *Captain Underpants*. I read the title aloud, and said, "This one is a bit of a stranger to me. I've got no particular feelings about it yet, and I know I can do better than that for myself before I begin to read it. Let me introduce this book to myself, to help me get excited about it. Hmm, this is the book lots of children in my class have read. *Captain Underpants*. The title is sort of, well, weird." I flipped it over and read the blurb on the back, commenting aloud to myself, "Well, it might be interesting to read, even though I'm not really into totally silly books, usually. Let me read a tiny bit to see if it is the right fit." Then I opened up the book and flipped through the pages, settling on a page where I read a brief excerpt."

> *The Flight of the Goofy Glider*
>
> Fluffy and Cheeseball had to admit that it was pretty cool flying over the city streets on a paper airplane. They didn't even seem to mind the fact that they were only about an inch tall each.
>
> But you can probably imagine the boys' concern when they started heading straight for a wood chipper.

COACHING TIPS

You'll note that I'm asking children to bring their books with them. By this point, hopefully your children are all matched to just-right books and they each have a container that holds a short stack of books. We think of these books as the pile that might be on a reader's bedside table. We encourage children to carry small collections of books with them so that there is as little gap as possible between finishing one book and starting the next. Then, too, the fact that a child keeps this collection of past and future reads on hand means that our conferences can take into account and also support more of a child's reading. We can notice patterns across several books.

"It feels like the right fit for me, not too hard or easy. I can tell it might be funny because the character looks so ridiculous. It's different than what I usually read. I think I could get into this. I'm going to pick it."

Debrief, pointing out what you did that children can do on their own, with their own books. Ask children to try the process you've demonstrated.

At this point, I looked up at my class. "Did you see what I did? I picked up a book that I might have just passed over, and I spent some time creating my own introduction to it, reading the title, the blurb on the back cover, flipping through the pages, reading bits."

"Now it's your turn to try it. Flip through your bin of books and pick one—not one you've already read. Now introduce it to yourself. Create a book buzz. Do what I did: Read the title and blurb, flip through and read a quick excerpt. Browse through the book, reading little excerpts to get a feel for the book. Try to build your own excitement for the book."

As children talked with each other, I listened in and prompted their talks when I felt it was necessary. I used quick, lean prompts such as, "It mattered because. . . ." "Say more about that." "Is there a part of the book that shows what you mean?" "Think about the title for a moment, or read the blurb on the back cover. What's the tone of the story like?"

If you go overboard and totally gush about a book, kids may distance themselves from you, saying, "That is too over the top. I could never be like that." Therefore, you may want your book buzz to be more modest and to show yourself being won over, your resistance abating. In this way, you'll be demonstrating for many readers, perhaps a few strugglers, how we give books a chance and allow ourselves pleasurable possibilities.

Not only do my voiceovers provide scaffolds for children who may need to say more, but I also implicitly demonstrate for group members different ways to get another person to say more about a text. I will, of course, explicitly demonstrate these strategies more throughout the units, especially as we move into Unit Four, Tackling Complex Texts: Historical Fiction in Book Clubs.

You and your children may decide that reviewing and recommending books is important enough to the classroom community that you create ways to share book buzzes (or call them book reviews, if you like.) Many people create online resources. Some teachers put pockets inside the back covers of books and invite children to slide folded reviews into these little pockets.

Remind children they can try this from now on, in their lives.

After children talked for not more than five minutes, we reconvened, and I shared some highlights. "Readers, you are natural book promoters. I heard kids say things like, 'The really amazing thing about this book is. . . .' I heard others say things like, 'This book gave me strong feelings like. . . .' and 'It was good right from the very first page' and 'People who like books about soccer would really get into this book.' These are really great ways to recommend books and create a book buzz."

"So readers, this is something you can do when you're looking for books. Instead of flipping through a basket in a droopy way, or in a way that is full of shyness of the unknown, like this." I modeled. "You can flip through with the intention of creating a buzz for yourself about a book. You can approach a basket of books thinking, 'I know I'll find a book here I want to read. If necessary, I'll take a moment to create my own book buzz!'"

Notice that again, to make a point of what to do, I dramatize what not to do. Not only do children often find this humorous and engaging, but also in demonstrating what not to do, I acknowledge a child's agency in choosing how to approach his or her reading life.

DIARY OF A KILLER CAT
Anne Fine
•Tuffy is an ordinary cat that does ordinary cat things like killing mice and birds. But what happens when you are owned by an animal loving family and a soft-hearted girl?
•Tuffy kills the negbors rabbit! How will the family get it to the neighbors yard good as new before the negbors see?
•Tuffy and the vet dont get along so well after Tuffy ruins the carpet.

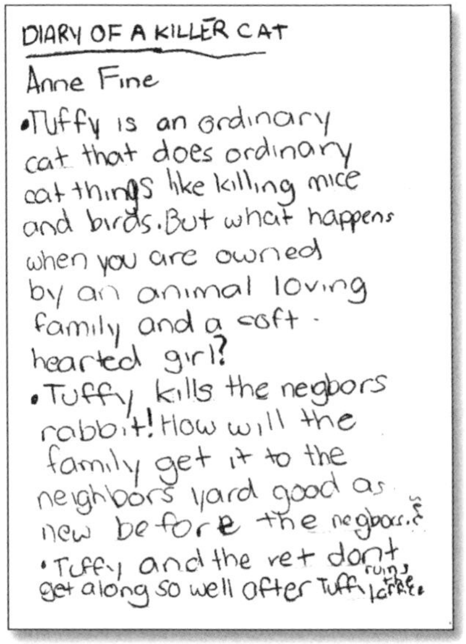

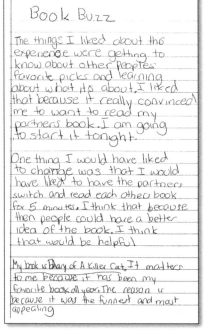

Figure VIII-3
Notice that Josh's writing has voice—that magic quality that suggests his personality is coming through. Perhaps that is because he is preparing to actually talk with friends.

The Missing Moose Mystery
By Dian Curtis Regan
In this book ghost twins Beka and Robbie try to help the new renter of their old house solve a mystery. The mystery of the town moose who's been missing for over 50 years! Jamie and the twins are nearly stumped, until clues start appearing in the famous Nell Makanda's painting other wise known as Jamie's grand mother.

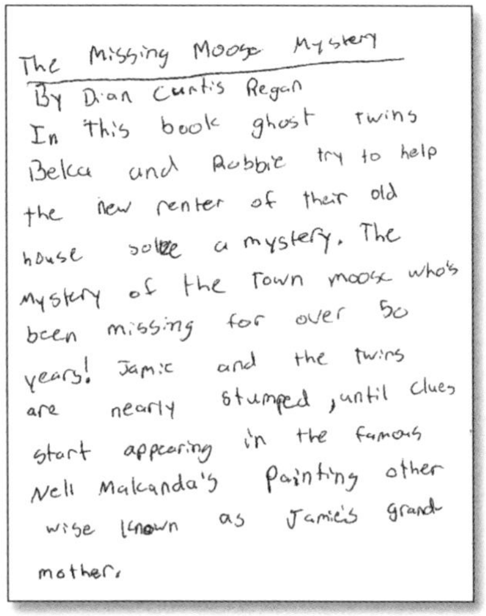

Figure VIII-4
Some children will end up making written book buzzes. Aly has clearly read book promotions and her writing bears the imprint of those mentor texts.

Book Buzz
• I liked the fact that it went a little beyond the covers and you got a little taste of each others favorite books. I also loved that as soon as we finished sharing we got to read. The last thing that for me was great was that I got to share my favorite books and let others know about it
• one thing I would have changed is that I I wish I could have looked at and heard of other books. Another thing I wish was that it was quieter in the room. It was very hard to hear Fallon and Amber and I had to listen harder to hear them.
• The Missing Moose Mystery mattered to me because it was the one book so far that I couldn't put down. It thrilled me. Infact I stayed up under the covers with a flash light during one of the scariest parts.

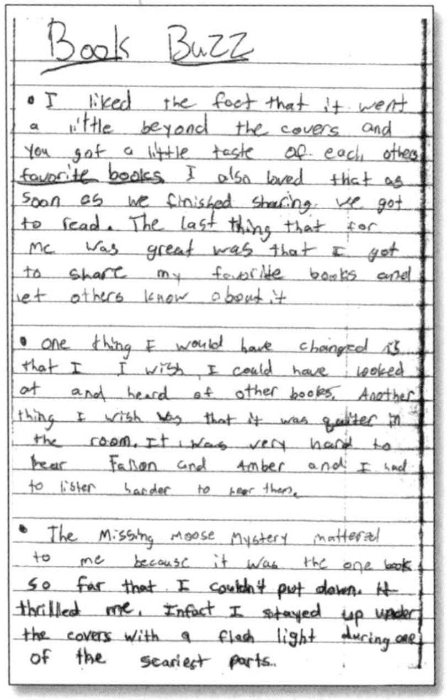

Figure VIII-5
One of the teachers who piloted a draft of these units asked her readers to reflect on the experience of doing book buzzes for each other. You probably won't ask your children to do this, but you'll be interested in these responses.

Book Buzz
The things I liked about this experience were getting to know about other peoples favorite picks and learning about what its about. I liked that because it really convinced me to want to read my partners book. I am going to start it tonight.
One thing I would have liked to change was that I would have liked to have the partners switch and read each others book for 5 minutes. I think that because then people could have a better idea of the book. I think that would be helpful
My book is Diary of A Killer Cat. It matters to me because it has been my favorite book all year. The reason is because it was the funnest and most appealing

Figure VIII-6
Generating enthusiasm for new books and authors

DRAFT

DRAFT
Choosing Texts that Matter

When it came time for my son, Miles, to write the essay accompanying his college applications, I felt sure he'd write about one of the service activities that had been so important in his life, or about his relationship with me, or with his brother, or with his grandfather. But to my surprise, Miles wrote instead about his relationship to characters in books. His essay began like this:

> When I enter college, I will bring my experiences trekking through the mountains of Vietnam and my memories of a 227-day stint in a lifeboat, accompanied only by a Bengal tiger. When I attend classes as a freshman, my role will bear the imprint of the tortuous hours I spent standing above the town square, a scarlet letter emblazoned on my chest. Reading has given me the water I swim in, the heroes I emulate, and the imagination to believe that I can make the world a better place.

For a long while, I have said, "My mission is to give all children what I give my own children." So it seems noteworthy to me that when Miles was asked to write about the whole of his life, the subject that he chose to write about was his identification with characters in books. For me, this is a reminder that one of the most important gifts of reading gives us is the feeling of walking in the shoes of another person, standing in a town square with a scarlet letter emblazoned on our chest.

There are students in our classrooms that lose themselves in books. The end of reading time comes, and these children walk, nose in the book, to the meeting area. But we tend to think of those children as if they were born that way, as if they are made of something different. We act as if we can't possibly *teach* children how to be nose-in-the-book readers. We can't imagine saying in a minilesson (to paraphrase a Ring Lardner quote), "'You can't read if you can't cry.' Watch me as I read this paragraph and bawl my eyes out. Now you try it. I'll read the next paragraph, and you let out a big sob." We can't imagine saying, not "Today will you use five Post-its?" but instead, "Today will you use five tissues?"

GETTING READY

- Ask readers to bring their "My Reading Life" folders and pens to the meeting area. During the minilesson, you might ask them to jot responses to questions you pose about their systems for locating books.

- Think about bringing props that support your talk about the need to develop systems for finding books.

- Bring your own planning notebook with you to the minilesson so you can record suggestions children make.

And so we teach kids to syllabicate or to find the main idea, but not to empathize with characters—with others.

This minilesson builds on the last few, encouraging children to read books with wide-awake appreciation, to read as if books are precious. This minilesson also rallies kids to join

> *We need to keep in mind that a book is just right not only because a child can read it with accuracy, fluency, and comprehension, but also because a child can read it with empathy and engagement, laughter and, yes, tears, as well.*

us in coauthoring the classroom community. Teachers tell me that children are up on their knees with excitement when they're asked to design a state-of-the-art calssroom library and that on the days after this minilesson, their classrooms glowed with kids' energy.

Frankly, I hope this session teaches all of us, teachers as well as kids, that it is not okay to give up on nose-in-the-

book reading. Helping kids care about books may not fit easily into the architecture of a minilesson, but this doesn't mean that we don't need to move heaven and earth to help kids know what it's like for a book to matter.

If we want to teach nose-in-the-book reading, we start by investing in the classroom library and encouraging schools to do so as well. John Guthrie recently completed a meta-analysis in which he synthesized 28 studies on comprehension. The studies showed that the single most important way to support comprehension is to provide children with more access to interesting texts. The next most important intervention involves giving kids more choice of books. Allington reports that another study showed that if you give high-poverty children even just ten books each summer, books that the children can read, that alone will have a much bigger effect than any of the major (and well-funded) comprehensive school reform projects that now exist in the world!

The American Library Association states that a library for a school of 300 kids should have 20,000 books and 10,000 other print resources, such as globes and maps. Title I schools usually have less than 20% of this, yet the children in these schools—unlike children in middle-class neighborhoods—rely on the school for 85% of their books. Libraries are crucial in all schools. They are especially important in schools serving high-poverty children. It is crucial that each of us becomes an advocate for libraries and crucial too that we spend much more time and energy trying to put the exactly right books into kids' hands. And we need to keep in mind that a book is just right not only because a child can read it with accuracy, fluency, and comprehension, but also because a child can read it with empathy and engagement, laughter and, yes, tears, as well.

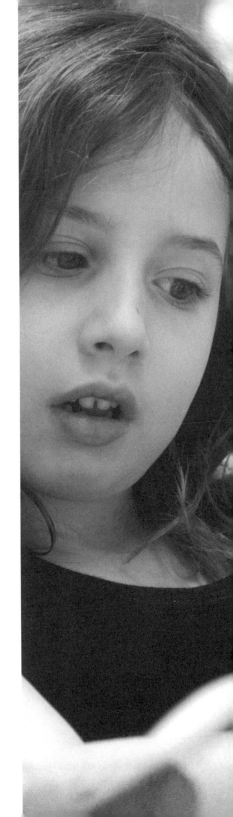

MINILESSON

Choosing Texts that Matter

CONNECTION

Share a story that tells about a reader (or a class) experiencing the power of enthralling books.

"I want to tell you about some sixth graders in a Harlem junior high. At the start of last year, these kids weren't sold on reading. A lot of stuff competed for their attention: music, friends, sports, video games. But then their teacher brought a series of books into the classroom, and within a month, the entire class was totally and completely lost in those books. The kids ended up writing the authors of the books, saying, 'We've never seen books that are so good,' and the authors ended up giving each and every kid in that class an entire set of those books. By the end of the year, those kids had each read dozens and dozens of books. And it all started because the kids got hold of books that mattered to them. This is what one kid wrote in her letter to the authors."

COACHING TIPS

When the school year drew to an end and I met with the teachers who had piloted the most recent draft of these units, most of them said that one of the great strengths of their year had been the systems that they had introduced during this minilesson, systems that lasted the year. Randi Bernstein's children, for example, decided during this session that they'd bring books from home to their classrooms to share, and they instituted a new ritual. If a child brought a book from home to share with the class, the school day would start with the child creating a book buzz, then putting the book in the basket where it belonged so it could be borrowed throughout the day. This ritual lasted all year.

Teachers, when you go to write your own minilesson, by all means draw on your stories of the kids you have taught in other years. Children absolutely love hearing true stories of other kids. Save kids' work. Remember the anecdotes. You are so lucky to be in classrooms all day, every day. Draw on the stories of your teaching when you want to invent a way to draw kids to listen close to your minilessons. Examples, anecdotes, stories, and quotes are more engaging then a lot of hot air. Don Murray reminds writers that good writing is built with information, not with the hot air of words. The same is true for good minilessons.

Dear Authors of the Bluford High Books,

This is so crazy but now that I have read your series, I enjoy reading. If you knew me from last year, you would know that if you gave a book to me, I'd think, "Why are you giving me this?" but now I am writing to say, "Please can you give me more books?"

When I read the Bluford High books that you have written, I feel like the characters are my friends. I feel like I've known Darcy for a long time, but really it is just that I have read three books with her in them and that is so cool. And I think Cooper is strong and tough at the same time. I think he would make a great boyfriend.

Your books changed my reading because I hardly stutter when I talk, I understand a lot more, and I think—no, wait, *I know*, my life has changed because of your books. Your books are like a movie that's too good to be in a theater. I'm like a spectator watching them and taking notes as they speak.

I also changed my habits. Now I read the back of the books where it says exciting sentences. For example, in *Bully* it says, "Tyray whipped out a knife and held it up to Darrell's face. 'Oh, no,' Darrell thought, 'He's going to kill me.'" See, that's exciting.

Are there any more books like the Bluford High ones? Maybe I'll even write my own book. At times when I feel bored, I write my life. I feel like I'm the main character in my own story.

Thanks for your books, Desiree.

"Readers, I'm telling you this because I want you to know that books matter. Desiree was smart to try to move heaven and earth to be sure she had a stack of books in her life that could turn her into a reader. Those Bluford High books are just right for her not only because they're easy enough for her to read them smoothly, but because they're exciting enough for her to read them with her heart pounding."

Sometimes in a connection I find myself preaching, as I do here. I am trying to inspire the readers who sit in front of me, to impress upon them the ways in which words on a page can hold so much meaning for our own lives.

Name your teaching point. Specifically, tell children that readers must develop systems for finding books we will love.

"Today I want to teach you that readers make sure we always have a stack of books beside us—and that the books are ones that can turn us into the readers we want to be. To find books that truly are just right for us, we need systems that can help us find those books."

TEACHING

Tell kids about a few systems other students have designed for promoting great books, letting kids know you will want their additional ideas.

"I was thinking that maybe we could work together to think about how we can develop systems right in this classroom for helping each other find just-right books. We've got a great classroom library, and you are starting to create book buzzes—that matters a lot. But I think we could maybe come up with some other ideas to be sure we each have the kinds of books that will really matter to us as readers."

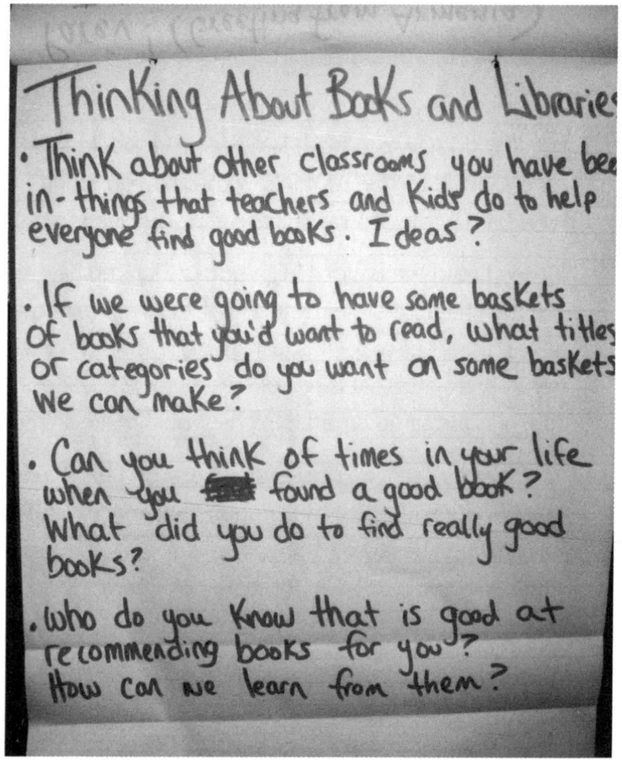

Thinking About Books and Libraries

• Think about other classrooms you have been in- things that teachers and Kids do to help everyone find good books. Ideas?

• If we were going to have some baskets of books that you'd want to read, what titles or categories do you want on some baskets we can make?

• Can you think of times in your life when you found a good book? What did you do to find really good books?

• Who do you know that is good at recommending books for you? How can we learn from them?

My teacher had bins that had labels like sports books to help me.

Figure IX-1

We had partners tell us about books we might like.

Figure IX-2

"Let me tell you about systems that other teachers have used, and then you can let me know if any of these sound like systems we should put into our classroom. Jot some of your own thoughts as we go along. I am hoping that together we can come up with systems to make sure each of us always has a good book in hand. Does that make sense?"

"One teacher I know searches for books she's sure her class will love and then introduces several of them at a time to her class She gives an overview of the book or the series, reads a passage, and says, 'This book is a lot like . . .' and tells kids other books that are similar. She says that her kids keep lists of books they want to read. If she spends ten minutes giving an overview of five series of books, usually by the end of that time, everyone will have added the title of one new series to their list. She'll do these book talks a couple times a week at the start of the year, and then after that, the kids end up knowing enough great books that they create book buzzes for each other and don't need her book introduction."

"In quite a few classrooms, the teacher and the kids work together to reorganize the classroom library so that the books are in categories or shelves that echo the kids' interests. So in one class, there is a shelf labeled 'Light Sports Books' and another shelf called 'Friendship Troubles.' Often there are bins for series books, too, so those are easy to find. As the kids reorganize the library, they find books that catch their interest."

Figure IX-3

One section of a library organized by genre

"Here's one last idea. You know how newspapers rate movies with one, two, three, or four stars? Well, in some classrooms, kids leave Post-it notes inside the cover of a book after they read it, saying, 'This is a three-star book' or 'This is a four-star book.' (If we don't like a book we'd just leave nothing rather than leaving an insult. Another reader might think it's a four-star book, since different types of books matter to different types of readers.) Kids sometimes write little recommendation notes on the Post-its, too."

ACTIVE INVOLVEMENT

Channel children to participate in a whole-class conversation in which they share ideas for the systems they can develop to help each other locate great books.

"Take a minute now to write some thoughts about systems we could invent that would help us all get lots of books that truly matter to us. We'll talk about what you are thinking in a minute."

After a time, I said, "Read over all that you've written and star the ideas that might be helpful to the rest of us." Once kids had done that, I said, "Let's discuss this as a class. Who can get us started?" Hands shot up around the carpet, and I said, "All eyes on Fallon."

Each child turned to look at Fallon. She said, "I have a lot of books at home that I love. Like all the Jacqueline Wilson books that my dad brings me from England. Oh, oh, like Anne Fine and Michael Morpugo."

I made a signal for her to get to the point. She giggled into her hand, then said, "So I'm thinking that maybe we could have baskets that we fill up with our favorite books, and they could say on the outside 'Fallon's Favorites' or 'Brianna's Best.'" As Fallon talked, I quickly recorded her idea in my planning notebook.

I gave three examples because I wanted to give children a chance to grasp what I meant by developing systems for helping each other find just-right books. I don't want to share many more ideas, though, or it won't be as easy for children to invent more.

Throughout this book, you will have seen that when I want to talk with children, I decide whether I'm talking as they continue working (rare at the start of the year) or whether I am asking for their full attention. When I want the class to talk together, as in this instance, it is important to me that children actually listen to each other and build on what other children say. In this instance, I ask them to look at each other just as I have often asked them to look at me. After working in many classrooms, my colleagues and I have come to believe that many children don't listen well with their ears only, so if I want the kids' full attention, I ask for their eyes, as well as their ears. It is natural, then, that whenever I want children to talk together in a whole-class conversation, I ask them to look at the child who is speaking, saying "All eyes on Fallon." This also signals Fallon to address her words not only to the teacher, but to all of her listening classmates. This may seem like a small detail—but it is not.

Sometimes it takes too long to record children's responses on chart paper. In these instances, be prepared to jot the gist of what they are saying in your notebook, knowing you can always record these on a classroom chart later.

When I looked up, hands were waving frantically. "Let's have a conversation without me calling on kids. Put your hands down. People jump in. If two of you start at the same time, one of you will just let the other person speak first."

There was silence and then Izzy said thoughtfully, "Well maybe we could have a basket filled with all of our favorite books from home and we could name the basket 'Class Picks.'"

Tyrell jumped up from his spot on the rug, almost upsetting a basket of markers in his eagerness. "Wait! I know—we could try reading a friend's favorite book!"

"No! No!" Lily said. "I've got it! We could have two people talk about books, maybe their favorite books, and almost debate them, like presidents would. We could say, 'Pick this book because. . . .'"

"And also, if we really, really want people to read a certain book, maybe we could vote on them, like having a Supreme Court of Books in our class!" Aly piped in.

"Last year, our teacher had a bin for all the brand-new books that just came into the store," Rosa said. "I always like reading brand-new books."

"I'm kind of the opposite," Jasmine said. "I like to read books that are old and tattered because that means a lot of people have read those books, so they must be good!"

Later you'll want kids to talk about books in this way, without you controlling the talking. This provides a model for that.

Be aware that there will be instances when a speaker steps on the heels of another, out of enthusiasm. Don't overreact to this. The last thing you want is for children in whole-class conversations to be obsessed over etiquette, worrying more about manners than ideas. You will have chances later to quietly coach (privately) rambunctious participants to be a bit more cautious.

Gabe had been waiting for a pause in the conversation to say quietly "I think we should invite special people in, like our grandparents or our neighbors, and they can give book talks to us." The class nodded in support, and Gabe beamed shyly, ducking a little to hide his eyes with his bangs.

The class continued with the conversation for a few more minutes.

It is fairly rare for a whole-class conversation to appear inside a minilesson. But in this case, the minilesson is all about communities working together, so it makes sense to conduct a whole-class conversation. Don't feel as if every child needs to contribute. Remember, the children were already part of smaller conversations, so they've all had a chance to share their thoughts.

LINK

Summarize your children's ideas and channel your students to put their ideas into action.

"My head is spinning! You all came up with so many ideas for how we could make it more likely that each of us has a stack of books beside us as we read, books that urge us to read voraciously. There are a couple of things we can get started on right away.

We need to scour the library and our homes for books that can go in 'books we love' baskets, like 'Fallon's Favorites' and 'Class Picks.'"

"And what do you think about the idea of rating a book with a Post-it note showing if it's a two-star, three-star or a four-star book? It'd be nice if you left your name, as well, so that your fellow readers could ask you for a sense of the book. Am I right that you'd like to promote books during share time when you feel as though you have a particularly hot read?"

In this link, I celebrate some of the wonderful ideas the class came up with and rally the children into action. After generating so much excitement and enthusiasm, it would be a shame if nothing comes from this lesson!

Remind children, that, as always, what they've learned to do today is something they can do always in their reading lives.

"All of that will get us started! Now you know what I mean when I say that readers figure out systems for getting ourselves and others exactly the books we need to read with enthusiasm! This is something you can do from now on—make systems with each other to solve your problems. In this case you are making systems to help us all find the books we need! It's been a longer minilesson than usual, so I'm dying for us to get to reading, aren't you? Let's all, together, head back to our reading spots, and to our reading logs and our books. Off you go!

Some of you might be thinking that your children aren't ready to be sent off all together—that you still need to dismiss one small group, then the next group, and the next. If that's your sense, follow your instincts, but be sure you are working toward the day when you can simply say, "Let's get started!" Children should ultimately be responsible for themselves during a transition, and before, long your class should be able to both gather and disperse without you micro-controlling the transition.

Figure IX-4

Early in the year, when you've just assessed readers and helped them know books that are especially apt to be just right for them, you might arrange some of your library according to levels. Later, you'll want categories—award winners, sports, books about family issues. Books will still be leveled but the levels are of subordinate importance.

CONFERRING AND SMALL-GROUP WORK

Plan for Your Conferences by Considering the Funds of Knowledge that You Can Draw Upon

Those of us who lead reading workshops invariably take a moment before an upcoming workshop to plan what we will teach in a minilesson. We wouldn't sit ourselves in the chair at the front of the meeting areas without a plan in mind for that minilesson. And because we definitely do not want to be empty-handed when we approach a minilesson, we're apt to lean on colleagues to help us prepare for this aspect of our teaching. We share ideas for powerful minilessons. However, we are far less apt to plan our conferences and small-group work, or to discuss this with our colleagues, and I think this is a problem.

I can hear your protest. You are probably thinking, "But, but, but aren't conferences created brand new, on the spot, in response to what a child is doing and saying?" The answer to that question is yes—and no.

Yes, it is true that in our conferences, we listen to the child, take in all that we can about the child's intentions and hopes and the child's efforts thus far, and then we teach in response to what the child shows us.

On the other hand, when we teach responsively, it is all the more important for us to be broadly prepared. There are lots of ways to prepare for conferences, and over the course of your work with these units of study, you'll learn many of these. For now, let me suggest that it is helpful to approach a day's workshop with some sense of the sort of work you're apt to be doing when conferring with children.

MID-WORKSHOP TEACHING POINT

Readers Give Books a Chance

"Readers, today we talked about creating systems for finding books we love. As I conferred with Issac just now, I realized that sometimes, when we are totally lucky, we might fall in love at first sight with a book. we get into the story from the very first pages and don't want to put it down. Right now, I bet each of you can think of a book that was like that for you, a love-at-first-sight book. But sometimes, we experience what's been happening to Kobe today. He already read one book he really liked this year *(Hatchet)* and he just recently started another book. He's in the second chapter, and he told me the book is 'just okay.' He hasn't fallen in love with it. But Kobe told me something that I think is a wise idea. He said that he realized from reading *Hatchet,* his last book, that sometimes it takes him a little while to get into a book. One of his goals as a reader this year is to push himself to find ways to give books a chance. He says one of his new systems will be to read at least the first three chapters because he wants to give the book a chance. I just wanted to share this with you, to suggest that some books are love-at-first-sight books and other books might require you to give them a chance, like Kobe does. You can get back to your reading now."

One way to prepare for your conferences is to remember that when conferring, you will essentially link the child to one fund of knowledge or another. It helps, therefore, to enter conferences aware of several possible funds of knowledge that can become resources for your readers.

Plan for Your Conferences by Anticipating that You Might Draw on Your Knowledge of Reading Skills

Your teaching might, for instance, draw on your knowledge of reading skills. For any reading skill that you will be highlighting in a unit of study, it is helpful for you to have a sense of what emergent work with that skill might be, what more developed work with that skill might be, and what even *more* developed work with that skill might be. For example, in recent minilessons, you have been helping children choose books that are just right and orient themselves to those books. Perhaps you imagine that children who are early on in this work will read the back cover blurb and the first page of a book, using those indicators to help them imagine what the book will probably be about. As children become more advanced, perhaps you expect that they will also draw on their knowledge of the genre to help them anticipate how the book might unfold. Your knowledge of what early and more advanced book orientations might entail allows you to work with readers along a line of skill development.

Of course, the skill of book orientation is one of many skills you're apt to be supporting early in the school year. Your conferences will also draw upon your knowledge of what it means to monitor for sense. At the most fundamental level, you'll want readers to notice when they have lost a grip on meaning and to say to themselves, "Huh?" Then you will want readers to read on, expecting their confusion to clear and if it doesn't clear, you'll want readers to go back and reread. As readers become more skilled at monitoring for sense, you might, for example, expect them to recognize that there are predictable times when texts are apt to be confusing. Recognizing this can help them deal with those times. For example, stories often begin mid-stream, and it can take the reader a few pages of reading to construct a clear sense of what is going on. Readers who know that stories often begin this way will still register that the start of the story is confusing, but these readers will also think, 'I've seen other texts like this one,' and draw on that prior experience with a similar sort of confusion to help them work through the early complexity in the text.

Plan for Conferences by Anticipating That You Might Teach Readers by Drawing on Your Knowledge of Genres

When you invite children to choose books that interest them and are just right for them (rather than expecting every child to read the same book), the consequence is that oftentimes when you pull a chair alongside a reader, you will not be familiar with the book that the child is reading. This can make you feel empty-handed. "How's your reading going?" you ask, feeling out of your league. "You like it? Can you make pictures in your mind as you read?" The child says she can. "Great," you say, feeling totally inadequate. "Any hard words?"

If you have felt that way, you need to know that you are not alone. But the good news is that, even when you do not know the book that the youngster is reading, your knowledge of genres can help you confer. For example, at this early point in the year, most readers will be reading realistic fiction. You can draw on what you know about the genre to ask probing questions. "Can you tell me a bit about the protagonist, the main character in your book?" You may follow up with clarifying questions: "Is the main character also the narrator? Is this written in first person?" You can ask about the main character's traits, nudging the reader to talk with more specificity and nuance, and perhaps asking for evidence of a trait. You

can expect the reader to be thinking about the main character's motivations; more specifically, you can help a reader recognize that often readers will first note an external motivation and will, upon reflecting, be able to identify a deeper underlying motivation. It may seem the character wants an invitation to the party, but really, what the character wants is to not feel rejected. You can anticipate that the main character will encounter struggles, and you'll hope the reader sees this, and also sees ways in which the protagonist will try, try, try to achieve what he or she wants and will change and learn in the process.

If a child is reading fiction, you can also know that the book will have a setting—a time and a place—and you can wonder why this particular author will have chosen to place this story in this setting. You can hope that the reader pauses to wonder how the book might be different if it had been set in a different time or place.

If a reader is reading a fiction text, you can also know that the author has deliberately made craft decisions to forward his or her deeper message, and you can ask the reader, "What do you think this text is really, really about?" Then you can draw on your knowledge of how fiction texts work to question how the central meaning of the text affects other aspects of the text—the lead, the ending, the title, the parts that are elaborated upon and those that are missing.

Of course, as you confer with children you'll find some are reading fantasy books or mysteries or graphic novels or historical fiction, and you can draw on your knowledge of any kind of book to conduct conversations. If this is a fantasy, you can ask about the quest. You can ask whether the book contains a map—or a world that merits being mapped. If this is a mystery, you can expect there to be a pattern in the class.

Plan for Conferences by Anticipating that You Might Teach Readers by Drawing on Your Knowledge of Talking and Writing Well about Reading

You could, on the other hand, decide that your conference will draw upon your knowledge of how readers talk and write well about their reading. If this is the case, you'll again draw upon a sense of the ways readers do this that are more elementary and ways that are more advanced. You might, for example, teach learners who are early in this continuum that when recording thoughts about a book, it is best to not record the facts that are in the book so much as the reader's response to those facts, something that will not be in the book as you saw in the Session 8 conference. Learners who are more advanced might benefit from being coached to entertain various theories about a story or text using phrases such as, "Perhaps it could be . . ."or "Then again, maybe. . . ."

Plan for Conferences by Anticipating that You Might Teach Readers by Drawing on Your Knowledge of the Unit of Study

As you confer, you can also draw upon the specific emphasis of the unit of study and work to be sure that children are using all that you have been trying to teach in your minilessons, mid-workshop teaching points, and teaching share sessions. For example, as you confer during this particular unit of study, you may well decide to help readers become researchers of their own reading, thinking about what works for them and what doesn't work, and thinking about how they can use this knowledge to help them fashion a reading life that works. You might suggest that a child look over his or her log, noticing times when he or she has done a ton of reading. If one child identifies a day when she read much more than usual, you could help the child think, "What was it about that one day that made reading really work for me?" and then, "So going forward, how can I use what I'm learning about myself to make my reading life the best that it can be?"

Alternatively, you can suggest that a reader work hard to be sure that she is reading herself awake, or is reading texts like they are gold, or is monitoring for sense and noticing when texts suddenly turn a corner and for a time seem confusing. Of course, once you are farther in the year, you'll draw not only on the learning from the current unit, but also on all the teaching from prior units.

As part of this work, you'll want to help readers use all the charts around the room as reminders to set goals for themselves as readers and to be consciously working to become stronger readers.

Plan for Conferences by Anticipating that You Might Teach Readers by Drawing on a Host of Other Sources of Information

This conferring section has highlighted a few sources of information that you can draw upon when conferring—and there are many more. For example, you may want to draw upon your knowledge of the level of book a child is reading, and I'll discuss this more later. You may want to draw upon your knowledge of what it means to live a readerly life, carrying books with you everywhere, talking about books often, reading in stolen moments of time, and so forth. In such a conference, you might ask a reader about when she reads, how often she reads, whether she shares her reading with anyone, and so forth. You may want to draw on your knowledge of reading-writing connections.

My larger point is that if you take just a moment or two to think about your conferences and your small-group work before the reading workshop begins, you can refresh your memory of all the possible sources of information that you are apt to draw upon when you pull alongside a reader or convene a small group of readers. When this knowledge is fresh in your mind, you will not feel empty-handed if you ask a child, "How's your reading going?" and the child blithely answers, "Great."

TEACHING SHARE

Readers Help Other Readers Find Great Books

Ask children to talk with their partners about their plans for setting up and using the systems they've invented today for getting great books in each other's hands.

"Your suggestions earlier that we share with each other our favorite books, our 'book picks' got me thinking how great it would be to record our book recommendations with ratings in a central, visible spot in the classroom for us all to use. So I created a bulletin board just for this purpose (and I pointed to a fresh board with a fancy gold border and the words 'We Highly Recommend:' written on top). Give me a thumbs up if you think of a book you could recommend on this board."

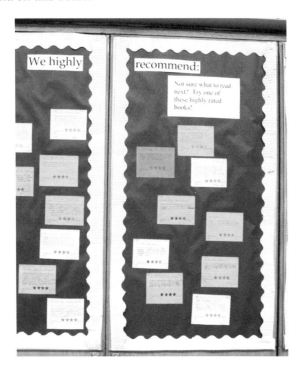

Figure IX-5

Creating buzz around popular books

"Turn to your partner now and share some more ideas you have for helping us all get great books to each other. Share also how you plan to get started using our new systems."

Learning New Words from Books

DRAFT

IN THIS SESSION,
you'll teach children that
when readers come to a
hard word, we try several
ways to figure it out so that
they can continue to follow
the story.

For the young readers in our classrooms, there is no dispute over the definition of a "hard word." It is, simply, a word that makes them stumble as they read. It is a word that requires work.

Children do not realize that the qualities that make a word hard are different for one learner than for another. If a child has grown up reading a lot or otherwise immersed in a sea of book language and if English is the child's first language, then when this child comes to an unfamiliar word—say, *philanthropy*—the challenge may simply be to sound out the word. That is, once that child turns the string of letters into an approximation of the word, saying aloud what might be a slightly garbled or awkward variation of *philanthropy*, such a child might possess the syntactic and linguistic knowledge necessary to be able to make meaning to accompany the word. Sometimes, once the child has said the word aloud, the word clicks because the child realizes this is a word he has heard before and just has never seen in print.

Other times, the child may not know what the word means, and the word as a whole may be unfamiliar to him, but he may be able to bring his background knowledge to bear on parts of the word. For such a child, the challenge when encountering a hard word is to relate what he sees to what he already knows, and to work with chunks of letters, turning those into sounds.

There will be other children in our classrooms, however, who will be reading words that they have never seen or heard, words that are part of an entire register of vocabulary that is unfamiliar. For these children, it will be harder to sound out words because they'll be less apt to recognize chunks of words. Many of our ELL children will belong in this category of reader, as will the children who have not grown up in a sea of academic language. How important it is for a teacher to understand that the work these children will be doing when they tackle hard words is qualitatively different than the work the first group of children will be doing.

GETTING READY

- Write a short passage that contains a tricky word onto chart paper. (We've selected a passage from *Esperanza Rising*.) Be sure there are context clues that could help an active reader figure out what the word means. Be sure to distinguish the challenging word in some way, maybe by writing it in red as is done in this minilesson.

- Add the word *tormented* to your word wall, if you've opted to use the passage from *Esperanza Rising*. If you've chosen another text, write the tricky word you've selected onto your word wall.

- Find other passages for readers to use to practice substitution strategies. Write them on chart paper and consider making individual copies. These passages will be used in today's conferring component. Look ahead to the conferring session to notice the ways we've chosen passages according to readers' needs.

- If you plan to conduct a small group for word-solving strategies, prepare by reviewing assessment materials in order to identify those children needing the support.

- Post the charts you created in previous sessions that relate to partnerships and partner talk, because today's teaching share calls on children to make choices about their partnerships based on all the work they've done together.

What is the best way to help these children? First, school needs to provide kids with that crucial chance to grow up in a sea of academic language. The entire school day offers invitations to teach vocabulary, and giving kids lists of words to memorize is the last way to do that! The single most important thing you can do is to immerse your classroom community in heady, engaged conversations about the stuff of the world. Read aloud bits of *New York Times* editorials. Discuss the issues that are before Congress. Assign children

> *The single most important thing you can do is to immerse your classroom community in heady, engaged conversations about the stuff of the world.*

to watch the news and discuss it with their families and each other. Channel kids to talk about gravity, inflation, global warming, and immigration during snack time.

Then, too, encourage approximation at all times. My oldest son grew up with an astonishing vocabulary. When I tried to understand why, I noticed that Miles would take words that he met only on the page and incorporate them into his everyday oral language. He read a book called, *The Reluctant Dragon*, and that evening, when I asked if he wanted to play tennis, he responded by saying, "I'm re-luke-you-lant to play because my racket has popped a string." He read in a book about *ominous* storm clouds rolling in and the next morning looked out at the day and said it looked "oh-min-ooose." How crucial it is to celebrate times when children pronounce words incorrectly because they are using words they have seen in print and yet have never heard anyone use in oral language. You can encourage children to take in the words they encounter in print by suggesting they record a few favorite words and keep them on a word card at the corner

of their desks. Encourage them to find any possible entrée for bringing these words into their conversations.

Of course, you'll also want to help children understand the meanings of words that are utterly new to them. A word of warning: Suggesting that children carry and consult dictionaries each time they encounter an unfamiliar word is like recommending that they carry water coolers for each time they get thirsty. This suggestion is potentially effective but cumbersome. This is especially true because the definitions of words contained in dictionaries often end up assaulting learners with yet more hard words.

Your best bet will be to provide kids with direct instruction in the power of context clues as a source of information. You'll tell children who are reading books that contain pictures to rely on the picture as well as the content of the story for help, and to think, "What would make sense?" Once children graduate from books with pictures, you'll shift the advice a bit, suggesting these children "Read around the word," or "Skip the word and come back to it later." Of course, the catchy phrases you use to teach children to rely on their emerging sense of the text's meaning to ascertain what a new word probably means will not be as important as your think-aloud demonstrations. As you read aloud to your class, pause at the hard words and let the children see you figuring them out, making your thinking visible as you consider the context clues that help you do so.

Through your demos, you're essentially saying, "Reading isn't about *knowing* all the words; it is about *figuring* words out as we meet them on a page." It is no coincidence that kids who are ravenous readers have the best vocabularies. These readers attack and conquer any word that gets in the way of their knowing how Jo's family will react when they discover that she's sold her hair for a wig or whether Harry Potter really dies in this book. In this session, you will honor the fact that a few hard words never got in the way of any serious reader, that plunging ahead often provides the context for figuring out the meaning that any single word stands for. After all, that's what readers do: We figure out meaning. No single word is so important in itself that it should get in the way of that!

DRAFT

INILESSON

Learning New Words from Books

CONNECTION

Tell an anecdote about a time you chose between avoiding and confronting a challenge.

"Yesterday, I watched a tiny ant as he made his way across my paper. To see what he'd do, I lay my pencil across his path. I thought he'd climb over it, like one of those monster tractor toys that climb up and go over a hurdle. Instead, the ant turned left, walking patiently along the length of the pencil. My thin pencil felt so high to the ant that he didn't even consider climbing it. Instead, he got sidetracked and started walking in another direction altogether. I felt sorry for the little guy, removed the pencil, and pretty soon, he found his scent trail again and moseyed off in search of lunch."

"I'm telling you this story as an example of what *not* to do in reading. When good readers come across a difficult word, we are not ants that get sidetracked."

Name your teaching point. Specifically, teach children to read on when they encounter a difficult word, knowing that upcoming context clues will help them determine the definition.

"Today I want to teach you that the best readers are like the monster tractors that climb over the hurdle of the hard word and read on, never taking a detour from the trail of the story."

DRAFT

Tell children that readers often read forward in a story to figure out the meaning of an unfamiliar word. Share an example from your own reading experience.

"I know that you already have ways to tackle the hard words you encounter as you read. You know you can look closely at the letters to figure out the word, and even look the word up in the dictionary. You can pause to really notice word roots inside a word and use these to help you. But today I want to tell you that mostly, readers are so dying to find out what happens next in the story that we don't let a single word sidetrack us. We know that reading *forward* will give us a better chance of understanding the word and larger story than reading *backward*."

"Wait a minute!" you might be thinking. You have just announced to the class that the meaning-making strategies that you might have painstakingly introduced in the past are often discarded when a difficult word appears in the text. You're suggesting that engaged readers sometimes don't stop to open dictionaries or pause to sound out words or reread in search of root words that can elucidate the new vocabulary word. This teaching point might appear to negate your previous teaching.

Read on! Previously in this unit, we also taught our kids that meaning isn't contained in any single word, but rather in groups of words. It follows logically that the most engaged readers plow forward. They remain focused on the larger meaning; they're dying to know what happens next. They certainly don't allow the appearance of one difficult word to sidetrack them into pondering specific strategies for decoding that one word.

"This happened to me. My best friend had just finished reading *David Copperfield* by Charles Dickens, and she recommended it to me. Since my friend and I usually have similar taste in books, I decided that I would read it. *David Copperfield* was written a long time ago and it's set in England, so the words and phrases the author uses are very different from what I tend to read. Even so, I liked the story a lot, but sometimes I encountered unfamiliar words that I couldn't define. I had no idea what they meant."

Here I am using an example from my own reading life, which I do frequently. I want children to know that growing as a reader is not something that we do only when we are in third or fifth or, even, twelfth grade. Of course, it will be much more powerful if you cultivate examples from your own reading life. Kids have a way of sniffing out authenticity, and when they sense that we are being insincere, they will sometimes tune out.

"Let me give you an example. The narrator is talking about his aunt who just found out that her husband had died. He says, 'Immediately . . . she took her maiden name again, bought a cottage in a hamlet on the sea-coast a long way off. . . .'"

"I thought, 'bought a cottage in a *hamlet*?' I've only heard of a play called *Hamlet*. I know Hamlet is a character, but that doesn't make any sense here. Hmm."

"I needed to figure out what the word meant, but instead of pausing in my reading and going back, I forged ahead. I decided to read on. While I read on, I carried the question—hamlet?—with me. I was pretty sure I would come upon more of the story that would serve as clues as to what *hamlet* means."

You might want to write the excerpt you choose on a chart so children can see it as you read it. Some of the teachers who piloted this lesson did write their excerpt and found it to be a helpful visual for many children.

"Let's see. Dickens, the author, says that the hamlet was 'on the sea-coast a long way off.' That makes me think a hamlet must be a place, like a town or village. Let me try that. Let me see if *town* makes sense. "Immediately . . . she took her maiden name again, bought a cottage in a *town* on the sea-coast a long way off. . . .' Good! I think I was right. *Town* is a good synonym for *hamlet*." Then, stopping the think-aloud and talking directly to the children, I added "When I got to school today, I double-checked with Mr. Feingold (he knows every word imaginable) and he told me that I was right: *hamlet* is a word for a small town."

"Did you see how I read on when I got to a word I didn't know? I didn't get side-tracked like that ant I told you about. I was a monster truck, working right through the obstacle. I read further, past the word, looking for clues to its meaning, and I found them. Now, if I ever see that word again, I'll know what it means. That's the bonus of reading in this way—you get to learn lots of new words! Just think about it. Your mind can become as filled up with words as a dictionary!"

ACTIVE INVOLVEMENT

Set children up to try this strategy, first trying to use the context clues to figure out the meaning of the unfamiliar, and then sharing and working with a partner.

"Now, you're going to try to read like a monster truck, working with a person sitting beside you. I've written a short passage from *Esperanza Rising* on chart paper. I'd like you to read the passage to yourself, paying special attention to the difficult word I've written in red. Maybe you've seen this word before, maybe not. Don't be totally knocked off track by the hard word. Instead, keep reading on in the story. Go right over the hard word so you can use the context of the passage—the words that come after the hard word—and the context of the passage (Esperanza just found out that her dad died) to figure out what that tricky word could mean. I'll give you a few moments to do this work in your head, and then I'll ask you to turn to your neighbor and share your definition of the tricky word."

The word I used—hamlet—is easy to pronounce. You may decide, in either your teaching example or the readers' practice example, to select a passage containing a word that is difficult to pronounce. In such an instance, you could show the kids how you might try a few different pronunciations. You could then say something like, "I'm not quite sure how this word is pronounced, but, for now, what I really need to figure out is what it means, so that I can understand this part of the story." We do want readers to build sight vocabulary, but in this lesson, we want them to develop their ability to figure out a word's meaning from its context. As children read more and more sophisticated texts, they'll need to be equipped with strategies for dealing with words they can't pronounce.

I've asked children to do this work, retelling, not sharing yet, to provide a space for everyone to do the work. We've all known kids who solve the problem almost instantaneously, and this can prevent other kids from having the time needed to process. By delaying talk time for a moment, we give all children the opportunity to contribute their thinking.

"Where's Papa?" she cried.

Miguel hung his head. Alfonso didn't say a word but the tears running down his round cheeks confirmed the worst.

Mama fainted.

Abuelita and Hortensia ran to her side.

Esperanza felt her heart drop. A noise came from her mouth and slowly, her first breath of grief grew into a tormented cry. She fell to her knees and sank into a dark hole of despair.

I chose an excerpt from Esperanza Rising, a text that is familiar to my students, and I offered a tiny bit of context as a reminder of that part of the story. Unless your students are familiar with Esperanza Rising, you may decide to use a short excerpt from Stone Fox or another text that your students know. The rationale for choosing a familiar text is that it provides the opportunity to not only think of synonyms for a tricky word but it also gives students a chance to think about how that word works in the text itself.

"Readers, after you've read on a little while in the passage, see if you can think of what this word (I gestured to 'tormented') means. Try putting a substitute word into the sentence and thinking about whether it fits. Put your thumb up when you've done that."

I waited a few moments as children did the mental work. As they thought, I called out, "Think about what's going on in this scene. Is this a happy or a sad part? What word could you substitute for the tricky word? Try that out. See how it fits with the rest of the sentence and the whole part."

After a minute I said, "Okay, turn to your neighbor and take turns reading the sentence with your synonym in place of the hard word."

I crouched down and listened in while Lily and Jasmine talked. Lily, the first of the two girls to speak, as usual, said, "I bet it's loud. She's crying loudly."

"Yes, loud, that's it, Lily!" Jasmine replied.

"What made you both think it was loud?" I asked them.

"Cause she made a noise," Lily said, with her customary frankness. "It seems big to me, you know, like when you're so upset it's just a loud sound, like an animal noise."

"Huh. You're onto something there. This isn't a soft cry. How do we know that? What else would describe how Esperanza is feeling in this moment?"

You'll find that some readers grasp the concept of word substitution. If they read about a brown bear ambling down the path, turning its colossal body away from the campsite, the readers can easily plug replacement words into the sentence in place of amble and colossal. Other readers don't know what they are being asked to do, or don't maintain a sense for the whole sentence while working with the puzzling word, and these readers find this very difficult. You'll want to provide some small group instruction to support readers who don't yet grasp how to use substitution when necessary. You could give readers a text with some words underlined, even familiar words, and ask them to provide synonyms for the underlined words quickly, on the run.

Notice how I nudge this partnership to say more. Often children will gesture toward saying something and, with an additional push, will land on more precise words to describe what they're thinking.

"She's sad her dad died," Jasmine said, looking mournful. I gestured for her to say more. "Her heart dropped. It's like she's heartbroken." She clutched her own heart.

"Yes. She's just lost her father. Imagine that kind of heartbreak. I can see that you both are feeling it. So, if you're heartbroken, what's a more powerful word than *loud* that might describe what your cry would be like? That is, what else might a 'tormented' cry mean?"

Lily jumped in and said, "Like a cry . . . a cry you don't cry a lot. Like only when something really, really bad happens to you. Like you're ripped open. Like when I lost my pet rock and starting crying, but then realized that my sister stole it so I cried even harder because that hurt me."

"Look at all the ideas you've generated and the work you've done!" I gave them a thumbs up and called out, "Readers, some of you aren't quite sure how to pronounce the word, and that's okay because the most important thing is that you read *forward*, giving yourself the chance to understand the word and larger part, instead of letting the word get you totally off track."

After a minute I convened the class.

"Readers, eyes up here. As I listened in just now, I heard a few of you acting out what you thought a tormented cry might sound like. That is such a smart idea! I also heard a lot of you give some synonyms for this word. I heard "desperate" and "hurt," and some of you said, "really upset." I even heard one person say, "agonizing." Those are all great synonyms for this word. Now that you know these are some synonyms for the word *tormented*, go back to the passage and find all the clues that let you know that."

Well, they kept her tied up in a chair for two hours while they ransacked the house. They took coats, cloaks, gowns, silk handkerchiefs, silver shoe buckles, a spyglass, two muskets, four halberds, and four hundred fifty pounds of gold, silver, and copper coins.

Here, too, I'm scaffolding this partnership to push their thinking. It doesn't matter so much that these children come up with a perfect synonym for this particular tricky word. More important is that they leave this day's lesson with strategies for how to address—and make sense of—difficult words. They can always look this word up later.

Although Lily's example of losing a pet rock is not akin to the loss of a parent, I know that the experience of this loss—and the further grief brought on by the discovery of her sister's betrayal—was for her, like being "ripped open." Thus, in her own way, she understands the word tormented.

If you have a lot of strugglers in your class, you may opt to have kids practice this strategy using a simpler text. For example, in this passage from Horrible Harry Moves Up to Third Grade, *the children are on a field trip to a museum where they hear a story about a robbery that occurred in a nearby colonial home. The museum guide describes the way the burglars "ransacked" the house and then goes on to describe all the items they stole, which effectively spells out the word's definition. Even though the word itself is tricky, the examples the author provides helps kids understand that "ransacking" means to turn a place inside out, taking everything in sight. Easier books tend to incorporate definitions alongside the tricky word, and more challenging books require readers to draw on larger stretches of text to infer what the word probably means.*

LINK

Remind children that readers read on in a text and use context clues to will help them determine the definition of an unfamiliar word.

Before sending children off, I said, "So, readers, when you are reading and come to a word that you don't know, read on, substitute a word that you think means about the same thing and see if it fits into the sentence, the story.

"You may also want to consider reflecting on your growth so far as a reader in this unit, especially as you look over and fill in your logs to begin the workshop. Perhaps you've notice that you have been reading more each day. Or perhaps your reading rate has increased. You might take note of these things today and reflect on that progress. Off you go."

CONFERRING AND SMALL-GROUP WORK

Teach Readers to Substitute a Familiar Synonym for a Tricky Word and to Figure Out How to Pronounce Tricky Words as Best They Can

Once a unit of study is launched, you'll typically find that you are apt to focus more of your conferences and small groups on children who struggle. One part of this will involve helping readers become more flexible and resourceful as word solvers. You'll want them to have a repertoire of strategies for figuring out tricky words. When readers aren't flexible or when they can't access a variety of strategies for figuring out challenging words, their ability to read an increasingly wide range of books is compromised. In short, it's essential that we are always ready to offer instruction on how to deal with hard words and unfamiliar vocabulary. Some of that instruction will be directed to the whole class during minilessons, mid-workshop teaching, or teaching share time, but more of it will be directed to small groups and individuals during reading conferences and small-group instruction.

To prepare for small-group instruction on word-solving strategies, you will want to look over your assessments so that you identify the children who need this support. You'll want to look for children who mumble when

MID-WORKSHOP TEACHING POINT

Readers Guess What an Unfamiliar Word Means and Then Carry that Word with Us, Letting Our Understanding of the Word Grow

"Readers, may I have your attention for a bit? Eyes and ears both?" Waiting till all eyes were on me, I said, "Right now I'm going to give you a minute to look over your reading and mark a difficult word, any word in your reading that made you stop and feel like that ant stopped by a wall of a pencil; a word that was tricky or confusing." After allowing a minute of silence for readers to locate a problematic word, I invited students to call out a few hard words.

"Respite," shared Ally.

"Vanquish," offered Fallon, her pronunciation slightly off.

"Placid," called out Jasmine, pronouncing it "plack-id."

"Readers, let's repeat our difficult word to ourselves silently." I paused and quietly repeated: "*Respite. Vanquish. Placid,*" allowing the words to hang in the air, before I began speaking again. "Remember, I told you about coming across the word *hamlet.* Although I'd heard it, I didn't know what the word *meant.* So I read on and guessed. I came up with the theory that a hamlet meant a town. And in my reading, I replaced *hamlet* with *town* and read on, making sense. But the *next* day I talked with a friend in school and she said it is a *small* town. I didn't just make a theory, read on, and forget about the word. That word—*hamlet*—kept buzzing like a bee in my bonnet, even after my reading finished. The more I carry a word, the more my understanding of that word grows."

"Today I want to teach you that readers allow words to buzz in our bonnets like bees even *after* we finish reading. We don't just forget a word the minute we guess what it might mean. Instead, we carry our theory about that word, not just in our reading, but also in the world. We pay attention to how that word is used in the world. And—listen to this, it is important—the best readers bravely begin using these words ourselves, in our writing and in our talk. Later today, as you talk to partners, you might share a word or two that's buzzing in your bonnet today."

they encounter difficult words or who skitter past the tricky words when they read. Remember to look at the running records you took when readers were reading too-hard texts. What was it that fell apart for this reader (or that one) first? You'll find that some children could continue up the ladder of text difficulty just fine if you were looking only for accuracy. They continued reading at 97% accuracy long after they stopped being able to retell the text. Those readers will be ones with strong word-solving skills and less strong comprehension skills—and others will be just the opposite. You'll inevitably find that a need for more help with word solving is an equal-opportunity problem. You'll find that some of your strongest readers are stymied by tricky words or in denial about them, in much the same way as your most challenged readers.

If you don't have time to study your students' running records and their spelling inventories, the good news is that early in the year, you won't go too wrong if you cluster readers together according to the levels of book difficulty that they can handle. Most readers who are working in J, K, L, M texts will need help with multi-syllabic words word solving. Most readers working with No, O, P, Q texts will need help with academic vocabulary and with literary language including irony, metaphor, allusions and the like.

Teach Students to Rely on General Sources of Information When They Encounter a Tricky Word

At the start of the school year, you can generally assume that many of your readers who struggle will probably need instruction that teaches them how to rely on meaning (or semantic cues) as they tackle difficult words. The sad truth is that many older readers who struggle will have spent far too much time during previous years holding onto books that are too hard for them, and these readers will probably not trust that pausing to think, "What would make sense here?" is a question that will pay off for them when they get to a tricky word. After all, that question won't pay off if the child has had to skip past huge chunks of the text, creating a Swiss cheese like text. On the other hand, because these readers will now be working with texts they can read with 96% accuracy, they will often be able to rely on sense to help with tricky words. Because these readers were often holding texts that didn't make sense for them many of them will have over-relied on sounding out words, and when they *have* sounded out words, they've done it in isolation, not simultaneously drawing on meaning. When sounding out alone hasn't worked, the students will have tended to keep on reading, even though the threads of comprehension were apt to be frayed at best and breaking down altogether at worst.

So our first priority for readers who struggle to incorporate other sources when decoding is to show them exactly what kinds of books are at their level and where they can find these books in the classroom library. This is absolutely essential for them to make rapid progress. Then, once they've accessed a steady flow of books that they can read with accuracy, fluency, and comprehension, we can teach them that they can, in fact, think about meaning to help them figure out the tricky words in their books.

Kathleen pulled together a group of four children, Gabe included, who tended to work briefly on sounding out tricky words, relying on grapho-

phonics only, and then after giving the tricky words a routine attempt using graphophonics, whipped past them. "Readers, let me begin by being honest with you. I noticed that you might be in a reading rut, and this happens to all readers now and then. Here's what I mean: I noticed that when you get to tricky words in your books, you tend to do the same thing every time, even if it doesn't work. You're in a 'tricky word rut.' When you get to a tricky word, you try your best to figure it out using the letters in the word, but the problem is that doesn't always help. Your work with the letters needs to be combined with another strategy, and that's what I want to teach you today. I want to teach you that when you get to a tricky word, you can look at the letters, but you also have to ask yourself, 'What would make sense?' That is the missing piece that will get you out of your 'tricky word rut.'

"Let me show you what I mean. I'm going to read a sentence that has a tricky word. Watch how I use not only the letters in the word to help me, but also think, 'What would make sense?'" Kathleen uncovered a sentence written on a chart paper that said:

Our next stop was the Baseball Hall of Fame. As we walked around, I learned about so many legendary players from the old days, like Babe Ruth and Mickey Mantle.

Kathleen read the sentence once, pausing at the word *legendary*. She modeled using graphophonics to no avail and kept on reading to the end of the sentence. "Hmm. That didn't make sense. Let me reread to figure out that tricky word." She began again, pausing at *legendary* and using graphophonics again to wrestle with the word. She then said aloud to herself, "What would make sense here?" Kathleen reread: "I learned about so many /l/l/leg players like Babe Ruth. They are obviously amazing and famous. It's some word that means *famous* and *amazing.* Leg. Lej. Legendary. Legendary! That makes sense. Let me reread it to check." Kathleen reread the whole sentence, this time decoding the tricky word and showing with her intonation the sentence now made sense."

"Did you notice, how when I just used the letters of the word, it did-n't help me? I *could* have kept doing that, but then I would have been in a 'tricky word rut.' But did you see when I used the letters AND I thought, 'What would make sense here?' I was able to figure it out?'" "Why don't you to try it. I wrote a little passage on this piece of paper. Let's read it together, and when we get to a tricky word, we'll think about what will make sense, and we'll also pay attention to the letters. I'll coach you."

We woke up in the morning to discover another mess. Our new puppy was naughty again during the night. She must have gotten out of her cage somehow because Mom's favorite plant was knocked over. Dad's slipper looked chewed and the living room rug had a big wet spot. What a mischievous puppy! What were we going to do with her? It looked like time to take her to Obedience School!

The group read the passage chorally. When they got to "naughty" they paused. "Okay readers, give it a go. Don't just look at the letters, but think also about what would make sense. When you figure out the word, give me a thumbs up." As the students worked at the word, Kathleen coached, saying things like, "Does that make sense?" and to another, "Is that a real word?" She prompted a couple of readers by saying, "Start from the begin-ning of the sentence: 'Our puppy had been . . .' What? What would make sense here?"

After a few moments all the students had their thumbs up. Kathleen said, "Let's read it together to check that we're making sense." They read the whole passage chorally.

Then Kathleen said, "So let's remind ourselves of the hard work we just did to get out of the tricky word rut. We got to a tricky word. We looked at the letters and tried to figure the word out by sounding out the start of it. When that wasn't enough, we then thought, 'What would make sense and would sound something like this?' Understanding the passage helped

us. That's total reading. Keep it up, and you'll be out of your tricky word rut in no time!"

Meanwhile, when you work with your more advanced readers, you'll also want to locate a passage that contains some challenges. But for these readers, you might find a passage that is studded with a couple of chal-lenging wordsso there will be several opportunities for the children to use their figuring out muscles. You might, for example, have gone so far as to duplicate a passage such as this one, passing it out to each reader (or each pair of readers) within this small group:

At dinner, Pa cleared his throat and announced that he received his back pay. He said we could go with him to the general mercantile in the morning. "After we buy the pro-visions on Ma's list," he said, "I'll have some pay left." Pa winked at Ma and then looked at us and smiled, "I reckon you can each pick something special."

The next morning, after shopping for Ma's list, Silas found some denim britches to replace the ones with threadbare knees. Mary picked a piece of cloth to make doilies for the parlor tables. I couldn't take my eyes off of the writ-ing set that contained a lovely pen with gold nib, a bottle of ink, and several sheets of fine linen paper.

"Don't dither, Louisa," Pa said to me. "Bring that writing set here so I can settle our account."

Although you will use different texts with your different small groups, the actual work you do with the different groups will not be all that dif-ferent, one group from the next, and the work will resemble the active involvement of today's minilesson. The big difference is that with just a small group of children around you, you can observe and coach them as they work.

Teach Readers to Use Context Clues to Figure Out Tricky Vocabulary

I pulled together a small group of readers who were reading books that I imagined would contain tricky vocabulary. "Readers, I've gathered you together because you're reading the kinds of books that are apt to contain a few tricky words. Books that are set in different eras, different times, often contain tricky words, and books that are set in different places, too, sometimes contain tricky words. I'm especially thinking you might run into words you can read, but you might not understand what they mean. This often happens to me in my books, too. It's a good problem to have, actually, because when you read words you don't know, you learn those words, and you can add them to your own life. Anyway, right now, I want show you what you can do when you get to words that you don't understand."

"We are going to read this text together, paying special attention to the difficult words I've written in red, just like we did in the minilesson. Remember, part of our job as readers is to use the contextual clues to figure out the meaning of the word. We are going to read for a bit and then stop and jot a word that could be a substitute, a possible synonym, for that word. Let's begin reading together aloud. Remember to use your best read-aloud voice. Let's get started."

I flipped over the chart to reveal the practice text I'd written and pointed to the first line with a pointer. I began to read with the group, but stopped so I could listen in as the children were reading. After we had read *mercantile,* I paused.

"Readers, think about what is happening so far. Now, think of a synonym and jot it on your Post-it note." I asked Lily and Jasmine to pass me their Post-it notes. I placed them on the chart above and below *mercantile.* One read *store* and the other read *shop.* "Lily and Jasmine suggested we substitute the words *store* and *shop* for *mercantile.* Right now reread the sentences to see if *store* and *shop* make sense." The children did and agreed that both words did make sense. "Jasmine, can you explain how you two figured that out?"

Jasmine leaned forward on her knees and paraphrased the passage, saying, "The dad got paid so he had money. He was going to go shopping the next day, so we figured mercantile means shop or store. I guessed shop, but store goes better with the word *general.* It's an olden days way of saying store.

"Wow, so the word has *mean* the same thing and *sound* right in the sentence. That's something for the rest of us to think about. Let's reread the sentence and be sure our voices match the meaning. Turn and read the sentence to your neighbor the way you think it should sound."

"Let's read on, thinking about what's happening and making our voices match the meaning." I pointed to the beginning of the passage and we reread chorally. I stopped the readers after the word *provisions* and asked the children to jot possible substitutions on Post-its and again we put two of their suggested words—*supplies* and *food* above and below the difficult word (*provisions*). I again asked children to reread the sentences checking to see if one or both of these suggestions fit. We continued to the end of the text, stopping at *britches, threadbare,* and *doilies* to consider synonyms and again reread, making our voices match the tone of the passage. At the end, I restated the teaching point, reminding readers of the strategy. "Readers, I want you to always remember that when you come to a word you don't know, think about what's going on in the text, and that will help you substitute a familiar synonym—a word that means about the same thing—in place of the hard word. Off you go."

TEACHING SHARE

Readers Pause to Collect New Words to Build Vocabulary as We Read and We Share Our Reading Lives

Offer a way to support children in developing their vocabulary as they read.

"Readers, as you continue to read, I want to encourage you to be like a favorite character of mine called Donavan. He collects words. He writes them down on cards with what they mean and puts them in his word jar." I held up the book *Donavan's Word Jar* so all of the children could see it and continued. "I've put index cards at the center of your tables. Use them to make word cards so you, can carry new words with you. Keep these word cards next to you so you can bring these words into your conversations not just at school but also at home. Instead of keeping these words in a word jar, like Donavan, we'll keep them in our book baggies so we can use them in our conversations whether we are at school or home."

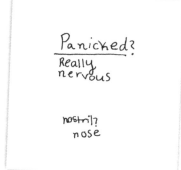

Figure X-1
Post-its where students have marked tricky words and written synonyms

Ask children to share with their partner something about their reading lives and recent reading work.

"Now, let's have you and your partner talk over the reading and reading work you did today. It might involve hard words or it might involve something else. Help each other figure out how to say your hard words, and figure out synonyms for them too."

As children worked, I circulated. I listened as Malik turned to Kobe and, as usual, spoke first: "It took me a while to figure out this tricky word today, so maybe one thing we could do is help each other with tricky words."

Kobe hopped to his knees and leaned in close to his partner and friend. "What word did you get stuck on?" Kobe asked, genuinely interested in Malik's word problem.

"Well, I figured it out," Malik replied proudly. "It was *photographer*."

"Oh," Kobe said. "You didn't know that word? I could have helped you. How'd you figure it out?"

"Well, I realized I knew the first part of the word—*photo*. It means *picture*. As I read on, I realized that someone was out of film. So then, I was like, 'Oh my gosh!' I bet that's a person who takes pictures. And then I knew it was a photographer."

Figure X-2
Post-its where students have marked tricky words and written synonyms

I leaned in and said, "What else could you and your partner do to support each other?" and I moved on to another partnership, Kadija and Issac.

Kadija, as usual, was searching the charts dutifully. "Another thing I'd like to work on," she said. "I don't know about you, Issac—is reading with more feeling. It's like I hear the words in my head, but sometimes they don't sound very pretty. I never really thought about that sort of thing before now." She pointed to the chart "Reading Strong and Long" and read "'Read with feeling so you hear a beautiful read-aloud voice in your head.' Do you have a beautiful voice in your head when you read?"

"Sometimes I do and sometimes I don't," Issac replied. Depends on the book I'm reading. So yeah, I could work on that with you."

"Make a plan for how you'll work on that together," I said. Then I reminded Issac of his plan of collecting a handful of books that he really likes so he can figure out what is just right for him and maybe he could recruit Kadija's help.

Once You've Matched Kids to Books, Now Your Assessments Must Be Personalized

omewhere in the middle of your first unit of study, your assessments will turn a corner. Until now, the need to calculate each child's 'just right' reading level will have been all consuming, leaving you with few assessment choices. But now that you have conducted running records on each of your children, for at least a window of time, your path as an assessing teacher is yours to fashion. Although you're apt to breathe a sigh of relief, thankful that the start-of-the-year assessments are behind you, don't catch your breath for too long, because now the deeply personal part of assessment will begin.

Make Your Assessment System Feel Like It Is Yours: Choose Your Priorities and Then Collect Data that Helps You Keep Your Eyes on Goals that Matter to You

From the very start of the year on, you will want to collect data that holds you accountable to goals that you each believe are important. There a number of key concepts in that sentence; let's look at the words that constitute this sentence and the concepts they crystallize. Let's look at the notion that '*you want*' to collect '*data*' that holds '*you* 'accountable and let's look at the idea that this is '*towards goals you believe are important.*'

"You will want to collect data that holds you accountable to goals that you each believe are important."

Let's start with what might sound like a preposterous idea. Could I truly be saying that '*you want*' to collect data? I think so, and there are a number of reasons why I think this. First, the emphasis on data based instruction is not going to go away. The question only is who gets to define the data that is counted, collected and valued, and I always think that it is better to be an active agent rather than a passive victim. If you and I start the year collecting and analyzing and learning from data, then we

are proactively contributing to the way data is being used to inform instruction, and to look at teaching and learning. More than this, research has shown that most of us actually do benefit from crystal clear goals, from concrete ways to gauge our progress, from a feeling that we can work with resolve to improve ourselves and then check in to see if systems are working, to self-correct when they aren't. Think about it—people who want to lose weight are channeled into systems where we count, we weigh, we chart, we note good days, bad days, we give ourselves pats on the back, scoldings. People who want to exercise more, run faster, play the video game with more finesse…subject ourselves to regiments that include keeping tabs on our progress. Why would we not want to keep an eye on our progress as teachers of reading?

"You will want to conduct data that holds you accountable to goals that you each believe are important."

Most of us, as teachers, feel unbelievably alone in our teaching. We go into our classroom, close the doors, and teach, knowing full well that the decisions we make, the actions we take have consequences that reverberate throughout children's lifetimes. We sometimes marvel that anyone could possibly believe that we have the knowledge it takes to actually make the decisions that are left in our hands. Should I allow this child to read this big fat book that she's clutching to her chest, or should I wrest it from her grasp, replacing it with an easier book? Should I regard this as the child's just-right level because he did alright on the assessments although I know full well that he loses comprehension when reading book-length texts at this level of difficulty? Is it really that harmful for this kid to mouth the words to himself as he reads, 'cause even when I suggest he stop, I still look over and see his lips moving? Should I continue to harp on that or shift my emphasis to support engagement in the content? What about the kids would are comprehending really well when they read silently, but messing up quite a few words when they read aloud—if they can still comprehend, does accuracy matter all that much? We can't help but think, "Shouldn't a Roving Expert cycle through all the classrooms in this world, telling us the right answers to the millions of questions that keep rising to the surface of our teaching?"

Of course, even if we luck out and find someone who can help us think through one handful of questions, other questions then rise to the surface. It is the nature of our profession that we will always be in situations that require judgment, and we will constantly need to go out on the thin ice of speculation, of conjecture, relying on whatever sources of information we can call upon, and on our best-guess intuitions.

But the good news is that we can check out those decisions, getting the feedback we need to know if our decisions help or hurt, as long as we get ourselves into the habit of collecting objective data that talks-back to our teaching, that confirms or questions our decisions, that gives us green lights and red lights—not summative ones, at the end of the year, but signals that act more as traffic signals, guiding our progress day to day. It is by collecting data and tracking progress on indicators that we especially value that we give ourselves a live-in coach, counseling us on what works, what doesn't work, in this particular situation.

"You will want to conduct data that holds you accountable to goals that you believe are important."

And what about the idea that we want to collect data that *holds us accountable*? To me, this is the one most concept of all. You and I want to collect data that hold US accountable. That is, this is not about counting and charting *how the kids are doing*. This is about us, and our teaching. We are counting and charting indicators that tell US how WE are doing. This is the most transformational idea of all.

The other day, a principal said to me, "It's interesting—I looked over the school's data and last year, the kids all went up a level in the fall, and they basically stayed the same in the spring." The principal made some joke about spring fever, and changed the topic of conversation. Later, I kept replaying the conversation over and over in my mind. It wasn't the observation itself that so struck me—that is, in fact, a pattern we've identified across many schools and is certainly one worth thinking about carefully. But no, what struck me was the distinct sense

I got that the principal felt this was a comment on the kids, on the nature of their learning curves, and the assumption was that it was outside his control. We collect data because that data functions as a mirror, allowing us to see ourselves. The bit of data that principal shared—the kids progress in the fall and flatline in the spring—clearly should create dissonance for that principal. Does test prep get in the way of progress in reading? Does the school support teachers engaging in running records in the fall and not provide similar supports for assessments in the spring, allowing kids to languish longer than they should at certain levels? Is there an emphasis on reading with volume in the fall, and perhaps that gives way to an emphasis on writing about reading, later in the year—and might the latter chase time away from reading and therefore slow progress?

That principal's comment is similar to remarks I hear all the time. "I've got a tough class this year. About a third of them won't read at home no matter what I say and their attention spans in school are like five or ten minutes." "Jane—oh yes, Jane. She has terrible comprehension. She's literal—totally literal. She doesn't infer anything. She just calls out the words." "He's an ELL so he mostly just looks at the pictures during reading time." I listen to these comments, and think to myself that if there was just one single gift I could give the teacher who talks in these ways about kids, it would be a firm, crystal clear belief that she is accountable for her kids' work. Until she grasps that her kids' work reflects her teaching, she'd denying herself the education of a lifetime.

My larger point is that collecting data, alone, doesn't add up to much—what matters is that we see the details we collect as OUR data, reflecting on OUR actions, providing feedback on OUR decisions, and we realize those actions and decisions can be accelerated or altered as of this minute, with the hope that the next round of data collection will show something different.

"You will want to conduct data that holds you accountable to goals that you each believe are important."

Finally, we need to collect data on goals *we believe are important*. So often, teachers are told to value goals that *others* deem significant. We resent that we are expected to fix our eyes firmly on the all-important test scores and want to cry out that we did not choose a career in teaching because we wanted our life work to be helping kids become more adept at bubbling in answers to multiple-choice questions. We want to scream that teaching kids how to understand questions that are worded "Which of these is not a good title…" is not the goal we want to live towards. We want to tell politicians who expect us to spend every minute of the year banging away on work that represents end-of-the-year standards that the only way to get there is through interim assessments tailored to the child. We become adept as forging passive aggressive relationships to the goals other people have for our teaching. "Okay, okay, you want me to post goals around our classroom that don't matter one wit to me?" we think. Fine. I'll do so, but I'll roll my eyes at the entire enterprise. "You want me to slap standards up alongside the work on our bulletin boards, to label that work as a 1 or a 2 or whatever you want—when I know intimately, exactly, precisely what this work does and does nor represent for the child who made it? Fine. You're paying me. I'll slap those standards or those number gauges all over the place. But don't think that a system that makes me post someone else's' goals and standards will make we live or teach towards your paperwork. I'll be collecting data in ways that resemble the tariffs, collected during medieval times for the distant landlord.

I know this script. I've heard spectacular teachers crying out these anguished pleas. And another time, I will write about the consequences I've seen when our teaching is racked by those feelings. For now what I want to say is that although I understand those pleas, I think it is better to try to turn ones back to the storm, to fix our attention elsewhere. When we get ourselves all worked up in resistance to what is done to us in the name of data-based instruction, then we deny ourselves the chance to reclaim assessments and to use them to help us achieve goals that we believe are important.

Even in a school whose very existence depends upon improved scores, there is no need to live and die for test-scores. The truth is, you can fix your gaze on entirely different goals and the test scores will follow, as day follows night (and I'll discuss those other goals that will yield strong test scores as a byproduct in a moment.) What is not okay is to give up on the idea that your teaching is all about achieving goals. It is not okay to plan teaching by thinking, 'What will fill up our time today?' and "What neat activities could be do that would be fun?' Powerful teachers have goals that are as important to us as life itself,

and those goals are all about the kids. We live for those goals; we think about them constantly; we look at everything through the lens of those goals. We drive ourselves and our kids towards those goals, and let them vitalize every moment of our teaching. What is not important is to let go of the urgent, goal-driven teaching.

Nor is it okay to give up on the notion that good teaching produces results. It just, simply, does. Read the study that Allington and Pressley did on proficient teachers.

Look at Allington's summary of that research in the article, "What I've learned about effective reading instruction from a decade of studying exemplary elementary classroom teachers" published in Phi Delta Kappan. Look at the tower of research that is now showing with crystal clarity: effective teaching is the most research-based strategy for improving achievement available. So yes—your teaching, if it is effective, will result in results, and those will be results that you can count and graph.

This of course brings home the question: what are the results that will pay off, that are worth counting and graphing? Each of us will have some of our own answers to this question—and it is important we pause long enough to get in touch with what we actually do believe matters, as our teaching will be enriched immeasurably if we teach from our own convictions, passions, and priorities, and collect and hold ourselves accountable to data we trust. Each teacher need not bring the same priorities to the teaching of reading—for one person, it is absolutely crucial that readers read as writers, noticing the craft decisions that a writer has made. For another teacher, it is crucial that readers read critically, paying attention to characters who have been silenced and to values that are embedded in texts and realizing they can read against the grain, bringing out voices of silenced characters and questioning values with which they disagree. If young people are lucky, they'll study with teachers who are not all the same, and different teachers will contribute their voices and values to the child's development.

On the other hand, those of us with responsibility to teach reading need to teach not just from our own personal passions but also from a research base. The good news is that there is research that tells us a few things that are important for growing readers—and better yet, the research really does not show anything that common sense doesn't support. If you want to learn in a nutshell what the research says about proficient teachers, look to the Allington article mentioned earlier.

Allington starts with this claim. The effective teachers in his study had "a reading and writing versus stuff ration that was far better than that which is typically found in elementary schools." These teachers had kids actually reading and writing for as much as 50% of the school day. In many classrooms, Allington points out that a 90-minute 'reading block' produces only 10-14 minutes of actual reading. Kids in the classrooms of effective teachers did as much as four times more actual reading and writing than kids in classrooms of less effective teachers.

Allington's second claim is that in the classrooms of effective teachers, there is a rich supply of books that kids can actually read. "Simply put, students need enormous quantities of successful reading to become independent, proficient readers."

It is important that kids read texts they can read with fluency, accuracy (96%) and comprehension, that they have access to books they believe are interesting, to books they want to read.

It is important that kids progress so they can read increasingly challenging texts—there are guidelines that suggest the level of text difficulty that kids should generally be expected to read well at different grade levels but if a reader is not where we wish he or she was, the only way forward is by progressing steadily up the gradient of text difficulty. It is important that kids can bring a sense of text structure to what they read, anticipating how different kinds of texts tend to go, and that they develop increasingly broad taste as readers, enjoying an increasing range of kinds-of-texts. It is important that they develop more proficiency with skills such as monitoring for sense, envisionment, prediction, inference, determining importance, interpretation, synthesis, and critical reading. It is important that readers can learn from texts, including learning vocabulary as well as world knowledge and literary knowledge, and that they can think between life experiences and texts. It is crucial that readers see themselves as increasingly proficient as readers, and that they choose to read, initiating reading in their own lived lives.

Yes, it is also important that kids show what they can do on standardized tests, but generally, if we as a profession keep our eyes on the real goals in teaching that will be a side-effect of our teaching. If it ever happens that we've taught towards all that we believe matters and we've stood on the shoulders of the research base, and yet our youngsters are not doing well on the state standardized test, then it is important to deconstruct that test with enormous care, looking between it and our teaching and our kids' work in order to ascertain what could be getting in way of our kids' progress on that standard of measurement. There are a few predictable answers to that question, and I address these in the chapter on standardized reading tests in *The Guide to the Reading Workshop*.

Make Every Effort to Mitigate the Hurt that Your Assessments Can Cause

Before you embark on assessment work that will be your focus during the second half of this first unit of study, you need to be mindful of the power that you and your assessments wield. Think of times in your life when you have been assessed, and for just a moment, focus on times when another person's assessments have belittled you in ways that continued to haunt you years later. In his beautiful and important book, *Choice Words*, Peter Johnston helps us understand that when we assess youngsters, we help them create identities for themselves. Teaching reading, then, involves teaching not just strategies but also roles, self concepts, identities….and those identities are more enabling or disabling than any strategy we could possible teach. Johnston writes,

> "When authors write novels, they create characters—people who say this sort of thing, do that sort of thing, and relate to people and things in those sorts of ways….This is not just what authors do, it is what people do with themselves (Bruner 1994a, 1994b, Harre and Gillet, 1994, Mischler, 1999, Randall 1995) They narrate their lives, identifying themselves and the circumstances, acting and explaining events in ways they see as consistent with the person they take themselves to me…..

He goes on to say,

> The way we interact with children and arrange for them to interact shows them what kinds of people we think they are and gives them opportunities to practice being those kinds of people. We provide them with what James Gee calls an "identity kit."

Once we have determined the level of text that each of our children can handle with ease, the challenge is to determine how we will talk about this information in ways that mitigate the damage done by assessments that essentially rank kids, with some falling into low categories, some high. A guiding principle is that when possible, it helps to talk about proficiency in reading as the result of experience and personal choice, and not as part and parcel of a person's identity.

Although it is hard to deny that the assessment system I've described slot readers into a reading hierarchy, with all the problems that poses, it is up to you how you will talk about the assessments, and the language and tone you use around them can make the world of difference. I recommend you think of the assessment system as a system for organizing the classroom library more than as a way to rank children. Consider an analogy, for a moment: the trails of a ski mountain. Some people haven't been out on the slopes for a while and therefore choose to ski the green dot trails—the dot signals that they'll be great trails for cruising down the mountain. Some are blue circle. They are more challenging, and better suited to more experienced travelers. The trails over there….Whoa! They are black diamond. Unless you are really experienced and have skied tons of those blue-circle trails, you risk your life going that way. Travel that direction with someone at your side, and when the other conditions are all with you. Let us know that you are going that way before you set off and if you take too long, we'll send a rescue team after you."

Your message can be similar in reading. Just as you suggest that only the most experienced skiers can tackle the black diamond trails, you've convey a similar message about the levels of text difficulty that are beyond reach for three quarters of your class. And some of your students will not have invested much time in reading yet, so those readers will want to look for the green-dot reading trails, where they can cruise along. "Some of you have not yet figured out how to get lots of books around you when you're at home, so you haven't done that much reading. You're going to find yourself more of a novice, and so for now, you'll want to read the books where you can really sail along—try these books with an orange dot, and a L or an M on the spine (the M's are a bit harder so try to start with the K's but either will probably be smooth sailing.) After you read a ton of those books, you'll going to be saying, "I'm ready for a challenge." When you've got lots more books under your belt, you'll be reading these N books—that might even be by Halloween, if you read a ton between now and then. You should aim for that 'cause there are some terrific books in the N bin."

Just as there are ways of talking that are helpful, there are also ways of talking about children that are best to avoid. It isn't helpful, for example, to accentuate the hierarchical aspect of matching kids to books by referring to group of kids as "My J-K readers" or "The U-V Kids." Even the slightest turn of the phrase helps—the phrase, 'Kids who are reading J-K books' suggests that temporarily, these kids are doing something similar (reading J-k books) rather than that these kids are this certain kind-of-readers. But in general, it's best to not identify groups of children through the level of text difficulty they are reading. The basal reading groups of yesteryear—the bluebirds, the sparrows—can be dressed up in new names —-the JK readers, the UV— readers—and the damage will be just as debilitating. Always pause for a moment and consider what it would feel like for you if your schools labeled teachers, and regularly called you to participate in the meetings that were only for the J-K teachers, with the L-M, N-Q and UVW teachers met in other rooms. Sometimes ways of talking that are initially intended as short-cut abbreviations and as handy ways to communicate become sources of unbelievable damage. We human beings are fragile, and none of us fare well when labeled.

Having said this, I do not think that attempting to mask levels of text difficulty help. I don't argue for hiding the letter of difficulty inside the front cover of a book rather than affixing it to the spine anymore than I recommend wrapping all books in brown paper bag covers or suggest strugglers hold *Harry Potter* and then set their *Frog and Toad* book inside that mighty tomb. I do not believe it helps to take children into deep corners of the room whenever talking with them about the texts in which they're apt to feel most at home as readers. First—none of those efforts to disguise the hierarchical nature of levels of text difficulties will work. The kids have eagle eyes and will quickly figure out what's going on. But more importantly, it does not help to act as if children should be ashamed of the amount of experience they've had as readers. Human beings are not all the same. Some of us can carry a tune, others haven't had a lot of help with singing and we marvel at what those to the right and left of us can do, and join in as best we can. Some people can draw horses so they look ready for a show; others of us make horses that look like sick cows. Some people can do tricks on a skateboard—others have never been on one, and would probably die getting from here to the corner. That's life. We get good at what we work on, and some people are just this year starting to work on their reading. It'll change really fast—you'll see. Meanwhile, anyone up for some skateboarding lessons?

Put Your Assessments to Use by Guiding Readers to Books They're Apt to Like and Creating Partnerships that are Apt to Be Supportive

How crucial it is for us to get into the habit of using assessments to guide our work—starting straight away. The first important way in which you'll do this is that you will use assessments to help you put books in your kids' hands that will be spell-binding for them, and you'll talk up those books in ways that draw kids towards them. When observing readers at work, we always think about whether those readers are drawing on many sources of information—and this is equally important for you to do. So when matching kids to books, draw on what you know about the levels of text difficulty that the reader is apt to handle well, but draw on more information that that, alone! Look for indications of interest, and consider even conducting a very quick survey to help you collect that information efficiently, from every child. Try questions such as this: Put several stars beside the books on this list you'd be most apt to like, fewer stars beside the runner-ups, and also show ones you'd probably not like at all.

Would you rather read…

- a slapstick, funny story about a wacky kid who gets into hilarious mishaps
- a fast-paced action story where one thing, another, another happens at breakneck speed.
- a mystery story that is written in such a way that you can practically find and put together clues alongside the detective, figuring out the answer to the mystery
- a beautiful story about relationships between kids, and perhaps kids and animals, that has sad parts that really get through to you, and happier parts too.

- a story that feels like it was written for readers who want to pay attention to the details, putting things together a bit like one puts together a puzzle, only this adds up to a whole world of relationships, adventures, and life-lessons
- a story that has lost of information and facts welded into it, so you read the plot but meanwhile you are learning about some new content—like life in that time and place, or life in the out-of-doors, or this particular topic/animal/sport/hobby.

When combining children into partnerships, it helps to think about putting children together who are apt to like the same books and to enjoy talking together. Oftentimes partnerships will be 'swap book partners.' Perhaps the two readers will decide to read Gary Paulsen books, and one reader starts with Woodsong, the other with The River. Then the readers will switch books. This means that often when talking about books, they'll be familiar with the book the other partner is reading.

Your assessments will help you to create partnerships that are aligned not only by the level but also by interest, and they will help you to channel high-interest books towards readers (and partnerships). In time, you will work to broaden each child's reading preferences, but at the start of the year, you'll use your assessments to make it as likely as possible that the students in your class read with engagement and pleasure.

Develop Informal Assessment Tools and Systems that Help You Track Goals that Matter to You

As I've said, from the very start of the year on, you will want to conduct data that holds you accountable to goals that you each believe are important. Of course, you and I could easily fill an entire wall of the classroom with lists of all the things that are important to us, but the art of teaching well requires that we are able to establish priorities, and this is never more important than at the start of the school year. Of all that matters to us, what matters most, and what matters first?

Assess Engagement

For me, my first priority in the teaching of reading will be that readers read with engagement. When I work as a staff developer, helping teachers teach reading well, one of the first things I try to do is to show teachers how easy and how crucial it is to simply step back in the midst of reading time and to scan the room, looking for evidence of engagement and disengagement. Time and again I'll say to the teacher, "Let's just look around the class and count how many kids, at this moment, are eyes-on-print, nose-in-book reading." This can be a sobering measurement. Sometimes, our instinct is to say, "Oh, but he's writing about reading." "Aw—she's choosing a new book, she'll be reading soon." "He's deciding what to read next." But the truth is, engaged readers will for the most part spend reading time, reading. If you and I were given forty minutes a day to return to a novel we'd been reading, and if the book was a splendid one, one that we'd gotten deeply engaged with, then during those forty minutes, we'd be glued to the book. The kid who takes ten minutes to sharpen her pencil so she can etch a few words out on a post-it that has been carefully lined up at the very bottom of a page, then adjusted so that it is less crooked….that child is taking that sort of time to record thoughts on the post-it because she is not engaged in reading.

Some teachers make this record of engagement more formal. If you have a student teacher or a teacher's aide, you may literally ask that extra person to take an official reading every ten minutes of which child from your class roster is engaged in reading, and which is not. The observer could have a whole coding system to record what the alternate activities are—is it writing about reading that is consuming reading time, is it talking that consumes time, day dreaming, or what? Then again, perhaps that is somewhat beside the point—and what you really want is simply an indicator of which kids are usually be engaged in reading, and which aren't….and what's your score for the class as a whole, this week. Next week?

There are other quick ways to take a count of this. Try this. Say to your children, "Readers, will you finish what you are reading right away and come to the meeting area?" Then scan the room to see how many children do as they've been told, snapping their books shut immediately—they'll be the disengaged readers! Look to see how many defy you and continue reading, at least to the bottom of the page, the end of the chapter (it is just another page) even going so far as walking to the meeting area, nose still in the book. That's engagement. Record what you see, and value it, and work with the children involved to help them know these indicators matter, and that this illuminates goals that could make the world of difference.

Similarly, watch for how long it takes kids to get themselves started reading at the beginning of a reading workshop. How many minutes pass by from your send off—"You can get started on your reading"—to the moment when the child is actually reading? That's another clear sign of engagement.

Ask your readers to let you know, on a scale of 1-10, how much they like their books, or how well they enjoyed that day's reading. Give children some free time to do any sort of school-related work they choose, and note how many choose to read. Again—keep your data. Record it, even if—especially if—it is depressing data. You'll get a really high two weeks from now when data suggests that on this most crucial quality of engagement in reading, you have already made palpable, observable, quantitative progress.

The important thing is that this sort of data takes on power if you collect it in a standardized way *over time*. Asking children to let you know how much they like their books or how well they enjoyed reading really is not all that interesting (some children are just prone to never waxing glowingly about anything) until you collect this sort of information over time. Think of how your teaching might change if you set out to alter those indicators—if you said, at the start of the week, I'm going to record observations three times a day of my students' engagement in reading, and see if I can't, by the end of the week, have a dramatic upswing in that engagement. How would your teaching change if your own sense of self-worth as a teacher was based on your ability to raise the scores—not on those standardized tests that come nine months from now and always seem somewhat out of your control, but on indicators that are right here, before your eyes, and very much within your control?

Assess Time Spent Reading and Progress Through Books

Chances are good that when you think of first things first, you will decide to value not just engagement in books, but time spent reading, and progress through books. Certainly the research is extremely clear that kids who read a lot will do better on all indicators (and here's one place where common sense and the research especially align themselves). Because this is such an important standard of measurement, my colleagues and I practically insist that any school in which we're working do the hard work necessary to make reading logs into viable instruments. I'll discuss the use of reading logs throughout many of these assessment write-ups, as these continue to be an important source of data across the entire year.

The idea of the log is that each child in each classroom in each grade (starting grade 2) logs the date, place (home/school), minutes, pages, titles, and levels of texts read on a Reading Log. There are sample forms on the CD. Most teachers find it helps to compile these logs into a two pocket folder, as the compilation of logs is a more substantial tool and more apt to be valued by kids. On the other hand, doing this makes it entirely possible for readers to lose weeks of data instead of just days of it, so some teachers devise other systems.

Certainly if a log is going to work in your class, you will want each reading workshop to begin with each child whipping out his or her log, filling in the data, title, starting page, starting time, and then each child keeps that log on the desk during reading each reading time, and at the end of reading time, the child fills in the ending time, ending page number, and perhaps the total minutes and pages read. You can decide whether the log is sent home for children to record in a similar way at home, or whether the records of home reading are recorded in school with the reading log remaining in school. That is, if yesterday Sari finished reading at page 110, today she is resuming reading at page 154, Sari therefore can fill in (while in school) that at home, she read p.110-154.

Actually training students to maintain these logs is not a small matter. Any parent who has tried to instill habits in his or her son or daughter can tell you that it takes consistent follow up over time in order to shape a child's life in such a way that certain things become habitual. How many times has the parent said, "Time for bed. Go brush your teeth," or asked, "Did you brush your teeth?" Instilling in children the habit of recording the number of minutes and pages read requires a similar amount of diligence, especially during the first few weeks of school. Become accustomed to watching as kids leave the meeting area, go to their seats, and get started reading. Do they begin by pulling out their reading log and recording the time and the starting page number? When reading time is over, do children as a matter of course take a second to record the page on which they stopped reading and the number of minutes read?

You'll find yourself taking the time to cultivate habitual record keeping on reading logs if you find yourself using those logs—so use them! Don't wait. The first way to use them is to check out the number of pages a minute the child seems to be reading. If you glide past a child's desk after fifteen minutes of the reading workshop, you can use the child's log (that is, the record of the page on which the child started that day's reading) and a quick glance at the page on which the child is reading right now to calculate how many pages the child has read in those fifteen minutes. The general rule of thumb is that usually a child should be able to read approximately ¾ of a page a minute (yes, the pages vary in length, but children's speed should be increasing as their pages become denser). So if you see that a child has read four pages in fifteen minutes, there should be cause for concern. Check back on other days—right there, on the log, you'll see a record of how many minutes the child had to read yesterday, and the day before, and you'll see a corresponding record of the number of pages read on those days as well. If you see that it is a pattern that the child is progressing slowly, then you and the child can talk about this, do an inquiry together, and set out a plan to change matters—tomorrow and the next day, with the child joining you in researching this. This is what data based instruction means—seeing a pattern in data across two or three days, letting that pattern lead you to look a bit more closely, sharing what you see with the learner right away, making tentative theories for how to address any problems…and being ready to watch the continued stream of new data.

I've mentioned that you can use logs to note the amount of time that a child takes to read a single page, and of course it will be equally or more important to look at the amount of time a child spends reading. One of the most important things you can look for in the logs is honesty. If you assign half an hour a night of reading homework and your readers dutifully record that they've read that exact amount each night—if each child reads 30 minutes, no more and no less—then you better worry! After all, you know for sure that this will not actually be the case. Some nights a particular child will be otherwise busy and not get a lot of time for reading, and other nights (hopefully) a child might be involved enough in a book that he or she reads beyond the requisite amount. Your goal for now must be that kids value accurate and precise data, and actually record the true story of their home reading lives in these logs. This means that when you have assigned 30 minutes a night of reading and you sit with a child whose log suggests she only read for 12 minutes, your response must be to appreciate the precise, scientific record, and to wonder, with the child, what may have informed the data.

Of course you will not want to settle for children never having the requisite time for reading, so yes, you absolutely need to use data to remind you that there are children with whom you need to talk about time for reading. Just make sure that you and the child are in solidarity over this, working as a team to think about ways the child can find ways to shoehorn more reading into his or her life. If you pressure the child too much, the data will all become a mirage, so by all means stay clear of doing that.

In all of these matters, it will be very important for you to get baseline data, even if that data is not showing that the child's engagement in reading, pace as a reader, or time spent reading is close to what you'd like to see. Remember that your responsibility is to help the child outgrow himself, herself, and to be able to show the child that he or she can grow and change and learn. If the baseline data is less than perfect, the one good thing about this is that it will be easier for you to show the child and others, including the child's parents and your administrator, that over time there has been growth.

Assess Readers in Need of Extra Attention

Before September is over, you're going to want to take special note of children who need extra attention. Your at-risk readers are going to need a more complete assessment, and this will almost surely involve using other assessment tools in addition to running records in order to disentangle the factors that are combining to make success elusive for this child.

Start with interest inventories. Ideally you'll be able to give all your readers such an inventory, asking questions such as, "What has been the best book you've ever read?" and "What do you like to do when you have time for fun stuff?" and "Has a teacher ever read you a book that you really liked?" and "If you were going to read one of these books (showing the child a stack of possibilities), which you appeal to you the most?" You'll need this information as quickly as possible so that you can move heaven and earth to make reading into the best it can be for each of your children who struggle with reading.

Then you are going to want to do the investigative work necessary to try to understand what's going on for the reader. You can tell from analyzing the running record that you took especially when the child was working at frustration level (not collecting the running record, but analyzing it) what the patterns are in the child's miscues. Chances are good that you'll see that the child either struggles with phonics (and accuracy) or the child struggles with comprehension (relying too much on phonics and not blending word work with attention to meaning or the type of word using sentence structure.) If the child struggles with phonics, you will want to give the child a spelling inventory, which is essentially a spelling test that aims not to determine whether a child can spell a word right or wrong so much as to figure out the child's developmental level as a word solver. Many of the teachers I know rely on the spelling inventory from Donald Bear's *Words Their Way*—this tool is on the Teachers College Reading and Writing Project website, with the directions necessary to use this in order to learn what aspects of phonics your child is using and confusing, and what aspects are well beyond the child's reach. Once you have determined what the child can do, and can almost but not quite do, then you can begin providing the child with the phonics and word-solving help that is exactly tailored to his or her needs. You'll want to reassess within a few weeks. Children who struggle with phonics profit enormously from increased time writing, and encouragement to draw on all they know about words as they invent spellings that will, over time, reflect their growing knowledge of letters, sounds, onsets and rimes.

If the child's struggles are with comprehension, not phonics, then you'll want to make sure that you are giving the child book introductions whenever possible. You'll want to engage the child in book talks constantly, to be sure you increase the quality and quantity of read-aloud experiences, to be sure children are orienting themselves to a book before reading it, stopping after reading chunks in order to recall the book, monitoring for sense and using strategies to fix up problems. As the year unfolds, you'll be able to research these youngsters more completely, but for now, you absolutely will want to do some extra listening to try to understand how you can tap into these learners/ interests, and begin to at least differentiate instruction based on whether this child is a learner who needs more help with phonics, or one who needs more help with comprehension.

DRAFT

Bringing Together Reading Lives, Texts that Matter, and Partners

PART THREE

Reading in the Company of Partners

IN THIS SESSION,
you'll teach children that readers help ourselves to build a reading life by working with other readers.

or a moment, think about your own independ-ent reading life. Now ask yourself, "How *inde-pendent* is my independent reading life? Did anyone recommend that last book I read? Did I talk about it with anyone? Lend it to anyone?" My hunch is that you'll quickly realize "independent reading" is actually "*inter*de-pendent reading." Alan Purves goes so far as to say, "It takes two to read a book." For me, it is true that the books that have mattered most to me are those that I have shared. And certainly, conversations and relationships are combed through all that I do and all that I am as a reader.

I would go so far as to say that most of what I do to teach comprehension is to teach kids to have conversations with others so they will learn to hold similar conversations in their own minds as they read. After finishing a shared book, two readers convene and one says, "That was a weird ending." The next agrees and muses over why the author decided to end it that way. The two readers start proposing different endings, weighing which is best. Another day, when one of these readers is alone with a book, she comes to the ending and says, in her mind, "Another weird ending." And then, because she recalls pursuing that line of thought in a con-

GETTING READY

- Prior to today's lesson, divide your class into long-term reading partnership relationships. Partners need to progress in sync through shared books, so take into consideration the levels of difficulty that partners can read, their reading interests, and their rate and volume of reading.

- Perhaps you'll communicate the partnership assignments when you convene children in the meeting area. You can write each partner's name on a card "tent" and use them to direct each reader to his or her new assigned spot in the meeting area. If you do this, write a large 1 beside one partner's name and a 2 beside the other's name, because you'll often ask just Partner 1 or just Partner 2 to do something.

- Rally a colleague, or perhaps a child, to participate in this minilesson with you. This person will ask you questions about your reading life. Set up the interviewer; he or she needs questions to ask, needs to be careful to listen well, and then should ask follow-up questions.

- As on other days, remind children to bring their "My Reading Life" folders to the meeting area. Today you will ask that they jot questions they plan to ask their reading partners, so you'll be glad that these folders contain paper on which children can jot ideas and that the children keep a pen tucked into one of the pockets of their folders.

- Either prepare to distribute sheets containing interview questions in the midst of the minilesson or write an enlarged version on chart paper.

- Create a chart titled, "Questions We Ask to Get to Know a Reading Partner" that offers readers tips for interviewing. You'll reference this chart during the teaching component.

- Create a chart titled, "Tips for Interviewing a Reader" for use in the teaching and teaching share sections.

versation, she begins the process of musing over why the author selected this particular ending rather than any others. "Maybe he wanted to show that...," she thinks. Then, talking back to that idea, she adds on, "Or perhaps it's that....." The work of thinking about a book is very much like holding an internalized conversation with oneself.

> *The best way to get reading partnerships off to a strong start is to make time and space for kids to get to know each other as people and as readers.*

This session spotlights the fact that independent reading is not independent at all. The content of the session is important, but the much more important thing is that this session marks the start of a new structure: partnerships. The partner relationships that you launch today will shape your children's experiences as readers throughout the upcoming year. Starting today, your readers will not travel through books alone. In time, these partnership relationships will undergird an even more complex social relationship: reading clubs.

It would be ideal if members of each partnership could always read from duplicate copies of the same book, progressing through the books together. We call those "same-book partnerships," and there is no question but that this is an ideal arrangement. What grand conversations these children can have! There are, however, very few classrooms that contain duplicates of every book, so chances are, the best

you can do is suggest that members of a partnership take turns reading books. We refer to these as "swap-book partnerships."

When children are in swap-book partnerships, the partnership often takes on a kind of book, such as books by Gary Paulsen or horse books. To get ready to read together, the two partners both fill their book bins with books the two of them have chosen that fall into the selected category. When one child finishes one of these books, it goes into the partner's bin. This means that when partners meet to talk about books, often the two of them will have both read the book under discussion, just not at the same time.

You should expect that children will meet to talk with partners during the last five minutes of almost every workshop. In another month or two, you'll alter some of the partnerships. Perhaps one child (and not the other) will progress to books at a higher level; perhaps a particular partnership will not have the chemistry necessary for it to work successfully. Although you can anticipate that your pairings will be tweaked over time, for now, communicate that it is well worth your time and your children's time to invest in the relationships.

The best way to get reading partnerships off to a strong start is to make time and space for kids to get to know each other as people and as readers. The author Avi once said, "If you're going to help me to write, first you need to love me." When you put youngsters together into reading partnerships, you won't say to them, "Before you can help each other to read, first you need to love each other," yet it is the case that for another person to help us outgrow ourselves, the relationship needs to be built on a foundation of respect. There is no better way to build respect than to share stories and hopes.

This session has been a great favorite for all the many, many teachers who piloted these units of study. The partnerships that begin on this day will become critically important to the social fabric of your classroom.

DRAFT

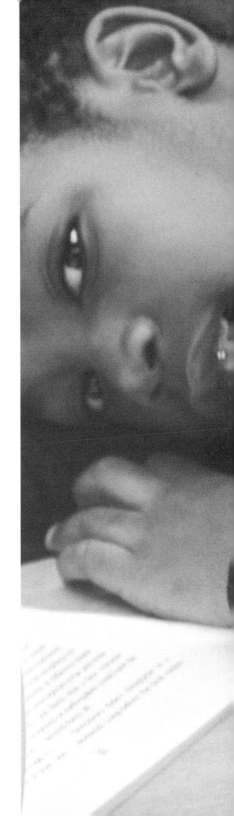

MINILESSON

Reading in the Company of Partners

CONNECTION

Tell the story of a time you realized a partnership would enrich an experience.

"Last summer, a friend gave me a bus ticket to Washington DC. I traveled down, went to the hotel, and got my room. I checked out the soaps and stuff in the bathroom and found the television inside a cabinet. Then I sat down on the bed and said to myself, 'Here I am.'" I whistled, looked around, and tapped my fingers across my knee. "Then I thought, 'I better go do something now that I'm in Washington DC.' So, I went across the street to a museum—it was all about newspapers. I walked around, pressed some buttons accompanying a few displays, and watched things light up. It was okay." My voice and affect conveyed that really, it was worse than okay. "But after about five minutes, I felt finished. And then I thought, 'What else should I do?' I knew I *could* go to a restaurant, but I thought it would be weird to sit in one alone. So I came back to my room and watched a not-great movie."

COACHING TIPS

When you write your own little life anecdotes for minilessons, there are some tricks to remember. One is that the language of minilessons is a kind of writing, and all the qualities of writing that you teach in the writing workshop are pertinent to your minilessons. For example, this little story about a trip to Washington DC, is written as a narrative, in a step-by-step chronological way, with lots of little details. The details are selected intentionally, though. If I'd provided details about the bedspread and the pictures on the wall and The Bible in the drawer and so forth, my example would be too long, and the details would distract from my point. I selected details with an eye toward those that would be engaging to kids and would help them create the bigger picture of my loneliness during the first portion of my visit to DC.

In writing this small moment, I have avoided summarizing my thoughts and instead, tried to relive the episode and to create it in a way will allow my reader to relive my experience. As part of this, I used direct quotes. That is, instead of saying, "I decided to occupy myself in DC.," I wrote, "I sat on the bed and said to myself, 'Here I am.' Then I thought, 'I better go do something now that I'm in Washington DC.'"

"I realized Washington DC is not all it's cracked up to be when you're by yourself. I got on the phone, called a friend, and convinced her to join me, and three hours later, she and I were back at that first museum. We had a blast there. We were laughing and talking about what we saw and asking each other questions to figure out what was going on in the displays. We didn't just press the buttons and walk away."

"I'll stop. I bet you can figure out my point. Washington DC is a great place to visit, but it's not that great if you are all by yourself. The trip is totally different when you're traveling with someone. This is true not only for trips to Washington DC—but also for trips to Narnia or to a potato farm in Wyoming."

Of course, the most important thing in this little story is the way it becomes a metaphor for talking about reading. I generally make the flip from a life story to a reading lesson in a concise manner. When I make these flips, I think of the turns I learned as a competitive swimmer. I'd reach the wall, touch it with one hand, and then summersault around, using my legs to push off in a giant whoosh, only this time I would be moving in the opposite direction. That's the image I have in mind as I flip from reflecting about life to saying, "And isn't that true also for reading?" By including Narnia and a potato farm in Wyoming in my list of destinations, I tell children that books allow us to journey to new lands. The flip between a life-story and reading occurs in half a sentence.

Tell children that today, to enrich their reading, they will begin working within long-term partnerships, and tell them these partnerships will work well if first, readers get to know each other.

"Today, I've given each of you a traveling partner. You and your reading partner may not already be the best friends in the world, but you will see that you will end up providing wonderful company for each other's reading. You can each make reading a whole lot better for the other. This begins by getting to know each other."

Notice that the bold heading here and the specifics of the mini-lesson do not constitute a teaching point. In a teaching point, I aim to teach learners something that they can draw upon always. A teaching point is instruction, not an assignment. This portion of the minilesson is setting up a new structure, but it is not teaching readers something they can draw on always throughout their reading lives.

Name your teaching point. Specifically, teach children that reading friendships begin with readers coming to know each other as readers, and then using that information to support each other's efforts to author reading lives.

"Today I want to teach you that having a reading companion makes all the difference in the world. And reading friendships start with people getting to know each other—as readers. We pay attention to each other's reading histories, reading interests, reading hopes, and by doing so we can support another reader's efforts to author a reading life."

TEACHING

Introduce your reading partner and set children up to research how that person interviews you.

"I have a reading partner. You already know Ms. Hanley. She and I recently discovered that we like to read the same kinds of books, and so we decided that starting today, we're going to meet regularly to talk about books. She's going to be my reading partner."

In the first version of this minilesson, Kathleen and I wrote, "If Ms. Hanley and I are going to help each other as readers, we first need to listen to each other. That's true in reading and true in life. If your doctor is going to help you, she can't just prescribe medicines to you. The doctor first needs to ask you questions and to listen. We can't really help each other unless we take the time to do a bit of listening." That is an apt metaphor, but just a few seconds ago, the minilesson described partners differently, referring not to a doctor-patient relationship but to traveling companions. The same partner can't be both your doctor and your traveling partner, so you need to select one metaphor and save the other for another year.

"If Ms. Hanley and I are going to be able to suggest books to each other, share funny sections of books, push each other to read more, we need to know something about each other as readers. So, Ms. Hanley is going to ask questions about me as a reader. (Later, I'll ask *her* questions, but you won't listen to that part.) The important thing to realize is that in a minute you will have a chance to ask *your* reading partner questions about his or her reading life. Although interviewing a reader sounds like no big deal, there's actually stuff a person can learn about how to interview someone really well. So you can research as Ms. Hanley interviews me. Jot your observations just like you do when observing our cockroaches during science. We'll wait until each of you has paper out and pens raised."

It will be important for you to tailor minilessons to suit your children. Katie Even, one of the teachers who piloted these units, taught a third-grade inclusion class, and she knew it would be too much for some of her children to take notes on the run as the interview unfurled. If your children, like Katie's, write too slowly to be able to jot quick notes while they also listen to the ongoing interview, then you, like Katie, will simply modify the minilesson, of course. The big point is that you teach toward student engagement and comprehension and that you always tailor your teaching so that you teach well.

Share some good research questions with the students.

Ms. Hanley signaled for me to look away, to not listen for a moment, allowing her a private moment in which she could talk to the kids. She leaned in close and said in a conspiratorial tone, "I jotted down questions I *might* ask your teacher, in case you want to see my possibilities." Ms. Hanley began circulating a stack of papers, one for each child. The paper listed these questions:

Questions We Ask to Get to Know a Reading Partner

- Can we look over your log and talk about how much you are reading at school and home? Are there times when you read more or less? Why do you think that happens?

- When you find books that are perfect for you, what do those books tend to be like? What should I know about the books in your life?

- What are your goals for yourself as a reader?

- If you think back over your life as a reader, what have the big turning point moments been for you?

- Can you tell me more about one turning point? How did your reading change during that moment? What did you realize about yourself as a reader?

- Who has helped you as a reader? What did that person do that was helpful?

It is entirely likely that you will have written these questions on chart paper rather than duplicated them. If the questions are written on chart paper, the person who interviews you may want to act as if she brought this list, clipping it to the easel and making an elaborate effort to turn the easel in such a way that the interviewer and the kids see the questions that are hidden from you, the teacher. That way, your colleague and the kids will be conspiring to think about the ways to interview you well. The kids will enjoy being one up on you in that fashion.

In the interest of expediency, you may need to forego this little bit of fun.

There are qualities of good charts, just as there are qualities of good narrative writing. When writing charts, I aim for the title to actually inform readers about the purpose of the chart, and I am willing to use more words in a title to be sure that it is as helpful as possible. Then I aim to be sure the bullet points are parallel in syntax and in their relationship to the audience. So these bullet points are each written to the interviewer, and each begins with an imperative verb: let, ask, listen. Brevity is important but never at the cost of clarity.

There are two types of charts you will make in your classroom. An anchor chart is one you return to again and again throughout a unit. The teaching points of minilessons or teaching shares become the bullets on an anchor chart, and thus the chart grows across the unit. The other kind of chart is more temporary; you may introduce it on only one day or over a couple days, and it is meant as a tool to help children hold onto that particular occasion, not across an entire unit. This chart is the latter kind.

With your colleague, demonstrate conducting a good interview and being a good interviewee. As you demonstrate, point out techniques kids can take away for their own interviews.

Ms. Hanley began and said to me, "Because we're going to be reading partners, I want to get to know you as a reader. Do you think it would be better to talk first about your reading log and what it shows, or about books that seem perfect for you, because I really want to hear about both of those. Which seems like a good place to start?"

You might be tempted to assume the role of the interviewer, uncovering information about your colleague as a reader instead of the other way around. If the colleague is someone that your class admires tremendously—say, your principal—then that might be a wise decision. But otherwise, you'll want to ask your colleague to do the questioning because the chance to hear the true details of your life as a reader will be precious to the kids. They do not really care about the reading history of some random adult, and you do want them to grasp that above all, the interviewer listens with enormous interest.

"Hmm, maybe we could talk about books first," I said. Ms. Hanley smiled, then she leaned in to the kids and whispered, "Do you notice how I let my partner partly guide the direction of our conversation? *And,* I am trying to make sure she can see that I am really interested in what she will say." Then Ms. Hanley turned back to me, and continued the interview. "So, tell me—when you find books that are perfect for you, what do they tend to be like?" In an aside, she whispered to the kids, "I definitely did not read off the question like I was a robot! I have to ask it in a way that shows my curiosity and gets her to *really* talk. I *do* really wonder what she likes to read. People are so different that way."

This entire unit has been designed to launch all the fundamentals of a reading workshop. Partnerships (and the regular interaction they provide for talk about books) are crucial to the children's growth in reading. Time to talk is not icing on the cake; it is not an expendable bit of curriculum. Numerous researchers such as Raphael and McMahon have shown that struggling readers, for example, need frequent occasions to talk to about books.

I said, "I really want to *like* the main character in a book. If the main character is energetic and hopeful, I want to read that book. But if the character is a depressed guy who hangs around bars and keeps to himself—living a curmudgeon lifestyle, I won't like the book." Then I added, "But I don't want everything to be too fairytale sweet either."

Ms. Hanley laughed, nodded, said, "Uh huh," and jotted in her notebook. She explained in a whispered aside to the class what she was writing. "I write notes to help me remember what she's said, and I jot questions I might want to ask her later. So far, I've written 'likeable characters,' 'not fairytale sweet,' and in the margins, I've written questions: 'Women?', the name of a mystery writer, 'Dick Francis?', and the words 'Where get books?' I may not ask all the follow-up questions now, but we'll talk about books on other days, too." Then she turned back to me and asked, "So where do you find the books you read?"

Initially, when Kathleen and I wrote this minilesson, we had me telling Ms. Hanley that I liked books that weren't too hard, that were smooth reads. I altered that later, thinking that it is really important to not overdo the emphasis on reading books that are easy enough to be accessible. Then, too, I want this to have the ring of authenticity, to emulate plausible conversations real readers could have. I am telling the truth about the books I do and do not like and I know that when I tell the truth in my teaching, kids hear it. They note the catch in my voice, the mistiness in my eyes, and this means more than any instructional overlay I could bring to this minilesson. Obviously, you'll tell your truths, not mine!

"Well, I get recommendations," I said, and Ms. Hanley gestured for me to say more so I added, "From my sisters, my Mom, and my friends. Mostly, I have kinds of books that I like, often about ambitious, visionary peopleor about families who pull together despite tough times."

Actually, I get book recommendations from other sources too, and initially I'd planned to deluge the interviewer with all the details I could dredge up. That's not unusual. Like many of you, I love the chance to talk about myself. Kids of course, are willing to sit and listen to those sorts of details forever. But time is always critical in a minilesson. And in this instance, the kids will actually learn less from long elaborate answers and more from the moves the interviewer makes, so I keep my answers clipped and allow the interviewer to show how she pulls more out of me, asks follow-up questions, and the like.

As I talked, Ms. Hanley recorded brief notes. Then she looked over her notes and thought aloud in a voice that the children could hear, "I'm just thinking if any of these things go together and lead me to deeper questions." Then, brightening, she said to me, "Lucy, you said you have kinds of books that you read. Do those kinds of books have kinds of characters? And are the characters sort of like you?"

This is actually a spectacular question. In an interview, it helps if the researcher builds tentative theories about the subject and then tests these theories out in some of the follow-up questions. You may not be able to teach your kids to do this, but you can try to learn this sort of interviewing yourself. Notice, too, that the interview doesn't hop all over the place. It hews a deep furrow.

"Interesting question," I responded. "Well, I recently have been reading Greg Mortenson's book, *Three Cups of Tea: One Man's Mission to Promote Peace…One School at a Time* and another book, *Leaving Microsoft to Change the World,* by John Wood. They are both about people who are starting schools in Pakistan and Afghanistan. I also just read Tracy Kidder's *Mountains Beyond Mountains* about an heroic doctor who is tackling health care on Haiti."

If you haven't read these beautiful books, I highly recommend them. They put the challenges we, as teachers, face in perspective.

"And do you feel like the characters are like you?" Ms. Hanley pressed, tucking in a tiny aside to the kids in which she said, "Did you see she didn't really answer my question, so I'm pressing a bit."

"Hmmm… I guess you could say they are like the me that I wish I was," I said. "They are more courageous than me and they inspire me!"

Ask children to list across their fingers three things they noticed the interviewer doing that they, too, could do. Then ask the interviewer to list what she hoped kids saw her doing.

Ms. Hanley stopped interviewing and stepped out of the role, even physically leaving her seat at the front of the room. I took up the reins of the minilesson again. "Readers, did you notice the wise moves Ms. Hanley made as she was interviewing me? List across your fingers three things she did that you could do as well when you interview your reading partner. And, truly, these are things you can always do when you interview someone, or talk with them intently."

I gave children time to think over what they noticed. Then I said, "Ms. Hanley, tell us what you tried to do." As she spoke, she displayed a chart that ostensibly she'd brought to the event: "Tips for Interviewing a Reader."

Tips for Interviewing a Reader

- Follow the person's lead

- Ask follow-up questions

- Record notes on the important things you learn and wonder

- Reread notes, look for patterns, grow theories, and turn these into questions

- Listen—really listen

Notice I am not asking the children to talk with each other about their observations. That would stretch out this minilesson, and it verges on being too long already. I simply ask them to list techniques they have gleaned across their fingers. Giving kids a chance to list the strategies across their fingers increases the chance that they'll hold on to this example when they return to their independent work.

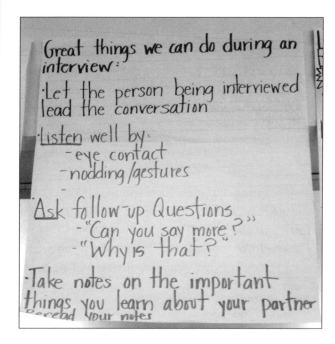

Ms. Hanley, said, listing across her fingers as she spoke, "First, I tried to let you lead me to good stuff to talk about. So I told you the main thing I wanted—to learn all about you as a reader—and told you a couple things I was wondering, but I let you take me to where you thought I'd learn some interesting stuff. I wouldn't ever have known to talk about kinds of books or depressing characters or anything, but you took me there.

"Then I tried to listen well. I didn't just act like I was listening. I tried to really think about what you were saying.

"Third, I followed up when you gave half-answers, which you did a lot, and I grew theories out of what you said and asked real questions that came from these theories."

These are sophisticated techniques that Ms. Hanley used, and if the class is operating at a fairly high level it makes sense for her to list techniques such as these. But if many members of the class are apt to lean back in chairs while a person talks, to not make any eye contact at all, to race perfunctorily through a list of robotic questions, then you'll want your colleague to cite some more obvious first steps toward improved listening.

ACTIVE INVOLVEMENT

Set up partnerships to interview and be interviewed.

"Readers, you're lucky. You won't be traveling through books alone. You've got a traveling partner. But before you can help each other make each reading experience great, you need to know about each other as readers. So why don't you do just as Ms. Hanley and I have done, and will partner one—the person with a number one beside your name on your name tent—take a few minutes to interview partner two. We'll switch off later today."

When my colleagues and I do staff development in schools, early on in our work with teachers, we are apt to point out that we usually repeat the exact words of a teaching point at least three times in a minilesson, if not more. Repeating the teaching point brings that point home to children. The need to return to the same teaching point in the middle—and at the end—of a minilesson is a technique that cajoles all of us into making sure that each of our minilessons illustrates and addresses a single main point. In this minilesson, for example, it would have been very easy to focus the connection on the pleasures of having a partner and the importance of knowing a partner well. It would also have been easy to focus the link of the minilesson on the importance of asking questions that extend a person's first answer. Such a minilesson, however, would have made one point and then illustrate an entirely different (but equally important) point. In my eyes, that's not the ideal way to teach. You may notice that in this active involvement section, as in all of the others in this series, I make a point of returning to the teaching point, reminding kids of the original intent of the minilesson, and in doing so, I embed the details related to ways people can conduct effective interviews into the larger context of partnerships and of the minilesson.

"Interviewers, give me a thumbs up so I know who you are. Take a minute to think about how you will start your interview." I was quiet, giving them a moment to begin imagining the start of the interview. Then I coached into their silent rehearsal. "You won't want to just read the questions off a piece of paper—your reader needs to know you really want to ask the question! What can you say that sounds like you are dying to hear from the reader?" Again I was quiet. "When you are interviewing, remember that it helps to let your reader lead you to the good stuff—so you might start by explaining that you want to get to know this person, and then share a few things you'd love to hear about, and ask your reader if one of those might be an interesting place to start. Remember, too, that once your subject responds by telling you about his or her reading, you'll need to ask the follow-up questions that will help you construct an idea of who this person is as a reader. Take notes to help you remember important parts and build theories!"

Then after a period of silence, I said, "Give me a thumbs-up if you are ready to be an interviewer." Children so indicated, and I gestured for them to start.

As children talked, I moved among them, whispering to the interviewer to lean in, to look at the speaker, to display their interest, to ask follow-up questions.

Name the work children have just done that is transferable to other times.

"Readers, in this class, every one of us will develop reading friendships—and throughout your lives you'll do that as well. Reading friendships begin with readers getting to know each other as readers. As part of that, we'll each need to learn to read *readers*—that is, to take in the words another reader says and to understand what the reader means. That means listening attentively and working to comprehend what another person says just like we work to comprehend what a book says. It also means noticing when we are confused and thinking, 'Huh?'

"Today you've been asking follow-up questions so that you can really make sense of what your reader has said. (When Kobe said, 'I've read less on Wednesdays,' Malik didn't just nod. No way! Instead he thought, 'Huh? That makes no sense!' and he asked follow-up questions to understand. He asked, 'Why? Why do you think you read less on Wednesdays?!') Smart move, to be so interested in really understanding that you ask for more information. Thumbs up if any of the rest of you asked follow-up questions, saying things like, 'Why?' or 'Can you give me an example?' or even just saying, 'Will you say more about that?'"

Often as children work with a partner during the active involvement component of a minilesson, I coach into their work. I tend to not stop what they are doing to speak with them, but instead voice over. That works if they are reading or jotting because my voice functions almost as the print captions on a split screen. In this instance, the children will be talking and will be trying to do some ambitious talk, so I don't imagine that voicing over will be helpful. Therefore, I ask the interviewer to mentally rehearse for the interview and do my coaching into this silent rehearsal. Remember that active involvement is not a time for me to simply hand the reins to the kids saying, "Go to it." This is supposed to be assisted practice.

Notice that only partner 1s have had a chance to conduct interviews, and only partner 2s have had the chance to share their reading lives. On this particular occasion, you'll give children a chance to switch roles in the teaching share, but often in a minilesson, it will be the case that one member of the partnership only does one particular activity, and the teaching share will not usually change this. Both partners learn—even when one functions only as the researcher, the listener, or the coach. Become accustomed to this. In the long run, children will have equal opportunities.

LINK

Send children off to fill out their logs and to read, doing so with the awareness that soon they'll talk about their logs and books with their new partners.

"You are so lucky because now you won't be traveling alone—you have a traveling partner. I hope that you'll do lots of listening to each other. It's great to have a partner who knows what you are trying to do. Let's go fill out our reading logs, and as you do so, keep in mind that before long, your partner is going to help you study your log. What will you and your partner notice together about your reading life? When you read today, keep in mind that before long you're going to have a chance to tell your partner about your book. Mark some spots you might want to talk about!" *[Figs. XI-1 and XI-2]*

Figure XI-1

Aly can bring a jotting like this to her partnership conversation and use it to chart a long conversation. Eventually she'll learn to capture her second thought, not just her first thought, on her Post-its.

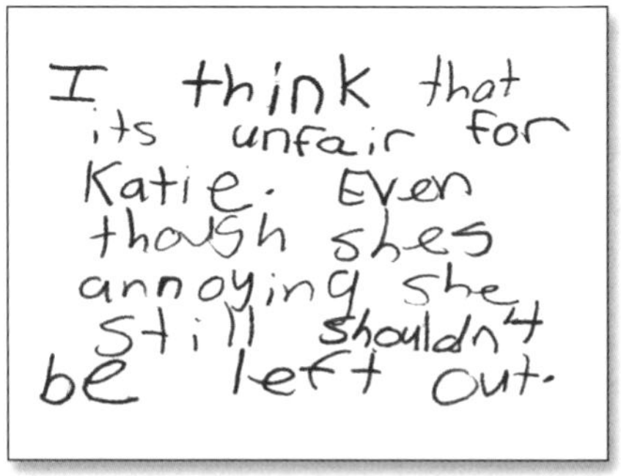

Figure XI-2

If you listen in on a reader sharing a Post-it like this with her partners, you'll want to help the partner celebrate the reader's effort to read critically. Readers who read against the grain are able to say, "I think otherwise." Bravo!

DRAFT

CONFERRING AND SMALL GROUP WORK

Help Readers Read Differently Because They Are In Partnerships

You will want to approach your conferring today intending to help readers read differently because they are in partnerships. You will want to think beforehand about the various ways you might support partnerships; rehearsing for a new line of conferring is one way for you to be sure you use your time to make the maximum difference.

Set Several Partnerships Up to Interview Each Other and Coach Into This

You may decide that although you've designed the day so that partners take turns interviewing each other during partnership time at the end of the workshop, you may mess up your own plan just a bit so that all of these conversations do not happen simultaneously, so you can coach more of them. Recently, I said to two partnerships pulled into a huddle, "Our plan is for partner 2s to interview partner 1s later, during share time, but if all of your interviews are at one time, I'll miss them. So let's have your interviews right now instead, and then you can read during share time. That way, I can listen in on your talks 'cause I am dying to know about you

> ## MID-WORKSHOP TEACHING POINT
>
> ### Readers Read Differently When We Can Anticipate Sharing Our Books with a Reading Friend
>
> "Readers, may I stop you?" I waited until I had everyone's attention. "When my friend joined me in Washington DC, we split up to explore the museum. As I stopped in at display and then another, I saved up stuff to show her. Then we got together and I said, 'You gotta see. . . .' I know you've done the same thing when you and a friend go places together. When you split for a bit, you travel with your friend in mind, saving stuff up to share with each other. As you are reading today, you should be thinking, 'This is a good part to share,' and then you will definitely want to mark those parts with a Post-it."
>
> "Right now, if you haven't already marked stuff that you'd like to show to your partner and talk about with your partner, do so right away—and you have only two minutes so do this quick as a wink."
>
> After two minutes, I voiced over as the children continued to finish marking spots to share. "I'm wondering what sorts of things you marked. Were they confusing places, funny places, places where your character seems to be changing, or what?" For a moment, children called out reasons they'd marked various sections.
>
> "In another twenty minutes, you'll have a chance to talk with each other, and I'm pretty sure you'll want to not only read sections aloud to each other, but also to share your thoughts about those sections. As you get back to your reading, let yourself read differently because you have a traveling companion."
>
>

as readers." As the children talked, my role shifted from listening (and demonstrating how to listen with responsiveness) to whispering in little prompts such as, "Ask her for an example."

If you do this, don't let yourself get so involved that you stay with these two partnerships too long. Others in the classroom also need to feel your presence. You have far more than these two to teach!

Confer to Support Children (such as ELLs) Who Could Struggle During Partnership Interviews

If you decide to conduct a one-to-one conference, you may want to help a reader who might otherwise struggle with his or her partnership conversation. You might decide to conduct what I describe as a "proficient partner conference" with this reader, wherein the teacher takes on the role of a partner, a wonderful partner. I knew that if I selected this kind of conference, it would give me the opportunity to set Rosa up for her partnership conversation.

Rosa's first language is Spanish. Rosa's understanding of English is strong, and she participates in read-aloud conversations as an active listener. I appreciate that when the whole class is talking, she looks at the person who is speaking. She rarely participates as a speaker, however. I am not sure, yet, if this is due to her comfort level with English or her lack of experience with book talks. I anticipate that if she and I talk as if we are partners, I can provide almost a rehearsal for the partnership conversation she will hold with a peer at the end of the day's workshop.

As I walked over to her, Rosa was reading the first book in the *Junie B. Jones* series. It looked like she had about five pages left. "Rosa," I said, "May I talk to you for a moment?" She nodded. "When we meet with our partners, it always seems like there is so much to say. I was hoping we could work together now to figure out some things you want say to your partner later on. I've read this book too, so let's talk about it together." Rosa looked up at me expectantly as she put the book down, holding her place by using her thumb as a bookmark. She didn't say anything, even though I left a long pool of silence.

"What are you thinking about your book?" I asked, realizing I needed to offer her some support. Rosa shrugged, offering a slight smile. "Can you tell me about a part you like?" I asked, reaching for the book, opening it up. "Let's go through it together. Are there parts that stand out to you?" I raised my eyebrows, expectantly. She shrugged. At this point, I altered my questions, so they would be easy to answer, to help her get started. "Did you like the book, Rosa?" I asked. In the long run, I wanted to hear a lot from her, but my more immediate priority was to help her be a conversational partner.

"Yes."

"May I look at it for a second? I'll put this sticky note on your page to hold your place." I thumbed through the pages slowly, holding the book so Rosa could see it. My intention was to help Rosa remember any thoughts she may have had as she read the pages she was now seeing again. "Flipping through it like this reminds me of the story," I explained. "This is where we meet Junie for the first time, and we realize she says whatever she is thinking. I remember this." I showed Rosa the page and looked up at her, expecting her to say something.

"Junie is nice but mean too," Rosa said.

"She is, isn't she? Junie just says anything she wants. She's probably even a little bit nervous at times, especially when she tries something for the first time. I know how that feels. I remember starting school and being very nervous and not being super nice to everyone because I was actually really sad not to have friends. Rosa, what about you? Do you sometimes act differently because you're nervous?"

"When I started school here."

"So are you a little like your character, Junie B. Jones, then?" I asked.

"I want to not be scared, but I am like her."

"I'm sorry to hear that you were scared here. I'm sure that you'll become less scared and more like yourself as the year goes on and you meet new friends. I wonder if you could even learn some ways to act less shy by studying Junie. This book can show you stuff about that, can't it?"

"Yeah," Rosa said, "I like how she stands like this," and she crossed her arms and tilted her head to the side, showing how Junie is tough. She showed me a page where Junie acted that way.

"Rosa, it seems like you like this book. You've already read so much of it, and you're like Junie already, vowing to push yourself to be less shy. It's making me think that you like to read books with characters that are like you a little."

"Yeah."

"Wow, Rosa. That's important information you just shared. It will be so helpful for your partner to know this about you. When you notice something about yourself as a reader, you can tell your partner. You could tell your partner you like books with characters who are like you, and then you can flip through, like we did, and show your partner the parts of the book where Junie B. Jones reminds you of you."

I hoped that the conversation that Rosa and I had together would serve as a rehearsal for the later conversation that she would have with her partner. "You could find more places where Junie B. acts like you, or like you want to act, and then you could share those with your partner."

"Okay," Rosa said.

# TEACHING SHARE

Readers Tell Our Reading Partners Our Histories and Hopes So They Can Help Us

Ask children to fill out their logs with the awareness that they'll soon talk with their partners; then ask them to begin talking and listening.

"Readers, please stop and fill out your logs. If, as you do so, you notice a pattern or a something interesting in your reading life—something you can imagine talking about with your reading partner when you have a chance—go ahead and star that."

After children had a minute to work, I said in a voice over, "In a minute, partner 2 will interview partner 1. Partner 2, remember that you can rely on questions that are up here on our chart or your own questions. *[Fig. XI-3]* Remember that you will probably want to tell your partner that mainly you want to know the big stuff about him or her as a reader. I'm pretty sure your partner can steer you to a territory that will be interesting. Once you determine the topic, remember, you want to show you are interested. To show interest, frankly, you need to *be* interested. You need to see significance in what your partner says. As I come around and listen to your interviews, I'm going to look for how you express your intense, honest interest. You may get started."

COACHING TIPS

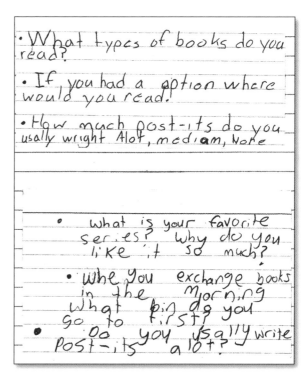

Figure XI-3

If you invite children to generate their own charts and lists, a few will do so and you'll want to share their suggestions with the class.

As children worked together, I moved among them. Above all, I mentored the listener in listening by paying rapt, responsive attention to whatever the interviewee said. Partway through the interviews, I took a break from listening in and stood in the midst of the room and said, in a voice over, "Friends, you're not remembering the pointers about being good interviewers." I gestured to the chart that recorded tips we'd talked about earlier. "Before you continue, partner twos, tell partner ones the tips you are going to try to use. Then continue." [Figs. XI-4 and XI-5]

If your children are fast, fluent writers then you may encourage them to jot some of what they learned through these interviews in the blank pages of their My Reading Life folders. Be wary about expecting too much writing from children who don't yet write quickly as this could chase away time for talk.

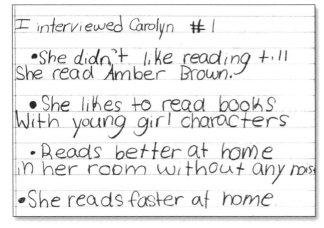

I interviewed Carolyn #1

• She didn't like reading till She read Amber Brown.

• She likes to read books with young girl characters

• Reads better at home in her room without any nois

• She reads faster at home

Figure XI-4

This partner has taken it upon herself to jot what she's learned from interviewing.

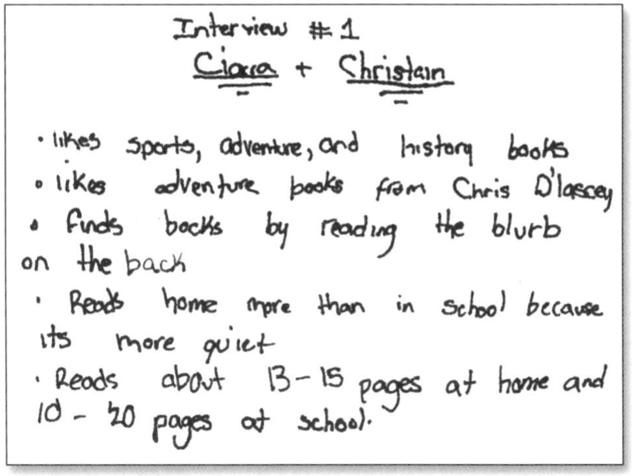

Interview #1
Ciara + Christian

• likes sports, adventure, and history books
• likes adventure books from Chris D'lacey
• finds books by reading the blurb on the back
• Reads home more than in school because its more quiet
• Reads about 13-15 pages at home and 10-20 pages at school.

Figure XI-5

Note the interesting discrepancy! The reader believes he reads more at home than at school because it's quiet, but data collected in the logs suggests otherwise. A great listener will see this and press further.

DRAFT

Thinking Over Stories with Partners

IN THIS SESSION,
you will teach students that when readers think and talk about our reading with others, we have more fun reading.

Each of your children now has a traveling partner on his or her journey into literacy. You'll give children lots of riches this year: books that can open new worlds and give them new areas of expertise; the time to become lost in texts and to let one text lead to another; the tools of the hand that will also become habits of the mind; responsive teaching that begins with recognition of what a child can do and takes children as far as they can go. All of those gifts will be precious, but none more so than the gift of friends who cherish books and words and use both to build relationships that are deep and real.

Robert Coles writes about the extraordinary power of bringing beautiful literature into a hospital, of sharing Earnest Hemingway's novel, *The Old Man and the Sea* with a cancer patient who is holding on for dear life. Somehow, the fact that books are being read in the midst of the intensity of life makes them matter more than ever. When books are read and swapped, passed from one child to another, interpreted and reinterpreted, all within the highly charged social fabric of a classroom, the books take on added resonance because of their placement within the high drama of elementary school classrooms. The bully in a book has a real-life corollary, as do the characters who stand by silently, and the one who betrays another, and the one who resolves to be kinder. And when books are not only *read* in the midst of the hurly burly of classroom life, but are also shared among other readers, the moments when one sees oneself on the page suddenly become invitations to intimacy.

Kafka has said, "Literature is an ice axe that breaks the frozen sea *within* us." I have found that literature can also be an ice axe that breaks the frozen sea *between* us. In classrooms where teachers read aloud books like *Stone Fox*, books that don't mince on the true drama of life, children learn that books can bring people together; books can help us realize that the human condition is a shared one.

Over the school year, you will often harness the social energy of partnerships, recruiting these beautiful relationships so that children are able to do with the support of

GETTING READY

- Remind students to bring their reading folders and writing supplies to the meeting area.

- Preselect four partnerships for a fishbowl activity in the teach section of the minilesson. You'll want to read ahead so you can set children up for this.

- If possible, have a whiteboard and marker available so that groups of children can jointly contribute to notes recording observations of the fishbowl activity.

- If you plan on special small group work, select students ahead of time.

- Create a chart titled, "Ways You and Another Reader Can Talk About Your Books" for use in the teaching share.

- By the start of Session XIII, you'll want to have read up to the end of chapter 7 in *Stone Fox* if you are using that book as your read-aloud.

another that which they cannot necessarily quite do yet on their own. Partnerships will provide children with scaffolds, with audiences for repeated practice, and with more time on a task because it's partners as well as teachers who nudge readers to think and rethink. As the series unfolds, you'll find that your minilessons often channel partnerships toward particular kinds of work. In this way, partnerships sustain the new directions, making them a bit less fleeting that they'd be if they were sustained by minilessons and conferring alone.

> *When books are read and swapped, passed from one child to another, interpreted and reinterpreted, all within the highly-charged social fabric of a classroom, the books take on added resonance.*

For now, at the very start of these relationships, the important thing is that you give partners a chance to do their own thing, to simply be together. These few days mark the start of new relationships between readers and texts. At weddings, the master of ceremonies sometimes asks the gathering, "Will you, the family and friends of this new couple, promise to give your support to the relationship, providing counsel and encouragement to it?" From across the gathering, there will come the resounding, "We will." In the same way, you need to take this as an occasion for you to give new partnerships your blessing—to encourage and support them. You'll do this by giving partners time to be together and space to talk in the most natural ways possible about themselves, the books they're reading, and the thoughts and feelings that might otherwise streak like meteors across the canvas of their responses to books.

How will you hope the talk goes between partners? What is it you're looking for? For today, above all, your hope is that the relationships are real—between kids and between kids and books. For today, you hope your children do not look over their shoulders every minute or two to see if they are performing according to your instructions, to see if they are reciting their parts just right. Instead, you want kids to be kids.

This will give you opportunities to assess ways children already talk with each other about books. There will be tons of time soon for you to lift the level of these interchanges. For today, assign yourself the job of finding stuff to compliment. Look for the ways children naturally support each other, and provide language for what you see that works. To one partnership you'll say, "I watched the two of you talking, and it was so great to see that the more you talked about your book, the more excited you got. You started sitting on your butts, then you got going and you were both on your knees, and now you're jumping between your knees and your feet. The two of you sure know how to build on each other's energy, don't you! What a partnership!"

You'll no doubt find that when children talk about texts, as when they talk about events that one or the other has lived through, they'll spend a fair percentage of time catching each other up on experiences. One sister has a sleep over with her cousin, and the other stays home. The two girls get together, and they swap stories about what occurred. "You wouldn't believe. . . . After that. . . . Then you know what she did? I wanted to say. . . . But after that, you know what?" Expect this sort of retelling and savor it. Over the next few days, you'll intervene to lift the level of these exchanges, but for now, enjoy them.

DRAFT

# MINILESSON

Thinking Over Stories with Partners

CONNECTION

Tell children that a lot of things in life, like movies, are better when we can enjoy them with another person.

"Readers, I've been thinking about something. How many of you go to the movies by yourself?" Give me a thumbs up or a thumbs down to let me know." The children all signaled that no, they don't go to the movies alone.

"That's true for me too," I said. "But last night, a friend kept bugging me about that. He kept saying, 'What's your problem? It's dark at the movies—no one can even see you are sitting alone.'" I tried to convince him that my hesitation is not that I'd be embarrassed to sit at the movies alone. Groping for an explanation, I finally said, 'The movie's just better if I'm sitting with someone.' When he heard that, my friend *really* looked at me like I was losing my mind."

"So I thought I'd see if any of you understand. Do any of you get why I wouldn't go to the movies alone? If you could, would you go alone?"

Throughout the room, kids leapt to my defense. "I definitely wouldn't go alone," one after another said. "No way." They were unanimous.

"Can you talk to me about that?" I said. "That way I'll have some way to explain this to my friend." I added, "I mean—I agree. But *why* is it? If you're just sitting there quietly, watching the show, what is the problem with sitting with a stranger on your right, a stranger on your left?"

The kids were clear: "'Cause we wouldn't have anyone to talk to afterwards. We couldn't tell each other the good parts, the scary parts.'"

COACHING TIPS

I'm pretty sure that the kids will be standing in solidarity with me by now, which is my hope. I want them to be really clear that absolutely it is much more fun to watch movies with a friend. And as you can imagine, I'll then try to turn their zeal over this into an equal commitment to the fact that it is much more fun to read with a friend.

Notice that minilessons are colloquial. When you go to write them, it helps to compose aloud, trying out the feel of a minilesson in your mouth, in the air. When minilessons are too literary, too written, they may be harder for kids to follow.

Remember that time is of the essence. You do not need to hear from nine kids. Your minilesson leaves spaces for a bit of call and response from the audience, but more is not better. Once two or three kids have piped up, then move on to your next point.

Name your teaching point. Specifically, teach children that much of the fun in reading comes from sharing a book with another reader.

> "You know what, readers? I'm realizing now that reading a book is a lot like going to the movies. A lot of the fun part comes after reading time is over, when you get to talk about what you've read."

TEACHING

Highlight the advantages of having a reading partner, suggesting that when we talk about a book, it's is similar to talking about an experience; we share what happened and our response to what happened.

> "Yesterday you each got a traveling partner for your journey through books. You had time to talk about each other as readers. By the end of today, you'll be clear why these relationships matter; you'll see that when you anticipate being able to share a book (or a movie or anything), it becomes more interesting. By the end of today, most of you will start swapping books with each other once you finish them. It will be cool because you'll hear about a book from your partner and then, if it sounds good, you'll get a chance to read the same book your friend just read. You'll even remember what your partner said about the good parts, so when you get to those parts you'll be able to think, 'She was right!' or 'Huh? Why'd she think this was so good?'

> "You already know a lot about talking about reading, because people talk about reading just as we talk about stuff we've done in our lives. If I was to tell you about my trip, caving, for example, I'd tell you what we did—how it started, what occurred, how it ended. My family and I each climbed aboard a little kayak, and we paddled through miles of streams that went right in the center of a mountain and we finally emerged into the sunshine. And I'd tell you my thoughts and feelings about that trip. When you and your partner talk together about books, you'll probably talk in similar ways. You'll probably tell each other what happened, and you'll probably tell each other your thoughts and feelings about what happened.

If your eyebrows are raised at this teaching point, and you're sputtering a bit of protest—saying, perhaps, that this is not especially academically rigorous—know that you are right. Today's minilesson doesn't up the intellectual ante by a whole lot. But this minilesson does give kids space to acclimate themselves to their new relationships, and it means that you don't establish partnerships and then immediately impose restrictive agendas on those relationships.

Shirley Brice Heath, the great language researcher who won a MacArthur Award (also known as a genius award) for her research, has suggested that one of the most important things an adult can do to support a child's literacy is that we can help children tell stories in which they re-create what they did earlier in another place. The challenge of doing this—to retell a trip with Daddy to the park, for example—nudges children to use language not only to comment on the here and now ("That's mine." "I want the big one." "Move over.") but also to use language to re-create another time and place, one that exists in the mind. When a child uses language to re-create a narrative that another author has written, the child is supported because the author's language exists, and child can incorporate some of that language into his or her retelling. On the other hand, the linguistic and intellectual work is all the more complex because the child is using language to create an event that, in fact, the child experienced only vicariously, only through language. This work is rigorous work. There are some who are disdainful of retelling—referring to this as regurgitation, for example. My own feeling is that retelling is one way to know. It is not the only way to know something, but there is no need to diminish this one form of intellectual work in an effort to suggest that there are yet other kinds of intellectual work that also have merit. And certainly, human beings are so constructed that the sharing of stories is a valuable part of what it means to live together. We get to know each other by sharing stories; we understand other perspectives by sharing stories; we extend our reach by sharing stories; we remember by sharing stories, so I would not want to minimize retelling.

In corners of the room, set up a few partnerships to demonstrate retelling—first an experience, then a story. Set up observers to record ways that sharing life and reading are, or could be, similar.

"Let's just get a feel for what book conversation can be like. At each of the four corners of our meeting area, one person in each partnership has agreed to talk for a few minutes about something he or she did once that was cool or weird or different. I'm going to ask you to research what people tend to do when we talk about stuff we've done. Then, after a bit, the person talking will stop talking about what he or she *has done* and start talking about what he or she *has read*. Researchers, I want you to listen to this second conversation, and think, 'When people talk about books, is it a lot like when people talk about life? Should it be?'"

"To help you research, I'm going to pass out white boards—one board and one marker pen for each of the four groups of researchers. If you see the person retelling what he did, or what a character did, one of you record what the speaker is doing: retelling what he did. If you see a person telling what he or she thought, record that: telling thoughts. And so forth. Later we'll have a chance to compare and contrast how we share a life experience and how we share a reading experience.

At the Teachers College Reading and Writing Project, this arrangement that has something happening at each of the four corners of the meeting area carpet is a fairly common one. In effect, it's an efficient way to form four small groups, each with a leader: Each child turns away from their teacher at the front of the room and toward the leader sitting in that child's corner of the carpet. In this instance, at each corner, a partnership is performing, and the observing children are taking note of their peers. You can use the "turn to your corner" method whenever this structure will come in handy for you.

You may notice lots of subtle ways in which I set children up to realize that one of the natural things people do when we have lived through an event—actually or with help from a book—is that we retell what we have experienced so others can grasp the experience enough to be interested in our thoughts about it. I'm championing retelling because now, at the start of the year, I will be helping readers to know that they should read in ways that allow them to be able to retell. That is, a reader may not choose to retell a story, but should grasp the essential infrastructure and the big pieces enough that she could retell the story if called upon to do so. I'm also going to suggest that, in fact, retelling is a very natural thing to do, and I'll encourage readers to do this within their partnerships.

ACTIVE INVOLVEMENT

Ask children to share with each other the things they noticed as they researched partners retelling an experience and retelling a story. Reconvene the class to share these observations.

"Researchers, what did you see your person doing when he or she talked about an episode from life? When he or she talked about a text? Turn and share your findings, as researchers, just to remember what actually happened and what thoughts you have about it." After children talked for a bit, I reconvened the group. "I heard you saying that usually people start by retelling. What else did you find out?" Many thumbs popped up. I pointed to Fallon, who had observed Izzy and Emma in one corner of the room.

Fallon began, "We noticed that Izzy told about exciting things that happened *both* in her life *and* in the book. It's like Izzy gets really caught up in whatever story she's telling and she gives a really detailed description of whatever happens."

"Okay," I said. "Pick someone else." Fallon looked from one classmate to the next and then ceremoniously pointed to Sarah.

"We noticed," said Sarah, "that Jasmine talked about how she was feeling in her story, and when she talked about her book she talked a lot about how the other characters felt about the main character."

I nodded and added, "It sounds like she really pays attention to the characters' and people's emotions." Then Sarah looked around the meeting area and called on Sam.

"I noticed that when Malik talked about his book he gave his opinion a lot." I gestured for Sam to say more. "He said things like 'I didn't think it was right. . .' and 'It wasn't fair. . . .' Stuff like that." I again gestured for more and Sam added, "He's kind of like that in our class too, wanting stuff to be fair." I asked a few more children to share their research.

Notice in this active involvement how incredibly spot-on the children's observations of each other are. Sarah's assessment of Jasmine as an empathetic, deeply feeling reader and Sam's understanding of Malik, the son of a police officer who often takes the high ground, as a socially conscientious person are incredibly insightful.

LINK

Send children off with the idea that readers tend to read more deeply when we are expecting to have opportunities for book conversations.

"Readers, when I teach kindergarten children, one of the wonderful things I notice about them is that they use talking to help them think. A five-year-old will be drawing a picture, and she mutters to herself, 'What color crayon should I use? Maybe blue. Blue, blue, blue, blue.'"

"I'm thinking that we can learn from those kindergarteners. We can become the kinds of people who know that if we plan to *talk more* we can help ourselves *think more*. If we know we'll have a chance to talk over an experience or a book, then every step along the way we say to ourselves, 'I gotta tell so and so about this,' and 'She's gonna ask about that.' Then when we get together with a friend to talk, we take the time to retell so we catch that person up on the experience, and we share thoughts, too. This can make the text come alive between you and your partner."

CONFERRING AND SMALL-GROUP WORK

Support Readers To Understand Pronouns In Order To Help Them Follow The Story

A key aspect of reading fluently is being able to automatically make connections between a pronoun and its antecedent, the noun to which it refers, so that sentences in a text weave together into a meaningful fabric.

I had pulled together a small group of readers whom I thought could use some support in this area, and I'd chosen an excerpt from *Horrible Harry Goes to Sea,* a level L book. All of the children I planned to call together had read the text before. When you choose a text for work with your own small groups, you will want it to be a text you know and love, one that you've spent time studying and that you know has great teaching potential. I chose the text for those reasons, and also because I knew it would work for Zayd, for his partner Max (who was reading level M books), and for the other partnership, Rosa and Gabe (both reading level N). Rosa was reading relatively fluently, but her retellings gave me the sense that she wasn't understanding her stories in great depth.

Gabe's tendency to read choppily and slowly was affecting his comprehension as well, and along with the fact that he often needed to stop to self-correct (which almost certainly affected his comprehension), I suspected that he wasn't always paying attention to how the sentences in his stories fit together. After sending the class off, I asked Zayd, Max, Rosa, and Gabe to stay with me on the rug.

"So, I asked you to meet with me for a few minutes," I said to the children as they settled in on the rug near me, "because I've noticed that sometimes when you are reading, you get confused about who's doing what in your stories. I want to help you take all the meaning you can from pronouns. When we understand them, the story makes much more sense." I brought out the copies of the excerpt. "We're going to read this bit of *Horrible Harry Goes to Sea* together, and we're going to practice making sure we know to what each pronoun is referring. Now, first, let's read this silently."

MID-WORKSHOP TEACHING POINT

Readers Know that Focus Matters When Talking About Both Reading and Writing

"In just a few minutes, you'll have a chance to meet with your partner to talk about each other's books. Make sure you've jotted some Post-it notes so that you'll be ready to talk."

After another two minutes or so, I said, "Right now, I am going to teach you how to share your thoughts with your partner." I waited until I had the class' attention. "First, you need to decide which partner will share his or her reading and thoughts. It won't be the same person every day! But if one person is bursting with ideas, start there. If partner 1 is sharing, then partner 2 will…what?"

Children chimed in, and I agreed. "That's right, if partner 1 shares her book, then partner 2's role today will be to be a powerful, active listener. Right now, work it out between the two of you—who will share right now, who will listen?"

"Thumbs up if you have that worked out. Good. There will be time at the end of reading time for the other partner to share today, but usually, you'll only share at the end of reading time, and you'll need to plan on there just being one partner who shares in a day (although if there is leftover time, the other can as well.)

continued on next page

"Boys and girls," the teacher said. "For the past few days we have been talking about our ancestors. Who can explain what that word means?"

"It means our dead relatives," Harry blurted out. Then he flashed his white teeth.

When they'd finished this text and a bit more, I told them that I was going to demonstrate paying special attention to the pronouns along the way so we'd know who was who and how the sentences fit together. I started with the first sentence:

"Boys and girls," the teacher said.

I point to the words *the teacher* and interjected, "*The teacher* means Miss Mackle." Then I continued, again pointing to the words and pausing at the pronouns: "'For the past few days we'—*we* means the boys and girls and Miss Mackle—'have been talking about our ancestors'—*our* is referring to whose ancestors they were—the boys' and girls' and Miss Mackle's. 'Who'—*who* means which boy or girl—'can explain what that word'—*that word* means *ancestors*—'means?'"

Before asking the students to try this out, I wanted to explain a bit about how this kind of practice could help them. "I know this sounds pretty ridiculous, right? Well, of course we don't usually read like that. It'd take forever and it'd sound silly. But defining those words out loud

---

MID-WORKSHOP TEACHING POINT

continued from previous page

"Now, sharing partners, listen up. When you share your reading, it is not that different from when you share a story from your life. When you are writing true stories in your writer's notebook, you don't just race through a million topics, do you? No, you think, 'Of all I could write about, of all I could focus on, what is the one thing that especially matters to me?' Then you zoom in on that, and talk and think with details about that one thing.

"This means, sharing partners, that you need to decide on the focus for your share. Take a second to choose an idea, a Post-it, to share. Choose an idea that sparks tons of thoughts, and then plan to also share the part of the book you've marked. And the two of you need to have a grand conversation about that thought and that part of the text, just like our book talks after a read aloud."

"Meanwhile, listening partners, you can talk amongst each other about how you'll listen especially well. Think of some gestures you can use to signal the sharing partner to say more."

After a moment in which listening partners exchanged gestures such as touching their ears, using hands to say "Come on, add on," and so forth, I said, "Partners, start talking."

---

gives our brains a chance to pay more attention to work that we're learning how to do silently and automatically as we read. When we're reading smoothly, our brains automatically do what I just did out loud. We can practice getting our brains to make those connections automatically by doing it out loud for just a little bit. Okay? Your turn. Let's look at the next sentence, and this time I'm going to ask you to help say what some of the words mean so that we can see how all of this fits together."

I read the next sentence out loud:

"It means our dead relatives," Harry blurted out.

Pointing this time, I said, "Okay, let's start with *it*. What does *it* mean in this sentence? You might need to look back to the first sentence for your answer."

Gabe paused, tugging on an untied shoelace, and then said, "I think it means the ancestors, right?"

"Let's try substituting that in to see if it makes sense. What if we said, 'Ancestors means our dead relatives?' Does that seem right?"

"Yeah," Gabe agreed.

"Let's keep going. How about the word *our*. What does that mean? Rosa, what do you think?" I prompted Rosa because she didn't tend to volunteer often.

"*Our* means it's theirs, the kids'," she said, flicking her hair out of her eyes.

"What's theirs?" I questioned.

"The ancestors."

"Yep! Make sense to you guys?" I asked the rest of the group, who nod-ded.

"Let's try the next sentence:"

> Then he flashed his white teeth.

"Who's *he?*"

Max said, "Harry, it's Harry. So's *his.*"

We continued on for a few more sentences, stopping at words that I knew they needed to pay attention to in order to hold the sentences together.

Before sending them off to read independently I said, "So when you're doing your own reading, of course I don't want you to clarify every little word along the way, but see if you notice yourself making connections automatically, in your head, as you go. And you can check on yourself every so often. If you find yourself reading along and then you realize you're not sure who *she* refers to in your book, or you're not sure what *it* is, go back and see if you can figure it out. Those little words are really important in tying all of the sentences together into a story that makes sense."

TEACHING SHARE

Readers Talk About Books Together—Wisely

Prepare children to talk with partners about their books by offering them a handful of tips.

"Time to stop reading and to start talking. This time new people will become sharing partners. Sharing partners, can I see who you are?" I made a thumbs up to show that was the signal I expected. "Sharing partners, remember you need to choose the text and the thoughts you'll share. Will you walk your partner through every Post-it you've used? No way! Instead, you need to ask that question that you ask all the time in the writing workshop: 'Of all that I have to say, what is especially important? 'Take a second to plan your sharing. Perhaps you'll put a star on the Post-its or parts you want to talk about.

"Before you do this, I want to introduce a new chart that will act sort of like a sister to our chart, "Ways You and Another Reader Can Talk About Your Reading Lives." This one will give you tips on ways to talk about not your *reading lives* but your *books*. I've put a few items on this new chart, based on things we've been doing in our reading work together this year. You may want to consider some of these things as you decide what to share with your partner today. We'll be returning to this chart again and adding to it."

Ways You and Another Reader Can Talk About Your Books

- Share passages that especially drew you in—parts that made you feel a strong emotion or exciting parts that had you on the edge of your seat.

- Share parts in which you really pictured what is happening, perhaps parts where you felt like you were in a 3-D movie—one with surround sound.

- Show each other parts of your books where the mental movie you made as you read got blurry, places where you thought "Huh?" and then talk about those parts, discussing what's going on in them.

- Figure out a tricky word by discussing what the word might mean and by using words you **can** read to figure out how to say this unfamiliar word.

COACHING TIPS

It is important to give readers choices and certainly it's as important to be able to choose how to respond to a text as it is to choose that text in the first place. On the other hand, many children won't imagine many possibilities. This teaching share attempts to provide possibilities while also supporting choice.

After about a minute I continued, "Sharing partners, you have just another minute to get ready. Listeners, remember to actually listen, and to try to understand what your partner is saying. That's not easy—and there will be times when you don't get it. When you are confused, register that on your face, and ask for clarification. If you are confused, you owe it to your sharing partner to say, 'Huh?' or 'I don't really get it. Can you explain?'. "

"Sharing partners, remember that it is always important in life, while telling the story of a book, to watch your listener's face. You should be able to read whether your listener really grasps what you are saying or not. Watch for confusion to cloud the eyes; when you see that look, go back and clarify.

"Also when talking about books, please be especially careful to actually use names for the people in your book because if you say, 'This guy, he goes to visit that guy, and the guy—not the first guy but the second guy,' it'll be very hard for anyone to follow. Use the character's name, and when you use it, add in a descriptor about the character so that you talk like this: 'Grandfather, an old potato farmer who is in bed with a broken spirit, looked blankly forward.'

"Okay, let's meet with our partners and remember that whether we are talking about our books or listening, what we say and hear needs to make sense. If it doesn't, we should say something like, 'What?' 'Who?' or 'I don't get it.'"

As partners talked, I went around and whispered into the listeners' ears, "'Aren't you confused? Ask her to explain.' or 'If you're really interested, you need to show that.'"

Notice that after I set readers up to work in partnerships, I'm apt to coach in ways that support the listening partner. I don't want to usurp this person's role, although it's conceivable that I might ask, "Could I take your place and be the listening partner for a minute and will you notice the ways that I show I am listening?

BE A GOOD LISTENER and HELP YOUR PARTNER GROW HIS or HER IDEAS...
- Gesture to get your partner to say more.
- Nod or comment to show you're listening.
- Ask questions.
- Say, "Can you say more?"
- Repeat what partner said.

DRAFT

Retelling Stories by Starting at the Beginning

hen my oldest son was three, I searched diligently for the perfect nursery school. My first visit was to the school that seemed to top the list of other parents in my town. I arrived early at the school. None of the adults were ready to speak with me yet, so I joined a few children who were working with play dough. One of the girls was using it to chronicle the story of how, the previous evening, she'd fed leftover pizza crusts to a few baby ducks. The youngster had made a duck family out of the dough (just one blob for each duck) and as I watched, she swam one baby duck toward a play dough blob that represented herself. "Quack, quack, quack," the baby duck said in a high voice.

"Here ducky, have some pizza," the little girl said, making the clay representation of herself move toward the baby ducks. The baby duck gobbled up the pizza crusts, then looked for the mother duck that had apparently swum away.

As the baby duck began its search for the missing mother, the director of the school joined me. "This is where it all starts," she said, gesturing toward the play dough. *This* is essential for writing, reading, the works."

My heart leapt. "Yes!" I thought. "She knows, she knows, she knows." I could have hugged her. But my heart leapt too soon.

GETTING READY

- Remind children to sit in their rug spots with their new reading partners.

- Before this session, read to the end of Chapter 7 in *Stone Fox*. You'll retell the text during this session.

- To provide additional support for today's minilesson, you may want to create a chart titled "Ways We Can Retell to Our Partners" that details today's strategy. If you decide to create this chart, you'll add more bullet points to it tomorrow.

- Readers will need Post-its for the mid-workshop teaching point, but presumably they'll have a stash on hand in their My Reading Life folders.

- During the mid-workshop teaching point, you will want to have your own independent reading book on hand so that you can do the work alongside children.

- Before you start Session XIV, you'll need to have read up to the end of Chapter 8 in *Stone Fox* if that is your read-aloud book.

The director held up her hand, and began to move her fingers in the air as if she were kneading bread. "Yep," she said, "It all starts here. We begin exercising their fingers with soft play dough, then move on to the stiffer beeswax clay, then to the stiff clay, and by that time, their fingers are strong enough to hold a pencil."

> *We live, and then we turn around in our tracks and retell the story of our lives.*

Finger exercises? What a tragedy it was to me that the teacher didn't choose the story-making, the retelling of the little girl's life, as the brilliant, generative, essential activity of the morning. In the end, it's not what we do that matters, but what we make of what we do. It is the most human thing in the world for us to experience something, and then to turn around in our tracks and to chronicle the story of what we have experienced.

Patricia MacLachlen says it well. "Other creatures have journeys far greater than ours," she says. The salmon crisscrosses the ocean many times, the monarch butterfly summers in Maine and winters in Mexico. Other creatures have journeys far greater than ours. But we are the creature that lives to tell the tale." We live, and then we turn around in our tracks and retell the story of our lives.

Shall we support that instinct in our schools with our children? Shall we tilt toward children, listening keenly to their renditions, their retellings of their lives? We can ask children to share family stories, to retell favorite movies, to reminisce over the preceding day. And we need to ask them to share the stories of the texts they read as well, and help them put all those various retellings into the world in ways that make sense, that invite others to share their thoughts and ideas—and yes, to share their own retellings as well.

Today, in this session, you begin the work of teaching children to make their retellings inviting, sensible, and deep so that they and their reading friends can gather around shared stories as people might gather around the campfire. It is by storytelling that we, human beings, create shared experiences—both firsthand and vicarious—and shared understandings. Through shared stories, we build relationships and understandings of the texts and of the world around us.

DRAFT

MINILESSON

Retelling Stories by Starting at the Beginning

CONNECTION

Talk about the human need to tell stories, referring to stories from those inscribed on ancient cave walls all the way to blogs. Suggest that just as it is natural for people to story-tell their experiences, so, too, it is natural to story-tell the books we read.

Zillions of years ago, when human beings were still cave men, people would return from hunts and journeys, and they'd use berries and sticks to capture the stories of those escapades on stony cave walls. Then after depicting the story on the wall, the wise old hunter and the young novice hunter would stand together, reminiscing and reflecting on the events.

Now, thousands of years later, young adults have Facebook pages and blogs, and these function like those stony cave walls once functioned. Instead of using berries and sticks to capture the stories, today's youth use writing. But either way, for as long as human beings have existed, we have always been the creature who not only has experiences, but who also pauses to recall those experiences. This is a big part of what makes us human. We go away for the weekend—and return home, full of stories. The family gathers to hear what happened.

"Every time you and I open a book, we head off on an adventure, and it is only human nature that when we return home to our reading families—to our partners and reading friends—we come full of stories.

"Yesterday, when you readers shared your reading with each other, a fair amount of what you did was that you retold the stories you've been reading. Then you talked over those stories. I want you to realize that what you did—sharing the stories of your books—is what people do with books all the time. The way you talked about your books is the way that people gossip, too. First, you say, 'Did you hear what happened to so-and-so at the such and such.' Then you dissect the sequence of events: 'I'm so surprised she said that.... I mean, what would drive her to...?'"

As I wrote this minilesson, Iranians were protesting a stolen election. While journalists and the media were arrested, driven from the public square, ordinary citizens in Iran became reporters, their reports broadcast across the world on CNN and MSNBC. Despite threats on their lives, the Iranian people did all they could to speak out, telling their story to the world. When the government shut down the Internet there, hundreds of thousands of Iranians discovered and used a special software—Global Internet Freedom Software—that for a time allowed them to erase their tracks and escape detection. They did all this to tell and retell their stories.

Alan Tizon, a journalist, wrote, "Stories give shape to experience and allow us to go through life unblind. Without them, everything that happens would float around, undifferentiated. None of it would mean anything."

The fact that children did something on the preceding day—in this instance, retold their books—is insignificant. The fact that they learned something is monumental.

The opening of a minilesson will usually recall the latest tool that has been added to the toolkit, often also recalling other tools that can be drawn on, as well.

"But it starts, 'Did you hear that so and so did such and such?' And sometimes, you can't just tell *the latest* catastrophe. Sometimes, you even need to back up and tell the *whole* story, right? So sometimes the retellings start like this. 'Well, it all started a few months ago, when. . . .'"

The biggest misunderstanding teachers have about minilessons is thinking of them as the forum in which a teacher rallies the kids to do the day's assignment, to jump through the hoops that the teacher has set out for that day. Minilessons are not assignments. The goal of a minilesson must be to add to a reader's repertoire of skills and strategies so the reader then has more to draw upon from that day forward. In a minilesson, the teacher often demonstrates a strategy that he or she has decided to advance and then gives kids help trying to put that strategy into action. Sometimes the teacher will go so far as to encourage children to use the strategy during independent reading that very day. But mostly, the point is that the new strategy will become part of readers' toolkits to be drawn upon as needed.

Suggest that retelling is helpful not only as a way to catch partners up on what they need to understand about a book, but also as a way to help ourselves synthesize and respond to the unfolding story.

"Readers, I loved listening yesterday as you and your partners retold your books to each other. Listening, I realized that we retell not only as a way to catch *someone else* up on a story; we also retell to catch *ourselves* up. We retell to remind ourselves of what's already happened and to see how the unfolding story fits together. That is, we retell to catch up—and keep up—with the story."

Notice the language I'm using. 'We retell to catch up—and keep up—with the story.' When we teach a minilesson, we are hoping that the words that we say to kids will make a lasting difference. We want our language to be memorable. It should not be surprising, then, that the minilessons in these books rely on the same literacy devices that persuasive speakers use. Although I'm no John Kennedy or Abraham Lincoln, I use rhetorical devices one finds in Kennedy's "Ask not what your country can do. . ." speech and in Lincoln's "Gettysburg Address." Above all, there is a lot of parallelism in minilessons. "We retell to catch someone else up. We also retell to catch ourselves up." It will help if you develop an eye for seeing parallelism and other literary devices in these minilessons, because although you will definitely want to paraphrase major portions of the minilessons, there will be some ways with words that may you want to hold onto.

"I realized something last night. You know how, at the very beginning of shows that are series, like for me it's this show called *Grey's Anatomy,* there's a narrator who says, 'Previously on *Grey's Anatomy. . . ,*' and then the narrator shows a collage of key moments from earlier shows? I've always known that the collage of clips helps me when I missed the last episode, just like your retelling helps when your partner hasn't read the book, but last night I realized that even when I *did* see what was 'previously on' those earlier shows, the 'previously on' prelude of *Grey's Anatomy* warms me up for the upcoming episode."

Your tone of voice and your delivery when you say "Previously on..." will make all the difference to your children. Be sure to draw out the first syllable—preee—as they do on television and to play up a sense of drama. If you say this phrase with the intonation children know from television, they'll reward you by taking to the phrase like bees to honey. For days, even months, afterwards, children will go around saying, "Previously on..." and this will channel them to do the retelling work that some children need.

"Sometimes right after the narrator says, 'Previously on. . . ,' there are a bunch of commercials, and I use that time to think ahead to the upcoming show. Last night, as I waited for the new episode to begin, I wondered why one of the characters on the show wanted to be a doctor, because she always seems so miserable at work."

Really play up the reference to "Previously on...." The kids will take to this and know exactly what you mean. Of course, I'm aware that children will be more keyed into Survivor *than* Grey's Anatomy, *but I do not know that show, so I can't reference it with any power. You'll find your own version of this.*

"This got me thinking about reading and retelling. As a reader, I realized that retelling what happens in my story doesn't only help my partner, but it also helps me as a reader to get ready for what's coming up and to grow ideas about what has happened so far. After all, when I retell, I'm recollecting the story for *myself,* as well as for my partner. This gives me a chance to think about the characters and the action, to gather my thoughts, and to get my mind warmed up for growing ideas about the story."

Name your teaching point. Specifically, teach children that readers retell to recollect the story and think more deeply about it, and readers also retell to help someone else join us in thinking about a text.

"Readers, today I want to teach you that readers often retell our books (up to the part where we're reading) as a way to lay the story out *for others* so we can talk it over. But we also retell our books as a way to lay the story out for *ourselves* so we can think it over. And that process of retelling and rethinking keeps the whole story primed in our minds."

Kathleen and I are convinced that the ability to retell is a necessary, if not sufficient, aspect of comprehension. Too many readers grab onto isolated bits of a text and react to those isolated parts without putting them into a larger context. Comprehension involves the ability to take in a text in such a way that one can reconstruct a synthesized, coherent rendition of it. Of course, the elements a child chooses to include in such a retelling are, to a large extent, negotiable, but a child who leaves out one of two main characters is apt to have comprehension problems. When readers read novels with an eye toward reconstructing the main elements in a coherent fashion, they are more likely to hold onto meaning—to comprehend.

Teaching

Demonstrate that one way to retell a book is to take big steps through the timeline of events, retelling only the important ones. Physically pace out a timeline of a shared text

"Let me show you what I mean. In this case, I want to talk with my partner about my book, and he hasn't read it, so I want to tell him the gist of it so far so. Then he'll be able to react and understand and talk with me about it. One way to retell a story is to start at the very beginning and then take big steps across the whole of the story so far, only telling the most important parts." As I describe this type of retelling, I jot it on chart paper.

When children are reading books that have an overarching storyline such as one is apt to find in level K – M texts, it's entirely reasonable for a reader to retell those books from beginning to end. That is not a reader's only option, but it is a workable one. Once readers begin to read longer and more complex texts, however, this sort of point-by-point retelling becomes less feasible and now readers need to rely on summary and synthesis more, or to retell in support of an idea, tracing the thread of the story that pertains to that idea.

Ways We Can Retell to Our Partners

- *Start at the beginning of the story and take big steps through the timeline of events, telling only the key parts.*

- *Tell parts of the story that make you want to talk about them. Make the text come alive between you and your partner.*

Standing up from my seat, I walked about five large steps away from my chair, to symbolize walking back to the beginning of my story. Standing under the flagpole, near the door to the classroom, I said, "(I will start my retelling by going back to the start of the book.) Willy and his dog Searchlight can't wake up Grandfather. (Now I'm going to step over some of the details until I get to the next big part.)" I took a big step, and then I said, "Willy gets Doc Smith, who tells him his grandfather is depressed," and I took another large step. (There are a lot of parts I'm stepping over, but I think the next thing I need to retell is,) "Willy finds out that his grandfather owes a lot of money in taxes." I took another large step. "Willy and Searchlight enter a sled dog race to try to win the prize money to save the farm and his grandfather."

Back where you started, recap what you have just done in a way that is transferable to other days and other texts. Then shift from retelling the text you've just read to sharing your thoughts about it.

"Readers, did you notice how I retold the timeline of the story? Moving in big steps through the sequence of big events, I quickly covered the whole terrain of *Stone Fox*."

"Now if I start talking about one part of the book, my partner will get what I mean; I've given some context. But you know what? I've not only *filled in* my partner, I've also *filled up* myself. I feel ready to share some ideas that I have about the story. Let me see. . . . Hmmm. . . . My thought about what I read is that Willy is so determined. I would have given up! And he is young to be so determined."

Teachers who have piloted these sessions often remark that it is surprisingly helpful to actually walk across the front of the room, taking one step for each big event in the timeline of the story. The truth is that every minilesson takes on new life if it involves a physical dimension. For this reason, I suggest teachers draft minilessons through improvisational drama rather than while sitting at a computer. In a minilesson that aimed to show the way charts and graphs need to link to the passage in a nonfiction text, for example, some teachers and I got in a line. The first teacher read one sentence from a passage and then, in an effort to show that one sentence linked to the next, that first teacher linked her arms with the next teacher in line, who read the next sentence aloud before she, too, linked arms with a third teacher, a third sentence, and soon one teacher in this chain linked arms with a related chart, a graph that needed to be brought into the chain of sentences. The teachers actually looped arms up to the charts in ways that brought the chart into the chain of sentences. This may be hard to visualize, but my point is that it is best to avoid writing minilessons at the computer. Minilessons are oral instructions, and when composed at the computer, they often lose their oral quality, and their intimacy. To write a minilesson, improvise and enact, then scrawl with a pen, adding stuff that feels right, although of course you can eventually type it for posterity or to share with others.

As you can see, I share my thoughts in a very underdeveloped way. I think of this as sort of a placeholder for later when I will show readers a whole lot more about what it means to share thoughts with each other. I'm not at this point in the unit wanting to elaborate on the importance of growing and sharing thoughts about a text, but I do need to point out that we don't retell texts for no reason. Instead, this serves as a prelude to rethinking and discussing the texts.

ACTIVE INVOLVEMENT

Set readers up to practice this strategy, retelling a story to their partners, helping them recollect the important parts of the story in steps.

"Readers, I see you are ready to try this kind of retelling with your own books! I want to point out to you that, in life, people do not actually take physical steps across the room while retelling a story. You don't see people in coffee shops retelling a movie they just watched while taking giant steps across the cafe. Similarly, reading friends do not actually walk across the room while we are retelling our books either. When we're just learning this, though, I do think it can help to pace out the timelines of our books. So, I'm going to ask a few of you to go (with your partner) to some empty space in the room, and to retell like I did, while walking. The rest of you will need to walk and retell while seated—like this." I made my hands 'walk' step by step on my knees.

Of course it is utterly optional whether you want to disperse a few partnerships. If you decide to do this, send your squirmy kids off—the ones who seem to have a hard time with the physical constraints of classrooms. Their energy is real, and it helps to allow them ways to use physical activity in the service of intellectual activity.

"Partner 1s, will you retell the book you are reading, right now. You can look back for a second if you need to do so. Figure out the parts—the big events—you'll include in your retelling. Partner 2, it will be your job to make sure your partner does his or her job of retelling *in big steps,* just like I did as I took big steps across the room. If you realize your partner is taking teeny, tiny steps through the story, telling every little detail, staying in just one part of his or her book—then you'll want to whisper, 'Take big steps, not baby steps,' and encourage your partner to step over more of the details and small events and to touch down only on the big, important events."

"Partner 2, when your partner gives you a thumbs up, that means your partner is ready to retell the story to you. You are going to be intrigued by the great stories you are about to hear!" I gave them several minutes to retell and talk.

Giving listening partners a job to do is a way to increase their' sense of engagement in this work. Asking partner 2 to listen in certain ways to partner 1's retelling gives partner 2 a role to play. Partner 1 will have opportunities to be the critical friend another time.

LINK

Send readers off, reminding them that there are many situations in life that call for a retelling. Remind readers that one way to retell is to start at the story's beginning and take big steps through the story, telling the key events.

"So now, readers, you know something you can try when you want to talk about a text that you know and that your listener does not know. You can give a 'Previously in…,' you can help your listener have a context in which to put the conversation you'll have together about the book. And the important thing that I hope you learned today is that actually, retelling can be a way for all of us as readers to recall the main outline of a book—to reconstruct the pieces into a coherent story flow.

"If we've been away from a book and we want to reorient ourselves to it, we can give ourselves a quick retelling, a 'Previously in. . .' that warms us up for reading further. And if, when we are reading, we find ourselves getting confused about how this new little piece fits into the bigger jigsaw puzzle of the whole story, then we can retell in an organized way, so then we have the whole story in mind and can figure out how the new piece might fit.

"Remember, when you do retell, that if you want to back up and retell the whole story, it is important to take big steps so that you step over the details and small events, and touch down on the big, important events. Even if you plan to zoom in on one particular point of the story, it can help to catch each other up on the main timelines of the books before zooming in on the intriguing subsection."

CONFERRING AND SMALL-GROUP WORK

Record Keeping Can Make Your Teaching More Assessment Based, Giving it Traction and Direction

By this time in the year, your kids are accustomed to carrying on independently during the reading workshop. They've got baggies full of books and Post-its, and most of them are able to move from the meeting area to their independent reading fairly smoothly, and to keep themselves going as readers while you circulate throughout the classroom, conducting conferences and leading small groups of various sorts. You've taken some time to give your strugglers extra attention and have even given your strongest readers an extra push as well. It is probably time for you to stop thinking for a bit about your readers and their reading and to think instead about you and your teaching.

It is hard to emphasize enough the importance of learning to confer well and to lead small groups well. When you do these quiet forms of teaching really well, things change. First of all, your teaching will have a new sort of traction. You'll be able to draw upon your deep gut-level connection with kids to make any teaching you do more responsive—more

intimate. You'll have what it takes to be able to revise the minilessons in this book and the one that follow it, to be able to author your own minilessons, mid-workshop teaching points, and shares. Then, too, when your children understand that you are going to help them actually put the things that you talk about and demonstrate into practice, they will listen with absolutely new ears. So often, kids have become accustomed to teachers teaching and kids doing their work, and the two things happening almost in isolation from each other. You won't want to wait before making sure that you do everything possible to change the message, making your classroom into one in which words matter, teaching sticks, and kids' work is always front and center.

The one single thing you can do that will most help you lift the level of your conferring and small-group work is to develop a system for making and recording and learning from formative assessments. This is always important when one teaches, but never more important than in the reading workshop.

MID-WORKSHOP TEACHING POINT

READERS PREPARE FOR THE CONVERSATIONS WE WILL HAVE WITH OUR READING PARTNERS

"Readers, may I stop you? All eyes up here, please." I waited. "Earlier today, I reminded you that you'll have a chance to share your book at the end of the day. I know you were listening, but I need to make sure you really *heard* me. Because here is the thing—eyes and ears up here because this is important—when you know you are going to have a chance to tell someone about a journey, the whole experience of that journey will be different. It is different because you are always thinking, 'I'm *definitely* going to tell him (or her) about this part.' That's true when you travel to places like Washington DC, and it is true when you travel in your mind's eye, through books. You read, thinking, 'She (or he) won't believe this part!' It is almost like you write your retelling and your ideas about the book as *you read*, so that you will be all set to share the book."

"Will you try that right now? Whatever part you are up to in your book, take this time to recollect what you've read. You definitely can look at the book if you need to recall important details." As readers began to do this, I pulled out my independent reading book and began to visibly, intently, do this same thinking work as I sat in the chair at the front of the room.

"Right now, look back over what you have already read and make notes (or leave Post-its) that will help you be ready when it comes time to share your reading. In a minute,

continued on next page

Fashioning a Record-Keeping System That Allows Your Teaching of Reading to Be Grounded in a Sense of the Reader's History

Think for a moment about ways in which teaching *reading* is different than teaching *writing*. The good news about teaching reading is that once you set things up right—enabling kids to work with books of their own choosing that work well for them—then children's resistance to reading will usually melt away. If you do the engineering necessary to create the conditions that support engagement, many kids will read, read, read. The bad news about teaching reading is that it is not easy for teachers to gets our hands on what kids have been doing as readers. Reading, unlike writing, is invisible. Perhaps a child will come to a conference with tons of jottings about a book and with a list of recently read books, but it is more likely that the child won't have many written records, or that the records the child has made won't come close to capturing the mental work the child has done with the text. Then, too, because children will tend to be reading, reading, reading before your interactions and after your interactions with them, it is easy for your instruction to feel like it's just a light touch, one that hardly ruffles the surface of children's ongoing work and that quickly dissipates. Especially when you are not teaching into the specificity of one specific text that you and the kids know well, if you do not take record keeping seriously, it may seem as if your conferences and small group work with readers comes out of and goes nowhere.

When teaching *writing*, in contrast, although it is a challenge to keep kids mobilized as writers, because your teaching is so necessary, you'll rarely feel as if it was expendable or as if your instruction doesn't have traction. When you teach writing, you can look at what children put on the page after your interaction (contrasting it with what they wrote before your interaction), and you can immediately see the fruits of your teaching. The concrete, visible nature of writing makes it very easy for any one day's instruction to extend the trajectory of development that was established on previous days.

The trick, then, when teaching reading, is that you will want to find a way to use formative assessments and record keeping to help you be sure that your teaching is not merely "blowin' in the wind."

Although you'll need to devise a record-keeping system that works for you, there are some systems that I do not recommend—and one of these is the system that most teachers I know use when recording their writing conferences! It is very common when teaching writing for teachers to carry a sheet of paper, clipped onto a clipboard, containing a full-page grid of boxes, one for each of your twenty-five or thirty children. Teachers then record your compliment and teaching point when you confer with a child, sometimes squeezing records of as many as two interactions into a child's box on this grid. The advantage of this system is that it helps you see at a glance which child has and has not received some assistance, and you needn't spend precious time shuffling through lots of pages to locate the particular place for recording work with a particular child. The disadvantage of this system is that is does not help you see and build upon one's prior instruction or assessments.

MID-WORKSHOP TEACHING POINT

continued from previous page

you'll have a chance to share your thoughts with your partner. But first, readers, let me give you a tip. Sometimes, when you have a thought about your book to share, you can't just come out and say it because your listener won't understand everything she needs to know about the significance of the part you share. Sometimes, you have to retell some other parts so your listener can learn the context. If you only know one part of a story, one piece of the puzzle, you can only appreciate that one part. You can't really get a sense of how the whole thing goes, can you?

"On the other hand, you also don't really need to know every detail of the story to appreciate the part your friend wants to talk about, right? You don't have to hear every detail of a story or scrutinize every puzzle piece to see the whole picture.

"So talk to your partner, and if you need to, do a 'Previously in. . . .'"

After a minute, I intervened. "You all have Post-its in your Reading Life Folders. Get a stack of them out and keep them beside you as you read on. I'm pretty sure there will be things you notice because you are getting ready to share with a partner one more time today. As you read on, if you find yourself thinking, 'I better pay attention to that so I can retell this bit later,' just leave a Post-it note on that part. Then later, before you do a retelling, you can glance back over parts you marked to prepare yourself. You can also use Post-its to record places where you have big important thoughts—reactions you want to share.

Remember that when you confer with writers, you always have portfolio of their writing to draw upon. Even if your record keeping does not establish a trajectory for each writer, the writer's notebook itself enables you to recall and follow up upon what the child had been doing. Children's reading logs and their writing about reading can provide you with sense of a reader's history, but your record keeping needs to provide more detail than logs alone can provide.

You may, then, be imagining that you'll keep a loose-leaf binder with a section full of pages devoted to each of your children, so that you can cumulate all your records for each child on the sheaf of pages devoted to that child. This is not bad idea—it definitely would allow you to reread your records from the previous conference or small group before moving to another teaching interaction and it will ensure you don't send kids off on one trail and then forget what you asked them to do as you jerk them in an entirely different direction.

Fashioning a Record-Keeping System That Allows Your Teaching to Be Informed By an Understanding of the Challenges That Tend to be Posed by Books at Particular Levels of Difficulty

Although I think a loose-leaf binder with tabs for each child is much more helpful than a class grid (because it allows a child's reading history to inform your teaching), I think there are even better systems than notebooks filled with what begin as blank pages for each child. Ideally, your record keeping will not only allow you to recall what you have already taught this reader, but it will also remind you of the content you expect you'll teach, the skills you'll develop, the strategies you'll demonstrate.

And unless you are super human, you will probably find it difficult to keep twenty-five to thirty utterly unique individuals in mind as you teach. Instead, you'll probably have a sense that, for example, if one of the goals that you are addressing right now is fluency, you have a handful of readers are at the low end of your fluency trajectory, needing help reading phrases that are more than two to three words long, and another handful at the high end of that fluency trajectory, needing practice deciding what to forward and what to subordinate in complex sentences. And you'll have in mind strategies that you might use so that you provide varying numbers of scaffolds to these different clusters of readers.

There is nothing magical about the goal of reading with fluency. You'll always have a handful of goals that you are spotlighting in a unit of study, as well as a handful of goals that you are spotlighting that are independent of the unit of study (these may have a lot to do with the levels of book difficulty that these children are reading or with writing and thinking about reading).

At this time in the year, when you have just assessed readers and matched them to just-right texts and when the thinking about reading work that you are supporting is still fairly minimal, you'll probably cluster your children based on the levels of text difficulty that they can handle. That is, because level J, K, L, and M books have a lot in common, your record keeping (not your seating chart!) may cluster together the children who are reading levels J to M. Similarly, your record keeping may cluster children who are reading levels N to P. Either way, you'll want to spend time anticipating the teaching you'll do in response to your assessments. If your records allow you to draw on prompts and reminders so that you can take into account what a child is saying and doing and then draw on a repertoire of possible next steps, allowing your teaching to be responsive, this will be helpful.

In A Guide to the Reading Workshop and on the CD, you'll see templates I recommend that can guide your teaching assessment work with readers working in four different bends of text difficulty. That is, for readers reading books leveled J-M, you will want to watch ways in which they use narrative text structure to link one chapter together with the next and the next. It won't have been long ago when these readers tended to read books that were begun and finished in a single day. Meanwhile, readers who are working with texts in levels U, V, and W will benefit from you watching to note whether they expect sub-plots to fit together into a coherent whole by the end of the text.

TEACHING SHARE

Readers Include Vital Facts So Our Partners Will Be Able to Follow Along as We Retell Our Stories

Set children up to practice monitoring for sense when listening to retelling. Retell the read-aloud book poorly first, then collect a list of ways to improve that retelling.

"Today, as you were reading along in your stories, your partner was on your mind. You were thinking about what you'd share with your partner. In a minute, you'll have a chance to share. You'll start with a 'Previously in. . . ,' recapping the key elements in your story so you and your listener are caught up. And listeners, you're going to need to listen keenly, trying to reconstruct the story based on the retelling.

"Let's practice being listeners who actually try to grasp the gist of the story from what we hear, okay. Pretend you haven't read *Stone Fox*. I'm going to retell the book. See if I give you enough information so you can reconstruct the story in your mind. If you can't piece things together, let's see if you have suggestions for how my retelling could be better. List those across your fingers.

"Here I go. There is this kid, this boy, and this dog, and they are in a dog-sled race, and, well, before that the boy's grandfather is in bed depressed, and that's because of the potato farm, and the boy and the dog, they are racing someone who always wins so everyone says 'Don't race.' That's the story! Can you picture how it goes? Give a thumbs up if you had a clear understanding of the story."

I overdo all the problems that are most common in children's retellings, knowing this will allow children to devise all sorts of suggestions for ways I can improve.

"I don't see any thumbs up. Quickly, turn and with your partner, list four things I could have done to make my retelling stronger. What would have helped?"

Do not give children a lot of time for this turn and talk, just thirty seconds or so, but do lean in to a few partnerships so you can find one or two that will answer in ways that will move the discussion along.

I listened in as children talked to each other. "Well," said Izzy, directing her comments at me instead of her partner, "you only talked about Willy and Searchlight, but you didn't even say their names, and you didn't mention Stone Fox. So how can there be a race without someone else in it? Plus, you didn't tell much about the Grandfather, and he's a big part."

"Ah, that's a great suggestion. I bet it will help my partner understand what's happening in a story if I include all the important characters in my retelling. I'm going to jot those ideas down. Is that all I need to make my retelling complete?"

Izzy's partner Emma leaned forward and added with excitement, "You have to say that Stone Fox is right behind them."

"Hmm. . . . That's a good suggestion, too. Otherwise, I'm not helping people feel the suspense. You are really helping me get more details into my retelling, and you are right that if I want to convey the tone of this part of the story, I need to show the cause of the rising tension. I'm going to add Emma's suggestion to my list of tips for retelling well," I said as I added to my own notes.

After listening in on one other partnership, I convened the class. "Readers, I listened into a couple of partnerships and got some great ideas about how to make the retelling so my partner would understand it. When I am retelling to my partner, I need to make sure that I tell *who* is in the story and *what* each of the main characters is doing, using vital facts like names, places, and so on. If I can do this, my partner can get the gist of my story—and I also am double-checking to be sure I'm not confused about my book as it's important to show story tension if it is there in the story.

"Right now, take a moment to think about how you'll retell to your partner. Think about the vital facts, like names and places, that will really help your partner understand the story." I gave them about ten seconds or so to think about this.

"Okay, Let's start with partner 2. Talk to your partner, retelling your story in a way that helps your partner understand and that shows that you understand all that's been going on so far."

After a few minutes, I said, "We just have a couple of seconds left in reading workshop, so let me stop you. Partner 1s, give me a thumbs up if you think you sort of understand how your partner's story goes?" They did so. "Now a real challenge. Partner 1s, you have only two minutes, so you need to do a *very* quick summary. Tell who the main characters are, explain what the main character had done up to this point in the story, and get to the main tension, the main problem, pretty quickly. Go."

Notice that when a child makes a specific suggestion for how the retelling on a read aloud text could have been improved, I reiterate the suggestion, only this time I say the suggestion in a way that makes it transferable to other days and other texts. This one move is something that I do scores of times in any one day's reading workshop. When I compliment a reader in a conference, I'm always complimenting something specific the reader has done but I always want to phrase my compliment in ways that make the reader's good work into something he or she could do another day with another text.

DRAFT

Retelling Stories by Starting with Now and Backing Up

IN THIS SESSION,

you will teach children that when retelling, readers need to synthesize and fit together all the parts that we've read that are pertinent.

his session teaches children that sometimes readers do not retell or recall by starting at the beginning of a story and pacing through the text. Sometimes, instead of starting our retelling from the beginning of the book, readers start by retelling what we've just read, inserting, as we go, asides that reference earlier parts of the text and that add meaning to the events as they are unfolding in this chapter. Why, you might ask, should we spend the time to teach such a complicated structure for retelling a story? In fact, why spend so much time on retelling, period?

It's true that many wise educators deride retelling, characterize it as "regurgitation" or as an "empty recitation," suggesting this is a facet of reading that is devoid of—and even pushes away—comprehension, synthesis, inference, interpretation, and critical thinking.

I couldn't disagree more strongly. As I've written throughout this series and the sister series, *Units of Study in Writing,* I believe retelling—retelling our texts and our lives—is fundamental to our human nature. Humans are tied to one another through the retellings of the stories of our origins, of our struggles, of our families, and of our homelands.

And there's more. While we all have thoughts—thoughts to be honored and strengthened and heard—our voice is not the only voice that matters. There is a place in the process of understanding where the main goal must be focusing on what someone else—someone outside ourselves—is getting at. What is that other person, that other text, communicating to me? What is it offering up? What's there, outside me? Sure, it is important for me to be conscious of what I think in response to that text, but there must

GETTING READY

- Before this session, you'll need to have read aloud to the end of Chapter 8, in *Stone Fox.*

- Be prepared to show the "Ways You and Another Reader Can Talk About Your Books." from Session XII.

- If yesterday you decided to make the chart titled "Ways We Can Retell To Our Partners," bring that chart to the meeting area today. Before gathering children, add another bullet point to it: "Start at the beginning of the chunk you've just read. Summarize only that part, adding in asides as you go about earlier parts of the story that add a layer of meaning onto the events of the chapter." This is the strategy for retelling you will be teaching today.

- Devise and practice a "harken back" gesture that represents the mental operation of harkening back.

- Prior to Session XV, be sure to have read Chapter 9 of *Stone Fox* aloud.

also be a place for the text itself. Inviting readers to retell, and then teaching them to do this well, invites them to synthesize the text, to take it in, so they can then reflect on what the text actually contains. One part of listening and of reading involves an effort to wrap our minds around what someone else is trying to say, not passively understanding, but actively making our own reconstruction of what we're taking in. At heart, that is retelling.

> *Humans are tied to one another through the retellings of the stories of our origins, of our struggles, of our families, and of our homelands.*

Retelling is also a way of forging connections with others, of collaborating. If I want to exclaim with you over a sword-fight in a part of *The Lord of the Rings,* I have to retell the story to you. If I didn't see how Anna reacted to her new stepmother in *Sarah Plain and Tall,* I need someone to retell it to me so I can join in processing how to help her adjust to the situation. The act of retelling puts a live text between us so that we can work together, even when I was not there in the flesh. Retelling can bring others into collaboration with you when they otherwise couldn't join.

Retelling puts a live text between people not only when someone missed out on the text, but also when a text is challenging to comprehend. A decade or so ago, several hundred New York City teachers met once a week in small reading clubs sponsored by the Teachers College Reading and Writing Project, and each of those reading clubs read Toni Morrison's beautiful and complex novel, *Beloved.* I studied what adult readers chose to do together as a way for me to begin to imagine what book clubs for our younger counterparts might entail. When we were reading *Beloved,* there was not a single adult reading club that didn't choose to reconstruct the text together. We needed each other's help keeping the story straight in our minds, seeing how the pieces fit together, understanding the through line that held one section of the text together with another. Yes, the text was complex for us and therefore required this extra work, but I can't help but think that for many young readers, the texts they read are equally complex for them.

Figuring how all the pieces go together to make a coherent whole is never easy work—even if the text is, in fact, ones own life experience. I recently decided to write the story of how I got myself a new puppy. Sounds simple, doesn't it? As simple as retelling the story, say, of *Junebug* or of *Journey.* But how do I begin? With waking up at 4 AM, and driving five hours to the breeder's home in Old Forge? Or with the day it began to dawn on me that I would soon get a puppy?

I'd traveled to my parents' home to pay my respects, and this time, when I asked how I could be helpful, my mother had an answer. "You could dig a hole to bury Flurry."

Hearing the request, remorse washed over me. Mum's shadow had died and I was so out of the loop that I hadn't even heard? And Flurry—Flurry was just the age of my Tucker. Now she was dead? Horrors. "Oh, Mum," I said, "I didn't even realize Flurry had died—I'm so sorry."

"She's not dead," my mother said, matter of factly. "But she'll die soon, and I figure we might as well have the hole ready."

DRAFT

So I went out and under the chestnut tree, where we have always buried the pets that have died, and I dug a hole. As I did so, my mother's old dog and my old dog and my old mother all stood mournfully at the hole's edge. As I tossed one shovel full of soil after another to the side, I realized that I needed, in my own way, to dig a hole, to ready myself for loss.

My boys are both flying from the nest, and the chapter in my life that was all about the boys, the dog we got together, and that family unit is coming to an end. So when the breeder, Pam, handed me a squirming ball of black fur and said, "She's yours," I felt a pang of loss. Getting a puppy is my way of digging a hole.

Of course, the story could have unrolled differently—starting with a different beginning. I could have started the story when I arrived at the breeder's house. Pam was there at the driveway's edge, puppy in her arms. She passed the dog to me, and I buried my face in Emma's soft fur. As I did this, though, I found myself trying to peek out the side of my eyes to see the other puppies that tumbled around at our feet—the ones who were not for me. Was Emma really the best? Might another puppy be better? I looked Emma in the eyes, and she glanced here and there—away from me. I felt this huge wave of regret. No eye contact. Driving away from the breeder, my new puppy in my lap, I phoned my husband, and detailed the emotional roller coaster ride I'd been on since arriving at the breeder's home. I talked on and on about myself.

"But how is *the puppy?*" John asked, wanting to hear about her, not me. "She's fine," I said, and realized that was it exactly. The puppy was fine. But I was scared to death that I wouldn't be fine, that I wouldn't be able to let this puppy into my heart. I realized then that I was hoping not only to get a new puppy, but to get a new Lucy. I wanted to drive away from that breeder as a new person, to buy a puppy and in doing so, to once again be the kind of person who walks through my days with my heart on my sleeve, aching with

care. And I worry that as my kids grow up and away, this part of me has dried up, that I may have grown crusty.

Then Emma crawled up against me, lay her head on my shoulder, her body going limp against mine. I didn't call John to tell him that she was fine, we were fine. After all, you need to drive carefully when you have a baby in your arms.

The act of putting a line through all the pieces, of somehow finding a way to tell the story, is far from mindless. Retelling is an act of composition

DRAFT

MINILESSON

Retelling Stories by Starting with Now and Backing Up

CONNECTION

Ask children to reflect on why their current reading work is important.

"Readers, as I was driving to school today, I set up a little puzzle for myself. I challenged myself to think of some retellings in my life that truly mattered to me. When I started out, I wasn't sure if I could do it, but in just one tiny second, I could think of so many important retellings: My colleague telling the story of a meeting she went to at the district office, my friend retelling an article she read about our president's plans for education, my aunt retelling, with a trembling voice, the awful review she read of a play she wrote, my brother retelling his date with a woman who kept burping at the table. These retellings were so important to me that it was easy to bring them to mind."

"I bet the same is true for you. Here, challenge yourself, now: Turn to the person next to you and list some retellings that have mattered to you lately—retellings about reading or retellings about life." I gave them a moment.

Remind children of the different ways readers retell stories, as was taught in the previous minilessons.

"Readers, will you look up here? Retelling is everywhere, right? As you are probably noticing as you remembered retellings in your own life, retelling can take many different forms. We know retelling can take the form of reminiscing over our books. In that kind of loose, casual retelling, we talk about our books with our partners, reliving them, feeling moved together by the beautiful parts (like Aly did over *The Giver*) or talking wide-eyed over the suspense the author puts us through (like Malik did with his *The River*) or enjoying the author's clever jokes (like Kobe did with *The Chocolate Touch*)—and so much more!"

COACHING TIPS

My intent is only to help children feel that the work they are about to do matters, and I want to imply to them, for now, that this work, as all work in our classroom, can and should weave into their lives. This is not the main point of this minilesson, so I don't spend much time on it, and I don't belabor the point.

Remember that the first part of a minilesson is called a connection because this a time to say, "listen up" and to be sure your kids lean in closely to really hear what you have to say. Use their names, cite their stories, weave your teaching out of the fabric of the classroom.

"We also know another kind of retelling—the kind we were working on yesterday. In that kind of chronological retelling, we started at the beginning of the story and took big steps through it, telling only the important parts from each big step and keeping the whole retelling short and to the point. So that's two different ways to retell so far, and today, I want to tell you about and help you try a third kind of retelling."

Name your teaching point. Specifically, tell children that readers can also retell by summarizing part of the book we've just read, and, as we proceed, adding in as asides, earlier parts that reveal the importance of the events of this chapter.

"I call this third kind of retelling (and of recalling) a 'synthesis retelling,' because although you start out only retelling the section you just finished reading, whenever your retelling gets to a part that has meaning that comes from earlier in the story, you add a reference to the earlier bit into your retelling, almost using parentheses to bring in the relevant background. So as you proceed through the retelling, you have to synthesize, fit together, all the parts you've read that are pertinent."

TEACHING

Offer an example of retelling by summarizing the most recent chapter you've read aloud, harkening back, when relevant, to sections from earlier in the book that make this chapter's events more meaningful than they would be on their own.

"Here, I'll try a synthesis retelling based on the chapter of *Stone Fox* we just read, to show you what I mean. (After I retell some in this way, I'm going to ask you to try retelling in this way with your partner.)

"In Chapter 8 of *Stone Fox*, Willy rode his sled to the edge of the town on the day of the race. He stopped—amazed to see so many spectators."

At this point I paused and dramatically threw my arm backwards toward the door of the classroom, where I had paced out the earlier sections of the text during yesterday's minilesson. And then, as if I was physically gathering up an earlier part of the story that related to this new development, I said, speaking parenthetically, "(This is the race Willy entered so he could get money to save the farm from tax collectors and save his grandfather from depression. It is going to be really hard for him to win it, though!)"

This connection is literally joining the previous days' work with today's new learning. I often try to make links between minilessons explicit when there is a distinct sequence between a string of minilessons.

Notice that when I want to use words that are technical, I go right ahead and do so. As you proceed through your retelling, you need to synthesize parts that are pertinent. In this instance, I made the decision that synthesize needed a synonym and that pertinent did not, but you could have supplied one for both terms or neither.

Notice that I set children up to know what they will be expected to do as a result of my demonstration.

The physical dimensions of this minilesson are important: Each time you harken back to an earlier section of the book, throw your arm backwards, as if to scoop up something behind you. Later in this series, you will build upon and incorporate this harkening back move, and you will want to be able to throw your arm backwards as a way to represent that mental operation. So establish the link now between the gesture and the operation.

Resuming my retelling of the latest chapter, I said, "Willy saw that one of the people who had come to cheer him on was Doc Smith."

Again I paused, this time long enough for the kids to anticipate that I was going to again throw my arm back to an earlier section of the story to gather up important information. Noticing that some children did not seem to be joining me in the mental work of this retelling, I repeated myself. "Readers, are you with me? I just said that in the most recent chapter after Willy got to the edge of the town and saw a mob of people who'd come to see the race, he specifically noticed *one of those people was Doc Smith*." I waited for the children to throw their arms backwards before I did so, and when they did, I nodded in agreement, also reaching my arm back as if to an earlier part of the story. I paused, giving children a bit of time to think for themselves what I would say next.

I again spoke parenthetically, saying, "(Doc Smith is a brutally honest person who told Willy he was nuts to try to find a way to help his depressed grandfather repay the tax bill, that he should put him in the old age home and sell the farm and give up his beloved sled dog, Searchlight. Still, she's at the race to cheer him on!) If I don't bring that earlier part of the book in here, then I'd miss something, wouldn't I? Otherwise, without that aside from earlier in the book brought in, the doctor just seems like anyone else, just anyone waiting in the crowd, ho hum. But, when I bring to my mind and to my retelling what came before in this book about her, then I can really get into the meaning of the story and the chapter! By bringing in past parts of the book, by synthesizing, I can help my partner understand that Willy must be thinking, 'Wow, even she is here to cheer me on—she who told me honestly I had no chance of helping my grandfather!' He must be hopeful and encouraged by that, and probably he doesn't want to let her down. I can really help my partner understand the book that way! And I help myself put the pieces together too, don't I."

Brian Cambourne, the great Australian literacy educator, once pointed out that for years, he's looked out his office window on a meadow and watched people hang gliding. He's seen countless people strap giant kite-like airplanes onto their backs, run a bee-line towards the cliff at the edge of the meadow, and then throw themselves over it, letting the giant kite carry them into the air. He's pointed out that even though he has watched that whole procedure scores of times, he would not be able to strap on the machine properly, and he does not know the way in which one actually casts off over the cliff. "Why?" he asks. "Because I watch without the sort of engagement that comes from saying, 'I am the kind of person who needs to know how to do this. I, too, am doing this same work.' My point is that when demonstrating how to do this complex sort of retelling, I definitely want children to have taken up this work and to be doing the same thinking alongside me. They can, then, contrast the actions I take with those they almost took or were about to take, and learn from every step along the way.

This section of the minilesson could become your active involvement. That is, instead of you doing this work twice as a demonstration, you could do it just once and then turn it over to the children. We haven't done this because we think that children will benefit from a bit more support, and also because we forgive long minilessons when their length comes from the fact that they contain large sections of the day's read-aloud. In any case, you can decide.

Name what you have just done in a way that encapsulates what it is you hope children have learned to do, doing this recap in a manner that makes the work transferable to other texts, other days.

"Readers, do you see that I started to retell by summarizing our most recent chapter, and I went and grabbed earlier parts of the story to add in, to help my summary of this chapter make all the sense it can make? That is something you will always need to do when you retell this way to yourself or to a partner. And this kind of retelling helps you truly understand the chapters you read, with all their layers."

"I'm thinking that these different ways we've practiced retelling to each other are really another way we can share our books at school or in our lives. So let's add this kind of retelling to our chart, 'Ways You and Another Reader Can Talk Aout Your Books.'"

Ways You and Another Reader Can Talk About Your Books

- Share passages that especially drew you in—parts that made you feel a strong emotion or exciting parts that had you on the edge of your seat.

- Share parts in which you really pictured what is happening, perhaps parts where you felt like you were in a 3-D movie—one with surround sound.

- Show each other parts of your books where the mental movie you made as you read got blurry, places where you thought "Huh?" and then talk about those parts, discussing what's going on in them.

- Figure out a tricky word by discussing what the word might mean and by using words you **can** read to figure out how to say this unfamiliar word.

- Tell the big things that happened to the main character so far, either by reaching back and starting at the beginning, perhaps saying 'Previously in. . . ,' or by starting with now and tucking in past events.

ACTIVE INVOLVEMENT

Ask children to help you continue with your retelling, adding in asides of important information they get from reaching back into earlier parts of the story.

"Readers, it's your turn to help out. I'm going to keep retelling, and when I come to a part that means more when it's layered with background, I'll signal for you to insert that key information. You will need to reach back and bring in earlier parts of the story that add depth to the part of this chapter we're retelling."

You will see that in this active involvement, the kids are not especially active. You could decide to teach this part of the minilesson differently. You could provide less scaffolding, suggesting children finish retelling the chapter on their own to a partner, making sure they reach back at least once to gather important information. You could alternatively suggest kids retell another text, including perhaps their independent reading book.

"Let's see, after Willy saw Doc Smith, the doctor turned and asked someone what happened to *his eye*," I said, being sure to emphasize the last two words. I paused, hoping this space in the retelling would nudge children to realize that background information about Willy's swollen eye was called for here, and that they could provide it by reaching back to earlier parts of the story.

As you listen to the retellings the children are doing, listen to see if they simply add in explanatory information, or if they allow the earlier parts to add depth to the events of the current chapter. They will probably start by just explaining the background, and you can eventually help them move to letting that background information affect and deepen their understanding of the event in the present chapter. It's not simply that Willy got the black eye from Stone Fox. It's all that this reveals an important dynamic between the two characters. When Stone Fox sees Willy is here this morning, despite the swollen-shut eye, and notes that Willy tells no one about how he got the swollen eye, this must mean something to Stone Fox.

In this instance, though, the children didn't show evidence that they'd recognized the cue I'd given them to reach back into the earlier text. I therefore repeated the sentence of my retelling, and after saying "his eye," I arched my arm up and back to where I'd earlier paced out a timeline of the story. "Turn and talk," I said, and let them support each other.

"Eyes up here," I said, ending their conversations. I nodded toward Kadija, who jumped up on her knees and called out, "Willy got a black eye when he went to see Stone Fox's dogs and Stone Fox thought he was going to hurt them." I repeated what she'd said, and when I came to the name Stone Fox, I used a questioning intonation as if asking, "who's he?" and gestured as if to refer backwards in the story. Kadija nodded, and added, "Stone Fox is the one who always wins these races, and everyone thinks he's going to win this one too."

Name what children have been doing that you hope they continue to do with other texts, on other days.

"Remember that one way to retell (or even recall!) your book is by starting with the section you just read, and then adding in earlier parts of the story to bring out the true, deeper, not obvious importance of what just happened."

I could have gestured back again, hoping to push Kadija or someone else to take this observation further, and you might choose to do this. One of the next events that happened in the story is that Lester tells Doc Smith that Willy bumped himself and got injured. A reader who retold that untruth will need to layer in even more back story! For today, I sensed this had been enough.

LINK

Send readers off to read independently, reminding them to pause and recollect the events of the story.

"Readers, remember that when you are feeling like there's just so much happening in your book that you want to pause and orient yourself, when you start feeling like something big is going on, or like the story is moving so fast you can't keep up, or that you just are bursting to tell someone what's going on, those are perfect times to pause and retell the book, to yourself or a reading friend. You might retell by just spilling out with all the parts you are dying to talk about, or you might retell chronologically, saying all of the big important parts that have happened so far, or you might retell the way we did today—by thinking through the part you just read and reaching back to add in earlier parts that add meaning to that passage." I gestured to the chart that listed optional ways in which readers were apt to retell and recall a text.

Ways We Can Retell to Our Partners

- Tell parts of the story that make you want to talk about them—make the text come alive between you and your partner.

- Start at the beginning of the story. Summarize by taking big steps through its timeline, telling only the important parts.

- Start at the beginning of the chunk you've just read. Summarize only that part, adding in asides as you go about earlier parts of the story that add a layer of meaning to the events of the chapter.

"The decision over when you retell and which way you do it depends on you and what your reading calls for! When you go off today, I know you will each make the choices that fit the life you are authoring as a reader."

Even though you have just taught one strategy during the mini-lesson and had all children practice it, you are not sending children off to their reading spots to spend their workshop time doing that strategy. That would make it an assignment or an activity, not a strategy—a tool to use when it is needed.

ONFERRING AND SMALL-GROUP WORK

Position Yourself to Scaffold Children's Retelling

You may notice, straight away, that although you are eager to support children's retellings, as the workshop gets underway, no one is actually doing this. Instead, they are all reading, nose-in-the-book. It even seems too early in their reading time to channel them toward Post-iting ideas. You'll probably find yourself pacing a bit, ready to pounce on whichever unsuspecting soul does pick up a pen and begin to jot. Of course, this is the very child who least needs your help with the work of the day!

Anticipate Ways of Supporting Children's Retellings

One answer, for starts, is that you mustn't ever hesitate to pull a partnership together early in a reading workshop and to say, "Would you two have your partnership talk now instead of later so that I can coach into what you do? Will you pretend it is the end of reading workshop and I've said, 'Get together with your partners and talk about your books,' and will you show me how the talk would go for you two?"

As the partners shift into their conversation, you'll want to decide straight away whether your conference will be a coaching conference or a research-decide-compliment-teach conference. If you decide to teach using the method of coaching, then as the children proceed through their

---

> ### MID-WORKSHOP TEACHING POINT
>
> #### Readers Make Space for Thinking About Their Books
>
> "Readers, I just was conferring with Zayd, who told me that sometimes it's hard for him to make a lot of his own thoughts when he is reading because he just wants to read, to get to the next part. Thumbs up if you feel that way too." A bunch of thumbs shot up. "So it seems like a bunch of us might be a bit like Zayd. You might get so involved in your reading that you forget to pause in places to recollect your story and to grow ideas about it. So here is a strategy I use sometimes. I take a few Post-it notes and place them every few pages in my book like this." I picked up a book and placed a blank Post-it every few pages. "When I come to a Post-it, I force myself to stop, pause, and think, 'So what has been happening in the story so far?' and then I retell it in my mind, and after that, I think, 'The thought I have about this is that. . . ,' and I record my thought so I can talk about it later with a friend. The Post-it note acts as a stop sign, as a reminder to stop, recall, and think. So for those of you that are like Zayd, for the next day or two try doing this, and we can talk about whether it seems to help your reading or not. So take a minute or so to set your book up with Post-its to force yourselves to stop, pause, and think."
>
>

work, you'll voice-over, inserting quiet directives. You might, for example, say, "Plan your talk. Who's sharing today?" "Decide how to retell, what to share." "Signal which sort of retelling you'll do (I illustrate the signals by walking my hands across my lap and by reaching back)." Once a reader is retelling, I might coach, saying, "Watch out, baby steps." or "Reach back."

Of course, you could instead (or in addition) speak only to the listening partner, promoting that child to essentially convey the same messages. Your coaching, then, would sound more like this: "Get her to signal the sort of retelling she'll do. You don't even need to talk. Use your gestures to ask whether she'll pace through the text or do a retelling that harkens back." "Tell her she's taking baby steps." "She's got it—give a thumbs up." "That's confusing, isn't it?"

You needn't set up a partnership conversation to confer into children's retellings. Instead, early in the workshop, you can circulate among children or convene a small group, and your teaching could be unrelated to the day's minilesson, grounded instead in ongoing assessments. Then again, you could coach into the ways that work can lift the level of rdg itself. For starters, you could convey that readers often orient ourselves for the upcoming reading by doing a mental 'Previously in. . . .' Often this involves scanning the text one has already read—another skill that some children need explicit instruction in. You can sit at a table, say, "May I have your attention?" and then, once all readers are with you, you can say, "I am so surprised to notice that you all are reading on in your books." The kids will look at you as if you are nuts, so you'll need to elaborate. "I mean, I thought you had learned that readers usually take a second at the start of reading time to give ourselves a quiet 'Previously in . . . .'"

You could say, "Would one of you be willing to do this work while the rest of us watch and learn from what you do?" And then you could coach one child.

In any case, once one child has done some retelling as a book orientation, you again will have choices. Do you want to ask each child to retell to themselves quietly? As they do this, you could circulate among them, saying as you approach a child, "Keep thinking, but do this aloud so I can listen in?" Or do you want to set children up to retell to each other, therefore externalizing their work in a way that allows you to listen in? Or do you want children (just for now, not usually) to make written timelines that capture their retelling?

However you maneuver things, if you want some of your conferring time to support children's retellings, you will want to enter the workshop with an armload of teaching points you could conceivably make. It helps, too, to have some sense of a learning continuum so that you ascertain what a child can already do and can almost but not quite do, and you then teach in ways that take into account the learner's zone of proximal development—that next stage of growth.

For example, the simplest thing to do will be to help a reader return to the start of a book and leaf through the pages, scanning them, and saying aloud the sequence of big things that the main character does (or that happens to the main character). This "who-did-what" retelling, scaffolded by the text, should be within reach for all your children. As children do this work, you can help them use the character's name and add in a few descriptors—some character traits. You can also help children realize that the things they tell should sort of make sense, showing not only what the character did but why. That often involves showing the character's motivations, or wants. In general, keep in mind that what you are asking children to do when you ask them to retell is to construct a miniature version of the story, and one of the most helpful things a child can draw upon in doing this is an understanding of story structure. A skilled summary of a story will generally mention the main characters and their motivations, struggles, ways of dealing with the struggle, changes, and lessons.

Plan to Especially Support Children Who Struggle to Retell—As This Suggests They Struggle Also to Comprehend

As I pulled my chair alongside Malik, I remembered that during the previous day's partnership conversation, Malik had seemed unable to tell his partner the storyline of his book. In that conversation, he had chalked his incomplete synopsis up to a bad memory and to the fact that that his mind sometimes wanders as he reads. At that time, I'd interjected that when my mind wanders and I lose chunks of a text, I reread to remind myself of whatever I lost. Of course, making a passing comment such as that is only the start of teaching a child, so I was pretty sure I'd need to support that suggestion today. Now, as I sat down, I said, "Malik, may I talk to you about your book?"

As Malik talked to me about the book, I assessed to see how much of the story he seemed to be holding onto. His retelling was skeletal; it lacked details, and when I prodded for more, it seemed he didn't have details in mind to draw upon. I was tempted to tell Malik that the book he'd selected was too hard. But because it had just been days before that I had assessed him as a level R reader and I was pretty confident of that assessment, I instead thought about how I could help him hold onto the text that he was reading.

Leaning in close, I said, "Malik, I love the way you summed up what is happening in your book. You told me the main character's name and about his relationship to his great-aunt and uncle, and you told me the big thing that is happening in the story—that Arthur is becoming friends with the interesting girl next door, Moira. As you are reading, it is *essential* to determine what seems most important. Nice job.

"I want to give you one pointer, though. Your retelling is a bit like a pen-and-ink sketch of the whole story. You've told the big, broad strokes, and you are right to do that. We talked about a retelling being the big steps through a story.

"But the thing is, readers usually have in mind lots of the details that sort of go with each of those big steps, and if we want to think or talk about them, we can. And for you, it sort of seems that what you hold onto when you read is just the big steps.

"I'd love to help you to continue holding onto the main storyline, as you are doing, but to also pay some attention to the particulars of a story because they are what make a story interesting.

"My suggestion is that it might help if instead of trying to retell the whole story all at once, you and I look over just the start of the story, and then you retell just that, and this time try to add in a detail or two. Then you could look over the next part of the story, and again, retell that next part of the story, again adding in a detail. Let me show you what I mean."

As Malik nodded, I picked up his book and read aloud the title of the first chapter, then looked at the picture and glanced at the page for help. With this help, I said, "The book starts…," and I told the gist of that chapter, including a detail.

Then Malik and I scanned the next chapter together, and as he retold it, I interjected a few scaffolds. At one point, I tapped a chapter title. At another point, I said, "And then what happened?" and when he didn't seem sure, I tapped a passage. As I concluded the conference, I restated the teaching point in a way that reminded Malik to try the same strategy as he continued to read on. "Do you see how it helped to retell just the first part of the book, and then add some details about it, then to move to the next part? And it helped to skim the book a bit to jog your mind, too, didn't it? Now you have something to share with your partner. Both of you can practice retelling like this. And remember, this isn't a memory test! Any time you retell, you can use those hints the author gives you. You can reread the title, look at the pictures, and glance at the text. The next few times you and your partner meet, begin by doing this kind of retelling. Off you go."

When I recorded the conference in my notes, I jotted a note to myself to help Malik, another time, to not only retell a part of the text and add a detail or two, but also to add a thought about what he had just captured.

Because Malik had seemed to pick up on my teaching, it seemed to me that when I conferred with him again tomorrow or the next day, I'd again be able to provide him with fairly light coaching with his retelling. I knew, however, that if his progress stalled and if he didn't seem to really understand that retelling requires him to almost delete the unimportant sentences and hold tight to the important ones, I'd need to provide him with some more concrete scaffolds.

For example, a year ago, I worked with a reader who needed extra help with this. That child was a great fan of the Horrible Harry series. I remember building an exercise around the "All Aboard" chapter from *Horrible Harry Goes to Sea*. I first summarized what had happened so far in the book: "Miss Mackle required the students to bring in information about their ancestors. Everyone brought in many different things and told about their ancestors. Ida brought in a box filled with artifacts from the Titanic, because her great-great grandmother sailed on the Titanic and was rescued. Everyone in the class wanted to read more about the Titanic."

Then I had this student read the chapter "All Aboard," in which the students become really interested in ships and decide to go on a sailing field trip. I had previously prepared several sentences written out on sentence strips (you could also just type them up on paper and cut them into small strips) that described events in the chapter. Some were big events, ones that would definitely be included in a strong retelling, and some were just little details that would be left out. After having the student read through the chapter, I gave her a handful of these sentences. I asked her to read through the sentences and make two piles—one of important, big events in the story and one of small details that wouldn't need to be included in a retelling. For some children, the physical sorting seems to help make these distinctions concrete. When she had finished sorting, I asked her to retell the chapter, using only the big, important events rather than including lots of tiny details.

In that instance, a reading specialist was also providing my student with some extra support after school. It is always important that children don't receive discordant messages from within the classroom and from the intervention teacher, so of course the after-school work this child received was tailored to support the agendas we addressed within the classroom.

Because the student struggled to reconstruct a sequential retelling of the texts she could decode fairly easily, the intervention teacher designed a few activities to help her. One was based around this same "All Aboard" chapter of *Horrible Harry Goes to Sea*. Knowing that my student had recently read the chapter in the classroom, the intervention teacher said, "After I've read a story, I like to think back and remember what happened. I've just started doing that for this chapter. I've remembered some stuff, but there are big things that happened that I'm forgetting. I was going to look back and see if that would help me remember them. Would you be willing to help?" Then the intervention teacher showed the youngster that she'd remembered the first two major events in the story: six students went to the library to check out books on the Titanic, and then everybody in the class started to get excited about ships too. She'd put those events on Post-its on the table in front of the student. The teacher told her that she knew some other stuff happened next in the story, before the class decided to go on a field trip on a boat (another Post-it, further down the line) but that she needed help figuring out what had happened. She showed the student two empty Post-its following the first two and asked her to help fill them in. With some prompting, the girl was able to fill in a couple more important events in the chapter, though not necessarily in sequence. The reading specialist was able to coach my student to generate important events on Post-its and then to reorganize them until the sequence of Post-its matched the sequence of events in the chapter. When she'd finished, the teacher asked her to retell the whole chapter, making sure to include all of the big events on the Post-its.

It can be invaluable to build collaborative relationships with intervention teachers that work with your struggling students. Because this student's intervention teacher and I were presenting her with multiple opportunities to do the same kinds of work in contexts that transferred from her classroom work to her outside work and back again, she was able to progress more quickly in her retelling.

Plan to Especially Support Children Who've Mastered the Art of Retelling—Push Them into More Challenging Work

Unlike writing conferences, where there is a tangible artifact in the form of our children's writing to glance at and refer to, a reading conference relies more heavily on our questions. We use these questions to dig deep and figure out the unseen mental work a child is doing in his or her reading—before we can coach into this. Routine retellings, however, provide us with a valuable alternative to always questioning the reader.

Instead of always stemming from whatever *we* decide to ask a reader, our conferences now have a chance to arise from our observation of how our students happen to naturally retell the story they've read. We scribble silent notes to ourselves as they do this. We take note: Is a student's retelling dependent on mindless regurgitation of facts that the text makes explicit, or does it reveal an awareness of details and themes implicit to the story? Similarly, we record answers to other vital research questions: Is a child able to hold on to the core plot, or does he get side-tracked by irrelevant details? Is the retelling sketchy, or does it allow the listener to see a mental movie—proof that the reteller, too, is envisioning as he reads. Is the chronology of events off, or can our reader recount facts with an appreciation for the cause and effect forces operative in the book's plot? These and other such observations provide us with a treasury of teaching points for conferring—and for future minilessons.

Interestingly, we are often more certain of what to do when students struggle than when they seem proficient at these skills. Our strong readers often appear as though they get it all. Yet as even our strongest, most fluent readers retell, they silently reveal numerous instances where we can teach them to deepen their appreciation and understanding of text—or to enrich the thinking that spirals from their responses to text.

Conferring with Aly, a strong reader, I noted that she had no trouble recounting the chronology of events in her story in exhaustive detail, nor in inserting her own observations and analysis into this retelling. My retelling conference with Aly, therefore, appeared to *reverse* all the advice I had recently given Malik, one of my strugglers. To him I had suggested, "Insert more detail." But to some of our stronger readers whose retellings are fraught with details, we might ask, "Are all those details necessary?" urging them to be more selective rather than providing a retell-all. Retelling the entire story is a lower-order skill than summarizing. The latter requires the reader to determine importance, reframe, and often compose afresh.

"I am impressed by your retelling," I told Aly. "You're doing all the good work we've learned earlier. You're opening yourself up to your book, telling me details that help me see the mental movie of your reading."

"I want teach you one more thing. When retelling the story of our book, readers have a choice. We can use the retelling time to recall and include as many details about the story as possible from start to finish, but often this will take too long, especially when we start reading bigger books. So once we're reading with strength, the way I can see you are, we decide what the story is really, really about and retell the big details or main parts from that angle.

"Let me show you the difference. I could retell Stone Fox like this." I launch into an exhaustive detail-ridden sequential account of the story: "There was a boy named Willie who lived on a potato farm in Wyoming with his grandfather, and normally they had a lot of fun and laughed a lot despite all the hard work. One day Grandfather wouldn't get out of bed. He just lay there looking sad. At first Willie thought it must be a trick Grandfather was playing on him, but when he realized that no, Grandfather wasn't playing a trick, he and his dog Searchlight tore over to Doc Smith's house. Doc Smith was a ... (sigh).

"If I retold in this way, it would take me forever! And the listener might not even get what the book was *about*. When we start reading longer books, it makes no sense to retell every detail. What we might do instead is retell in this way." I proceeded to distill Stone Fox into a summary, making my voice energetic and crisp. "Stone Fox is a book about a boy's determination and about a dog's love." In a whispered aside, I added, "See how I started upfront with what the book was about?" In my crisp voice I resumed: "Once Willie discovers his grandfather is in debt, he—with the help of his dog Searchlight—harvests an entire crop. To raise the money to repay the loan, he enters a race, where he faces Stone Fox as a rival."

I paused to lay out what I had just done so that Aly would understand the difference between a start-to-finish retell and a summary. "Did you see what I just did? I didn't just begin from page one and start repeating everything that happened in the book. I started with what the book was really *about*. And then I retold the big things, trying to fit the whole story into a few sentences so that my listener would get the most information in less time."

In nudging Aly away from a classic retell—which she had clearly mastered—I introduced a new teaching point altogether, one involving an advanced version of the work that less proficient readers in the class were doing. Through our conferences, we have a unique chance to differentiate instruction. We walk around the room, clipboard in hand, silently listening and watching to ascertain which of our students can do what well without our help—each student's zone of proximal development. Then we step in and push them up to the next level, *expecting* that this zone will differ for different learners.

TEACHING SHARE

Readers Push Ourselves to Pause, Retell, and Have a Thought About Our Reading

Set Partners up to do retelling—one shares and the other listens.

"Readers, may I have your attention? I've been watching you, and it is great to see that you are actually reading longer, stronger, and faster than you were at the start of this year—congratulations. I think you are ready to hear something that a wise reading researcher once said. Mortimer Adler said, 'Some people think a good book is one you *can't* put down—but I, I think a good book is one you *must* put down— to rethink, to muse over, to question.'"

"So readers, it is time now for you to talk and think together." I waited. "Remember that before you do so you need to think, 'Which partner will share?' Think about who shared last and about who feels like you have tons of stuff to talk about. Right now, decide who will be the sharing partner and who will be the listening partner."

"Sharing partners, remember that you are probably going to start with a 'Previously in…,' where you get your partner caught up. You can choose any way to retell. Will you do a chronological retelling?" I made pacing-out motions, walking my hands across my lap. "Or will you do a synthesis retelling (remember, the one that harkens back to stuff that already happened in the book that is relevant to the part you've just read)?"

Make sure the sharing partner has picked a specicif idea to share and that the listening partner knows to ask questions in order to make sense of the text.

"After you retell, you'll want to share your thoughts, sharing partner, but you won't want to just yammer on about this Post-it, that one, and the next one. You'll need to think, 'Of all I could talk about, what is particularly interesting?' and then make a choice. Start with one Post-it, or two that go together, and with the part of the text it represents. If you haven't chosen an idea that you'll share with your partner, do that now."

Children reread their jottings and their book, and I waited for a minute, then spoke in a quiet voice-over to the listening partners. "Listeners, remember, you are going to actually try to reconstruct a sense of the text based on what you hear, and you'll ask for clarification if you need it. Hopefully, you'll get enough sense of the text that you and your partner can actually converse about whatever he or she is thinking. The talk should go back and forth between you, like a tennis ball goes between two people."

"Okay, get started."

Learning to Listen Intensely

IN THIS SESSION,
you'll teach students that intense listening creates a force field in which ideas grow.

After Don Graves and I had finished the National Institute of Education Study that we embarked on together almost three decades ago—a study that was heralded by many as the groundbreaking study that opened the whole field of teaching writing—both Graves and I took the data we'd collected from observing a dozen kids for two years, and we headed off to our separate spots to write about those data. Graves took his copy of the student work and the data with him to Scotland, where he devoted a sabbatical year to writing his version of the story (and I, meanwhile, took my copy of the data to New York City to work in a similar fashion.) One evening, talking about our parallel tasks, Don told me about how a Scottish farmer who lived across the moor had looked over the reams of student work, spread everywhere, and said to Don, "Wouldn't ye rather be writin' a love story?" Talking about it afterward, Don and I agreed that, in fact, what we were doing was just that. We were writing a love story. It's a work of love to listen respectfully to another person's work and to allow that work to leave a mark.

The best teaching involves a lot of listening. That is true whether the teaching occurs in a classroom or in a home, and whether the teacher is a grandparent, an aunt, a parent, a classroom teacher, or a peer. In this session, you will be helping youngsters step up to the job of listening well to each other, listening so that an idea that at first seems small and green can, in the sunlight of a good listener, grow and ripen.

To teach this session well, you'll need to remind yourself of the truly transformative power of good listening. Think about times when a person has helped you grow, some one who has tapped powers in you that you didn't even know you had. Chances are good you thought of a person who listened. There is a reason the times in your life when you have felt heard stand out as turning points. It is important to feel respected, validated. But it is more than this. When another person honors us by listening well, we actually hear ourselves. We unfold and grow.

To teach this session well, you'll also need to remind yourself of how hard it is to trust that we can help another person simply by listening. So often in our efforts to provide

GETTING READY

- Before you start this lesson, be sure to have read through Chapter 9 of *Stone Fox*.

- Readers will need one Post-it note from each of their independent reading books, perhaps placing them on the covers of their books as they enter the meeting area.

- Prepare to unveil a chart during today's active involvement titled, "To Listen Well, We…" that will be used again in the share.

- In the share session, you will finish *Stone Fox* by reading "The Finish Line."

the wisest counsel to our young readers, we wrack *our* own brains, searching *our* memories, *our* skills, *our* bank of experiences in hopes of finding that which will take the learner farther. Meanwhile, of course, we are turning away from the goldmine of teaching points seated in front of us—the student himself, herself. When we listen, really listen, to the student in front of us, we hear much more than the words she utters. We sense who the child is, how she views life,

> *When another person honors us by listening well, we actually hear ourselves. We unfold and grow.*

what she already knows and what she wants to accomplish. Listening well means hearing all the learner isn't saying, too, and coming to understand her fears, needs, and hopes.

Our children troop into our classrooms, bringing funds of knowledge that we must explore, celebrate, teach from, and expand. The best conferences, therefore, are the ones that advance goals the student was already trying to achieve and develop capacities the student was on the verge of accessing. The truth is that if we want to provide wise counsel to our students, the place where we are most apt to find treasure is within the memories, skills, and bank of experiences that our students bring to the conversation. The single most important thing we can do to teach well is to listen.

Once you have reminded yourself of the importance of

listening, and of the teaching power of listening, and once you have also recalled the many temptations to forego listening out of an interest in being helpful, then you'll be ready to teach from the heart. That will be important to do because you want your minilesson to get through to kids, to touch them, and to change them.

When you teach children to listen well, you will also be teaching them to read well. This session starts by spotlighting the importance of partners listening to each other in ways that help each other grow ideas, an emphasis that provides a context for you to convey that reading itself is listening, and for you to suggest that readers need to listen not only to the words of a text but also, to their own first responses and thoughts.

Such teaching requires ears informed by the heart. In Paul Tillich's words: "The first duty of love is to listen." Just as the best writers are always readers *first*, those who speak most wisely are the people who know first how to listen.

If we believe that the teaching of reading is important, we have to believe also that the art of listening is one that we need to master as teachers—and to teach to the kids in our classroom community. Here in this last bend in the road of this unit, we've introduced partnerships in the hope that conversations among kids will lead to growth and that higher-level thinking will take root during discussions about books.

But to hear themselves "think," kids require the privilege and audience of a real listener. In this session, you stress that a true conversation—indeed all communication—requires quality listening. This is a skill that is scarcely taught explicitly the way reading and writing—or even speaking—are taught because we assume that it is a skill that will develop organically. The truth is that our students need explicit instruction on how to listen well.

One of the beautiful things about teaching literacy is that the essential moves that a teacher makes are also essential moves that a writer makes, a reader makes, a learner makes, and a person makes.

DRAFT

MINILESSON

Learning to Listen Intensely

CONNECTION

Retell experiences you've had in listening—when you talked to someone who was distracted, contrasting with times you've talked to someone who listened intently.

"I'm sure you've had it happen to you. You start talking to someone. You are all welled up with tons of stuff to say, and you get started, talking with great urgency about these ideas that seem so huge and interesting. Then half way through a sentence, you see the other person's eyes are following something else in the room. You try to ignore the fact that his attention is elsewhere; you take a big breath, continue talking. But he's clearly distracted, and now you are too. 'Go on, go on,' he says, his head still bent, his eyes still far away."

"Suddenly what you thought you wanted to say doesn't seem worth the effort. What was your point anyhow? The ideas that had seemed so good feel like they amount to nothing. Whatever had you been thinking, getting so excited over those stupid ideas? You feel like one of those balloons after its whirled all around the room and now it is lying on the floor, deflated. 'Aw, never mind,' you say. 'I forgot what I was going to say anyhow.'"

"There isn't a person in this room who hasn't had the experience of talking to someone who isn't listening and suddenly finding that we have nothing to say."

"On the other hand, we've all had the opposite experience too. We've all known what it is to have just a little scrap of a thought, and to say it aloud, not sure it really amounts to anything. Our friend leans in, listening. We see our thought register. We see our friend turn our thought over in his mind. We can see a new glint in his eye, and when he says our words back to us, mulling them over as he says them, we mull them over too, and suddenly the one thought multiples, spawning all these other insights that come fast and furious."

COACHING TIPS

As we share personal experiences to make a connection with our readers, we don't just say the story, but we can act it out, dramatizing some parts to make it come alive. In this connection, I dart my eyes as I talk about it, take a deep breath when one is mentioned, and I pause for dramatic effect.

Name your teaching point. Specifically, teach children that readers benefit from talking with a person who really listens. Such a listener helps a reader grow ideas.

"When we are reading, and also when we are listening to other readers' ideas, we need to make sure that we're listening with our minds and hearts open. We don't want to listen like curmudgeons. We want to listen reminding ourselves that there are deeply brilliant ideas about to be made, ones that just need a little listening to grow."

Teaching

Extol the value of listening, saying that if we listen intently, others will learn from being heard, and hearing, and the class will become stronger and wiser.

"We need to begin right now, becoming powerful listeners. It's not easy or automatic, you know. There are things we can do to grow ourselves into better listeners. If we in this room *really* listen with patience and intelligence and open-heartedness, then each one of us will experience the way that listening can create an energy that opens us up to ourselves and to each other and makes us all wiser.

"And I think if we have been listened to, then a day later or so, we'll be listening to someone, and instead of picking at our teeth, scanning the room, saying, 'Go on, go on,' as we look and think elsewhere, we'll lean in, and we'll get that glint in our eye."

Annie Lamott, author of Bird by Bird, *has written advice for writers that can be rewritten into advice for teachers. And the advice works whether the teacher is a grown up or a child. Listen:" I honestly think that to be a teacher you have to learn to be reverent. If not, why are you teaching? Why are you here? Let's think of reverence as awe, as presence in and openness to children, to young people. The alternative is that we shut down. Think of the times when you've read poetry in such a way that it gives you a fleeting sense of being startled by beauty or insight, by a glimpse into someone's soul. All of a sudden, everything seems to fit together (or at least for a moment to have meaning.) This is our goal as a teacher, I think to watch our students at work and to be startled in just that way by beauty, by insight, by a glimpse into someone's soul."*

Teaching well involves reading children's work with—please forgive me—wonder, seeing things anew, things that catch us off guard, that break in on our small, bordered world. When this happens, everything feels more spacious. I think this is how we are supposed to teach—present and in awe.

Demonstrate listening well and ask children to notice the strategies you use as you do so.

"Let's try it. Okay, I need one of you to be our guinea pig and to leave the room for just a minute while we plan the work we're going to do with you. Who would like to be our guinea pig?"

A few hands shot up. "Okay, Sam, why don't you go out in the hall? Sam, take my copy of *Stone Fox* with you, and while you are out there, jot a Post-it note or two containing a thought you have about the chapters we've just read?"

Sam stepped out into the hall and I closed the door behind him. I leaned in and spoke to the children in a low voice. "Okay, so, readers, in a few moments, Sam is going to come back in and he is going to talk to me about the thoughts he had from *Stone Fox*. I want you all to research the ways I listen so intently to Sam that he ends up saying more, thinking more."

"I'm going to first try to say very little and give him the space to talk and think and talk some more. Then watch, and you'll see that I'll do a bit more. I'll gesture to him, or I'll say, 'Can you add to that?' Watch to see if that helps Sam say more or not. You'll be the scientists, collecting data on this experiment. Then I'll go a step further and repeat back some of what he's said. Sometimes that gets a person to say more, when he can hear himself and think about it more. Again, collect data on, jot down, whether that seems to help him feel heard. Then I may ramp things up and do even a bit more, asking him a few questions to help me understand exactly what he is trying to say, and what he hasn't said yet. There are brilliant thoughts in all of us. We just need to have time to let them grow—that's what a good listener can offer. I can let Sam hear himself think so he can figure out what his little idea can grow into!"

"Are you ready? Take notes on what I do, and how it works."

In the classes that piloted these sessions, most of the children were totally confused by why a child was being called a guinea pig. What did a squeaking little rodent have to do with anything? You'll notice that I haven't altered the term based on kids' confusion—I think it's fun to use and explain technical vocabulary and colloquial expressions. The term guinea pig *doesn't have quite the novelty of* curmudgeon, *but it has its own appeal!*

You'll notice that this minilesson borrows on some of the same aura as the earlier one, when a colleague interviewed me about my history as a reader. In both that session and this one, an adult colludes with kids around some secret knowledge that only the insiders have access to. That's one way to signal to kids: "Listen up." If your technique for drawing kids in is to take on this affect—go for it. Play this up. When you are sharing a secret with the kids, do so in a stage whisper. The kids will know this is partly just in fun, but it will work. Meanwhile, you and the kids will have some fun. Always bear in mind that student engagement is the end-all and be-all of your teaching. You can be the most brilliant teacher in the world, but if no one hears you or notices what you are saying, your brilliance won't amount to a hill of beans.

As Sam entered the room, he tipped an imaginary hat, earning himself a few giggles from his classmates. I motioned for him to sit next to me. "So, Sam," I said. "Tell me your thoughts about *Stone Fox*," and I gestured to the book, but said no more, giving the talking space over to Max.

"The dog's name is Searchlight."

"Ah, I see." Pause. I nodded and again made clear the air was for him to fill.

It will be very easy for them to observe the interview without noting the techniques you are using—and silence, especially, is a technique that could easily be overlooked. Be aware, though, that if your listening is just a show, then your listening won't actually create the energy that will lead the child to say things that end up being powerful. So try to make the listening real enough that it will work its magic.

"Yeah." Long pause. Nothing more seemed forthcoming. I nodded, letting him know he could take the time he needed. The silence greatened.

I gestured for Sam to say more, to elaborate once he was ready.

He added, "I never heard of a dog named Searchlight. It's not really a name, is it?"

I nodded thoughtfully, wondering where he'd go with that observation. Long pause. After a bit, I tried another way to hear what he was trying to say. This time, I repeated what Sam had said. "So you were saying that you've never heard of a dog named Searchlight?"

"No—it's a cool name."

I again nodded.

"Well, sometimes people name their dogs by the way they act or look. You know, like if I had a dog that was really good at sports, like me, like really good at catching Frisbees and stuff, I might call it Gretzky or Beckham."

"Yes, I can see that." I said, showing him I was with him and ready for more.

You will find that the child says something, like Sam has just said, and you're apt to think, "This is not going to lead to anything good at all." You are apt to feel a bit frantic, thinking, "Geez, this conference is not on a path that'll produce any nice insights, and I won't really make my point." The secret is to trust that "all roads lead to Rome." Whatever the child says is like the end of a string, and if you keep following that string, it absolutely will lead to something important. (Actually, this is not totally absolutely the case, but for certain, you are more apt to find something significant by trusting that whatever the child says is, deep down, important than by feeling frantic for the kid to somehow say something better, think something better, in the first place!)

"Maybe Willy's dog got that name because she liked to search around, so they named her that."

I waited, nodding, and when Sam said nothing more, I again tried simply repeating his words. "Hmm, she liked to search around?"

Sam nodded. "Yeah, like you know, when kids are lost, they use those big lights. I think they're called searchlights. They're like big flashlights."

"Oh, huh. I see what you mean," and I signaled with my body language that I was still ready to hear how this idea would build.

"Willy's only ten and Searchlight pulls him all over the place. She takes him to a school that's really far and waits there for him. And she races from town to home at night with Willy on the sled. It's dangerous, but Searchlight knows the way."

"I'm not sure I see where you are going."

"It's like Searchlight is the light on the front of the sled. She protects him from bad stuff—not just on the road, but in life, like the man with the gun. She will never let anything bad happen to him. She even plowed the potatoes. She's his. . . ."

"Yes? She's his what?" I'm not sure if this is the case, but I suspect my eyes had that glint in them. I knew Sam was onto something, and I make sure he can feel my excitement.

"She's his light in life!" Sam said, visibly excited by this description.

I mulled over Sam's words, letting them in, repeating them to myself, and said, "Wow, Sam. Holy moly."

For a moment we just basked in the glow of the idea, and then I began processing what had just happened. "You went from talking about the dog's name to talking about the role she plays in Willy's life and in the book. I am impressed at how much you grew that idea. You just kept layering it and layering it and I've never thought of Searchlight's name that way before! That is a new insight for me!" Sam smiled and said, "Thanks!"

Notice that the class is present, but my focus is totally on Sam and the conversation we're having.

Notice that I am not taking what he has said and running with it, adding my own interpretations, coauthoring meaning. Once Sam gets going on all this good stuff, it is tempting to do so. Refrain!

Name what you have done to help yourself listen well. Describe your moves in ways that are transferable to another day, another conversation.

Then I added, "I want to let you in on a little secret, Sam. While we were talking, the class researched what I did to help myself listen to your ideas in a way that would help me truly deeply understand what you were getting at—not just listening to what you said, but listening in a way that helps *both* of us understand your idea. Let's look at this chart I made earlier and see if it actually lists the strategies I tried when I was listening to you, or if I tried whole new ones." I read each item on the list aloud and said to the class, "If you saw this work, will you give a thumbs up?" Children indicated that they'd seen all but the final one of these listening strategies.

Once again you will notice that I'm colluding—sharing secrets as a way to keep kids' interested.

To Listen Well...

- Let there be some quiet around what the other says.

- Let there be some time around what the other says.

- Let the other know we understand so far, if we do.

- Show the other we believe he or she is quite likely to grow a good idea out of whatever has been said so far.

- Ask questions if we are confused.

- Reflect back what the other says so he or she can hear himself or herself and figure out where to go next.

- Invite the other to say more, or take more time, or collect more evidence.

"Thanks, Sam. You can go back to your seat," I said.

ACTIVE INVOLVEMENT

Channel the children to talk with their partners about their thoughts about a book, practicing the same listening techniques to encourage their partners to say more.

"Okay, now it's your turn. In a minute, I'm going to ask you to see if you can listen in a way that creates energy, allowing the speaker's ideas to grow. First, though, you will need the reader to have a seed idea, a thought. So right now, find a Post-it from your independent reading book that has an idea on it. Signal to me when you are ready with an idea."

After a minute, many children had signaled. "Partner 2, you share your idea, and Partner 1, you work on listening well. Listeners, push yourself to really listen with your whole heart to what your partner is saying and trying to say—help your partner hear himself or herself with your hard listening! If you aren't sure how to listen harder than you are, use the chart to remind you."

As I listened, Grace spoke of *Baby,* saying, "They didn't name the baby because they couldn't deal with the way she died."

Nicole nodded, saying nothing, but looking intently at her.

Grace added, "And now they don't know whether to love this new baby that has come to them, 'cause they are afraid she might die."

It's likely that some sets of partners will forget and will start talking back and forth conversationally instead of trying to actively listen and be listened to. You may need to say again to the group "One partner's role is to be just the listener, not to add in your own thoughts. You are interviewing the speaker."

After a few more minutes, I said to the group, "I know you all are just getting going and that you could talk for the rest of today's workshop, but I want to make sure we have time to read independently and then talk about *that* reading.

LINK

Remind children that good listeners listen with open ears, minds, and hearts. Such listening helps ideas grow. Send readers off to read, pausing to recollect and to grow ideas.

"I hope that you're coming away from today's minilesson resolved to do the sort of intense listening that will help others find themselves saying and thinking stuff they never even knew was on their minds. We can listen to books like we are curmudgeons, and we can listen to each other that way as well. But we can also make a different choice, and we can read and listen in ways that allow other people's words and ideas and stories to get through to us. I didn't do anything all that miraculous with Sam. You watched exactly what I did—and it was nothing that you couldn't do with each other. And the thing is—the results *were* miraculous. Sam ended up thinking ideas that are profound and important. He did that simply because we listened."

"I want to make one last suggestion. When you or I are the recipient of powerful, responsive listening, let's agree to acknowledge that listening. Sam just said, "Thanks," to me, and I think he was right to say thanks. In life, we thank people when they share cookies with us at lunch or lend us their sweatshirt for recess, but we don't always thank people for listening—and yet that is a true gift. I think we should change that. I think we should become accustomed to saying, "I really felt as if you were interested in my ideas, thanks," or 'Your listening worked that magic we talked about in class, and it really helped.'"

CONFERRING AND SMALL-GROUP WORK

Thoughtful Response to Reading is Worth Teaching Toward

There will be days when you enter the workshop already anticipating that you're going to need to devote a good deal of your time to the work you have been teaching. Certainly, during these sessions in which your mini-lessons have channeled children not only to retell but also to think about their books, sharing their thoughts with each other, you probably entered the workshop already anticipating that much of your conferring would revolve around supporting the work you had invited children to do.

Conferring and Small-Group Work to Support Thinking and Jotting in Response to Reading

A good portion of your conferring time today will probably not support retelling but will instead support children in thinking about and responding to their books. You'll probably think of these conferences as supporting Post-its, but of course Post-its are just the physical manifestation of what really matters, which is thoughtful reading. Again, you'll want to enter the workshop anticipating the sorts of conferences that are apt to help children be more thoughtful. One way to do this is to give yourself the time to hold a few really strong conferences around Post-its, knowing these con-

> ## MID-WORKSHOP TEACHING POINT
>
> ### Readers Cultivate Ways to Listen to People and Books
>
> "Readers, I've been admiring the listening you've been doing. For example, I watched two of you talking, and even though I couldn't hear a word of what you were saying because I was across the room, I saw all these zillions of signs that you were listening to each other. It was so beautiful. When one of you was talking, the other would nod, and lean in and gesture, 'Say more' and if you jumped in to talk before the other was finished, I could see from your gestures, it was as if you were saying, 'Oh, oh, so sorry. Finish what you were saying,' and then you'd tilt in to hear each other. I wonder if you have any idea how precious this sort of listening is to a reading community—because of how we learn from one another and because reading is really listening with that sort of intentness to an author. The way you listen to each other says so much about the way I bet you listen to authors. Some time during the next part of the workshop, will you take a moment to look around and admire the listening to each other we're all doing? When you admire it, think to yourself—'Is that a kind of listening I could try? Could I try it not only with my reading partner but also with my book? Could I try it elsewhere in my life?' We will be listeners our whole lives, to people and to texts, so taking time to improve our listening will help us forever."
>
>

ferences will teach you as much as they teach the students.

As I pulled my chair up to Kobe, I asked, "Could you finish reading the section you're in so then you and I can talk?" Kobe nodded and then lowered his eyes to finish reading. As he read, I made a note that he was reading *The Chocolate Touch,* a book that is considerably easier than the level R books that I'd channeled him toward earlier in the month. I do the same—reading books that are easy for me—and lots of kids do this. It is not a problem, of course, but on the other hand I am apt to expect a higher level of thinking when the book is probably easy for a reader. Also, if Kobe rarely reads level Q and R books, I'd intervene. I also noticed that although Kobe was near the end of the book, he only had two Post-its. I'd only emphasized Post-iting for a few days, so I wasn't surprised that this might require more attention from me, and I already knew that Kobe tended to do his work quickly. As he finished reading the passage, I glanced at his log and noticed that he had been reading two and often three books a week.

"So, Kobe, I notice you are almost near the end of your book. What kind of work have you been doing as a reader?"

"I kinda like this book 'cause John was *obsessed* with chocolate and now he's getting over it!" Kobe said.

I noticed that Kobe talked first about whether he liked this book, which made a lot of sense to me because until now I had been working especially on his engagement in reading and choice of books. Seeing that his engagement seemed to be better, perhaps related to the fact that he was reading a book that was easy for him, I developed a hunch that I might use this conference to support his thinking about books. I don't know *The Chocolate Touch,* so I knew I needed to listen to his current thoughts about the book with especially rapt attention. "I'm not sure I'm grasping what you are trying to say. Why does the fact that the character loves chocolate make you love the book?" I asked, pressing.

"I guess it's that I like the book because John was pretty greedy, but he's getting better."

"It is interesting isn't it when you notice a character changing." I said. "And what have you been thinking as you read, other than being glad that the main character's changing?"

Kobe shrugged, and repeated, "That it's good?"

I again noticed that Kobe now had a two-book-long run of liking reading, and at this point, I found myself feeling clear that he could use help thinking more as he reads. I wondered, though, whether he had any plans to do this once he reached the end of the book, so I said, "It looks like you'll be done pretty soon. What do you think you'll do after you get to the last page of this book?" I was not terribly surprised when Kobe raised his eyebrows at the question and said, as if his answer was the most obvious thing in the world, that when he finished, he'd get another book."

I constructed a pretty clear sense of the way Kobe tended to go about thinking in response to his books. When I begin to form a tentative theory about a person, I find it helps to share the theory, asking for feedback on it. So I said, "Kobe, I'm trying to understand your reading so I can help, and what I'm noticing so far is that your real aim is to keep going as you read, to get through books. You try to follow the main storyline. It seems like you are eager enough to get to the end of a book and start another book and that you are not all that keen on Post-iting. You'd rather read." Then I said, "Do you think I've got it right, or am I missing something?"

Kobe shrugged and admitted, "Well, when I do write Post-its, they are kinda lame."

"Lame? As in you have a hurt foot?" I said, objecting to his suggestion that a lame Post-it meant a generally inferior one. "If I'm right, you don't mean lame. I think what you are trying to say is that when you *do* Post-it, the thoughts you record don't seem all that worth returning to, all that worth holding onto, and for that reason you'd just as soon read on?"

As Kobe nodded, I glanced at the two Post-its he'd collected. He was right: both simply made a sweeping comment about what occurred in the book. *(Figs. XV-1 and XV-2)*

At this point, I felt ready to shift from researching Kobe to teaching him something. The important thing to stress is that as soon as I drew my chair alongside Kobe, I knew he didn't have many thoughts recorded on Post-its. I could have simply leapt to teach him to record more of his ideas as he read, and frankly, there are times when I would have done that because I don't have the luxury of time enough to inquire further. But in general, my rule of thumb is that I not only need the research portion of a conference to take me to the general terrain I'll address in the conference (which in this instance revolved around Post-iting). I also want the research portion to help me understand what the learner already knows, already tries to do, and already struggles with related to that general terrain. That way my teaching can have far more nuance. I won't simply blanket Kobe with the same instructions I no doubt gave him and all the others a week ago. Saying "Record your thoughts" clearly is not enough for Kobe. He is not sure his thoughts are worth recording!

Figure XV-1

Figure XV-2

"Kobe," I said. "I think you are exactly right when you say that the thoughts you have been recording aren't worth holding onto—so it has been wise of you to say, 'I'm not going to waste my time recording stuff that isn't worth recording.' The Post-its you have here just sort of comment on and note the events that occurred in the story, and the events are already in the book. You don't need to record them. What's not in the book, though, are your own deep thoughts, and I can show you how to think thoughts that you'll want to hold onto, if you are willing."

"Okay."

"The first thing is to do more of what you have already been doing. You already stop from time to time to have a thought about the story. Right now—have a thought about it."

Kobe's brow furrowed as it always did when he was deep in thought." "Hmm. . . John is too greedy about chocolate? 'Cause he always wants more and more chocolate, and he can't get enough. He is a greedy person."

"Interesting idea. That really gets me thinking. Now here's the thing. Instead of recording the first idea you come to, you are first going to grow it. The way to do it is to hold that idea as you read on, carrying it with you almost as if you are carrying a football as you run down the field. Holding onto that idea (I tucked it under my arm as if the show I was carrying it like a football), keep reading, and this time, after you read a bit, I'm going to ask you to think more about your idea that John is too greedy about chocolate and that he's a greedy person in general." Keep reading from where you left off, but this time, read aloud please." I said.

After he read a passage which seemed to me to elucidate Kobe's idea, I stopped Kobe and prompted him by saying, "*Now,* I'm thinking that John. . . ," trailing off to signal to Kobe that he needed to finish the thought.

"If John learns his lesson to be less greedy and obsessed with chocolate, then it'll help him grow up."

"Say more," I said and gestured.

Kobe added, "I think he'll ask his dad for help. And that makes me think he's changing for the good."

"Interesting. So he's reaching out for help. And that is a sign he wants to change things. Good, Kobe. Jot or read on?"

"Jot." Kobe jotted the idea on a Post-it, altering it in the process. He wrote, "John has been very greedy and now he is starting to maybe regret that. . . I hope!" (*Fig. XV-3*)

"Now *that's* an idea worth remembering, isn't it. You will still want to carry it with you as you read on, and your next jotting might be almost the next chapter of this idea, or it might be a whole new idea. Remember, though, you do not need to jot the first thought that comes to your mind. You can read on with the thought in mind, and then stop yourself and push yourself to think more, saying 'Now I think. . . .'

John has been very greedy and how he is starting to maybe regre that...I hope

Figure XV-3

"And Kobe, you are going to find that the whole feel of reading changes for you when you do this because the stuff that happens in your mind will become more thoughtful, deeper. So reading won't be straight plot. It'll also be an intense sort of thinking. This is the big work that you need to be doing as a reader. Some people say 'reading is guided thinking.' The text guides you—but *you* do the thinking. And doing deeper and more thinking needs to be a huge goal for you this year. It'll mean, for sure, that you won't have any more naked books. Next time I'm going to see loads of Post-its. But more than that, you'll feel your reading changes."

A conference such as that can put a child on course—and can also provide you with your mid-workshop teaching point.

I still had time for another few conferences, so I pulled up a chair beside Emma, who was reading the last bit of *The Great Gilly Hopkins* by Katherine Patterson. She continued reading as I sat nearby, and this gave me a second to glance at her reading log in hopes of providing myself with some context. Emma had just finished her last book and begun *Gilly Hopkins* the previous day, and she was already well into this wonderful book—none of which was surprising to me, given what I was coming to see as her pattern. For a second I wasn't sure whether to celebrate her avid reader habits or not. I love that she reads in great gulps. And yet I also want to encourage a bit more lingering, more slowing down to think hard. I made a quick decision that I'd probably angle the conference toward continuing to support her responses to books. I still needed, though, to hear her own self-assessments and plans. I opened the conference with the question, "Tell me how it's going for you as a reader."

"Well, I'm in the part right now that Gilly is in yet another school and she's thinking, like, 'Hmm, this teacher, this Miss Harris, doesn't seem to give me the attention I'm trying to get.' Because, you know, Gilly is used to getting into trouble and causing a scene, and this teacher isn't really giving into that. Gilly has moved around a lot and been in foster care, that's why she's in a new school."

"Emma, I would love to have you as my reading partner because when I asked you how your reading is going, you gave me such a quick but detailed, too, overview of what you've read. And you even backed up to fill in stuff I needed to know to understand the events—like when you said, 'Gilly has moved around a lot and been in foster care so that's why she's new.' Your partner and any reading friend you ever have will be so lucky if you always do that work of filling us in on the story. And that way, you and the other person can really dive into a real conversation about your ideas about the book." I said, trying to be sure that my compliment supported reflective reading and would be transferable to any partner talk about any book.

"Emma, the other thing I noticed is that you always have a book in your hands and are ready to jump into it whenever you have a spare moment. You have all the qualities of a true book enthusiast. But I think you are realizing your tendency to read faster and faster, on and on is both a good thing and a hard thing. It is great that you are always into a book. But to go the next step as a reader, you need to temper your eagerness to get to the next page with a willingness to be really thoughtful, and to savor your book, to really get into it.

I know I've talked to you about this before and already this year you are starting to actually change right before our eyes, becoming someone who can not only race on as a reader but can also pause to savor. I just need to remind you again to do that. It's like when you like eating something really delicious, like, say, the most delicious kind of cake. You can eat it super fast, and barely even taste it, or you can eat it a bit more slowly, really tast-

ing it and appreciating all the flavors it has. Can you see that you've begun to be the kind of reader who takes time to actually taste the cake?"

"Hmm, well, last year I read the second most books, in my old school, but we didn't do Post-its then."

"Emma, I don't want you to slow down completely, but I do think it would help you if you took a breath here and there to savor the story. Something that helps me is that I just plop Post-its at intervals in the book, and when I get to them they are like stop signs. Even if I do not want to do so, I stop and push myself to have a thought. Of course, you could also let the book signal when it is a good time to pause, and stop at parts in the book that seem really important, parts where the book is begging you to stop and think. Which system would make more sense for you?"

"I think I would want to stop at the juicy parts, cause there are a lot in this book."

"Try that right now. Find one of the parts in *The Great Gilly Hopkins* that you could savor."

"What about the part where Gilly is not sure why the teacher isn't responding to her, and Gilly is getting frustrated."

"Jot down what you're thinking about it. Here's a Post-it."

Emma immediately bent her head to jot. She still fingered her necklace with one hand, and with the other she quickly wrote out her idea. After a moment she said with triumph, "Okay, so I jotted, 'Gilly must be really frustrated by the teacher's reaction. I know she must be thinking, 'Argh! I'm crying out for help here!!!'" *(Fig. XV-4)*

"Smart work. You noticed an important part and pushed yourself to have a thought about Gilly's feelings. And you were really specific, too, thinking about how exactly you can capture the precise nature of her frustration. Now this Post-it could be a stepping stone to a big conversation.

After this, will you continue to develop systems that help you to savor the important parts of your books?"

Figure XV-4

Conferring and Small-Group Work to Extend Questions Readers Have in Response to Reading

When conferring with a reader, you want to listen to what that child is saying about the work that he or she is doing, but you *also* want to get information by looking quickly through his or her Post-its. Sometimes the Post-it work can lead you into your compliment or your teaching point of a conference.

Be wary of the fact that when conferring with readers, our inclination is to teach into something we *don't* see children doing rather than to extend what they are doing. Perhaps it's because it is easier to see deficit, or maybe it's because we aren't sure how to deepen what children are doing. In any case, it's important to strengthen our own abilities to see potential in what children *are* doing.

As I approached Aly, I saw that she was reading from our bin Books Recently Published. She had chosen the book *When You Reach Me* by Rebecca Stead. I saw that there were a few Post-its sticking out of her book. I know that she is having a hard time stopping to pause her reading to jot her thinking, so I am eager to see what she has jotted.

I sat down next to her, but she didn't seem to notice. "Aly, how's it going?"

"This is such a good book."

"Why?"

"I can't figure out what's really going on. It seems like realistic fiction, but it also is a mystery and fantasy maybe, but I'm not sure," Aly said with a puzzled look on her face.

"I see you started it last night and you are almost finished it."

"Yeah, it's short and so good. I want to read to find out what's really going on."

"Aly, will you tour me through your Post-its so far?"

"Okay, but I stopped a few times."

I looked through Aly's jottings and saw a place or two where she had done some character analysis and a few where she had asked questions. I decided to teach into questioning, but first I complimented Aly on her new efforts to pause her reading and to jot her thoughts. I wanted to celebrate her attempts. I chose to ignore that they were few and far between. I also chose to tackle at another time that they didn't even come close to the rich thinking she had a tendency to expresses during partner talk or whole class discussions because I wanted to first get her into the habit of Post-iting.

There are many ways to ratchet up students' work around questioning. I could teach a reader who is only asking questions of the main character to extend that work to secondary characters or to think about secondary characters' relationships with the main character. I could also teach that sometimes one question can lead a reader to ask another question and another so that the questions become more refined. I might also encourage the reader to gesture toward an answer to her question. Since Aly was racing through this book to find out what was going on, I thought teaching into trying to answer the questions she was having could help her become the kind of reader who reads to figure out what a book is all about before the book tells one. My goal was also to help Aly linger and think more deeply as she was reading, since I knew she struggled to do so.

"I noticed that you asked questions while you were reading. Let's look at one of them together. Can you find one and read it to me?"

"Sure." Aly flipped through her book and then read, "Who keeps leaving her those weird notes?"

"One thing readers do when they ask questions is try to answer those themselves. One way to do that is to think about 'maybes' or 'perhaps.' When you do this, you are trying to figure out what's going on before the author tells you. For example, in *Stone Fox* remember when we were wondering why grandfather wouldn't get out of bed. Some of us thought that perhaps he was dying and he physically couldn't, while others of us thought maybe he was too depressed to get out of bed. Then we read on and got more information and we definitely thought it was depression. This helped us to think more about what we'd read to come up with an answer, and then it spurred us on to confirm or revise our thinking. Why don't you try it with your question?"

"Okay, well maybe it's Sal because they used to be such good friends, but now he isn't talking to her because he was humiliated in front of her, and this is the way he is communicating with her now. It could also be him because this person knows a lot about Miranda's life, and Sal would know where she hid the spare key to her apartment."

"Anyone else?"

"Well, maybe it's Julia and she is messing with Miranda because she is jealous of her new relationship with her best friend Annemarie."

"Or. . . ."

"Or the notes talk about the trip being hard and how the person will not be himself or herself when they get there. So I don't know if it's a boy or girl but the notes are weird sounding. So maybe it's Marcus because he's kinda weird and he believes in time travel, so maybe that's the trip the person in the notes is referring to."

"I like the way you are really thinking about who it could be based on what you read so far. Now you can read on carrying these possibilities as you read, looking for evidence that would support one answer over another."

"I can do that."

"So Aly, whenever you are reading, I want you to continue to pause your reading, stopping to jot your thoughts down. And when it is questions you are having, one thing you can do to figure out what's happening is to gesture toward answers to your questions and then carry those possibilities on as you read, looking for evidence that supports one answer over the others." *(Fig. XV-5)*

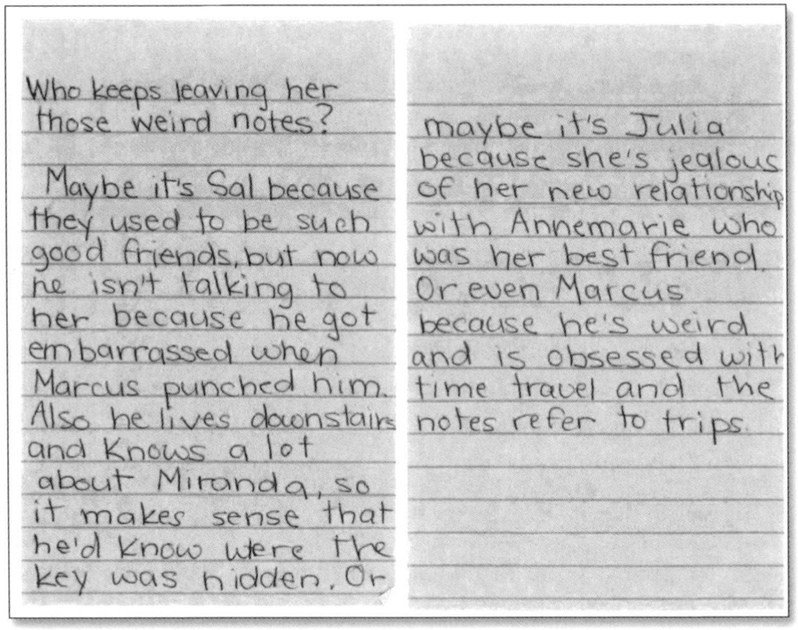

Figure XV-5

# TEACHING SHARE

Readers Open Our Hearts and Minds to the Characters We've Come to Know

Remind children that readers listen to texts as carefully as they listen to each other. Read through to the end of the read aloud, letting silence fill the room at the book's end.

Today we've talked a lot about listening—listening to each other and listening to our own emerging ideas. Let's end today's workshop in a special way. Let's remember that reading, itself, is listening, and the goal is to listen in such a way that the book gets through to us, with our minds and hearts open. I'll read straight to the end of *Stone Fox,* and then we'll talk.

> The crowd cheered madly when they saw little Willy come into view at the far end of Main Street, and even more madly when they saw that Stone Fox was right on his tail.
>
> "Go, Searchlight! Go!"
>
> Searchlight forged ahead. But Stone Fox was gaining.
>
> "Go, Searchlight! Go!" little Willy cried out.
>
> Searchlight gave it everything she had.
>
> She was a hundred feet from the finish line when her heart burst. She died instantly. There was no suffering.
>
> The sled and little Willy tumbled over her, slid along the snow for a while, then came to a stop about ten feet from the finish line. It started to snow – white snowflakes landed on Searchlight's dark fur as she lay motionless on the ground.

We usually think of listening as something you only do in conversation, but to talk about it as a way to be as a reader is an interesting twist and something you may want to carry forward across all of the units.

The crowd became deathly silent.

Lester's eyes looked to the ground. Miss Williams had her hands over her mouth. Mr. Foster's cigar lay on the snow. Doc Smith started to run out to little Willy, but stopped. Mayor Smiley looked shocked and helpless. And so did Hank and Dusty, and so did the city slickers, and so did Clifford Snyder, the tax man.

Stone Fox brought his sled to a stop alongside little Willy. He stood tall in the icy wind and looked down at the young challenger, and at the dog that lay limp in his arms.

"Is she dead, Mr. Stone Fox? Is she dead?" little Willy asked, looking up at Stone Fox with his one good eye.

Stone Fox knelt down and put one massive hand on Searchlight's chest. He felt no heartbeat. He looked at little Willy, and the boy understood.

Little Willy squeezed Searchlight with all his might. "You did real good, girl. Real good. I'm real proud of you. You rest now. Just rest." Little Willy began to brush the snow off Searchlight's back.

Stone Fox stood up slowly.

No one spoke. No one moved. All eyes were on the Indian, the one called Stone Fox, the one who had never lost a race, and who now had another victory within his grasp.

But Stone Fox did nothing.

He just stood there. Like a mountain.

His eyes shifted to his own dogs, then to the finish line, then back to little Willy, holding Searchlight.

With the heel of his moccasin Stone Fox drew a long line in the snow. Then he walked back over to his sled and pulled out his rifle.

Down at the end of Main Street, the other racers began to appear. As they approached, Stone Fox fired his rifle into the air. They came to a stop.

Stone Fox spoke.

"Anyone crosses this line – I shoot."

And there wasn't anybody who didn't believe him.

Stone Fox nodded to the boy.

The town looked on in silence as little Willy, carrying Searchlight, walked the last ten feet and across the finish line.

Ask children to process their ideas and emotions at the completion of this book, either by talking in partnerships or by talking as a whole class.

I closed the book and exhaled, as if collapsing under the weight of what had transpired in the story. "Turn and talk," I said to the sea of tear-streaked faces.

"I know a lot of you are thinking, 'Why did the book have to end this way? Why did John Gardiner make Searchlight die?'"

Through their tears, the children nodded in agreement. "Yeah, how come it had to be so sad?" they all seemed to say.

I let that thought hang in the air. After a long silence, I said, "I guess we're not made of stone, are we? It wouldn't hurt so much if we were stone?"

The room went quiet as we tried to pull ourselves together. Through the sniffles, one person said, "But *was* he really stone? I don't think so."

Others joined in. "He probably felt like crying too."

"I think the book is saying we don't need to be stone. Grandpa didn't need to be stone. Stone Fox didn't."

I nodded. "Even though I'm sad, I'm glad I'm not stone. I don't want to be a stone statue. I want to be open to books, and to my life."

Aly piped in. "I'm SO sad but it is not a bad-sad, it is, like, a, like a. . . beautiful sad."

I nodded, and for a moment no one said anything. Then I said, "Remember how I told you that a man named Kafka, a famous writer, once said, 'A book must be an ice-axe to break the seas frozen inside our soul.' Maybe that is what we have learned—more than anything—during this unit and this book."

The teachers who piloted these lessons said that the ending crushed their children, as it did them. The conversation was longer than usual. No one kept track of time.

Using a quote at the end of a teaching share may seem a bit unusual, but this teaching share is not just an ending to a session. It also serves as an ending to this beloved read-aloud and to the unit. This quote really hits home the bigger point of this unit. If we want books to matter, then we have to find ways that speak to their relevance in our lives.

SESSION XVI

IN THIS SESSION,

you will celebrate with your students the reading and learning of this unit. Readers write to make sense of and remember reading experiences. in this session, we'll be creating two pieces of writing—one to hold onto our memories of a cherished book, and another to hold onto the memories of our learning.

Celebration

DRAFT

his session is a celebration. As you end this first unit of study, you will help your children savor all they have experienced and take ownership of all they have learned. Your hope is that on this final day, you will remind the learners in your care of the essential content you hope they have incorporated into their sense of themselves and into their mental toolkit. That is, your aim today is to invite children to pack their identity kits and their strategy toolkits so that they go forward into the upcoming unit with a sense of personal agency, convinced that with resolve, enthusiasm, good books, and good company, they can author lives in which reading matters.

You might want to reread Byrd Baylor's beautiful picture book, *I'm in Charge of Celebrations,* before you enter into this first celebration. I'm not suggesting you read it to your kids—though that, too, would be great. But I'm suggesting you may want to read it to yourself. Let Byrd preach to you a bit about the topic of celebrations. If you are at all like me, you could read the upcoming session and think to yourself, "This all sounds a bit hokey to me." You could worry that the kids of today the digital age, cooler than life, multitasking, prematurely adolescent kids of today will roll their eyes at any attempt to create a solemn occasion that is saturated with meaning. If you undermine the event with your own worries, your kids will never get caught up in it. Try to remember times when you were little and you were part of ceremonies that meant the world to you—a funeral for a dead rabbit, a celebration when your older cousin graduated or got engaged. I suspect there were occasions in your childhood that left an imprint on you, that are forever part of your

GETTING READY

- Today you'll be reading aloud Paul Auster's *Invention of Solitude* in the minilesson and you might want to flag a few passages of *Stone Fox* to reread. If you have extra copies of the book, have them handy for children to write from.

- Bring a new reader's notebook for every child, ready to be distributed after the short activity. The type of notebook you choose to present to your students is up to you. You might find a stack of beautiful green spiral-bounds at the dollar store, or you might use the typical mottled black-and-white notebooks. Children can decorate them with pictures and cover in contact paper to protect them. Style doesn't matter—so long as they are full-sized notebooks, big enough to last a while!

- Create a bin for each table filled with magazines and catalogs of books, glue sticks, scissors, and other art supplies children will use to decorate their notebooks.

- Bring your white board and marker to the meeting area so you can jot your reflections on it.

- Ask children to bring paper and pen with them to the meeting area today.

244

memory map. This day can mean as much to your children—if you believe it will.

Of course, you will revise this session so that it is tailor-made to your own classroom community. If one child in the class has a bookbag that has been the envy of everyone, perhaps you'll gather together materials that will allow all your children to make themselves bookbags. If you do so, then you'll want to be sure that the tool becomes a symbol.

> *The books we read and the work we do as readers leave lasting impressions on us. We are different because of what we have read and what we have learned. We carry books and insights with us as we journey on.*

Readers need bookbags so we can carry books with us everywhere and use stolen moments to read, never wasting a second before we resume where we left off. Bookbags hadn't been the fad in the classrooms in which Kathleen, the pilot teachers, and I taught this session, so you'll see that we chose a different tool, a different symbol, but my point is that you will tailor this celebration so that it serves to cumulate the lived experience of your own class' first unit.

You'll see that the biggest message of this unit is that learners hold tight to all that we have learned. Some readers come to the end of a book and snap the book shut. But readers who know that books last a lifetime, that reading changes a person, know that we don't actually snap shut a book—or a unit of study. Instead, both resonate. The books we read and the work we do as readers leave lasting impressions on us. We are different because of what we have read and what we have learned. We carry books and insights with us as we journey on. Because *Stone Fox's* ending is so emotional and because the class will have collectively experienced that story, you'll start this session by reviving all the intense feelings that surround that book. "We're not going to ever forget this book," you and the class will say together.

You'll then take that same energy and intimacy and resolve, and help children look back on all they have learned and to resolve, "We're not ever going to forget the lessons of this first unit."

You'll give children a tool that will help them look backward, savoring all they have learned and making a monument out of it: reader's notebooks. You'll want to do everything possible to make it likely that they bond with these notebooks, just as they have bonded with their writer's notebooks. Often, writing about reading is something children do on command only, for the teacher. Your message will be that these notebooks are personal, that each notebook will be as unique as the reader it represents, that as children author rich reading lives for themselves, by themselves, these notebooks will mirror those lives and invite them to pay attention to their own emerging identities as readers and to reflect on what they see. You'll distribute notebooks, knowing that no tool is as conducive to reflection as the pen and the page.

Kids are accustomed to *our* goals, *our* standards, to their *parents'* expectations, their *peers'* judgment. Today you'll be silently teaching that it is possible to hold oneself accountable to one's *own* growth, creating a valuable, protected island of time in which kids ponder—and quietly articulate—their own identities as readers.

DRAFT

MINILESSON

Celebration

CELEBRATION

Explain that one way to hold onto memories is to make something new out of them. Offer an example.

"So, readers, we've come to the end of *Stone Fox*. It's hard to believe, isn't it? We've been living with Willy and Searchlight for a long time now. And *Stone Fox* is not the only thing that's ending. We've come to the end of the first month of the school year and of our first reading unit, too."

"*Stone Fox* has meant a lot to me—a lot to all of us, I think—and I don't want to let it just slip away into the past. I want to remember *Stone Fox* and think about it for the rest of my life. Today will be our celebration of *Stone Fox* and of this whole unit—a celebration to help us deeply, truly, really remember the parts of both that have mattered to us."

"One author, Paul Auster, used an interesting way of helping himself remember the details and the feelings of his own childhood. It works so well that when you read it, it's almost like you experience the things he's remembering, too. He used a really simple technique – he just starts with the words, "He remembers. . ." and then describes something he remembers in as much detail as he can so that when we read it, the memory is practically recreated, clear as a bell. I'll read part of it, and you'll see the way his invention works. We'll try it ourselves, in a minute, but first listen to this."

COACHING TIPS

Many children are deeply affected by the ending of Stone Fox. *Because being affected by books is a crucial component of being a good reader, it's important to honor this feeling by giving more time and attention to this moving story and letting the feelings the book evokes live longer in the room, over days and weeks.*

There are many authors who have written patterned ways of putting together memories and recollections, and in fact, writing a litany of memories is a common and wonderful technique that many writers use to get themselves goin . When I Was Young in the Mountains *by Cynthia Rylant is another example of a book that is patterned in a similar way.*

I then read aloud this selection from Auster's *Invention of Solitude:*

> He remembers learning how to tie his shoes. He remembers that his father's clothes were kept in the closet in his room and that it was the noise of hangers clicking together in the morning that would wake him up. He remembers the sight of his father knotting his tie and saying to him Rise and shine little boy. He remembers wanting to be a squirrel and have a bushy tail and be able to jump from tree to tree as though he was flying. He remembers looking through the Venetian blinds and seeing his new-born sister coming home from the hospital in his mother's arms. He remembers the nurse in a white dress who sat beside his baby sister and gave him little squares of Swiss chocolate. He remembers that she called them Swiss though he did not know what that meant.

I left a bit of silence so that the children could let the words sink in. "Do you see how using this structure – "He remembers. . .", makes the details of Paul's childhood come back to life in your mind?"

Ask children to create a piece of writing from their memories of the read-aloud text, in this case, *Stone Fox*, using the example as a template. In this case, the template leads them to create a list poem of sorts of their memories.

"Let's try together using this format for our memories of *Stone Fox*. First I'll help you get your mind back on that book." I opened *Stone Fox* and read about the day Grandfather wouldn't get out of bed.

> [Willy] never slept late again, after that.

> That is, until this morning. For some reason, Grandfather had forgotten to call him. That's when Little Willy discovered that Grandfather was still in bed. There could be only one explanation. Grandfather was playing. It was a trick.

> Or was it?

I paused and then flipped ahead to a bit when Doc Smith encourages Willy to put Grandpa in the nursing home with the other sickly folks.

Doc Smith shook her head.

"I think you should consider letting Mrs. Peacock in town take care of him, like she does those other sickly folks. He'll be in good hands until the end comes." Doc Smith stepped up into the wagon. "You can come live with me until we make plans." She looked at Searchlight. "I'm sure there's a farmer in these parts who needs a good work dog."

After pausing briefly, I read Clifford Snyder's threatening remarks and then turned to the race scene and read a snippet from that. Finally, I reread the very last two pages of the book, beginning with Willy asking "Is she dead, Mr. Stone Fox? Is she dead?" and ending, gravely, with the description of the end of the race at the end of the book. "The town looked on in silence as little Willy, carrying Searchlight, walked the last ten feet and across the finish line."

I closed the book slowly, put it in my lap, and said nothing. Then I picked up a marker and wrote on the white board:

"She remembers Doc Smith and Willy, riding back to the farm. She remembers...." And then I whispered, "Now you keep going on your own!" and gestured for the kids to start writing on their paper, just as I was writing on mine. The immediate scratch of pens could be heard, but several children seemed stymied. I distributed a couple of copies of the book to them to help get them going and then I continued writing: "She remembers Doc Smith saying, 'He's healthy as an ox.'" After a bit, when I could see that everyone had written at least one—and in most instances, several—memories, I stopped them.

I said in a soft voice so as not to disturb *Stone Fox*'s hold on us, "When I point to you, please read us one of your memories." Looking at Lily, I quietly pointed to her to indicate that she should begin,

Lily glanced through her long list of memories and then offered, "She remembers Willy riding his sled in the night with the snow in his eyes."

I smiled and then dramatically pointed to Malik, who said, "He remembers Searchlight pulling the plow to harvest the potato fields."

Next came Jasmine who said a little tearily, "She remembers Little Willie lifting Searchlight up and carrying him across the finishing line with tears streaming down his face."

I let those words linger in the air before I pointed to Tyrell. He said, "He remembers Stone Fox punching Little Willy in the face."

I pointed and Emma said, "She remembers Little Willy seeing Grandpa's shadow in the window as he was racing,"

Brianna was next. "She remembers Little Willie combing his Grandfather's hair and telling him about how he was going to save the farm."

David offered, "He remembers Clifford Snyder showing Little Willie his gun."

I continued that way until every child had a turn and then I paused to let the silence fill up the room.

"*Stone Fox* can be with us forever, if we let it, if we choose to be the kind of people who carry important stories with us into the future. Reminiscing and putting our memories into one place, putting the memories together into a new shape (like this gathering of important parts we made with the 'he remembers' and 'she remembers' pattern) always helps keep those memories with us. It helps carve a place for them in our minds. It's like making a photo album or a scrapbook. You see what I mean."

The more elegantly you point and use pauses, the more of a celebration this becomes. Take up the space wisely. Create a mood! This worked beautifully for many of the teachers who piloted the study, though less well for others, depending no doubt on the chemistry in the classrooms. You will need to tweak this so it fits your class' chemistry.

Ask children to create a piece of writing from their memories of their work in this unit, again using the example as a template for the new form. Again, in this case, the writing they create will be a list-poem of sorts.

"Now then, just as we've come to the end of *Stone Fox,* we've also come to the end of our first reading unit. Since we want to keep hold of all the amazing things we've learned just like we want to hold onto *Stone Fox,* let's try doing something similar with our memories of this unit. To help get your minds ready to pick out the parts of the unit that you want to hold onto for the future, take a few moments to prepare. Go through your reading logs, look at your post-its, think back over your independent reading books, the read aloud times and the conversations you've had about reading so far this year. Refresh your memories about how you've changed and what you want to remember. Talk with your neighbor about what you might say."

I gave everyone a moment or two to cast their minds over the whole unit. Then I added, "As you're getting ready, you might also want to think about the little ah-has and discoveries and insights you've made about yourself as a reader, and about what it means to author a reading life. And then start, just as you did before, by writing, 'He,' or, 'She remembers. . . .'"

As the children started writing, I did as well. On the white board, I wrote: "She remembers realizing that she was reading really slowly, and deciding to speed it up." Noticing some children were struggling a bit, I said, "It is a smart idea to use our charts as reminders of our learning in this unit." I pointed to those hanging up around the classroom. "Those charts remind us of strategies to try and ways to read."

After giving them a few minutes to record their memories, I raised my arm, getting ready to lightly point at Aly to start off our reading again. Aly saw my expectant look, and so she cast out the first line, "She remembers playing a movie in her mind as she read."

I nodded and tipped my hand toward Grace. "She remembers before this year when she didn't read that much."

Soon there were others. Gabe: "He remembers finding parts and reading them like gold."
And Rosa: "She remembered her first chapter book." After all the children had spoken at least once, I again paused to let the words soak in.

"Wow. That was amazing, it was sort of like an out-loud scrapbook of our first unit! I bet that doing that will help us hold on to what we've learned."

With ceremony and celebration, distribute new reader's notebooks into which children can put these two new pieces of writing, and the writing about reading to come. Ask children to decorate and begin to fill these notebooks to reflect their reading identities.

"Now, with *Stone Fox,* our class' first read-aloud book, and with this first unit of study both finished and alive in our minds, I have something I want to give each of you.

"I have here new reader's notebooks for each of you that will give you much, much more room to write your thinking than on the Post-its you've mostly been jotting on so far."

As I began to hand out the new notebooks, I continued, "This will be *your* reader's notebook, and it won't be like any other you might have had in other years; this notebook will be so uniquely yours, about you and your reading life now, that it'll be like your fingerprint. No one else will have one exactly like it. This is where you'll both record and create your reading identity.

Gesturing to Fallon to pass a stack of notebooks back, I said, "Things *happened* to you during this read aloud and this unit. You learned things, you changed, you collected the new images and ideas and emotions that are making you into a new kind of reader. This notebook will be one place to help you hang onto what you're reading, and what you're thinking as your reading. Just like you put your memories of *Stone Fox* and this unit into a new format to hold onto it, (the 'he remembers,' and 'she remembers' format) you can put your learning from all your reading into this new format—writing or sketching in this notebook. Turning thoughts into writing is another way to make things stick in your mind and carry on with them."

"So let's turn on some music and bring out the snacks, and let's celebrate. It's time to make your readers' notebooks your own – we want them to show who we are as readers, what we are interested in, what we value. I've got stacks of magazines and catalogs that you can cut apart that I've left in bins at the centers of your tables, plus scissors and glue. You may also want to sketch or write on the cover and first few pages—that's up to you. You have collected material in your My Reading Life folder, and you've got Post-its that hold amazing ideas and timelines. Some of that belongs in your notebook—your reading scrapbook. Prepare this reader's notebook in ways that say, 'This is who I am as a person and as a reader.' Talk with your friends, and they'll remind you of things you need to include. Go ahead, let's enjoy setting up our notebooks so we're ready for the next unit!"

As the celebration goes on, you will want to mill around, intending to help students reflect on who they were as readers, who they are as readers, and who they want to become as readers. Point to their sketches and initial decorations and say "Tell me something about what that says about you as a reader." Use the time to reminisce with your children over the important moments of the month!

As the end of the reading time approaches, ask students to share the best of their work.

"Readers, in my extended family we have an On Turning Ten celebration. On each child's tenth birthday, he or she is given his or her very own photo album, containing pictures that capture the child's first ten years of life. And the family looks through the photo album with that child, reminiscing—you know, with stories that start, 'Oh I remember when....' Well, it feels like to me that we have created such an album of ourselves as readers. What treasures!"

"Now, will each of you find a page that says something significant about you as a reader and hold it up to so we can see each other's." I allowed a moment of enthusiastic murmuring in which we looked at and appreciated each other's notebooks. "These notebooks are just right, aren't they! They will truly help us hold on to this year of reading and to carry it forward into our lives!"

Teachers, you may choose to ask children to lay their notebooks out as if they were on display in a museum, along a window, or in the chalk ledge. They could even leave their notebooks out on the tables while they walk around looking at each other's notebooks. They might even leave notes behind to comment on what they see.

Works Cited

Adler, Mortimer J. 1972. How to Read a Book. New York: Touchstone Books.

Allington, Richard. 2005. What Really Matters for Struggling Readers: Designing Research-Based Programs. Columbus, OH: Allyn & Beacon.

Bear, Donald, et al. 2003. Words Their Way: Word Study for Phonics, Vocabulary and Spelling Instruction (4th Edition). Upper Saddle River, NJ: Pearson.

Calkins, Lucy. 2001. The Art of Teaching Reading. New York: Addison-Wesley Longman.

Dreyer, Lois G., Ehri, Linnea C., Flugman, Bert, Gross, Alan. "Reading Rescue: An Effective Tutoring Intervention Model for Language-Minority Students Who Are Struggling Readers in First Grade." American Educational Research Journal, Vol. 44, No. 2, 414-448 (2007).

Gentry, Richard. 2002. The Literacy Map. Guiding Children to Where They Need to Be (4-6). New York: Mondo Publishing.

Guthrie, John and N. M. Humenick. 2004. Motivating Students to Read: Evidence for Classroom Practices that Increase Motivation and Achievement. In P. McCardle and V. Chhabra (Eds.) The Voice of Evidence in Reading Research (pp. 329-254). Baltimore: Paul Brookes.

Guthrie, John. 2002. Preparing Students for High-Stakes Test Taking in Reading. pp. 370-391. In Alan E. Farstrup & S. J. Samuels (Eds.), What Research Has to Say About Reading Instruction. Newark, DE: International Reading Association, Inc.

Hall, Donald. 1983. "Four Kinds of Reading." Thinking in Writing. 2nd ed. (Eds.) Donald McQuade and Robert Atwan. New York: Knopf.

Gardner, John. The Art of Fiction. New York: Random House Inc.,1983

Harste, Jerome C., Kathy G. Short, with Carolyn Burke. 1996. Creating Classrooms for Authors and Inquirers. Portsmouth, NH: Heinemann.

Uris, Leon. 1983. Exodus. New York: Bantam Books.

Krashen, Stephen. 1993. The Power of Reading. Englewood, Co.: Libraries Unlimited.

Works Cited
(continued)

Murray, Donald. 2003. A Writer Teaches Writing (Rev. ed.). Boston: Heinle.

National Center for Education Statistics. (2004). The Nation's Report Card: Reading Highlights 2003. Washington, DC: U.S. Department of Education, Institute for Education Sciences.

Purves, Alan C. and Olive Niles. 1984. Becoming Readers in a Complex Society. The National Society for the Study of Education.

Raphael, Taffy and McMahon. 1994. Handbook of Teaching the English Language Arts by James Flood. 2003. Hillsdale, NJ: Lawrence Erlbaum.

Rasinski, Timothy. 2003. The Fluent Reader: Oral Reading Strategies for Word Recognition, Fluency and Comprehension. New York: Scholastic.

Tillich, Paul. 1999. The Essential Tillich. Chicago: The University of Chicago Press.

Tizon, Alan. Telling True Stories: A Nonfiction Writers' Guide from the Nieman Foundation at Harvard University. Ed. Mark Kramer, Wendy Call. London: Penguin Group, 2007.

Topping, Keith J. 2006. Building Reading Fluency: Cognitive, Behavioral and Socioemotional Factors And the Role of Peer-Mediated Learning. pp. 107. In Alan E. Farstrup & S.J. Samuels (Eds.), What Research Has To Say About Fluency Instruction. International Reading Association, Inc.

Wood, John. 2006. Leaving Microsoft to Change the World: An Entrepreneur's Odyssey to Educate the World's Children. New York: Collins Business.

Children's Book List (Partial)

Abbott, Tony. 2002. *Secrets of Droon* series. New York: Scholastic.

Blume, Judy. 2004. *Fudgeamania*. New York: Berkley Books.

Bulla, Clyde Robert. 2004. *Shoeshine Girl*. New York: HarperCollins.

Cameron, Ann. 1987. *Julian's Glorious Summer*. New York: Random House Books for Young Readers.

Christopher, Matt. 2006. *Sports Classics* series. New York: Little, Brown Young Readers.

Dahl, Roald. 2007. *The BFG*. New York: Puffin Books.

Dahl, Roald. 2007. *Matilda*. New York: Puffin Books.

Danzinger, Paula. 2004. *Amber Brown* series. New York: Scholastic.

Degross, Monalisa. 2000. *Donavan's Word Jar*. New York: Scholastic.

Gardiner, John. 1992. *Stone Fox*. New York: HarperCollins.

Lobel, Arnold. 2004. *Frog and Toad* Series. New York: HarperCollins.

McDonald, Megan. 2002. *Judy Moody*. Somerville, MA: Candlewick.

Osborne, Mary Pope. 2002. *Magic Treehouse* series. New York: Random House Books for Young Readers.

Paulsen, Gary. 2006. *Hatchet*. London: Aladdin.

Park, Barbara. 2001. *Junie B. Jones* series. New York: Random House Books for Young Readers.

Pennypacker, Sara. 2008. *Clementine*. New York: Hyperion Books.

Rylant, Cynthia. 2000. *Henry and Mudge* series. London: Aladdin.

Rowling, J. K. 2006. *Harry Potter* series. New York: Scholastic.

Sachar, Louis. *Marvin Redpost* series. 1992. New York: Random House Books for Young Readers.